The Melting Pot in Israel

D1040233

SUNY series in Israeli Studies

The Melting Pot in Israel

*The Commission of Inquiry
Concerning Education in the Immigrant Camps
during the Early Years of the State*

Zvi Zameret

STATE UNIVERSITY OF NEW YORK PRESS

Revised version, translated from the Hebrew by Jonathan Chipman and Yohai Goell

The Hebrew edition (not including Chapters 12–14) was published by the Ben-Gurion Research Center and the Ben-Gurion University of the Negev Press, Sde Boker, 1993.

Published by
State University of New York Press, Albany

© 2002 State University of New York

All rights reserved

Printed in the United States of America

No part of this book may be used or reproduced in any manner whatsoever without written permission. No part of this book may be stored in a retrieval system or transmitted in any form or by any means including electronic, electrostatic, magnetic tape, mechanical, photocopying, recording, or otherwise without the prior permission in writing of the publisher.

For information, address State University of New York Press, 90 State Street, Suite 700, Albany, NY 12207

Production by Kelli Williams
Marketing by Patrick Durocher

Library of Congress Cataloging-in-Publication Data

Tsameret, Tsevi.
    [Yeme kur ha-hitukh. English]
    The melting pot in Israel : the commission of inquiry concerning education
in the immigrant camps during the early years of the state / Zvi Zameret.
        p. cm. — (SUNY series in Israeli studies)
    Translated from Hebrew.
    Includes index.
    ISBN 0-7914-5255-7 (alk. paper) — ISBN 0-7914-5256-5 (pbk. : alk. paper)
        1. Children of immigrants—Education—Israel—History.   2. Jews—Cultural
assimilation—History—20th century.   3. Israel—Emigration and immigration—
History.   4. Israel. Va ͨadat hakirah ͨal hinukh yalde ha- ͨolim, 1950.   I. Title.
II. Series.

LC3747.I75 T7313 2002
303.48'2'095694—dc21   2001049303

10 9 8 7 6 5 4 3 2 1

CONTENTS

BOOK II

ABBREVIATIONS

AHH	Archives of Hakibbutz Hameuhad, Yad Tabenkin, Efal
ARZBI	Archives of Religious Zionism, Bar-Ilan University, Ramat Gan
ARZMHK	Archives of Religious Zionism, Mossad Harav Kook, Jerusalem
BGA	Ben-Gurion Archives, the Ben-Gurion Research Center, Sde Boker
BGRC	The Ben-Gurion Research Center, Sde Boker
CAHJP	Central Archives for the History of the Jewish People, Jerusalem
CZA	Central Zionist Archives, Jerusalem
GHA	Archives of Mapam and Hashomer Hatzair, Givat Haviva
ISA	Israel State Archives, Jerusalem
LMA	Labor Movement Archives, Lavon Institute, Tel Aviv
MA	Mapai Archives, Beit Berl
RKA	Religious Kibbutz Archives, Kevutzat Yavne
YBZ	Yad Izhak Ben-Zvi, Jerusalem

"In the world they say: The Jew has succeeded.
This is a nation that in blood forged for itself a state,
But we know the truth: this is
still a state that must forge a nation."
—Nathan Alterman, from "The Seventh
Column" (Hebrew), *Davar*, October 1949

"We have come to the Land of Israel to build and be built [a popular Zionist slogan] Many of us interpreted 'to build and be built' as eradication of memory, as complete transformation, and as uniting with this territory; in other words, 'a normal life' as it was customary to call it."
—Aharon Appelfeld, from *The Story of a Life*
(Hebrew) (Jerusalem: Keter, 1999), 107

PREFACE

This book, which is primarily an extended introduction to the Frumkin Commission Report, is based upon copious documentation that has been brought to light, mostly in recent years, in most of the major archives throughout Israel. The Central Zionist Archives in Jerusalem contain the full mimeographed report as well as detailed records of the Commission's discussions and investigations. Documents relating to the early years of the Ministry of Education and Culture are contained in the Israel State Archives (ISA), although these are neither complete nor sufficiently organized. Also deposited in the ISA are relevant documents of other government ministries—including those of the Prime Minister's Office and religious government ministers. Most minutes of cabinet meetings, ministerial committees, and Knesset committees from the early years of statehood are still closed to the public; a few have recently been made available.

Information for this work was gathered primarily at the Ben-Gurion Research Center in Sde Boker, where I was privileged to work for an entire year. There I had access to Ben-Gurion's diaries, his correspondence (both incoming and outgoing), summaries of his meetings, and the totality of his writings, lectures, and speeches. I likewise found there photocopies of documents from the Mapai Archives and from the archives of the Histadrut (General Federation of Labor).

Examination of the documents of those two organizations was supplemented at the Mapai Archives in Beit Berl and the Labor Movement Archives in the Lavon Institute in Tel Aviv. It should be noted that the documents of Mapai are more accessible to scholars than those of any other political party. As a result, Mapai has at times been more open to criticism than any other party. Mapam (a more left-wing party) also has an archives at Givat Haviva, but numerous minutes of party discussions are as yet unavailable to the scholar (or perhaps did not survive). I found some Mapam documentation in the archives of Hakibbutz Hameuhad at Yad Tabenkin in Efal.

The situation is even more serious with regard to documents of the right-wing parties. The General Zionists do not have any archives, while those of Herut, deposited in the Jabotinsky Archives in Tel Aviv, contain little material. In this case, too, it is difficult to ascertain whether all available material is at the disposal of scholars. I also examined documents of the Religious Front housed at the Archives of Religious Zionism at Mossad Harav Kook in Jerusalem and at the similarly named Archives of Religious Zionism at Bar-Ilan University. Unfortunately, I was able to consult only some of the documentation of the ultra-Orthodox movements Agudat Israel and Poalei Agudat Israel, since their archives too are not organized, nor are they open to every scholar. I was able to find only a handful of documents at the archives of Agudat Israel in Eretz Israel and World Agudat Israel, both in Jerusalem. Some additional aspects were supplied by an examination of the documents of Hever Hakevutzot [the Kibbutz Union] at Kevuzat Hulda and the archives of the Religious Kibbutz Movement at Kevutzat Yavne. I wish to express my thanks to the directors of all of the institutions mentioned and their staffs, and particularly to my friends at the library and archives of the Ben-Gurion Research Center.

Certain *personal archives* were a treasure trove. Interesting personal material of Nahum Levin was deposited with the Central Archives for the History of the Jewish People on the Givat Ram campus of the Hebrew University of Jerusalem. In addition to personal archives deposited in central public archives, I also received for examination documents in the possession of private individuals, such as Ms. Paula Avreikh, Judge Hadassa Ben-Ito, and others. To all of them, I express my deepest gratitude.

To complement the archival material, I read through the newspapers of the period—all of the dailies and most of the periodicals. I was greatly assisted in the task of assembling material from the press by Nurit Meir, a student in the departments of education and history.

Once I had comprehensive knowledge of the written sources, I also turned to oral interviews. The limitations of oral documentation are well known; nevertheless, I did arrive at a number of extremely important insights that would have been impossible without judicious use of this methodology. I wish especially to thank Dr. Nana Sagi, who assisted me in the interviews within the framework of the oral documentation that she coordinates at the Hebrew University's Institute of Contemporary Jewry and at Yad Izhak Ben-Zvi.

My introductory study of the Frumkin Report certainly has some shortcomings. I am well aware of one—I deliberately made abundant use of quotations. This I did for several reasons: (1) Since the subject of the study is still an extremely sensitive issue, I wished to present it, as close as possible, in a reasoned, balanced manner. I believe that the use of quotations—even if only selected ones—leads to a more neutral presentation of the episode; (2) It seems to me that the quotations themselves are particularly interesting, and that many readers may be specifically interested in the actual wording used in those days, though it obviously loses something in translation; (3) Since it is difficult even today to clearly decide which side of the debate was correct, it is necessary to present the various viewpoints, beliefs, and approaches of that period.

A central methodological question in any historical study is that of *objectivity*. This has been discussed by many historians of all periods. Thus wrote, for example, British historian E. H. Carr in his discussion of Italian philosopher-historian Benedeto Croce: "All history is 'contemporary history', declared Croce, meaning that history consists essentially in seeing the past through the eyes of the present and in the light of its problems."[1] In my study of the Frumkin Report, I made a great effort to present an "objective" picture of the past, however, I am aware that I also view the events of the past from the perspective of contemporary reality.[2]

The late Professor Menahem Stern, one of the great Jewish historians of the Second Temple Period, murdered by an Arab terrorist, once said in a colloquium on historiography:

> *I do not believe that it is possible to arrive at an overall depiction of history that will be acceptable to all.* This is only possible if we educate people in certain frameworks that will accustom them to accept uniformity. It is the nature of historical writing not to be uniform. *We intend that at least the facts will be correct as far as possible.* Even here we are limited by our sources, and by the possibility of comparing and analyzing them. In any event, there is a difference between *the historian who truly aspires to objectivity,* and the one who from the outset, on the basis of his political or social beliefs, consciously forgoes even the attempt to describe the facts as they are and to evaluate the issue dispassionately. . . . Obviously there is a difference between a historian who attempts to get to the roots of the matter, to examine the facts properly, and to give a balanced view to the best of his ability, and *the historian who a priori has chosen sides.* I do not believe that there is any historical work—at least I do not know of any— that is accepted by all with complete agreement.[3] (emphasis added)

Stern made this declaration during a discussion of the Zealots and Sycarii of ancient times. It would seem that his words hold doubly true regarding modern history and contemporary Jewry. There is no doubt that many readers will sense much contemporary relevance in this book, and that many will judge it on the basis of their own worldview and affiliations. I nevertheless wish to assure the reader that I have made a great effort to get to the root of the facts, to examine them properly, and to provide to the best of my ability a balanced picture of a complex and exciting reality.

A few words are in order to the readers of the English edition of *The Melting Pot in Israel*, to whom some or many of the institutions and concepts mentioned in this book may be unfamiliar. These include: the peculiar nature of the Israeli party system, both before and after the creation of the state, and its interrelation with a gamut of nongovernmental agencies; the multi-party system in the Knesset, necessitating coalitions to establish majority governments; the traces of pre-state institutions in the early years of the state, including a school system organized on the basis of ideological streams established by the major political movements in the Yishuv; and the role of major nongovernmental bodies: the two most notable are the Histadrut (General Federation of Labor), the umbrella labor organization that functioned not only as a mega-union but also as a provider of health care, cultural, and social facilities as an entrepreneur and owner of economic enterprises, and so forth; and the Jewish Agency for Palestine, which acted (and still does) as the executive arm of the World Zionist Organization in providing services relating to the bringing in and absorption of immigrants. All of these concepts or institutions are explained, where necessary, in the Glossary at the end of this book and are designated by both an asterisk and italics upon their first appearance in the text.

The English edition could not have been published without the initiative of my friend Dr. Tuviah Friling, director of the Ben-Gurion Research Center, and his active support of the book in all of its stages. I also am greatly indebted to Professors Rachel Elboim-Dror and Yosef Gorny for their encouragement and valuable comments regarding the manuscript.

This book could not have been executed without the willingness of my wife Tamar and our children, Re'ut, Ma'ayan, Amitai, and Carmel, who spent a unique sabbatical year with me in the development town of Yeruham to assist in my research work, conducted primarily at the Center in Sde Boker. Our familiarity with the region went back many years, and we returned there for this period of research with much love and enthusiasm.

This book is dedicated with great affection to my friends and students at Kiryat Shemona. A period in our life that we treasure greatly was spent engaged in educational work in that northern city. There we saw some of the implications of the educational system of the early years of statehood, which awakened in me the intense wish to know more about and to delve more deeply into the historical-cultural roots of Israel's existential problems.

NOTES

1. E. H. Carr, *What Is History?* (Harmondsworth: Penguin, 1964), 20–21.

2. See on this matter, as but one example, Y. Eram, "The History of Education," in *Reshafim*...(Tel Aviv: Tel Aviv University, 1991), 105–120.

3. M. Stern, "The Zealots and the Sycarii," *Cathedra* 1 (September 1976): 55.

BOOK I

INTRODUCTION

The "Frumkin Commission":
Its Assignments and Significance for Today

On 17 January 1950, the government[1] of Israel appointed a state commission of inquiry charged with investigating "educational matters in the immigrant camps," appointing Gad Frumkin, a former Supreme Court justice, to head it. (I shall refer to it as the "Frumkin Commission" hereafter.) This decision was made during the government's third meeting devoted to that issue in the course of one week, the first on 10 January and the other two one week later. The appointment of the Commission came after months of complaints lodged by religious circles who claimed that, in the course of educating the children of the new immigrants—particularly those from Islamic countries—anti-religious coercion had been practiced in the camps where the immigrants were temporarily housed immediately following the creation of Israel.

Investigation of anti-religious coercion was not the only assignment of the Commission. Its charge was threefold: (1) "To investigate all accusations concerning religious coercion in the immigrant camps." The government's intention, of course, was to investigate all kinds of coercion—religious and anti-religious alike. Though the writ of appointment referred only to immigrant camps, not mentioning immigrant villages (*moshavei olim*), in practice the Commission extended the scope of its authority to include the latter as well (where its members found some very disturbing phenomena); (2) "To clarify the accusations published in the press and those responsible for them." This referred to accusations—mostly on the part

3

of religious circles—leveled against the state and its leaders regarding what was happening in the immigrant camps; (3) "To examine the sources of the propaganda abroad concerning the accusations in question." According to Prime Minister David Ben-Gurion, the Commission was to determine "the source of agitation in America." Evidently Ben-Gurion and his colleagues hoped to pin the blame on certain persons or movements.[2]

After conducting investigations for about three and a half months, the Commission submitted a detailed report—published almost in its entirety in this book[3]—including the conclusions it reached on all three subjects. In relation to anti-religious coercion in the camps, the Commission unequivocally asserted: "There was no intention on the part of the government of [engaging in anti-]religious coercion." Nevertheless, the Commission did level severe criticism against the Department for Language Instruction and Cultural Absorption among Immigrants of the Ministry of Education and Culture—also referred to simply as the Culture Department—for conducting a system of "uniform education" for immigrant children. According to the Frumkin Commission, the objective of uniform education was to rapidly assimilate the immigrants to the pioneering-socialist model of Israeli culture, and in doing so to undermine religious and traditional values. According to the Commission, the educational arm of the department was unsuited for the "customs and way of life of the immigrants" and accorded "superficial treatment of the religious problems of the immigrants and the children." Moreover, staff members of the Culture Department sought to quickly assimilate their pupils to the ideal image of the "New Israeli" (a pioneer, of European origin, and secular), adopting the most severe methods to achieve this goal: "cutting off *payot* [sidelocks]*—this was done systematically and not accidentally"; "interference with religious studies was also systematic"; "they were not sufficiently assiduous about the observance of the Sabbath and prayer, and there were also cases of interference with prayer."[4] The report included other specific accusations and led to the speedy dismissal of Nahum Levin, acting director of the Culture Department, along with two of his staff, and to the transfer of responsibility for the education of immigrant children to the Education Division of the Ministry of Education and Culture (which had until then been responsible for the education of all children in Israel, excluding those living in immigrant camps). In the long run, these findings were among the major factors leading to the replacement of the first minister of education, Zalman Shazar, and to a severe shake-up in the first government confirmed by an elected Knesset, indirectly leading to a vote of nonconfidence in the government by the Knesset and to its defeat.

Regarding the other two assignments of the Commission—"to clarify the accusations published in the press and those responsible for them," and "to examine the sources of the propaganda abroad concerning the accusations in question"—the Commission's conclusions were of no significance. Concerning the press, the Commission stated that, "Responsibility for what was published in the local newspapers lies, in the usual manner, with the newspapers and their correspondents, and, insofar as the paper is the organ of a specific party, with that party as well." No accusations were leveled against the religious circles, whom many in the Labor movement had hoped to find guilty of agitation against the state. As for propaganda abroad, the Commission found that it did originate among religious circles in Israel, but added that Diaspora Jews have the right to know what is going on in Israel and "to take an interest." The Commission's stand was a compromise formula between the view of Ben-Gurion who, as we shall see below, demanded that Jews who wished to influence events in Israel should come to live there, and that of Diaspora Jews, who wished to be involved in the "internal affairs" of the state.

Prime Minister Ben-Gurion's main objective in appointing a commission of inquiry was to prevent the defeat of the *coalition** a mere few months after it had been formed. At that time the government relied primarily upon two parties, which together constituted a majority among the Knesset's 120 members: Mapai (an acronym of *Mifleget Poalei Eretz Israel*—Eretz Israel Labor Party, forty-six seats) and the Religious Front (sixteen seats). This coalition, formed in March 1949, also included the Progressives (five seats), the Sephardim (four seats), and Arab Knesset members affiliated with Mapai (two seats). However, the commission of inquiry only enabled the coalition to survive for about one year after the Commission's appointment: in February 1951, it fell on a motion of no confidence. Over the long run, the findings of the Commission widened the breach between secular and religious Jews in Israel, and in practice they still weigh heavily upon relations between the Israeli Left and the religious public half a century later. This is one reason it is important to revisit the findings of this investigation and to survey and analyze them from a historical perspective with the help of archival documentation that has become accessible in recent years.

One reason for the contemporary relevance of the Frumkin Commission's report is that, because of its findings we can more fully understand the process of the absorption and education of hundreds of thousands of immigrants during the early years of the state. In the first two year of Israel's existence—from the declaration of its establishment in May 1948 until the submission of the conclusions by the commission of inquiry in May 1950—almost 500,000 immigrants arrived in Israel, about one-third of them from Islamic countries. These included about 45,000 from Yemen, 30,000 from Turkey, 20,000 from Libya, 27,000 from Algeria, Tunisia, and Morocco, 11,000 from Egypt, and the first 7,000 from Iraq, who were to be the vanguard of mass immigration from that country.[5] The Commission's report examined the process of "adjustment" and absorption in the immigrant camps, primarily among immigrants from these countries.[6] To this day, the issue of cultural absorption during Israel's early years—especially of immigrants from Islamic countries—is heatedly debated. The Commission's report may provide pertinent facts and information about this debate.

A second reason for the current relevance of a study of the Frumkin Commission's report is that one can learn a great deal from it regarding the shaping of the Israeli educational system until the present day. In my opinion, the abolition of secular educational streams affiliated with political parties, on the one hand, and the continued politicizing of the *state religious educational system*,* on the other hand, are both related to the manner in which immigrant children were absorbed during the early years of the state. I believe that the process—then called "soul snatching in education"—exposed by the Frumkin Commission hastened the transformation of education from partisan to more of a state system. At a certain stage, the workers' parties, who were a majority, relinquished their ability to influence and determine the frameworks of religious education. One reason for this step was that they had lost the moral authority to do so in the wake of the criticism directed against them by the Frumkin Commission for their acts of anti-religious coercion.

Third, interest in this period of Israeli history has recently been reawakened by the issue of Yemenite children who allegedly disappeared from immigrant camps and, according to the accusations currently being lodged with renewed force, were in some cases falsely reported dead and improperly given over for adoption. A commission of inquiry has recently reopened these questions, following three earlier investigating committees that lacked legal authority. The issue also has been the subject of a series of in-depth investigative articles in the prestigious daily newspaper *Ha'aretz*.[7] Public attention to the issue has been aroused through a series of violent acts by a hitherto unknown religious sect led by Uzi Meshullam. Those arguing a connection between the two affairs refer primarily to the attitude of haughtiness and arrogance displayed in both cases toward the Yemenite immigrants.

A fourth reason for the contemporary relevance of the Commission's report is that it leads us to an understanding of the roots of Shas, the Sephardic ethnic-religious party that has appropriated to itself a central role in Israeli politics from the mid-1980s until the present. Shas is to a great extent a belated reaction, after a few decades, to the anti-religious coercion and ethnic snubbing that characterized Israel in its early years. The reader, I hope, will end up with a better understanding of the political movements and ideological controversies in Israel, both then and now.

CHAPTER 1

EARLY INCIDENTS OF RELIGIOUS-SECULAR CONFLICT

THE "TEHERAN CHILDREN" AFFAIR

About seven years prior to the appointment of the Frumkin Commission, during World War II and the Holocaust, the attention of Jews in Eretz Israel and abroad was engaged by what came to be known as "The Teheran Children Affair." Who were the "Teheran Children"? As a result of the Stalin–Sikorski agreement signed in 1942, it was hoped that several thousand Jewish orphans from Poland who had fled to the Soviet Union during the early phase of the war would be able to leave the Union of Soviet Socialist Republics (USSR), via Iran, and be brought to Palestine.[1]

On the eve of the children's arrival in Eretz Israel, the Mapai Secretariat discussed where they should be absorbed. Arye Bahir, a member of Kibbutz Afikim, proposed that "the children first of all be divided among the workers' collective farms [i.e., *kibbutzim* or *moshavim**], because we need to attend to the social character of the operation; these are the young vanguard of the Diaspora in Eretz Israel." Pinhas Lubianiker (Lavon) added: "The main role of the *Histadrut** and of the party [i.e., Mapai] is organized absorption of the children, which will allow for supervision of their education and provide hope for their full absorption into the life of the country." Ya'akov Uri, of Moshav Nahalal, was of a similar opinion: "For me these children are not only an object for rescue, but also one of the cornerstones of our future." Not everyone shared his view. During that same discussion there were those who thought differently, expressing fear of what the future might hold. Yona Kosoy said: "We should not monopolize. . . . There will be a political complication of the first order. . . . General registration within the entire Yishuv* [all of whose sectors will wish to adopt the refugee children] is essential."[2] About two weeks later, Ben-Gurion, at the time chairman of the Jewish Agency Executive and leader of Mapai, once more raised the question of the anticipated problems related to the children's religious education. In a second discussion of the issue in Mapai, he said: "It will be difficult to obtain the agreement [of religious circles in Eretz Israel and abroad] that they be immediately brought up as aetheists. On the other hand, we cannot forego having them educated in our settlements. This confronts us with an extremely serious question. We have seen how the [nonreligious] settlements resolved the problem of their own [religiously observant] parents by establishing synagogues and kosher kitchens. . . . We must find a solution by which the children will go to our settlements, while simultaneously meeting the demands of religion."[3] I shall discuss below at greater length the policy adopted by Ben-Gurion, who did not compromise on educating toward the values of the Labor movement, but at the same time refused to enter into a head-on confrontation with religious circles and their values.

The first 1,228 refugee children from Teheran arrived in Palestine on 18 February 1943.[4] Of these children and youth, 719 were placed in various frameworks of Youth Aliya*—primarily secular settlements—and it was this that gave rise to the protest that later became an "affair."[5] A delegation appeared before Henrietta Szold, then head of Youth Aliya, demanding that education of the Teheran Childen be entrusted entirely to religious circles. Its members threatened that should their request be rejected, the Ashkenazic Chief Rabbi Isaac Halevi Herzog would turn to "all those who put on phylacteries daily, to all women who light Sabbath candles, and even to those who attend the synagogue only on Yom Kippur" to launch a struggle for religious education of these children. Rabbi Herzog hinted that he would not hesitate to address international bodies as well to pressure the Jewish Agency Executive to alter its policy.[6]

After a few months, in the wake of the harsh public controversy between religious and secular circles, Ben-Gurion and his colleagues were forced to agree to the appointment of a commission of clarification to deal with the Teheran Children issue. The commission was initially composed of Yitzhak Gruenbaum, Dr. Werner Senator, Rabbi Yehuda Leib Fishman (Maimon), and members of the Jewish Agency's Immigration Department. However, after a further public uproar and complaints that it was inconceivable that those responsible for immigration "investigate themselves," a new commission of three was appointed by the court of the Zionist Congress in the spring of 1943, consisting of attorney Shmuel Ussishkin, Dr. Yeshayahu Wolfsberg (Avida), and Dr. Shmuel Friedman. The commission was charged with collecting testimony about whether acts of anti-religious coercion had in fact been committed regarding these children and presenting the leadership of the Jewish Agency with its conclusions regarding a suitable educational framework for the Teheran Children. In the summer of 1943, after about two and a half months, the commission presented its report which concluded, in brief, that the severe accusations regarding treatment of the Teheran Children were unjustified, though nevertheless noting that "the majority of the youth leaders were not religiously observant. They showed no interest in developing a religious aura and lifestyle in the children's house, and did not evince any initiative in this direction." Furthermore, there were youth leaders who interfered with the prayers of their charges, did not bother to provide them with kosher food, and more.[7]

Even as the commission of clarification was being appointed, attempts were made by the Jewish Agency Executive to arrive at compromises regarding the practical problems of educating the children who had reached Teheran, particularly regarding educational frameworks for those who had already been brought to Eretz Israel. In the spring of 1943, Youth Aliya set certain guidelines according to which "each child should be educated in a manner compatible with the atmosphere in his parents' home." It was likewise stated that "children from the age of 14 up will be afforded the right to decide for themselves the kind of religious education they wish to receive." Actually, 124 of the first group of Teheran Children had been orphaned of both parents.[8] For them—especially the younger ones—it was difficult to remember their family background. In other cases, there were those who were "convinced" to transfer to a secular framework; in practice, the guidelines set down were not really strictly observed. Actually, there were dozens of cases of children from religious backgrounds who were transferred to secular educational frameworks, especially in secular kibbutzim. In the final analysis, even Youth Aliya officials admitted that "in 93 cases there were appeals concerning the place [of absorption], and it turned out that there had been mistakes. In 27 cases the appeals were justified."[9]

It should be noted that the Teheran Children affair involved tension not only between the religious and secular camps but also between the two religious movements, *Hamizrachi** and *Agudat Israel*.*[10] Agudat Israel strongly protested the transfer of children from religious families to Hamizrachi institutions, demanding that half of the children be educated in their own institutions.[11] In fact, 278 of the Teheran Children were sent to Hamizrachi institutions, while only forty were transferred to ultra-Orthodox ones.[12] Hamizrachi, for its part, accused Agudat Israel of attempting "to seduce children among those who came from Teheran and others to switch over to Agudat Israel,"[13] protesting against such attempts and warning that "we cannot under any circumstances accept such interference with our work."[14] Meeting with Rabbi Yitzhak Meir Levin, the political leader of Agudat Israel, Ben-Gurion openly told him that it was incumbent upon himself and all Zionists to safeguard good relations first and foremost with Hamizrachi, since that movement supported Zionism, while other religious circles opposed it. Ben-Gurion emphasized that he wished to tighten cooperation with Agudat Israel as well—but not at the expense of Hamizrachi.[15]

Rabbis Isaac Herzog and Ben-Zion Ouziel (the Ashkenazic and Sephardic *chief rabbis*,* respectively) were very much involved in the "Teheran Children affair," and it was they who to a great extent fanned the fires of conflict. Rabbi Herzog was the more insistent of the two. At a meeting on 24 June 1943, between representatives of the Jewish Agency Executive and the Chief Rabbinate, he said: "It is incumbent upon the people of Israel to care for those children who have come here without parents. They are a pledge entrusted to the people; they do not belong to one party or another. . . . The Israelite nation is a religious nation. . . . There is no suitable education for these children other than a religious one, such as we received from our fathers." His unequivocal conclusion was that, "There is one absolute authority in matters of religion, namely, the Chief Rabbinate, and it is the Chief Rabbinate that is responsible for religious education."[16] About a week later, Rabbi Herzog sent a personal, handwritten letter to Ben-Gurion, in which he condemned secular education as being "heretical and rowdy . . . that will ultimately dry the roots of our national life from within, and deny [the nation] those powers by virtue of which it has existed for thousands of years." Herzog demanded that Ben-Gurion apply the full power of his influence and acquiesce to "the voice from above," and "make tremendous efforts to save, at least, those tens of thousands of refugee children who are yet to come . . . that they not be caught up in the surge of secularism, but grow up as a healthy and health-giving element, in the spiritual and moral sense."[17]

Ben-Gurion's files do not contain a reply; one may assume that none was written, perhaps to not stir up further controversy. Since Ben-Gurion expressed his own principled position in all of the discussions, he felt no need to respond directly to the religiously zealous letter of Rabbi Herzog. His position contained several basic principles from which he was unwilling to back down: (1) There are different beliefs and principles within the Jewish people. "I have no common language with those who claim that the Israelite nation is only the Jewish religion." (2) A non-religious Jew is not a "deformed Jew." Secular circles also have principles and are prepared to fight for them "to their very souls." (3) One must avoid fraternal warfare, because "Judaism cannot exist without Jews." (4) The way to prevent fraternal warfare is acceptance by all of the rules of mutual respect and the principles of not imposing either secularism or religiosity. (5) Every decision must be reached by a majority. One must emphasize "the rule of the people and not the rule of the rabbis."[18]

Sephardic Chief Rabbi Ouziel, somewhat less militant than Rabbi Herzog, stated: "We have not said that we specifically wish to raise the children in the *yeshiva*;* we will send them to religious kibbutzim. We do not insist that they come and pray like us every day, but that they should observe the Sabbath, that they should know that there is such a thing as prayer, that a Jew prays to God, and does not turn away from his God."[19] When dealing in a later chapter with the controversy over the education of children who came in the mass immigration of 1948–1951, we shall once again encounter the forcefulness of these chief rabbis and again distinguish between the more powerful demands of Rabbi Herzog and the more moderate position of Rabbi Ouziel.

When all of the controversies had ended, it turned out that far fewer children than had been anticipated were rescued via Teheran. The great hope of saving a myriad of refugee children from the Holocaust was not to materialize, and the debate over their education remained an open wound, mainly ideological in character.

From then on, the affair of the Teheran Children was to become a symbol for the ultra-Orthodox public. Years later, one of their members would write that "like the *Cantonists** in their day, these children too will serve in the history of Israel as a symbol of terrible spiritual and physical destruction."[20] "Teheran Children" has since then become a concept and slogan for ultra-Orthodox Jewry in its struggle with secular Jews who, it was claimed, wished "to distance the nation from the authority of the Divine Torah."[21] It was repeatedly argued in ultra-Orthodox circles that these children "were forcibly stripped of the ornaments of their faith in the God of Israel and His Torah; they were forced to deny their Judaism and educated to a life of lawless impiety."[22]

THE AFFAIR OF THE YEMENITE CHILDREN DURING WORLD WAR II

From the very beginnings of immigration from Yemen in the late nineteenth and early twentieth centuries, it was claimed that the veteran Yishuv was "spoiling" the Yemenite immigrants and interfering with their religiosity.[23] In late 1943 and early 1944, various religious personalities complained of "a new affair involving immigration, worse than that of the Teheran Children." This time the issue was the absorption of some 4,500 immigrants from Yemen, who had arrived during the period 1942–1944, and acts of anti-religious coercion committed against them.[24] Religious circles demanded an "authorized examination and investigation by the Jewish Agency Executive whose conclusions will be made public."[25] As early as November 1943, Moshe Glickman-Porush, of Agudat Israel, wrote in the ultra-Orthodox *Kol Yisrael*: "When the 'Teheran Children' arrived in the Land of Israel a great row was aroused concerning them, and everyone felt that an extraordinary injustice had been done to these children, in that they were given over into unreliable hands. This week [the Yemenite children] came to the Land of Israel . . . and thus far no one has heard of any effort on behalf of these children."[26] In January 1944, an instructor in a Yemenite *yeshiva* wrote in *Hatzofe*, the newspaper of Hamizrachi, that an instructor in an immigrant camp "between Karkur and Kfar Pines" had mocked the prayer of the Yemenites, that he "conducts anti-religious propaganda among them," and that he "shaved off their *payot* [sidelocks] with a razor ... saying: 'in the Land of Israel one needs to be clean like soldiers, and it's not fit to grow *payot* as in the Diaspora.' "[27] *Kol Yisrael* quoted the report from *Hatzofe*, adding: "A second edition of the 'Teheran Children affair' is in the making.... This is not a matter of 'affairs,' neither of the 'affair' of Teheran or that of 'Yemen,' but of a systematic uprooting of what is most precious and sacred to our people from our holy land, of a war against religion, an anti-religious inquisition."[28] About two weeks later *Hatzofe* reported in a similar vein that there were those in the immigrant camp near Karkur who "strive to completely uproot the religiosity of the new immigrants," and that the camp had "become the site of inquisition for immigrants from Yemen."[29] The religious press became filled with headlines and news stories phrased in an extremely pained, aggressive style, such as: "Abuse of the Religious Sentiments of the Immigrants"; "He Who Goes to Prayer Is Expelled"[30]; "Insulting and Offensive Attitude to Religious Immigrants Regarding *Kashrut** at the Karkur Camp"[31]; "Youth Leaders from *Hashomer Hatzair** Snatch Up the Souls of the Olim Like Beasts of Prey"[32]; "Histadrut members must be clearly told.... Do not ensnare innocent and ingenious youngsters in order to distance them from religious life and observance of the Torah and the commandments. This is a shocking crime [tantamount to] kidnapping. 'Do not harm My anointed ones!' "[33]; "Oppression of Yemenite Children"[34]; "They Cut Off *Payot*, Don't Allow Them to Pray, Feed Them Non-Kosher Food"[35]; "Parents [who wished to send their children to a kindergarten of *Hapoel Hamizrachi**] were threatened that their furnishings would be taken away, and they would even be denied work"[36]; and "The Scandal of the Oppression of Jewish Children."[37]

In February 1944—following political pressure by all of the religious circles— an investigating committee was sent to the camp in Karkur. Its members, who belonged to the Association of Yemenites—a movement that had officially joined the Histadrut one month earlier—declared: "Rumors and published accounts that ... [the Yemenites] have been coerced into shaving off their sidelocks or have been fed non-kosher meat are completely unfounded." The committee, however, noted that the Yemenites "are in great need of a spiritual mentor who will visit them regularly to teach them and encourage them [to live] in the spirit of religion." Its members also stated that there was a need for a Yemenite cook, holy books, and religious artifacts.[38]

In April 1944, Rabbi Meir Berlin (Bar-Ilan), leader of Hamizrachi, demanded of Ben-Gurion that the investigating committee's conclusions refuting charges of anti-religious coercion in the immigrant camps be made public, but

Ben-Gurion evaded this call, and in fact refused their publication.[39] Apparently Ben-Gurion was aware of the fact that despite the report exonerating those involved with the immigrants from all guilt, there was nevertheless at least some partial basis to the claims. A letter written on his behalf to those engaged in the absorption of Yemenite immigrants at the same period read in part: "Comrade Ben-Gurion wishes to know who appoints the instructors for these camps. Is it not possible nevertheless to provide them [the Yemenites] with instructors in their own spirit?"[40] This is another instance of the policy that would characterize Ben-Gurion several years later: he did not want to exacerbate the conflict between the religious and secular public, but he wished to attract the new immigrants to his party and its ideology by friendly means, as much as possible without coming into conflict with their basic lifestyle.

Religious circles, however, did not cease to complain about the absorption of Yemenite Jews. On 20 April 1944, Rabbi Yihya Netanel Alchech wrote to Ben-Gurion: "Does not your hair stand on edge when you hear the cries of the immigrants, who are upset and agitated by what is being done to them in the spheres of religion and education?"[41] Ben-Gurion does not seem to have replied. On the other hand, the Histadrut published responses to complaints of religious coercion on billboards throughout the country. Thus, for example, the Secretariat of the Workers Council of Herzliya informed that city's residents: "It has been brought to our attention that certain circles have begun inciting against the Histadrut . . . regarding the handling of the Yemenite immigration. . . . The immigrants from Yemen, both veterans and newcomers, know very well who truly cares for them and who exploits their distress to stir up controversy and conflict."[42]

The fact that the wave of immigration from Yemen was limited and came to an end in mid-1944 while the religious camp was divided and limited in influence enabled the Labor movement to ward off the charges. The fact that all of this was happening during World War II, when there was great public concern for the fate of European Jewry, likewise affected matters. Notwithstanding the complaints, the absorption process of the religious immigrants from Yemen—conducted mostly by secular Jews, almost all of whom were members of the Labor movement—did not change as a result of the criticism and controversy. Some of these Yemenite immigrants remained in the camps until after the establishment of the State of Israel, and the policy of cultural absorption remained unchanged: to try to integrate them into the Land of Israel "melting pot."

CHAPTER 2

ABSORPTION OF MASS IMMIGRATION IN THE EARLY YEARS

FACTS AND FIGURES

Between the establishment of the State of Israel in May 1948 and mid-1950 nearly half a million new immigrants entered Israel. About 102,000 arrived during the War of Independence, from May 1948 until the end of that year, while 17,200 had already come during the first months of 1948, until the end of the British Mandate on 14 May.[1] There were another 240,000 during 1949, and an additional 100,000 during the first half of 1950.[2] In most months, the average number of immigrants did not drop below 20,000, and there were those in which it reached 30,000.[3]

THE FIRST PERIOD OF ABSORPTION: MAY–DECEMBER 1948

Even though part of this period coincided with the bloodiest battles of the War of Independence, it was in some respects the easiest era of immigration absorption in comparison with those that followed. During this initial time, immigrants to Israel were predominantly of the "saved remnant"—those who survived the Holocaust in Europe.[4] From 15 May 1948, until the end of the year, 86 percent of the immigrants came from Europe, and a few hundred came from America.[5] During that same period, about 100,000 new immigrants were settled in houses in abandoned

Arab villages, in abandoned neighborhoods in mixed cities (Jerusalem, Haifa, Jaffa, Tiberias, and Safed), or in cities that had been entirely abandoned (Acre, Lod, Ramle, and Migdal-Ashkelon). This also was a relatively easy time with respect to employment, compared to the years that followed, since there was a scarcity of laborers due to military service and wartime mobilization. As for the educational system, it too absorbed the children of these immigrants more easily, for several reasons: first, there were fewer immigrant children than in the subsequent period; second, most of the children came from Europe, making their cultural absorption easier for the teachers, most of whom were themselves of European origin; third, since many of the immigrants were absorbed in urban neighborhoods alongside the veteran population, not an inconsiderable number of immigrant children were placed in regular, already existing classes.

THE SECOND PERIOD OF ABSORPTION: FROM THE BEGINNING OF 1949 TO MAY 1950

This was the "period of the immigrant camps," which in several respects seems to have been the most difficult time of absorption. The year 1949 was the peak one for immigration to Israel, one in which the relative proportion of immigrants from Asia and Africa greatly increased. Some 111,000 immigrants—47 percent of that year's total—came from Oriental countries. Moreover, whereas at the beginning of 1949 only 28,000 lived in immigrant camps, by mid-year, that number had grown to 60,000, and the total neared 100,000 by the end of the year. Dr. Giora Josephtal, head of the Absorption Department of the Jewish Agency, told his colleagues in Mapai that some three-quarters of those living in the camps were Oriental Jews.[6] Many of the immigrants from Asia and Africa were young—about 37 percent of them were under age fourteen.[7] Thus many of those living in the immigrant camps were children from Islamic countries of an age for whom education was compulsory.[8]

Physical conditions in the camps were extremely difficult. The immigrants were housed in cinder-block structures with tin roofs that had formerly served the British Army as storehouses, in large huts, or in tents. Entire families lived together under conditions of great crowding, and most of them did not leave the camps, even to work. Journalist Arye Gelblum was the first to describe conditions in the immigrant camps in a series of fifteen dramatic reports in *Ha'aretz*, entitled "I Was a New Immigrant," beginning on 13 April 1949. In the first article, he wrote:

> I open one door after another, and everywhere I see exactly the same
> sight: dozens of beds along the sides of the "hall," near the walls, and
> in the middle of the "hall." Beds, beds, beds, one bed touching the

next—and in between, large crates containing some of the possessions of the new immigrants, on top of which there are clothing, rags, cooking utensils (the crates also serve as tables), while in every space between the crates—more beds. Some of the beds are empty, most of them are unmade, dirty, while on the others lie women, old men and women, young girls and boys, and even children—all idle.

Gelblum's description reflects to a great degree the difficulties of life in the immigrant camps. Moreover, sanitary conditions and general cleanliness in the camps were abominable: entire camps, housing thousands of immigrants, were put up with hardly any plumbing, with only a few water faucets, without showers, and with scant toilet facilities. Many camps lacked sufficient public buildings, creating a great shortage of available places for classrooms or for prayer.

As noted, many of the inhabitants of the camps were children and youth below age eighteen, mostly from Islamic countries. In the spring of 1950, when the Frumkin Commission was conducting its investigation, only one-third of the children who were of compulsory education age were in fact studying at any school. A report written by Dr. Ephraim E. Urbach, who was appointed head of the Department for Education in the Immigrant Camps on 16 May 1950, states: "When we assumed [responsibility for] education in the camps, there were, according to notification received from the Central Bureau of Statistics, 12,570 children [up to age fourteen] in immigrant camps of various kinds. Of these, only 4,451 children, that is, 35 percent, were actually studying in the schools."[9] There were numerous reasons so many children were not studying in any educational frameworks in the camps. The major ones were: (1) the organizational inability of the Ministry of Education to meet the challenge of absorbing the large numbers of immigrants; (2) a great shortage of teaching staff and instructors; (3) severe budgetary problems; (4) lack of public buildings; (5) many parents and children suffered from severe health problems; (6) the heterogenous nature of the great wave of immigration, and the fact that in many of the ethnic communities people were not accustomed to studying in and attending organized schools; (7) the economic and other difficulties of the parents, who needed the assistance of their children and therefore did not send them to school.

THE THIRD PERIOD OF ABSORPTION:
FROM MAY 1950—THE PERIOD OF THE *MA'ABAROT*

The term *ma'abara* (pl. *ma'abarot*,* or "transit camps") was coined by Levi Eshkol, who also introduced this form of absorption.[10] The first *ma'abara* was set up at Kisalon, in the Jerusalem corridor, in mid-May 1950. The objective was to change the way of life in the immigrant camps in several major areas. There were no longer surrounding fences, and the *ma'abara* was a settlement like any other in Israel, no longer a closed, isolated "island." Collective kitchens were closed down, and the free distribution of food by Jewish Agency officials was stopped. The inhabitants of the *ma'abara* were expected to find employment in its environs and to feed their families through their own efforts. The *ma'abarot* were converted into separate administrative entities or combined with existing local authorities. In many cases, the special educational and cultural frameworks of the immigrant camps were abolished and integrated into the educational system of greatest geographical proximity.

The government commission of inquiry, which is the subject of this book, was primarily related to the first two periods of absorption, although I shall discuss the implications of its conclusions—and the degree to which they were implemented—for the period of the *ma'abarot* and later.

CHAPTER 3

WHY WAS A GOVERNMENT COMMISSION OF INQUIRY APPOINTED?

The decision to appoint a government commission of inquiry came in the wake of strong pressures applied by the new immigrants, the religious public in Israel, and Jews in the Diaspora (primarily in the United States).

Though pressure by new immigrants was not the major factor that led to the appointment of the commission, it is nevertheless deserving to be the first element discussed. We should note that at that time, most immigrants from the Islamic countries were disorganized and lacking in political influence, so their agitation concerning anti-religious coercion did not make a very strong impression. The strongest ethnic community, whose efforts and influence concerning religious education were most effective, was the Yemenites. What made this community especially influential?

UNREST AMONG YEMENITE IMMIGRANTS REGARDING THE EDUCATION OF THEIR CHILDREN

The Jews of Yemen and Aden were the first to complain about anti-religious coercion in the immigrant camps. They were brought to Israel during Operation "Magic Carpet" (the popular name for what was officially called Operation "On Wings of Eagles"), which began in December 1948 and intensified during the latter half of 1949. During 1948, only 300 Jews came to Israel from Yemen and Aden; in 1949, there were an additional 38,100 immigrants from those countries, while another 9,100 came in 1950.[1] They were religiously observant Jews and were generally acknowledged as such within the Yishuv.[2] This ethnic group, unlike most other Jewish communities in the Diaspora, had been isolated for centuries and was hardly aware of the "secrets" of modern times—the Jewish Enlightenment and the attendant crisis it caused in traditional society. Rabbis and sages were the recognized and honored leaders of the Yemenite immigrants. They were primarily concerned with problems relating to religious matters, complaining about issues such as the lack of Torah scrolls, the absence of ritual baths in the immigrant camps, the paucity of synagogues, and particularly the lack of religious education for their children.

Unlike members of other ethnic communities, who were dispersed in immigrant camps throughout the country, the Yemenites were concentrated in four distinct camps: Athlit, Ein-Shemer, Beit Lid (the entire camp was divided into seven sections, immigrants from Yemen being housed only in Beit Lid B) and Rosh Ha'ayin.[3] Many of the new immigrants had relatives who had come to the country from Yemen in 1881 during the *First Aliya,** during the *Second Aliya** (the group whose immigration was helped by Shmuel Yavnieli), between the two world wars, and during World War II. All told, prior to Operation Magic Carpet there were already some 40,000 Yemenite immigrants and their descendants in Israel.[4] Along with the newcomers, the size of the Yemenite community in Israel was about 80,000 (out of a total Jewish population of less than 1 million) by the middle of 1949.[5] All of these factors taken together—the concentration of the Yemenite immigrants in specific, isolated camps, their large numbers, and the fact that they found many of their countrymen upon arriving in Israel—greatly enhanced the influence of those who came on Operation Magic Carpet relative to immigrants from any other ethnic community. However, these would evidently not have been sufficient were it not for the political consolidation of the Yemenite immigrants—albeit in several political frameworks—and were it not for the fact that an active leadership had already developed in the immigrant camps.[6] Their political power also was enhanced by the widely accepted image of the Yemenites as industrious, easy-natured, and disciplined persons, traits that made them popular with the public and leadership in Israel.[7] Side by side with these positive attitudes were many negative stereotypes of Yemenite Jews,[8] such as Yemenite immigrants being excessively pliable and easily directed, ideologically and politically.

When the State of Israel was established, the Yemenites were already organized in a number of political organizations. Despite the splits in the community and harsh personal disputes, three Yemenites were voted in to the first elected Knesset—over and above the proportional representation of any other Oriental

Jewish community.[9] The three Knesset members of Yemenite origin were Zecharia Gluska (the Yemenite Union), Avraham Tabib (Mapai), and Hayyim Meguri-Cohen (Herut). Yemenite strength is indicated by the fact that when Tabib died at the beginning of 1950, Mapai instructed twenty-six (!) of its members who were on its Knesset list to withdraw to enable him to be replaced by another Yemenite—Israel Yeshayahu.[10] Interestingly enough, it was precisely the religious parties that made no effort to have a representative of the Yemenites in their Knesset factions, nor in most of their other decision-making forums.

The Yemenites, as we noted, were the first to complain vociferously about their religious tribulations. Their complaints, particularly concerning the education of their children, were conveyed to the authorities by various religious personalities and elected representatives of the political parties (particularly those of the Religious Front). Thus, for example, Rabbi Zadok Ben-Shalom Yitzhari wrote to Prime Minister David Ben-Gurion:

> I was one of the first immigrants in Operation Magic Carpet.... As a religious person, I joined Hapoel Hamizrachi and was assigned the task of caring for matters of religion and tradition at the immigrant camps [on behalf of Hapoel Hamizrachi].... The government of Yemen never oppressed in regard to religion. On the contrary, as a religious government it recognized our rights, our religion, and our faith. How shocked we were to see that even here in our own country, in our own state, in our own government, we have once more been persecuted on account of our religion and our faith.... The *activists*,* the administrators, and the supervisors in charge of the immigrant camps—it is they who pursue us, it is they who scorn us and our Torah and those who study it, it is they who have greatly sinned, and it is they who have become the abusers, vituperators, and blasphemers of the works of the living God.... Some of the immigrants have bitterly complained to me of acts that are shameful and terrible in their eyes, as they see people who are called Jews angering them by desecrating the Sabbath before their eyes. And [they complained] about the order given to send their children to a school of which they do not approve, in the charge of teachers who remove their hats and cut off their sidelocks. They went on to tell me that those who attend to them [in the camps] curse and blaspheme them and the traditions of their ancestors.... And now, Mister Prime Minister, the eyes of the entire community are turned towards you.... Keep an eye on those whom you rule.... Do not allow those among the people who cast off the yoke to act harshly against His flock.[11]

Zecharia Gluska, the Yemenite Union Member of Knesset (MK), was the first to raise the trials and tribulations of the Yemenite immigrants in the Knesset, but he did so rather late—only in the summer of 1949—after public complaints had already been circulating for several months. At a Knesset session, he argued: "The community of Yemenite Jews is the first victim. Those responsible in the government forget that an entire community of 50,000 Jews is oppressed. Among them are fathers who worked as porters and mothers who washed clothing in the boiling sun for the Ashkenazic lady, and both father and mother did so for only one purpose—to provide their son or daughter with a suitable education." Gluska went on to warn: "For the moment they protest silently, but this silent protest may become an open and stormy one. The day is not far off when a great cry will break forth from the mouths of these people."[12] It seems that Gluska was well aware of the problems faced by his community and reported them accurately. But his warnings were to no avail, and a few months later his bleak forecast came true.

COMPLAINTS BY LIBYAN JEWS

Another Jewish community, most of whose members were religiously observant and firmly committed to tradition, was Libyan Jewry.[13] During the years of the great wave of immigration (May 1948–December 1951, known in Hebrew as *Ha'aliya Hagedola*—the Great Aliya), 32,271 Jews immigrated to Israel from Libya.[14] They began arriving in Israel in March 1949, and they too were initially concentrated in specific immigrant camps: in Beit Lid, Beer Ya'akov, Ein Hatkhelet, near Netanya, Yad Hama'avir, and Ashkelon.[15] A particularly high percentage of immigrants from Libya were children and youth of compulsory school age.[16]

Though Libyan Jews were of course also affected by the process of "uniform education" in the immigrant camps, their voices were hardly heard in public. They vocalized their complaints primarily within their own community, and these also found their way back to the Jewish community still in Libya. Thus, for example, *Hayyenu* (an organ of *Bnai Akiva** and *Bahad** in Libya)[17] published a letter to the editor by A. H. Gabizon, head of the Jewish religious court in Libya, which read in part:

> "Where are you from?" Everyone in the Land of Israel asks this question. . . . We too are Hebrews and observe the law of the Torah— where, then, is Hapoel Hamizrachi, the party that claims to support those who observe the Torah??? . . . The Tripolitanians must care for themselves, and if I am not for myself who will be for me [a Rabbinic aphorism, from the tractate *Avot* 1:14] and organize a committee representing them, that shall come and go before them . . . so that the congregation of the Lord shall not be like sheep without a shepherd

[after Num. 27:17, which refers to the qualities of Joshua as the successor to Moses].[18]

Gabizon's main complaint against his community—that it was disorganized and hence lacked strong representatives, such as the Yemenites—was true. There can be no doubt that this factor greatly weakened the force behind the demands raised by members of the Libyan community. In another letter to the editor of *Hayyenu*, explicit mention is made of the "soul snatching in the immigrant camps." The writer calls upon his fellow Libyan immigrants: "We are returning proudly to the Holy Land . . . and how can we, children of the Lord our God, dare to turn our backs on our origin and betray our holy and perfect Torah, our only heritage? Let every man take care to distance himself from all these [anti-religious] instigators and those who lead astray."[19]

Only occasionally did representatives of the new immigrants from the Oriental Jewish communities make public appearances at conferences of political parties and various other institutions. One of those few was Joseph Maimon, formerly of Tripoli. At the Eighteenth World Congress of Hamizrachi,[20] Maimon complained that the future of immigrants from his community, as far as religious life was concerned, was particularly disturbing. He claimed that even Hapoel Hamizrachi did not do enough to prevent discrimination between the immigrants from Libya and those from Europe, and that religious youth and groups of religious *halutzim* (pioneers) were not being absorbed in Israel.[21] Maimon also approached Youth Aliya, firmly demanding that emissaries from nonreligious parties not be sent to Tripoli.[22]

It has already been noted that the protests of Libyan Jews in Israel against acts of secularization made little impact. This may be one of the reasons, in the winter of 1950, that Mapai rejected the demand of the Religious Front and refused to agree that all Libyan immigrant children should receive a religious education. Mapai was only willing "to forego" Yemenite children, declaring that all Yemenites would be considered religious Jews and educated in the religious school system, but refusing to concede in the case of Libyan children. I shall elaborate upon this matter later.

COMPLAINTS BY OTHER ORIENTAL COMMUNITIES

We have little evidence of complaints by new immigrants from other Islamic countries—such as Morocco, Tunisia, Algeria, and so on—concerning their children's absorption in the educational system. Such complaints were of course part and parcel of their other objections concerning the way they were absorbed during the period 1948–1951. We also have little specific information concerning their complaints regarding anti-religious discrimination. For several reasons these are almost completely lacking from surviving written documentation, some of which I shall enumerate:

1. Those who arrived during the period of mass immigration were absorbed by a population, the vast majority of which was comprised of Ashkenazim.[23] All in all, throughout the entire British Mandate period until 1948, a grand total of some 60,000 Jews immigrated from Islamic countries.[24] The Yishuv had difficulty understanding the language of the new immigrants, whose culture was strange to them.

2. The immigrants were housed in immigrant camps, which to a great extent were a kind of new exile within the State of Israel. The camps were surrounded by fences, placed under special guard, and declared "off limits." Under such circumstances, few complaints came to the knowledge of the veteran population in the country.

3. The immigrants were without financial resources. Lacking even the most elementary means of subsistence, they obviously did not have the means of producing their own media. They were dependent upon the "establishment" for everything—for the most part, political parties, and these of course had no interest in publicizing the misfortunes and complaints of immigrants.

4. Most immigrants differed ideologically from the established Yishuv. Their immigration was primarily motivated by distress, not by Zionist-pioneering ideas. For all of these reasons, and perhaps others as well, there is no more than scattered written evidence of complaints by new immigrants from Oriental countries.

A series of articles by Arye Gelblum, published in *Ha'aretz* during the spring of 1949,[25] placed a severe stigma on all immigrants from Islamic countries, particularly those from North Africa. He did not distinguish among immigrants from Libya, Morocco, Tunisia, and Algeria, leveling claims bordering on racism against them all. "We have here an extremely primitive people. The level of their education borders upon total ignorance, and even more serious is their total inability to comprehend anything spiritual," wrote Gelblum. He also categorically stated that, "Unlike the Yemenites, they also lack roots in Judaism" and "are entirely subject to the play of the most primitive and wild instincts," including knifing, fighting, playing cards, drunkenness, and prostitution.[26] Few of the new immigrants responded to these accusations. One of them, the founder of a Zionist association in Agadir and Tangiers, related his own severe personal hardships, noting that: "My situation was complicated by my being a Moroccan, for as such I can barely open my mouth to speak since people see me *ab initio* as a kind of habitual criminal."[27] The other few reactions published also argued that Gelblum was guilty of generalization and defamation. Most of those who came to the defense of the new immigrants were themselves longtime settlers who had immigrated years earlier from the same countries, or Zionist emissaries who had come to know those Jewish communities before their mass immigration.

An assembly consisting of "some fifty immigrants from North Africa, representatives of the immigrants in the camps" convened in the summer of 1949. This was to a large extent in reaction to Gelblum's articles and the public opinion that they helped create. *Davar* reported:

> All the speakers expressed the bitterness of the North African immigrants towards the institutions, the government, the Ashkenazic communities, and the Yishuv as a whole, for the contempt which they encounter wherever they turn. They are convinced that there is discrimination against Sephardic Jews in general, and the North African immigrant in particular. . . . One of the speakers . . . did not hesitate to say that the Yishuv as a whole relates to North African Jews with "racist antisemitism."

The speakers demanded that they be allowed to live in Israel, following "the Jewish lifestyle of North African immigrants."[28]

Almost no one listened to the complaints of the Oriental communities in general. In practice, the little attention paid was primarily to complaints by the Yemenite immigrants. I have already enumerated what led to a greater degree of response to the Yemenites: their geographical concentration, large numbers, and political influence; their leadership in Israel, which comprised both veterans and newcomers; and their great devotion to religious practices relative to members of all other communities. Nonetheless, the Yemenites were not really listened to; rather, the authorities succumbed to their relative power but simultaneously continued to wage a cultural war against their value system.

The powder keg of cultural confrontation in Israel between secular and religious Jews had been loaded for many years and was doomed to explode at one stage or another. The Yemenites evidently "lit the fuse" of a network of relations, which would in any event have crumbled at a later stage. During the early years of statehood, the entire relationship between the secular integrating public and the religious-traditional community that was being integrated, between one world of values and another that differed from it, hung on a thread. The members of the Oriental communities, particularly the Yemenites, merely exposed the fault line already inherent in the process of cultural-educational absorption during the pre-state period and Israel's early years. Until the establishment of Israel, the new society in Eretz Israel had been molded along secular social and cultural lines. However, the large numbers who came during the period of mass immigration altered the norms of behavior that had emerged over the course of decades. The *Kulturkampf* between the new culture in the Land of Israel and the traditional one was largely inevitable. The immigrants from Yemen, who refused to forego their religiosity, were the decisive catalyst against the "melting pot" that alienated people from religion, and they swept with them the Jewish public and society in general.

PRESSURES OF THE RELIGIOUS PUBLIC PRIOR TO THE APPOINTMENT OF THE FRUMKIN COMMISSION

Religious circles were already aware in 1948 of anti-religious coercion in the education of new immigrant children, however, they did not launch a campaign regarding this matter until late 1949. I shall try to clarify the reasons for the restrained policy of the Religious Front, which continued for about one year.

The most significant internal discussion known to have been held concerning the education of immigrant children took place on 15 December 1948, in the offices of the World Center of Hamizrachi. The first speaker was the chairman of its education division, Y. Bernstein, who had called the meeting "to find a way to *save something* of the immigration that is flowing to our country for Hamizrachi education" (emphasis added). Dr. R. H. Etzion, the chief supervisor of Hamizrachi education, informed those present—perhaps for the first time—of the "uniform education" in the immigrant camps, stating:

> The Jewish Agency has appointed Mr. Nahum Levin, of the Culture Department of the *Va'ad Haleumi*,* to coordinate this activity. He, of course, does everything as he sees fit. The Jewish Agency officials work on behalf of the Histadrut, and the education system in the camps is on behalf of the Histadrut. True, this is a temporary educational system, but nevertheless it is education for the benefit of a particular stream. . . . The people involved in immigration and absorption and those working in the camps on behalf of our organization must find a solution to this serious problem.

What is striking is that Etzion related to the issue as a limited, specific problem. He did not blame the Mapai leadership for unified education, nor did he consider it more than a temporary problem. Similarly, at that same meeting, Dr. M. Kurtz stated: "All the claims made concerning the Jewish Agency won't help. *This is a fact against which we are powerless to fight.* I don't see a great danger in the fact that education within the camps was entrusted to Nahum Levin. *This temporary education cannot damage us; this activity within the absorption camps is not what will determine things*" (emphasis added). Kurtz and others proposed concentrating the main efforts upon educational absorption of the immigrants outside of the camps, in their permanent places of residence. Many of the discussants stressed the lack of coordination among the various religious groups and the fact that information concerning the absorption of the Great Aliya was not transmitted from one religious body to another. Some had recourse to sharper language. Joseph Goldschmidt, for example, called this state of affairs "chaos." The meeting adopted a resolution to establish a kind of general staff—"a committee which will determine guidelines and carry out everything."[29]

Following this discussion, Moshe Shakdiel, director of the Education Division of the World Center of Hamizrachi, who was present at the meeting but did not take an active part therein, wrote a personal letter to Rabbi Y. M. Kobalski, a member of the Directorate of Hamizrachi. Holding a different view than some of his colleagues, in his letter he vociferously condemned uniform education in the immigrant camps:

> Thousands [of immigrants] arrive every week. They are put in the reception camps run by the Jewish Agency, where their children are formally provided with a kind of uniform education by the Jewish Agency and the state. A few months later the immigrants leave the reception camps for the cities, the villages, and abandoned Arab [villages and neighborhoods]. Both the parents and the children have already been properly "processed," and it is only literally by the skin of our teeth that it is possible to save something for our religious education.[30]

For Shakdiel, uniform education, notwithstanding its temporary nature, was of decisive influence. We do not know what response was received by Shakdiel, but one fact is clear: despite knowledge of the facts, for many long months no special effort was made by Hamizrachi's leadership—or any other religious body—to change them.[31]

The vast majority of the religious public in Israel was unaware of what was being done in the immigrant camps. Only in the spring of 1949 were the first isolated reports concerning anti-religious coercion in the camps published in the religious press. Even these were extremely mild in comparison to those published only a few months later. Thus, for example, on 5 May 1949, *She'arim* (the *Poalei Agudat Israel** daily) published a lengthy report concerning the "national conference of new immigrants." In that report, Yosef Pfeffer, director of the Absorption Department of Poalei Agudat Israel, was reported as saying in passing that "the lifestyle in the camps is not Jewish." In *Hakol* (an organ of *Pagi–Poalei Agudat*

Israel in Jerusalem*) on 20 May 1949, in the context of a report entitled "With the Immigrants from Aden," the correspondent mentioned, again in passing and phrased with moderation: "I saw with my own eyes a painful sight (which should be brought to the attention of the minister of immigration), that in the middle of the Sabbath a convoy of buses arrived at the camp carrying new immigrants. . . . Now you ask yourself: Was it not possible to detain the immigrants at the airport until the end of the Sabbath?"

At the end of May 1949, religious groups began a campaign to change the conditions of education in the camps. At that time, Y. Bernstein of the Education Department of the World Center of Hamizrachi wrote on this subject to Dr. B. Ben-Yehuda, director of the Education Division of the Ministry of Education. Bernstein noted that, "According to information which we have collected, those engaged in this matter [i.e., officials of the Culture Department, headed by N. Levin] explicitly object to religious education." Bernstein went on to write: "We cannot agree that education be provided in the camps . . . in any form whatever of uniform education, even to those children whose parents request religious education." A copy of the letter was sent to Minister of Education and Culture Zalman Shazar and to two of the ministers from the Religious Front, Rabbi Maimon and Mr. M. Shapira, along with a request that "the Ministry of Education solve the problem as fast as possible."[32] The letter indicates that the problem was raised, but even then no constant pressure was applied to lead to its solution.

One may assume that there were a number of reasons for the restrained reaction of the religious camp and the paucity of pressure applied by its leadership until the middle of 1949. The first was the attempt to negotiate with the leadership of Mapai and to change conditions in the immigrant camps by "quiet diplomacy" and persuasion. Some religious leaders believed and hoped that their counterparts in Mapai—particularly David Ben-Gurion and Minister of Education and Culture Shazar—would protect the immigrants from this aggressive secular coercion.[33] A second reason was economic and party interests that led religious leaders to aspire to preserve the coalition with Mapai and to refrain from exacerbating relations with it. It was clear to them that the decisive part of the economic power belonged to the Histadrut and the dominant political party, with whom they thus needed to maintain good relations. A third reason was their concern over the supply of religious needs and over religious autonomy in education. The Religious Front—all of its factions—believed then that the only way to ensure this was by being part of the coalition.[34] Moreover, all of its leaders thought that the proper way to ensure religious education was by the system of educational streams. They feared that a split with Mapai would lead that party to form a coalition with *Mapam** and/or the *General Zionists*,* who would jointly abolish the streams in education. A fourth reason was the small number of religious immigrants until the end of 1948 and the growth in their numbers only from the beginning of 1949, when the flow of immigration from Islamic countries greatly increased. A particularly decisive factor was, as mentioned, increased immigration from Yemen in the summer of 1949. There also would seem to have been a fifth, additional reason that may have been more decisive than the four preceding ones: the religious parties were explicitly Ashkenazic and thus were distanced and alienated from the Oriental communities. I believe that they would not have stood for the same degree of anti-religious coercion, which they covertly allowed toward immigrants from Asia and Africa, being applied to immigrants from Europe and America. I shall elaborate on this last point.

As we have seen, the religious parties were up in arms during the Holocaust period over the affair of the Teheran Children. There is no doubt that the public uproar over this affair was far greater than that aroused by the anti-religious coercion of the Yemenite children, who arrived in Eretz Israel a few months later and greater than that generated by the educational absorption of Yemenite children during 1948 and early 1949. In my opinion, this state of affairs also is the outcome of the degree of affinity or estrangement sensed by the rabbis and leaders of the religious parties toward members of the different communities.

It should be noted that there had always been numerous accusations that Ashkenazic religious circles looked with disdain upon the Yemenites. Such testimony has been presented by members of the earlier waves of Yemenite immigration:

> When we first came to Israel, the Ashkenazim expressed doubts as to our Jewishness. . . . They evidently thought of us as *"Gibeonites"** who had disguised themselves as Jews. . . . They looked down upon us. They were reluctant to give their daughters to our sons [in marriage], and did not eat our slaughtered meat. . . . However, our daughters and wives served in their homes.[35]

To a large extent, Yemenite educational institutions, notwithstanding the objection of some of the Yemenites, were subordinated to Hamizrachi's educational system—and complaints that the directors of this stream did not recognize the special character of the Yemenite schools were heard continuously from the beginning of the 1920s.[36] Since the mid-1940s the "Yemenite Union" claimed that it was not given any representation on the committee that supervised Hamizrachi's educational system, despite the fact that Yemenite *Talmud Torahs** accounted for about 25 percent of that system.[37] There were those who argued:

> It was the contemptuous attitude of the religious parties . . . which pushed this public into the arms of the Histadrut, even though its leaders were free-thinkers. The disdain with which the religious leaders treated the Yemenites is as old as the history of the Return to Zion,

when a Yemenite Jew was considered unfit to complete a *minyan*,* and [an animal] slaughtered by a Yemenite rabbi was considered unfit. The discrimination against them in the assignment of religious offices and the low status assigned to their rabbis even after the establishment of the state made it clear to this public that they only found favor and were good for casting their votes at election time, without any representation or compensation.[38]

Rabbi Zadok Yitzhari, who, as we have seen, was one of the leading Yemenite activists in Hapoel Hamizrachi, abandoned that party after a relatively brief period of time and went over to the Yemenite Union, claiming contempt and discrimination toward the members of his community within Hapoel Hamizrachi.[39]

All of these cases are indicative of the discriminatory attitude of the religious public toward the Yemenites, but they also exhibited a similar attitude toward other communities from Islamic countries. Take, for example, what Y. Raphael, director of the Absorption Department of the Jewish Agency, and an observant Jew, said at a closed session of the Zionist Executive devoted to Jewish immigration from North Africa: "We would not wish this to be the only source of aliya."[40] About two weeks later, he made a similar statement: "Everyone agrees that we are not prepared that this be the only aliya."[41] There were similar statements as well, both by himself and others.

Some religious leaders tried to prod their movements into changing their attitude toward the Oriental communities. Thus, for example, at the Fifth Convention of Poalei Agudat Israel, MK Binyamin Mintz said:

> We too are not all of one fabric. We have Jews from Germany, Hungarian Jews, Romanian Jews, and Lithuanian Jews . . . so too there are Yemenite Jews, Afghani Jews, etc. They each have their own forms [of prayer], and we must not hold them in disdain. We have no other Jews. The Jews of Hungary should not think that they are *dos oibershte fon shtoisl* [lit., "the top layer of what is being crushed in a pestle," i.e., the best, the most refined]. The Master of the Universe has not yet told us who is *dos oibershte fon shtoisl*, and no Jew has the right to disqualify any other Jew. We do not know from what tribe the Messiah will come.[42]

But even such a call reflects the fundamental attitude of superiority of the religious parties toward the Oriental Jewish communities.

In summary, we may say that, until the final months of 1949, the faint response of religious political circles to anti-religious coercion in the immigrant camps was the outcome of a number of factors. There would seem to have been a combination of political considerations, economic interests, and social and cultural motivations. During Israel's first year, none of the religious parties perceived education of immigrant children to be as substantive an issue as it became during the second half of 1949. They were more concerned about other issues and religious laws then under discussion—such as the Sabbath laws, *kashrut* (i.e., kosher food), military conscription, and so on—which they deemed more critical. There is no doubt that this factor made it much easier for the labor parties to continue cultural-educational absorption in the manner that had been practiced for years.

REPORTS IN THE RELIGIOUS PRESS DURING THE SUMMER AND FALL OF 1949

During the summer and fall of 1949 the Israeli press carried numerous reports and complaints concerning the "soul snatching" conducted by the various educational streams, and not only among children of new immigrants. In particular, there were numerous complaints, by both the General Stream and the religious streams, that the Workers Stream was expanding and taking over strongholds—by both threats and temptations—at the expense of the other three. And indeed, the Workers Stream, which during the 1947–48 school year had only 384 educational institutions with 28,343 pupils, doubled its strength within less than two years: by 1949–50, it boasted a total of 668 institutions with 55,639 pupils.[43] Many of the complaints particularly emphasized the political and economic pressures for the new immigrants to send their children to study at Workers Stream schools.

Thus, for example, *Hakol*, the organ of Pagi–Poalei Agudat Israel in Jerusalem, published an editorial under the heading "Is This Freedom?" that argued in part:

> In order for the State of Israel to become a "Histadrut State"—or, more correctly, a Mapai State, since the Histadrut no longer exists as a uniform body—all that is necessary is for the Histadrut to dominate education in the state. All other areas of life in the state are either entirely in the hands of the Histadrut, or it imposes its authority upon them. Only education remains substantially outside of its domination.

The article goes on to cite several examples of Workers Stream domination of schools, particularly in those of the new aliya, and it concludes with a demand for "a fundamental non-partisan investigation of the numerous complaints made recently concerning pressure and other improper means." Otherwise, "We will be forced to conclude . . . that all talk about freedom to choose the stream desired is no more than pulling the wool over the eyes of innocents."[44]

In mid-August 1949, Hamizrachi held its Eighteenth World Convention in Jerusalem. The education of immigrant children was an issue barely raised in any of its sessions. Only in the Convention's resolutions, among dozens of others, do we read:

> Hamizrachi cannot consent to the provision of unified education in the immigrant camps, as has been recent practice ["uniform educa- tion" had been provided in the immigrant camps for about a year and a half, since March 1948—author]. The World Center of Hamiz- rachi is to immediately address the Jewish Agency Executive and the other bodies involved and insist that in every camp the pupils be clas- sified and that religious classes be arranged if the parents so wish. The World Center of Hamizrachi is to make the effort necessary to receive this right to conduct religious classes within the immigrant camps.[45]

These were unequivocal resolutions, but precisely at this time the true center of power in the movement was beginning to move from the World Center to the party leaders who represented the religious public in the Knesset.[46] The pressure applied by the religious leadership in the Knesset at the end of the summer in 1949 constantly increased and took shape.

At the beginning of September, the four Religious Front leaders met with Minister of Education and Culture Shazar—evidently for the first time—to dis- cuss the education of immigrant children.[47] At the end of that meeting, the four obtained the minister's signature upon a commitment to "ascertain that both in the cultural work in the Yishuv and in that carried out in the immigrant camps . . . Or- thodox Jewry would not be deprived of its share." In exchange, MK Pinkas, chair- man of the Knesset Finance Committee, promised "to extend to the minister of education all help necessary to receive the sum required for the Torah institute . . . from the approved budget."[48] Shazar, who was notorious for his organizational in- eptitude throughout his term in the Ministry of Education and Culture, did not carry out his signed commitment to these four religious leaders. We do not know whether MK Pinkas fulfilled his promise.

In the fall of 1949, *Hakol* carried the headline: "To Save the Immigrant Chil- dren for Torah Education." The author of the article castigated Orthodox Jewry for its "criminal apathy toward the children of the new immigrants," but argued that "the ice is finally beginning to move a bit." He informed his readers of the fi- nancial mobilization within Orthodox circles and the collection of "*redemption money*"* that had begun in Jerusalem.[49]

Yehuda Dominitz published a series of strongly phrased articles under the title "How Are Children Educated in Israel?" in *Hatzofe* beginning 23 October 1949. In the first installment, he sharply criticized, among others, the Religious Workers Stream (*zerem Haoved Hadati*), arguing that, "whether deliberately or unintentionally, Haoved Hadati has lent its hand to unthinkable acts, to convert

Jewish children from belief in their Creator." The second article was entitled "Thus Is the Soul of the Child Snared," with subtitles reading "Changes in the Size of the Streams," "The Battles between the Various Streams," "Threats and Promises," and "Misleading Parents."[50] In a third article, Dominitz dealt with the education of immigrant children, complaining of "the plague of uniform education in the camps" and of "the Histadrut propaganda—threats and denials." In an interview, the author told us that he was instructed to write this series of articles by S. Z. Shragai, who was then in charge of public information in Hapoel Hamizrachi.

Several days after the publication of Dominitz's articles, the Tenth Convention of Hapoel Hamizrachi in the Land of Israel was held in Jerusalem. It is difficult to know to what extent his articles influenced the delegates. In any event, among the hundreds of resolutions adopted—filling nineteen pages—two related directly to the education of immigrant children: "The convention views with anxiety the paucity of religious teachers in the immigrant camps and calls upon the Actions Committee to forcefully insist upon the employment of religious teachers in numbers corresponding to the proportion of religious persons in the immigrant camps, and the establishment of separate religious schools in places where there are large concentrations [of religious persons]." The second resolution read: "The convention protests the tendency of the Ministry of [Education and] Culture to set up only institutions of general [i.e., secular] study in the immigrant camps. The convention demands the establishment of institutions of religious education in the immigrant camps, under the supervision of Hamizrachi, by the above-mentioned Ministry of Culture."[51]

The publications in the religious press indicate a new stage in the struggle against anti-religious coercion upon which the Religious Front decided to embark. It seems that more than in any other papers, except perhaps in the left-wing *Kol Ha'am* (Communists) and *Al Hamishmar* (Mapam), there was a great deal of coordination in the religious press about what would be published and what would not be, and political leaders exerted direct pressure on the papers and journalists. In any event, from the autumn of 1949 on, the issue of anti-religious coercion toward new immigrants was one of the main subjects reported in the religious press, being dealt with constantly.

PRESSURE BY RELIGIOUS POLITICAL LEADERS IN LATE 1949 AND EARLY 1950

As we have seen, public information activity late in 1949 by religious elements "did not begin in a spontaneous manner, but as a systematic and organized struggle, deliberately decided upon by the political leadership of the religious camp."[52]

Who comprised the political leadership that decided to step up the propaganda offensive? To answer this question, I need to elaborate somewhat upon the composition of the Religious Front in the First Knesset. Even though most of the religious movements united in one front during Israel's early years, the historical differences, controversies, and rivalries among them continued as before. Above all were the differences between the Zionist and non-Zionist factions (who were represented in the First Knesset by ten and six Knesset members, respectively). Second, even among the religious Zionist factions, there was still a severe controversy over certain issues between Hapoel Hamizrachi (seven Knesset members, led by government member M. Shapira) and Hamizrachi (three Knesset members, led by its minister, Rabbi Yehuda Leib Fishman [Maimon]). Ultra-Orthodox, non-Zionist circles were represented in the first government by Yitzhak Meir Levin of Agudat Israel, whose faction totaled four Knesset members. There also were two representatives of Poalei Agudat Israel.

Most of the public controversy over education of the children in the immigrant camps was raised by Religious Zionist circles and their Members of Knesset (and not by the ultra-Orthodox circles, who were predominant in many of the later public controversies).

The two Religious Zionist parties—Hapoel Hamizrachi and Hamizrachi—were both part of the world movement of Hamizrachi, whose supreme governing body was the World Center of Hamizrachi. This body was responsible for the Hamizrachi educational stream and "formally had the authority to decide every matter concerning the educational policy of the Zionist-religious camp."[53] The World Center was deeply involved in organizing the struggle of the Religious Front.

On 4 December 1949, members of the World Center and the Hamizrachi Knesset faction met jointly to discuss the education issue. Anti-religious coercion in the immigrant camps was highlighted, and a decision was made that "public opinion must be cultivated on behalf of our educational system. . . . The religious public must be encouraged to support our stream. Pressure and public opinion will likely be to our benefit."[54] Summing up the meeting, Rabbi A. L. Gelman, chairman of the World Center, who had immigrated to Israel some two months earlier,[55] proposed "*to begin a campaign in the press and to arouse public opinion here*" (emphasis added). Such a resolution was adopted. The chairman also believed that an effort should be made to mobilize the Jews of the Diaspora—particularly those in the United States—to support the campaign of religious circles in Israel for the provision of religious education for immigrant children.

Five days later, on 9 December 1949, Rabbi Gelman wrote a letter of complaint to David Ben-Gurion containing Hamizrachi's explicit demands. The two basic principles included in the letter were: "a) The state must refrain from all coercion and prevent any coercion—in any form—of religious parents to send their children to schools which are unacceptable to them; b) The state must refrain from turning the administration of religious schools and the handling of their matters over to non-religious people." The writer argued, on behalf of his movement, that "there is a tendency in the Histadrut to extend the Workers Stream of education to large sectors of the people, not only by persuasion but by means which seem to us improper and opposed to the principle of freedom of conscience." He went on to claim that "there is evidence of economic pressure being applied against parents who are Histadrut members—on the part of Histadrut members who are excessively zealous and adroit—to enroll their children in schools of the Workers Stream. According to our information, such unrestrained 'propaganda' is applied among the new immigrants, who are as yet unfamiliar with the nature of the education provided by the different streams—whether in immigrant camps or in immigrant neighborhoods." Rabbi Gelman strongly condemned "the creation of a new stream—a religious stream within the Workers Stream," arguing that this is "a violation of the law, which recognizes only four streams" and leads to excessive splitting up and weakening of religious education. In conclusion, Rabbi Gelman explicitly stated that, "One of the principal conditions of the government coalition which the Religious Front joined is the autonomy of religious education. Such autonomy has been promised by the government, but its nature has not been defined." He noted that the autonomy of religious education "may be realized through one of the following means: through a special ministry for religious education with its own minister," or "through an autonomous department for religious education within the Ministry of Education and Culture." He recommended adopting the second option. This would entail "a unique internal structure of such a department, different from that of the other departments."[56] In other words, the intention of splitting the Ministry of Education in two, with a separate section for religious education, was already broached in December 1949.

The central figure who most encouraged the Religious Front and the conflict over the education of immigrant children was MK D. Z. Pinkas of Hamizrachi, who served as chairman of the Finance Committee of the First Knesset and represented his party on the Knesset Committee on Education and Culture. Pinkas was one of the outstanding parliamentarians and chosen by Knesset reporters as "man of the year."[57] In 1949, he energetically fought for leadership of Hamizrachi, seeking to replace the elderly Rabbi Fishman (Maimon) and take his place in the government as well.

With the adoption of the Compulsory Education Law in 1949, "Mr. Pinkas was of the opinion that education of children in the camps should be provided by the Education Division [and not by the Culture Department], and within the framework of the above-mentioned law, since the camps are an inseparable part of the State of Israel."[58] Pinkas made this claim at a meeting of the Knesset Education Committee on 15 November 1949. At that meeting, Dr. Baruch Ben-Yehuda, director of the Education Division, expressed his opinion that all educational matters should be transferred to the Education Division, noting that he had suggested this idea to Minister Shazar, who approved it.[59] When the anticipated changes in the educational framework in the camps did not materialize, Pinkas did not relent, and again he presented "new facts and difficulties in the camps" at subsequent meetings of the Knesset Education Committee.[60] In mid-December, he wrote to Ben-Gurion: "I was very much impressed by your statement that any attempt at spiritual coercion must be totally uprooted," and he insisted that the prime minister put this stance into effect in relation to a specific case that he raised in the letter.[61]

Pinkas demanded rapid changes. When these were not forthcoming, at the end of December he changed his mode of action.[62] He submitted a parliamentary query to the Education Committee of the Knesset, which he deliberately worded in a harsh, threatening manner. Some of what he wrote in that query—which served as a decisive catalyst for all of the later struggles by the religious public—follows:

> What is being done in the immigrant camps, to use the mildest possible language, may be termed *coercion of conscience and inquisition against the Jewish religion.* . . . Destructive acts are being perpetrated against the Jewish religion. I claim that there has never been such a state of coercion and exploitation of the unfortunate situation of the people in the camps. *They are attempting to make them abandon their religion and their beliefs.* . . . The other day the Treaty against *Genocide* was discussed in the Knesset. I claim, with full responsibility, that the activity of Mr. Nahum Levin and his staff is *cultural and religious murder,* and that if this matter does not cease immediately, *the coalition known as the State of Israel will fall apart at the seams.* At this moment I represent the Religious Front and I declare that *we will launch a civil war, a truly bloody war,* if this does not cease immediately. . . . I propose the appointment of a commission of inquiry with the participation of several members of the Education Committee.[63] (emphasis added)

Pinkas' parliamentary query, which received much publicity due to its harsh formulation, led the Knesset Committee on Education and Culture to almost immediately set up "an investigating committee," which consisted of Knesset members Devora Netzer, Esther Raziel-Naor, Rahel Cohen, Yizhar Smilansky, and David Zvi Pinkas himself and was chaired by Shoshana Persitz—who was chairperson of the Knesset committee. According to the Frumkin Commission, "The investigating committee met for one session, on 12 Teveth 5710 (1 January 1950) . . . and decided not to investigate by itself the material which had been submitted by MK Pinkas, but to request the Ministry of Education to investigate the facts. . . . The material was passed on to the Ministry of Education, and the investigating committee did not continue its activity."[64] In reality, the process was somewhat different and rather more complex: Minister of Education and Culture Shazar refused to acquiesce in the appointment of an investigating committee by the Knesset committee, and he wrote to Shoshana Persitz that "a complaint which has not yet been proven cannot serve as a basis for the appointment of such a committee and for widespread publicity in the press."[65] The minister—who until then had not bothered to undertake a careful investigation of the issue—now committed himself to investigate the problems relating to the education of immigrant children and to act to solve them, should anything be uncovered that required correction.

Though it was the leaders of the religious Zionist circles who led the campaign against anti-religious coercion in the immigrant camps, the reaction of the ultra-Orthodox, non-Zionist circles also is worthy of scrutiny. There is no doubt that their reaction at times served as an influential and even a decisive factor that spurred the religious Zionist camp.

The first gathering of "all the heads of the *yeshivot* in the Land of Israel" "to rescue education in the immigrant camps" took place on 29 November 1949.[66] A "reliable messenger" spoke of "the inquisition prevailing in the camps due to the leftist camp." He presented his impressions of three camps: Athlit, Ein-Shemer, and Rosh Ha'ayin. Various proposals were raised at this gathering of rabbis, and "there were those who thought that at such a time and in this case one needs to make an uproar, to demonstrate and to protest, and in general to adopt drastic steps."[67] Among the resolutions adopted:

> The gathering denounces the trampling underfoot of the demand of thousands of religious immigrants and the demands of religious Jewry in Israel and throughout the world—[concerning] the withholding of religious education from the immigrant children, [the condition] prevailing in the immigrant camps regarding that education which is holy and sanctified to us.... The gathering heard with sorrow about cases of attacks upon Torah students, who made the effort to go to the immigrant camps to teach Torah to the children who thirst for the word of the Lord, and demands an explanation on the part of those responsible for this.... The gathering addresses those who have the power and the responsibility to do so to immediately correct this shocking injustice. ... The gathering calls upon ... the Chief Rabbis and the religious ministers [in the government] to rise up against this horrid action and to prevent spiritual destruction from being wreaked upon Jewish children, and a terrible desecration of the honor of God.... The gathering demands that the immigrant camps be opened to religious teachers.... The gathering obligates the *yeshivot* to make an effort to expand their absorptive capacity, so that they may receive additional students from

among those leaving the camps. . . . The gathering requires *yeshiva* students to contribute of their precious time, no less than two weeks a year, for the goal of disseminating Torah, education, guidance, and the fear of God within the immigrant camps.[68]

These resolutions were directed both inwardly, within the religious camp (i.e., greater recruitment and more resources) and outwardly, as demands addressed to all of those engaged in the absorption of the immigrants.

A week later, *Hakol* devoted an editorial to that same gathering that read in part: "One thing was attained: the great Torah sages in Israel openly and clearly declared that responsibility for the education of the immigrant children to observance of the Torah and its commandments lies with them. No longer is this matter entrusted to the party activists who, whether or not their intentions were acceptable, frequently their acts were not."[69] *She'arim* provided a similar report of this meeting on its front page, adding: "In addition, the gathering complained about the apathy prevalent among the religious public regarding this burning issue, and called upon it for alertness and action in order to set up locales of religious absorption and institutions of Torah education."[70] The two papers repeatedly admitted that the issue of educating immigrant children had not received the attention it deserved, either on the part of the rabbinic leadership nor the political religious leadership, and that the religious public in Israel was generally apathetic toward what was being done to the religious immigrants.

PRESSURES EXERTED BY DIASPORA JEWRY

Increasing reports of anti-religious coercion in the immigrant camps began to be spread abroad as well at the end of 1949. One may assume that the Religious Front leaders encouraged propaganda abroad, utilizing it to pressure the government in Israel. We may say with certainty today that the strong Jewish reaction in America and Europe was one of the elements that most influenced the government—and, of course, Ben-Gurion—to appoint the state commission of inquiry. The government of the young state was very apprehensive about the antidemocratic light in which it had begun to be seen due to the harsh publicity concerning its action in the immigrant camps. It also was quite disturbed by the effect that this publicity was liable to have on fund-raising abroad and its influence on the marshaling of potential contributors and investors.

A lengthy report concerning the processes of absorption in Israel was published in the London *Times* on 23 November 1949. The correspondent quoted one official in the camps as saying that 80 percent of the Yemenite Jews had forgotten their belief in the Messiah and transgressed the Ten Commandments cynically, in a way that shocked even the sentimental materialists. The official went on to say that without religious support and understanding of the obligations imposed upon the citizens of a modern state, the Yemenites are an anchorless community.[71]

On 13 January 1950, the London *Jewish Chronicle* also published a harsh item concerning the education of immigrant children in Israel. Critical reports were published simultaneously in the United States. As a result, on 14 January 1950, the government of Israel received a telegram of protest from United Jewish Appeal officials in England. Two days later, another telegram came, this time signed by most of the Orthodox Jewish organizations in the United States, reporting a planned demonstration in Manhattan and demanding that the government reexamine the issue of the absorption of the children to prevent a miscarriage of justice to the children and their parents and to the foundations of religious Judaism in order to avoid a worldwide scandal.[72] The government's decision to appoint the commission of inquiry was made one day after receiving this telegram.

Even though the decision to appoint the Frumkin Commission had already been made, religious pressure from abroad continued unabated. On 23 January 1950, a mass demonstration was held in Manhattan by Orthodox Jews, with giant ads in the American press on the day of the demonstration. This was the largest Jewish demonstration in the United States since the establishment of Israel. Thousands of protesters participated, and for the first time representatives of most of the traditionalist Jewish organizations in the United States demonstrated together to protest acts by the Jewish government in Israel. The demonstrators demanded that "an immediate end be put to all forms of pressure intended to impose non-religious education upon the immigrant children, particularly upon those who have a definite religious background." Hope was expressed that, "The firm steps that have been adopted by the religious ministers in the Government of Israel will move the government to prevent the repetition of such anti-religious incidents."[73]

The demonstration in Manhattan fanned the flames of public outrage in the United States. In its wake, more and more telegrams containing protests and demands were sent to Ben-Gurion. They conveyed a clear message: "You are requested to fulfill the just demands of Orthodox Jewry and its representatives. An ideological conflict within the Yishuv and a split in the government at this critical hour is liable to lead, Heaven forbid, to a split in the Jewish people as a whole, and cause great damage to the joint efforts for the building up of the land"; "A special meeting of the Religious Front with the participation of all the religious federations and circles in America was greatly agitated by the difficult and harsh condition of religious education of the children of immigrants in Israel."[74]

Ben-Gurion rejected all pressure from abroad—in language that offended some—but it is clear that he was nonetheless influenced by it. To the united religious group in America, he wrote, among other things, "You may be certain that nothing will be done under the pressure of threats, if the matter is not justified and necessary of itself. If you wish to directly influence the direction which the State of Israel [is taking] and to strengthen a particular group among us, the most effective means of doing so is for you and those in whose name you speak to come to us and settle in the country."[75] His letter, of course, did not convince them, and they again wired and informed him that their letter was not a threat but an expression of deep concern for religious Jewry. Israel, they claimed, was very dear to them, and that as far as they were concerned the Land of Israel, the People of Israel, and the Torah of Israel are one, and they would be ready to sacrifice for them as they had in the past. They also made it clear that they represented more than 1 million Jews in America. Their oft-repeated, unequivocal demand was that immigrant children be provided with a religious education.[76]

MK Pinkas claimed that the foreign protests were not organized from Israel,[77] but it is very difficult to accept this at face value. It clearly emerges from the archival material that most of the religious leadership in Israel was in constant contact with the Orthodox leaderships in the United States and Europe, and that these relationships intensified unrest in the Diaspora and the pressures brought to bear by Diaspora Jewry upon the government of Israel.

CHAPTER 4

THE COMPOSITION OF
THE COMMISSION OF INQUIRY

It was Prime Minister David Ben-Gurion who decided in January 1950 to appoint the commission of inquiry, and he and Minister of the Interior Moshe Shapira seem to have been the dominant figures in determining its composition.[1] As this commission was intended to mediate between the religious and secular camps, it was decided from the outset to appoint a committee that was more or less balanced between the two, made up of persons Ben-Gurion and Shapira believed were most suited to this purpose.

Former Supreme Court Justice Gad Frumkin, the only Jew who had served in that capacity under the British Mandate, was appointed commission chairman.[2] Frumkin's appointment came after the government had committed itself, at its session on 30 August 1949, to appoint him as a member of "one of the appropriate government commissions."[3] Apart from the commitment that he had received, there were two additional major reasons for Frumkin's appointment as chairman of the commission: (1) He was well versed and experienced in procedures of the law and legal examination, including the conduct of commissions of inquiry. Twenty years earlier, Frumkin had already headed a commission of inquiry appointed by the British mandatory government to investigate "the practice of ritual slaughtering and burial of the dead by the Jewish communities in Palestine"[4]; (2) His neutrality, and the fact that neither religious nor secular people opposed him. Gad Frumkin often was involved with subjects that were accepted as having some bearing on religious life and served on committees with Orthodox persons.

For many years he had served as chairman of the Executive of the *Hevra Kadisha* (Burial Society) in Jerusalem, from which he resigned on 25 October 1949, to be replaced by MK Rabbi A. H. Shaag.[5] In later oral testimony, Israel Yeshayahu claimed that an additional reason influenced the choice of Frumkin: "He had a certain relationship with the Yemenites, because his father, who had been the editor of *Havatzelet*,* was greatly involved in the absorption of Yemenite immigrants in Jerusalem during the period of the First Aliya. Thus from this perspective he had a certain relationship and connection to the subject."[6]

The original intention was to appoint two Mapai members to the committee, but due to pressure from the Sephardic Party, which was a coalition partner, only one Mapai Knesset member was appointed—Izhak Ben-Zvi. Ben-Zvi, who later became the second president of Israel (1952–1963), was one of the outstanding figures in the Labor movement. Among other public offices, he had served as chairman (from 1931) and president (from 1945) of the Va'ad Haleumi (National Council). His appointment seemed natural, as he had the necessary qualifications: public recognition of his extreme honesty and scrupulousness, a special attitude toward the "dispersed of Israel" in general and to the Yemenite community in particular,[7] and respect for Jewish tradition.[8] Nevertheless, there were those within the Labor movement who were concerned about Ben-Zvi's naiveté, fearing that he would succumb to pressure applied by religious elements. Ben-Gurion responded angrily to all those who questioned the composition of the commission of inquiry. Addressing Ben-Zvi directly during a meeting of the Mapai Knesset faction (to which other central members of Mapai also were invited), he requested: "It may be that one of our loyal members did something that was improper. I appeal to comrade Ben-Zvi, who is a member of the commission, not to cover up for him, but to denounce him. It is not Ben-Zvi's task to safeguard him, but to safeguard the truth." MK Devora Netzer added at that same meeting: "I know one person who is objective, and that is Ben-Zvi." Ben-Zvi replied: "I hereby declare that it is not my intention, as a member of the commission, to cover up facts or to hide anything. . . . Had I thought that I was being sent to the commission in order to protect somebody, I would not have accepted. I was sent to clarify things according to my own conscience."[9]

The third member was MK Avraham Elmaleh of the Sephardic Party. The original intention had been, as noted, to appoint two members from Mapai, but "Shitrit[10] made a row and insisted that they include a Sephardi, and hence Avraham Elmaleh was included."[11] Elmaleh was an author, a journalist, and a public figure. From 1921 on, he had been a member of *Asefat Hanivharim** (Elected Assembly) and thereafter also a member of the Va'ad Haleumi and the Jerusalem Municipal Council. Elmaleh was one of the first emissaries to be sent from Eretz Israel on an educational mission to the Jews of North Africa.[12] In justifying his appointment to the commission, Ben-Gurion stated: "Nevertheless, these [the new immigrants] are groups, the majority of whom are not Ashkenazi, and it is only right that one person who can speak their language participate [in the commission]."[13] One may assume that Ben-Gurion chose him specifically because he belonged to that sector of the Sephardic Party that tended toward Mapai.[14] El-maleh's long-standing connections with the Jerusalem Yemenite community also may have stood him in good stead.[15]

All three secular members of the commission then had a positive attitude toward traditional Judaism. I believe that it would have been imprudent to appoint secular members with a less positive attitude toward religious tradition, because the very purpose of setting up the commission was to overcome severe controversies between secular and religious people. I do not agree with the claim that the composition of the commission predetermined its conclusions, even though its secular members were doubtlessly also inclined, a priori, to lend an ear to the claims and complaints of the religious circles.

Dr. Aaron Barth and MK Rabbi Dr. Kalman Kahana were originally intended to have been the two representatives of the Religious Front. Barth had been president of Hamizrachi in Germany since 1920 and enjoyed a reputation as a jurist, an economist, and a religious ideologist. Appointed Director General of the Anglo-Palestine Bank in 1947, he was among the architects of Israel's financial policy during its early years of statehood. He was held to be a reliable person, with an affinity for the Labor movement. The government decision of 17 January 1950, states: "If Dr. Barth is unable to participate, the prime minister, with the agreement of the minister of the interior, will appoint a replacement."[16] And indeed, Barth announced that he declined to accept this commission, and Rabbi Avraham Shaag was appointed to replace him. Shaag also was one of the leaders of Hamizrachi, but in an internal discussion within Mapai some were of the opinon that "the situation was worsened" by Shaag's appointment, and that Barth was "more qualified than the candidate proposed in his stead to examine things objectively."[17] Shaag himself thought otherwise, and he took pains to declare at the first meeting of the commission of inquiry that "even though I belong to one of the religious circles . . . here in the commission of inquiry . . . I have taken [it] upon myself to be completely objective. Here I must free myself of all extraneous opinons and influences . . . it is like a court."[18]

The second representative of the Religious Front on the commission of inquiry was MK Rabbi Kalman Kahana, in those days a member of Kibbutz Hafetz Hayyim—one of the few kibbutzim of Poalei Agudat Israel—who enjoyed particularly friendly relations with many Labor movement leaders, including Ben-Gurion.[19] He represented Poalei Agudat Israel in the Religious Front, held a Ph.D. from the universities of Berlin and Würzburg, and wrote several works dealing with *halakha* (Jewish law).[20] By Kahana's own testimony, "Ben-Gurion assumed . . . [that] he could rely upon me not to specifically serve [partisan] interests . . . Ben-Gurion liked me."[21]

The secretary of the commission was a member of Mapai who in later years would become a member and then Speaker of the Knesset—Israel Yeshayahu, a person of Yemenite origin. Yeshayahu's appointment deterred many of the Yemenites; nevertheless, the Frumkin Commission, which reviewed the appointment, confirmed it. In any event, it was not opposed by the Commission's religious members.[22] Many years later, Yeshayahu recounted:

> He [Ben-Gurion] told me: "You will be the secretary of the commission." Of course, this appointment implied a certain intention to safeguard the commission and to assist it to arrive at the truth, because there were tremendous efforts made to flood the commission [with partisan testimony] and to arouse great incitement by means of the testimonies. . . . The members of the NRP [National Religious Party, an anachronistic reference to the Religious Front], especially the late Moshe Shapira, opposed me. One day I sensed that he had gone to the chairman of the commission (I assume that he also went to Ben-Gurion) to tell him that the secretary was not objective—that he was a Mapai member who was involved in the matter [under investigation], that many of his colleagues are active in the field, and he must be replaced. But . . . apparently Ben-Gurion expressed his opposition, calmed them, assuring them that I was objective and there was no need for worry. I sat on this commission, and I heard many lies and distortions that were brought before it, and it did not help me that I was shocked. More than once I said to myself: I will throw over this business and go; what do I need this for? But on the other hand, I thought that perhaps I would be able to somewhat balance and restrain it. But to no avail.[23]

Yeshayahu then admitted that his task was "to safeguard the commission . . . to somewhat balance and restrain it," but the Religious Front feared that he would do more than that. In a letter to the chairman of the commission dated 23 February 1950, it repeatedly complained that immigrants were afraid to testify before it, knowing that Yeshayahu served as its secretary.[24] Replying to the Religious Front's "Actions Committee in the Camps," Frumkin wrote: "There is no reason to question the loyalty of Mr. Yeshayahu as secretary of the commission of inquiry, nor is there reason to fear that any harm will be caused on his account, directly or indirectly, to any witness who testifies before the commission."[25] These lines were only partially convincing. In an internal list perpared by the commission, fifty-eight witnesses were called to testify but did not show up. We may assume that at least some of these failed to do so out of fear that they would be harmed by testifying.[26] In the private notebook of Gad Frumkin, deposited in his private archives, he relates that on several occasions he asked

Yeshayahu to prepare various materials for the commission, and that they were not readied. It may be that Yeshayahu also delayed some of the commission's work through technical means.[27]

MAPAI'S COMPLAINTS AGAINST THE COMPOSITION OF THE COMMISSION OF INQUIRY

Immediately following the appointment of the Frumkin Commission, harsh criticism of its composition was expressed in Mapai circles. MK Israel Guri stated that, "The composition of the commission of inquiry is a pogrom. From here on it is but a step to concessions—this is a disaster."[28] At a meeting of the Mapai Knesset faction, to which other central party members were invited (with a total of eighty-four particpants), and at which the main discussion of this issue was held, Guri related that "comrades who discussed this matter among themselves were unable to comprehend why the government decided to man the commission specifically in this manner, and we related critically to the committee." He claimed that "there was no need to appoint a commission with this specific composition, so that among its five members there would be only one laborer." MK Pinhas Lubianiker (Lavon), who a short time earlier had threatened to resign from his position as secreatry general of the Histadrut due to a severe controversy with Ben-Gurion, withdrawing his intention only a few days prior to the meeting, also firmly criticized the composition of the commission of inquiry as determined by the prime minister. He declared: "If two decent religious people could be on the commission, then it should have also been possible to find two decent members of the Histadrut. . . . The composition of the commission is not as it should be in a matter as serious as [being dealt with by] this commission of inquiry." Zalman Aharonowitz (Aranne), Mapai's secretary general, who was generally among those closest to Ben-Gurion, specifically supported Lavon in this debate. He said: "I am in full agreement with him [Lavon] that this commission of inquiry could have been composed of Histadrut members, honest people who would not cover up detestible acts."

Ben-Gurion responded in great firmness to those who questioned the composition of the commission:

> I do not accept Pinhas [Lavon's] theory that we ought to enlarge the commission so as to be safe. . . . What is the difference between us and others? . . . The difference is that we are the state, while every other party is a powerless minority. A member of a minority or an individual may do something wrong, this won't shock the world . . . but if the state commits an injustice, this jolts the world. The state cannot be

forgiven. We are the state! Whoever is a member [of Mapai] and acts
on our behalf has greater responsibility. . . . Power carries obligations.
We are the state! The situation in the state is not like that in the committee, as Pinhas noted, in which there is only one [working-class
member] out of five. I would not be afraid even if there were not even
one, since the task of the commission is only to examine facts. We are
not such *Nebekhels* [Yiddish: "unfortunates"]—everything in the state
is in our hands. If our emissaries, who are emissaries of the state, exploit their power badly this is likely to destroy the state, because this
state cannot be founded upon injustice and oppression. The task of
our members on the commission is not to cover up actions, if bad acts
have been committed.[29]

Ben-Gurion's remarks indicate that he sincerely wished to counter anti-religious
coercion, reports of which he also had received from his own confidants, as we
shall see. Yet his efforts were not enough. It may be that he considered the
Frumkin Commission a deliberate, albeit circuitous, means to reduce the harm
done to religious circles, which is why he encouraged Ben-Zvi to publicize the
truth that was revealed to him. To Ben-Gurion, far more than to his colleagues
and other senior party leaders, it was clear that such a harsh blow to the basic
rights of a large sector of the public was likely to be dangerous for both the state
and its leading party.

   We shall nevertheless see that Ben-Gurion did not for a moment believe that
the facts to be uncovered by the Frumkin Commission would transcend isolated
acts of anti-religious coercion. It may be that, on the basis of his experience in earlier, similar cases, such as those of the Teheran Children or Yemenite children during the World War II period, he thought this was just another investigation,
similar to those with which he had already been acquainted. Ben-Gurion's position in principle, to be clarified in the following chapter, was that one needs to better understand the immigrants from Oriental countries and gradually guide them
to adopt Labor movement values. Ben-Gurion thought that the religious customs
of the new immigrants—such as growing sidelocks or donning phylacteries, which
he believed would in time disappear by themselves—should not be the object of a
frontal attack. He believed that an insistence upon members of these communities
to rapidly adapt to the lifestyle of "labor Israel" (Israel's pioneer elements) was only
likely to alienate and push them into the arms of the religious circles or extreme
parties, both on the Left and on the Right.

CHAPTER 5

BEN-GURION'S STAND ON THE EDUCATION OF IMMIGRANT CHILDREN

During Israel's first years, David Ben-Gurion was the dominant figure in the government, in the Knesset, in the largest political party—and ipso facto in Israeli society as a whole.[1] In the words of historian Yosef Gorny, Ben-Gurion was first and foremost a "utopian pragmatist."[2] He held an ideal utopian worldview that he wished to impart to the entire nation. During the early years of the state, more than in any other period of his leadership, developments in most of the basic areas of life in the state seem to have been determined on the basis of his views. This also was true for education, including new immigrants. However, as we shall see in this chapter, over a period of several years he unsuccessfully tried to impose certain basic tenets that he considered important for education, relating to educational frameworks. This failure is doubly striking in light of the fact that for many long months he did not succeed in convincing most of the leadership of his own party to change their dogmatic position to immediately "remake" the new immigrants. Most of them saw things differently—and in the final analysis, the activity of his party members in their direct contact with the immigrants was determined by the position of his opponents.

As early as April 1947, about a year prior to the establishment of Israel, Ben-Gurion laid down plans for the future state in a lengthy entry in his diary, in which he detailed what was to be done from an educational viewpoint and how the nation was to be shaped. Among other things, he wrote: "There is need for *Zionist* control of the public. There is need for a channel by whose means the message of Zionism will be transmitted to every man and woman" (emphasis in original). It would be necessary to establish "a framework of young people that will be at the command of the nation. One cannot expect the pioneering youth movements to encompass the majority of the youth"; "One must plan state alternatives to the pioneering youth movements, which will educate in the spirit of the labor movement in the Land of Israel." Were these perhaps his initial thoughts about reshaping the *Gadna**(Youth Battalions), or a state youth movement?[3] "Once a month one needs to publish something good to be sent to every branch (to explain biblical passages!). . . . There is need to give shape and style to the festivals, a horn and trumpet-flourish of our own." Ben-Gurion's program emphasized, in its most basic lines, educating the people "from above." The familiar pioneering frameworks no longer satisfied him, and he wished to accomplish the task of educating in the values of pioneering and labor through state agencies as well. As we have said, Ben-Gurion held a coherent and cohesive educational vision: the education of the entire nation—not only a minority within it—according to the Zionist labor pioneering ethos.[4] This was a logical extension of Ben-Gurion's tendency to fashion a new Hebraic culture: anti-Diaspora, rooted in the soil and in Jewish labor, and one familiar with the Bible and connected to the periods of Jewish independence in the Land of Israel, with new patterns of culture and celebration of the holidays, bearing Hebrew names, and so forth.

In January 1949, at a gathering of members of the free professions, Ben-Gurion declared that the three great challenges of the day—security, immigration, and settlement—"are impossible without a great educational thrust." The army—he argued—"is fundamentally an educational enterprise." "And there will not come into being among us an army which will fulfill its function in our historical circumstances, if it is not accompanied by a tremendous educational effort, more than in all the armies of the world. The army must serve as a school for maturing youth, a crucible shaping the unity of the nation and its might and culture." Regarding the new aliya, he stated that, "It will not be absorbed without a great educational effort . . . among both the veteran inhabitants of the country and the immigrants." The outstanding models that he wished to convey to the new immigrants were "the people of Petah Tikva and Rehovot, of Sejera and Ein-Harod, of Nahalal and Kfar Vitkin." As for immigration, "without pioneering education, this abandoned and desolate land will not be built up."[5]

In a proposed platform for his party, in anticipation of the first elections that were to be conducted at the end of that month, Ben-Gurion suggested that "the fusion of communities from various Diasporas into a cohesive Hebrew unit" be made the underlying objective of education. The proposal was accepted and formulated in a similar manner in the platform.[6] In a meeting with writers and poets about two months after the elections, he again spoke of what was later to be called the "melting pot" approach. Ben-Gurion stressed the need for "a process of forging and fusion of the nation," and he called for the shaping of *"an image of a unified, free Hebrew nation"*[7] (emphasis added).

In September 1949, at the height of the mass immigration, Ben-Gurion submitted the Military Service Bill to the Knesset. In a discussion preceding submission of the bill, Ben-Gurion stated: "We will take it [the youth] to agricultural training, and also provide it with teaching, and vision, and models, and Hebrew, and reading and writing. We have at this moment a historic opportunity, and the State of Israel must do something that has not been done by any country in the world—to obligate its youth to undergo agricultural training."[8] The law stipulated two years of compulsory service in the Israel Defense Forces (IDF), of which nine months were to be spent in agricultural training in the settlements. Addressing the Knesset, Ben-Gurion again emphasized the educational power and importance of state agencies. In his view, the Military Service Law was intended to impart to the army "two basic characteristics required for our security: military ability and *pioneering ability*" (emphasis added). "After initial military training of several weeks—between a month and a half and three months—they will be sent . . . native-born and new immigrants, young men and women, to agricultural training, combined with intensive cultural activity . . . [intended] to impart to the entire younger generation an ability for service, for cooperation, for mutual assistance, for responsibility, for order and discipline, for knowledge of the land, for living with nature, for fighting, and creative service."

It should be noted that the Military Service Law was passed by the Knesset by an absolute majority of sixty-two votes without opposition, with twelve abstentions (most of these representatives of the Religious Front who objected to the conscription of girls but supported the service and education of male soldiers in the working settlements). The Knesset vote is indicative of the broad public support from the Left and the Right, of both secular and religious persons, for Ben-Gurion's belief that agricultural training and education in the agricultural settlements were important in shaping both the IDF and each and every Israeli youth.

At a "consultation to clarify issues of cultural activity within the IDF" conducted by Ben-Gurion at General Staff headquarters in Tel Aviv on 19 September 1949, he said: "Why do we need agricultural training? Because our nation is not similar to other nations. We are a hodgepodge. Even the veteran Jewish population in Israel is a hodgepodge. . . . The ingathering of the exiles is a very important matter, and the army can be a great instrument in creating a unified nation, in shaping its cultural image. . . . If we know how to exploit this year wisely for appropriate educational purposes, this can be a historical turning point in the education of the youth. . . . The uniting of this *human dust*,* that which is in the country and that which comes from abroad, into one nation, a cultured nation with a common goal—this can be a revolutionary factor in shaping the character of the nation."[9]

As we have seen, Ben-Gurion believed that the IDF was the most important educational instrument, apart from the schools, and that it was "incumbent upon it to be the forge that will shape the pioneers of the nation and the cultural tool for the fusion of the Diaspora Jews, their unity, and cultural elevation."[10] It was Ben-Gurion's intention that in the IDF "melting pot" "that human mixture which is flowing from many exiles, be smelted, refined, and purified of its foreign and worthless dross." There is no doubt that, for him, this "dross" included many of the commandments conditioning the behavior of man toward his Maker, which Ben-Gurion did not value and which, he was convinced, would completely disappear within a brief historical period.[11] Ben-Gurion wished for the Labor movement to be "the core and future image of a new Hebrew nation."[12]

When Ben-Gurion enumerated the educational values that the army should impart to its ranks in addition to military values, certain ones that would have immediately come to the mind of every religious Jew were conspicuous because of their absence. Ben-Gurion emphasized the inculcation of what was common to all, completely ignoring the fact that there was no national consensus about what this entailed. According to Ben-Gurion, "It is incumbent upon our army to impart to the youth which is subject to its guidance, beginning with the youth brigades and up, the basic values of physical and moral purity, knowledge of the language and the country, bodily and spiritual alacrity, love of the homeland and loyalty to one's comrades, bravery of spirit and creative initiative, discipline and order, the ability to work, and a pioneering impulse."[13] At the above-mentioned "consultation to clarify issues of cultural activity within the IDF," on 19 September 1949, Ben-Gurion also stressed these same values. He spoke there of the "basic Bible" that every soldier needed to know before being discharged from the army. He emphasized the physical, ethical, and social-pioneering values that would contribute to the building of the homeland and to striking roots therein. He called for far-reaching involvement of the army (as one of the agencies of the state) in areas that democratic states generally leave to individual freedom and pluralism.[14]

In internal discussions with influential members of his party, Ben-Gurion's position tended to statism, insisting that Mapai must be "a vehicle that guides the state."[15] In a meeting held in his office with a group of chosen colleagues on 8 April 1949, he sought "a party that rules by the power of persuasion. . . . It persuades the majority of the people that its path and vision are the path and vision of the people." It was the members of the kibbutz movement (who then accounted for about 5 percent of the Jewish population of Israel) who, according to Ben-Gurion, were the vanguard of the Labor movement, who should guide and direct the state.[16] "I see a need for government ministers to be kibbutz members (I don't say that it is obligatory). The heads of staff of the Navy, the Air Force, and the Ground Forces should be kibbutz members. The same holds with regard to directors-general of government ministries. Leadership of the government, fishing in Eilat, the airfield in Eilat, a rest home in Ein-Gedi—all are part of one pioneering body." According to Ben-Gurion, whereas the state could assist in the establishment of a pioneering movement, this could not be effected by law. "The state has the authority to obligate every young man and woman of a certain age to undergo one or two years of agricultural training, but this is not *halutziut*,* but rather something that brings one close to it. That is the basis. The rest needs to be added by the party ... by the power of its ideals and of its example." Ben-Gurion aspired to a pioneering esprit in the spirit of the Labor movement, which would be imparted to the entire nation. He was not satisfied with a "pioneering movement ... limited to those young boys and girls who wear shorts and go to Eilat or Ein-Gedi or join the Navy from the kibbutz," but hoped "to also introduce *halutziut* into the factories, and in those places where a pioneering movement is unnecessary in order to work there ... to those places where people go to work to earn a living." In other words, Ben-Gurion wished to add voluntary elements to state compulsion and to create a uniform product of the educational system that would be imbued with the pioneering ideal in the spirit of the Labor movement and its settlements. "The party must be present in every neighborhood, and particularly in the poor Oriental neighborhoods." The members of the party as a whole "should constitute an alert force that is active, constantly discussing and clarifying, one which exemplifies the path adopted by the state."[17]

In numerous additional discussions, Ben-Gurion reiterated the special role to be played by his party, Mapai, as the vanguard party in the state. He generally repeated that theme while stressing its superiority and the consequent obligations imposed upon party members. On one occasion, for example, he stated: "We are not a party like all the other parties. ... We are the state, while every other party is a powerless minority. ... We are the state! Whoever is a member [of Mapai] and acts on our behalf has greater responsibility. ... We are the state! ... everything in the state is in our hands."[18] For Ben-Gurion, Mapai was, in the formulation of Anita Shapira, "a center of command and education, of organization and indoctrination."[19] Or, in Ben-Gurion's own words, "Without a guiding and ruling party, the state is like a ship carried on waves without a rudder and a compass."[20]

There can be no doubt that Ben-Gurion was the creator of the policy of mass aliya, and that to a great extent it is to his credit that so many immigrants came to Israel during the first years of the state. But he also was apprehensive about the Great Aliya—although only on a few isolated occasions did he admit so publicly. He said at a meeting of authors, which was convened in March 1949:

> We confront an aliya that differs, not only in numbers, but also in quality, from previous *aliyot* [plural of aliya]. ... *The character of the Yishuv*

is liable to be negatively affected and its pioneering image to fade. . . . We will have to make great efforts to shape a national unity. . . . *We need to reforge this Jewish human dust . . . to shape a Hebrew character and style which did not exist,* which could not have existed . . . in the state.[21] (emphasis added)

He seems to have particularly feared the mass immigration from Muslim lands—although he would not admit this either. Prominent Israeli sociologist Moshe Lissak has argued quite justifiably that this approach was shared by most of the leadership:

> As opposed to nostalgic descriptions, which are today in vogue, the absorption of the immigrants produced a very tangible trauma among those who implemented it. It therefore should not surprise us that they toyed with all kinds of ideas, which to a large extent expressed their disappointment at the human quality of the immigrants and their deep suspicion with regard to what the future held in store, and all this accompanied by a feeling of weighty responsibility which was translated into an all-encompassing sense of patronage towards the immigrants in general, and to those from Islamic countries in particular.[22]

Indirect allusions to this apprehension are found in various incidental jottings in Ben-Gurion's diary. Thus, for example, in the course of a conversation with "Sh." (evidently David Shealtiel, a high-ranking army officer), in which some comparison to the French people was broached, he wrote: "With us everything is fluid. The composition of our state is changing, and we do not know how the Oriental communities will be absorbed and how many gangs of criminals will be organized that will operate among us together with Arabs."[23] At a meeting of the Zionist Executive in Jerusalem in April 1950, Ben-Gurion warned that, "We cannot build an inferior state. We will not be able to withstand our enemies and implement the Zionist vision unless we build a *lofty civilization*" (emphasis in original). He argued that the state could not develop without the best scientists, technicians, and managers—and that all of these could only come from immigrants originating in Europe and America.[24] In a letter to Chief of Staff Yigael Yadin, following a visit to a transit camp of Yemenite immigrants, he expressed his view of this community of new immigrants. After expressing his respect and affection for the Yemenites (they integrate easily, they love work, they are not enticed by the city, they are rooted in the Hebrew language and in Jewish tradition, etc.), Ben-Gurion expressed his concern over their condition:

> It [the Yemenite community] is two thousand years away from us, if not more. It is lacking in the most basic and rudimentary conceptions of civilization (as distinct from culture). Its attitude to children and

women is most primitive. . . . For thousands of years it lived in one of
the darkest and most wretched Diasporas, under a regime that was
even more primitive than an ordinary feudal and theocratic regime. As
for its transfer to Israel—nothing can be compared to this revolution in
the lives of people, a profound human revolution . . . [in which] all
human values undergo a fundamental change.

His enumeration of the characteristics and problems betrays a sense of superiority on the part of a man of the West in relation to the Oriental, combined with
great concern. Nevertheless, Ben-Gurion had great faith in education, believing
that the party, the Labor movement, and the state could influence the molding of
members of all communities. He wrote to Yadin concerning the IDF's mission as
a "constructive force—builder of the nation and of the land." He advised the army
to exert influence upon the Yemenites and to change them gradually: "One cannot
do away with this [their system of study] simply by giving an order. One must understand the Yemenite mentality and relate with respect to his practices, *but they
must be transformed through pleasant, gentle means and by personal example*"[25] (emphasis added). Ben-Gurion was convinced that the Yemenite community should
be helped to bridge a gap of thousands of years. Yet he felt that this could be done
primarily through personal example and extensive conversations. He repeatedly
demanded that his party members—especially those from the kibbutzim and
moshavim—volunteer for this task.

In a discussion with the Mapai leadership on 26 January 1950, he referred to
the education of Yemenite children, which was then the issue on which the
Frumkin Commission was focused. His basic stand may once again be inferred
from his remarks on that occasion. As we have seen, Ben-Gurion wished to absorb
the Yemenite immigrants into the Labor movement, but he was prepared to do so
gradually, without clashing head on with their traditional religious principles. The
main thing, from his point of view, was that the Yemenite immigrants "take root
in labor, in agriculture, and in the life of the country. . . . We need to guide them
towards this. It won't happen in one day, it is a protracted process."[26] Despite the
differences between them and the veteran Israelis, what was important was that
the Yemenites should absorb general knowledge, geography, and so on as well as
what they could be taught about agricultural labor, worker solidarity, specific
trades, pioneering, and "the unique character of the State of Israel . . . in this light
and not another." The labor-pioneering society was meant to "embrace" the community of immigrants and gradually convey its "light" unto them.

In a polemic with Ya'akov Halperin, one of the leading educators of the Workers Stream, who criticized Yemenite educational practices (i.e., learning by rote,
teaching children Bible cantillation and the weekly portion before they knew how to
read, etc.), Ben-Gurion firmly argued: "They are coming and they are not bad . . .

They too have some traits which are not so bad. . . . They love the weekly portion [of the Pentateuch] and the Bible, they love *payot*. I can live without *payot*, and I can live with a Jew who grows *payot*. . . . Halperin has a religion called pedagogy. Why should we insist that this religion of ours absorb the religion of the Yemenites?" Ben-Gurion warned against being "fanatical religionists" and to be prepared to accept most of the Yemenite customs. He warned the members of his party that if they were not tolerant of these customs, the Yemenites would be pushed into the open arms of the other parties—Hamizrachi, the Communists, and Herut.

Nevertheless, Ben-Gurion added that there were certain practices of the Yemenites that he intended to combat stubbornly, such as polygamy—"but this is a fundamental matter which we can explain to them." There are some things which one must meet head on, but one may leave most matters to time. Rhetorically, he asked himself: "We shall encounter this Judaism, which comes from an entirely different intellectual and cultural climate, from a climate filled with a traditional atmosphere. Why should we be unable to approach them without harming this atmosphere? Is a religious atmosphere detrimental to our values?" Ben-Gurion asked his colleagues to relate with respect and propriety to "their customs and views, and to accept them with love." For example, he suggested treating respectfully—even if only as a tactical step—the practice of donning phylacteries, an unnecessary one as far as he was concerned.[27] He compared how one related to donning phylacteries to one's attitude toward wearing neckties: in both cases, he believed, no more than an outward feature was involved. In the present stage, the encounter between new immigrants and old-timers, one must "skip over" external features and gradually draw the Yemenite Jews to identify with the values of pioneering Israel. Later on, as a matter of course, they themselves will remove their *payot* and cease putting on phylacteries.

Ben-Gurion's main protagonist on various issues, including the education of immigrant children, was Histadrut Secretary Pinhas Lubianiker (Lavon), who was supported in this matter by other senior Mapai members such as Secretary General Zalman Aharonowitz (Aranne). Lavon asked why only religious teachers should be allowed to educate the Yemenites. He argued:

> I do not know why the administration of the school [for Yemenite children] must be in the sole control of religious people, who have received ordination from the Chief Rabbi. It is unacceptable to me that every teacher in such a school must be religious; I do not accept that principle. I understand that a Bible teacher must be religious, but why must a music teacher be a religious person? Why must an arithmetic teacher be religious?

Lavon claimed that both he, a secular person, and his fellows in the secular labor settlements were entitled and obligated to teach the children of Yemenite immigrants. "Non-religious persons also have the right to come into contact with these immigrants," he stated.[28] He repeatedly warned that, "We are entering, not slowly but quite rapidly, upon a condition in which the clerical claws are beginning to show behind the *talit* [prayer shawl] . . . and this disease is spreading."[29]

Ben-Gurion countered: "[Even the math teacher] needs to be religious, and not only that. He needs to be such a Jew that the Yemenites will see in him and his approach one who is close to them in all things, and that they should not sense any threat or fear of something alien." There was a need for religious teachers who were most akin to them, and from this point of view the ideal teachers and principals were Yemenite immigrants who had adjusted to the new spirit of Israel ("colleagues of Israel Yeshayahu," to use Ben-Gurion's phrase). Such teachers would be the most suited to encounter them without arousing any apprehension, without deterring them or seeming foreign to them. Ben-Gurion called for the rapid training of dozens of teachers from Muslim countries. He demanded "to appoint . . . Yemenites, religious of course, as principals of some schools."[30]

Ben-Gurion did not even rule out teachers from the Labor movement who might pretend to be religious. As he put it: "I myself would be unable to be a religious teacher, because I could not lie to myself in that way. I would nevertheless go, because I believe the absorption of the Yemenite immigration to be more important than the cleanness and purity of my conscience." He called upon his comrades to befriend the new religious immigrants among whom, as opposed to the veteran religious community in the country, "the spirit of zealotry is totally absent."[31] In a direct reference to the Religious Workers Stream in education, he said that he was very happy that it existed, though he had some doubts about it. He demanded that "a religious Jew be able to feel himself at home in the Histadrut and within the party," and that there should be rabbis among the Mapai membership. In his opinion, there is need for "a little bit of heresy against the 'heretics.'" Extreme, head-on secularism must be more open to others who see things differently. "I demand," thus he concluded, "more understanding, more concern, and comradely adjustment regarding spiritual matters which are not detrimental to our own spiritual concerns. I demand this so that we may impart our values to them with greater success and credibility."[32] In the final analysis, Ben-Gurion's position was not accepted by the forum that heard him out, and the Mapai leaders determined by a decisive majority that not all teachers of Yemenite children needed to be religious. Due to the force of events, this decision was to be revised only a few weeks later under pressure from the Religious Front.

Whereas Ben-Gurion spoke of the need to exert gradual and gentle influence in the education of new immigrants, many members of his party did so through coercion, intending to cut short the process. In practice, Ben-Gurion did not at all try to counter the dozens of acts of anti-religious coercion that came to his attention. Only in an internal discussion in the Mapai Secretariat did he for the first time relate to one of the incidents that had been extensively discussed in the press and the Knesset. Religious circles claimed that in this incident instructors of *Tnu'at Hamoshavim** imposed Workers Stream education upon the Yemenite inhabitants of the village of Amka. What happened in Amka was turned into a symbol by religious circles. They claimed that the inhabitants were not allowed to open an Agudat Israel school in the village, and that anyone who requested that his children be educated in that educational stream was prevented from working, and even from buying from the local grocery.[33] In the Knesset, Ben-Gurion completely denied what allegedly had happened in Amka and claimed: "I know for a fact that part of the allegations are false, though I cannot swear to their falsehood because I was not an eyewitness."[34] On the other hand, he admitted the facts to the party Secretariat and angrily asked his comrades:

> They pester the Yemenites in this village who wanted an Agudat Israel school, starving them, and threatening them, and forcing them to close down this school. Is that how we want to meet this tribe, the Yemenites? Is the Yemenite who wants to live in a moshav not allowed to maintain a school according to all the fine points of the *Shulhan Arukh?** . . . Do you need to arouse this entire tribe against us? I don't understand this concept. I don't understand the considerations of the movement.[35]

It is certainly no coincidence that Ben-Gurion's reaction was voiced around the time that he was presented with the report of the Frumkin Commission though, as we shall see, he refused to accept the facts presented in the report regarding anti-religious coercion.

In his public statements Ben-Gurion adopted a purportedly completely neutral stance regarding the issue of molding the new immigrants, and he called upon those engaged in their integration to put aside "the redemption of their souls." The new immigrants should not be objects of pity, he claimed, nor persons upon whom views were imposed or who were dragged into political debates and partisan arguments. "Let us leave it to them to determine things of the heart, limiting ourselves to providing economic and physical support. Let us not so hastily be concerned about the redemption of their souls—they themselves are qualified to do so."[36] This contradicts what we already know: that Ben-Gurion held clear educational goals. He explicitly wished to influence the immigrants' thinking as well, and to fashion them in a particular ideological tendency—albeit using methods more indirect and less coercive than those in which many of his colleagues at times believed.

At a meeting of the Mapai Political Committee at the end of December 1950, Ben-Gurion again spoke at length on the issue of anti-religious coercion of the immigrants. This time—after more than a year of heavy accusations directed against his party and government concerning these matters—he condemned more firmly those who performed coercive acts:

> If it is a fact [that religious children are provided with a secular educa-
> tion], and I have the impression that this is the case in many places . . .
> this is an injustice and a serious political error. . . . I suspect that it is not
> due to class consciousness [that most of the immigrant children regis-
> ter in Workers Stream schools], but that there are many acts of coer-
> cion in this matter. . . . I believe that in many places our members use
> coercion and threats—regarding work and settlement—and so [the im-
> migrant children] register. I know of such cases, because comrades
> have told me that they have done this—good comrades, upright, and
> honest, and very dedicated people from agricultural settlements, who
> do this out of loyalty.

Ben-Gurion admitted that members of other parties did likewise, but that "others
must be forcefully prevented from doing this," while with members of his own
party, he sought to convince them of the damage they were causing. He added:

> One should not do this—to use economic power where it exists—and
> I tell you that this power will be taken from us if we use it in that way.
> . . . I believe that this is an extremely serious matter for the State of Is-
> rael, because if already from the outset it relies upon violent robbery—
> and this is violent robbery, the exploitation of a man's weakness—if it
> will not actually destroy the State of Israel, it will destroy the possibil-
> ity of labor class hegemony in the state.[37]

Ben-Gurion did not intend to take legal steps to prevent the "violent robbery"
being perpetrated against the new immigrants, even though he was aware of its
existence. He only sought to convince his own party members that this policy
would act as a boomerang in the long run and damage the party. But these attempts at persuasion did not influence many of those holding vital positions in the
moshavim, in the immigrant camps, in Histadrut institutions, and in government
offices. Many of them did not mend their ways, and Ben-Gurion was evidently
well aware of this.[38]

Ben-Gurion, who was particularly concerned with the long-run effect,
thought about how to integrate members of the Oriental communities into the
future fabric of the state, paying particular attention to developing leaders and
training senior army officers from among the new immigrants, particularly those
from Oriental countries. His repeated statement that he hoped to see a Yemenite
Chief of Staff is well known, and special courses to prepare officers of Yemenite
background were conducted at his initiative.[39] At the same time, he was concerned
about providing special military training for all Oriental immigrants. Thus, for example, he told the Mapai Secretariat that he had been present at the graduation
ceremony of a battalion commanders course, and that when looking at the faces,
he saw "only one race, our Ashkenazim. . . . I know of no greater danger than this."

He also told the Secretariat that he wished "to gather about a hundred Yemenite, Moroccan, and other youth, and to sit them down to study for an entire year in a special place, to learn Hebrew, history, math, and geography, so that afterwards it will be possible to send them back to the army and make them at least sergeants, perhaps officers as well."[40] He believed that the preparation of a cadre of future leaders was the gradual, proper, safest, and most certain way to educate the immigrant generation.

When Ben-Gurion summed up what had occurred in Israel during the first years of the state, he wrote:

> A deep and fundamental change has occurred in the lives of hundreds and thousands of Jews . . . a deep revolution in the image and way of life of the Jew. . . . The Jewish human dust who lived on foreign soil in a state of dependence, wandering, and enslavement was shaped into an independent, sovereign entity upon entering the homeland, becoming involved and rooted in its glorious past, and adhering to the vision of the end of days that will be manifested in national and human redemption. . . . From the tree trunk of ancient Hebrew civilization sprout the branches of a new Hebraic culture, permeated with Jewish and human values and with no barrier dividing the man and the Jew. . . . Another example of such a human revolution is hard to find, a revolution that touches upon all those returning to Zion—those that come from the countries of Europe and America, and those who return from the lands of Asia and Africa.[41]

There can be no doubt that, more than it portrays historical fact, this is an expression of hopes and expectations.

It was the intention of Ben-Gurion and his colleagues during the early years of statehood to bring about a "human revolution"—to create a "new Hebraic culture," but they were only partially successful. It seems that already in the period 1952–1953, Ben-Gurion had realized that his educational ideal was not so practicable, and so his hopes changed as well, however, this is not our present concern.

CHAPTER 6

ATTITUDES OF VARIOUS PARTIES TOWARD THE COMMISSION OF INQUIRY

MAPAM

From the party's inception in January 1948, Mapam was the most zealous, unqualified supporter of education in the spirit of labor values. Mapam believed that socialist education—particularly of the type provided in the Workers Stream schools in the kibbutzim of Hashomer Hatzair and *Hakibbutz Hameuhad*,* which Mapam believed was the optimal education—should be imparted to all children in Israel. It was nevertheless clear to Mapam leaders that their hope for "uniform workers education" throughout the country was only a dream that might be implemented sometime in the future. Until that time they saw themselves as the zealous guardians of the educational institutions that belonged to the Workers Stream. Mapam invested great efforts in a variety of educational activities, and its affiliated party and settlement movements sent numerous active members on educational missions throughout the country, including to the immigrant camps. Mapam supported the Culture Department's system of uniform education in the immigrant camps—which, as we shall see in the next chapter, reflected a definite tendency to transmit Labor movement values—and many of its members were involved as teachers and instructors, or in other capacities in support of this activity.

From the establishment of the state, and to an even greater extent after the creation of the first elected government in March 1949, Mapam severely criticized Mapai for "turning its back on pioneering labor values" and for its "constant policy of appeasement, backing down, and acquiescence to religious blackmail." Mapam believed in principle in a democratic-secular state, severely criticizing Mapai's tendency to compromise on religion-related issues such as its opposition to a constitution and civil marriage, agreement to the enactment of Sabbath laws, consent to exempt religious girls and yeshiva students from military service, and more. Mapam demanded "to free the state from the shackles of religious law ... to bring our nation to a condition of a healthy nation in a healthy state—a nation that grants individual freedom, freedom of conscience, and freedom of faith, and which makes an absolute separation between the life of the state and the laws of religion, which a person may only fulfill of his own free will."[1]

Their opposition to the very appointment of the Frumkin Commission was a direct continuation of Mapam's opposition to Mapai's attempts to preserve its partnership with religious circles. The following is one expression of Mapam's interpretation of the events leading to the appointment of the Commission:

> The Religious Front has launched an attack on the Workers Stream in education. They do not balk at any step. Their newspapers are full of horror stories about "hunting" for children. Educators of the Workers Stream are referred to as criminals, accused of encouraging children to heresy and to the abandonment of religion. Rabbis in Israel and in America have rallied for a holy war and to rescue the young generation. ... For months, the religious camp has carried on unrestrained incitement. ... [They] attempt ... to impose a regime of religious coercion upon the State of Israel, and in this insolent attempt they do not refrain from any provocation, including the organization of armed attacks upon workers in the camps, incitement against the State of Israel among the new immigrants, both in the country and in the Diaspora, and attempts to undermine the fund-raising campaigns. ... Clearly, Mapai is paying the price of its coalition with the religious camp, and this price is also paid, together with Mapai, by the State of Israel—and by the working public as a whole.[2]

Mapam's policy on the appointment of the Commission, then, was unequivocal: there was no need to investigate what was being done in the immigrant camps. All of the accusations leveled by religious circles were no more than wicked, reactionary libels to be rejected out of hand.

Mapam was convinced that the kibbutzim were the most suitable locales for educating the immigrant children. The Mapam Council issued a call to widen the framework of Youth Aliya to absorb children and youth in preparatory programs in agricultural settlements and to establish youth villages with the aim of transferring those trained in them to the settlements.[3] Mapam sought the welfare of the immigrants and believed that in the settlement movement "there awaits them a home, a school, a guiding hand, and an atmosphere of a homeland being built." They decried the "despicable situation, in which thousands of children and youth are being kept in the camps under impoverished conditions because the Religious Front prevents them from being sent to the labor settlements."[4] In an internal party forum, they proudly related how they had managed to circumvent religious opposition and bring hundreds of immigrant youths to be educated in kibbutz schools. Nevertheless, the report was accompanied by an aura of sorrow over the fact that it applied to only a few hundred of them.[5] In the spring of 1950, when religious agitation against "soul snatching by the Left" had increased, members of the kibbutzim agreed to give Youth Aliya a commitment that "there would be conditions for observance of the Sabbath and the holidays, and a kosher kitchen for the pupils" even in the kibbutzim of Hashomer Hatzair, which were known for their anti-religious attitudes, and all this so that Youth Aliya should send more children to the kibbutzim.[6] It is quite likely that the kibbutz members knew that they would be unable to carry out this commitment in full, but the the very fact that they made it emphasizes the extent to which they were interested in absorbing more children and youth in their institutions.[7]

It is noteworthy that all of this occurred at a time when negotiations were being conducted among Mapai, Mapam, and the General Zionists to discuss the possibility of setting up an alternative government coalition without the participation of the religious parties.[8] Even according to the accounts of Mapam leaders, the negotiations, conducted between Mapai and Mapam at the end of 1949 and the beginning of 1950, were serious and "responsible, not like [those] at the time when the incumbent government was established," during January–March 1949.[9] Even Meir Ya'ari, the leader of Hashomer Hatzair, said that "there is a serious turn in Mapai towards an agreement with us. Even the optimists among us did not believe that Mapai would be so willing to meet our demands."[10] Naturally the coalition talks covered a variety of issues relating to foreign, defense, and domestic policies. Regarding the specific issues of religion and education, there was considerable agreement between the representatives of the two parties. In practice, the two sides were in agreement on the democratic-secular character of the state, but the coalition negotiations failed toward the spring, primarily because of differences regarding questions of foreign policy and defense. The failure of the talks, of course, exacerbated Mapam's opposition to the "clerical-reformist" government, one of whose means to enable it to remain in power was the appointment of the Frumkin Commission.

CENTER AND RIGHT-WING PARTIES

Before the establishment of Israel and during its early years, center and right-wing parties repeatedly argued that the division into party streams was the root of all evil in the Jewish educational system in the country.[11] These parties received only one-fifth of the votes in the elections to the First Knesset and were thus powerless to have their principled position against the streams in education adopted as government policy.[12]

In their speeches, the leaders of the Right and the Center repeatedly attacked the "curse of partisan streams." Thus, for example, in a discussion of education in the Provisional State Council, Arye Altmann (Revisionist Zionists) said:

> Nothing will destroy the country more than the multiplicity of streams in education. . . . [One must] appoint a committee and charge it with the task of setting up one universal school system for all the children of Israel. . . . We need to learn from the healthy nations. In every normal country there is universal education. If someone wants to establish something special, let him do so at his own expense, but the state should have only one uniform school system.[13]

The comments of Dr. Stupp, a representative of the General Zionists, were in the same vein:

> Today it is ten times more difficult for us to understand why there is this division in education. We were all present in this house when we spoke about another body, also important to the state, when we discussed the army, and we all understood that this particularism is a terrible thing and that we need to return to a unitary form, to a unitary administration [i.e., command], to a unitary body. In our humble opinion, education is no less important than the army.[14]

As mentioned, most leaders of the Right and the Center believed in uniform education for all children in Israel. Only at a later stage did they admit the possibility of separate state educational systems for secular and religious children.

When discussions began in the Knesset concerning a Compulsory Education Law, right-wing and center parties initiated public pressure upon Knesset members by creating a movement of educators and public figures in support of uniform education.[15] In September 1949, during the Knesset debate on this bill, MK Israel Rokah of the General Zionists once again appealed, "Give us state schooling in which all the children in Israel will be educated, without any connection to the status of their parents."[16] During the final hours of debate before the adoption of the law, his party colleague, MK Shoshana Persitz, chairwoman of the Knesset Committee on Education and Culture, demanded "to delete the shameful clause stating that 'every father shall be required to declare to which stream he wishes to send his child.'"[17] Members of Herut also sharply criticized the legitimization that this law would give to the four partisan streams. After its adoption, they swore: "We will not cease fighting against it until it is done away with, until the legal status of education in our country is similar to that of all other states and nations, in that we will have not only free compulsory education, but also *uniform* education that assures the unity of the nation, just as the army of the state must guarantee the unity of the nation" (emphasis in original).[18] Once again, when speaking in those days of uniform education, one generally referred to a single educational system for both religious and nonreligious pupils, but there also were those who suggested that there be several trends within it, including a religious one.[19]

Uniform education in the immigrant camps—even though tending more toward the values of the Labor movement—generally did not alarm the center and right-wing parties. Indeed, many of them were even happy about it, seeing this as a harbinger of the creation of a uniform educational system throughout the entire country. MK Yizhar Harari of the Progressive Party proposed that a special law be passed establishing "a uniform state school in the immigrant camps."[20] An editorial in *Herut* stated: "One should praise the initiative to create a uniform school in the immigrant camps. We see this as a first *breakthrough* into the divided educational system. . . . This experiment must . . . also be founded upon the quest for a uniform curriculum, common to all opinions and outlooks found in our country. . . . Would that the new immigrants will be privileged to be among those who break through the fences and walls dividing the nation into educational streams" (emphasis in original).[21]

The opposition parties would seem not to have been particularly concerned over the issue of anti-religious coercion among the immigrants. Thus, for example, *Herut* repeatedly denounced the "coercive regime of Mapai" in general, while arguing that the religious parties assisted Mapai and enabled it to continue its system of coercion. In other words, parties that felt they did not receive their due argued that the system of party rule that discriminated against them was the result of a coalition between Mapai and the religious parties. Thus they were more concerned over the injustice they felt was being done to them than by discimination against religious circles.[22]

When the polemic between Mapai and the religious parties became sharper on the eve of the Frumkin Commission's appointment, the centrist and rightist press also began to deal with the issue of educating immigrant children. One example is the following item in *Ha'aretz*: "There are opposing claims. Hamizrachi complains bitterly about a regime of coercion, while the Left accuses Hamizrachi of scheming to 'monopolize education of immigrant children.' The aspiration to make conquests stands out in both camps, but regarding the Yemenite immigrants it should be clear that this is a very religious Jewish community that will inevitably react negatively to any attempt to wean its youth away from traditional ways."[23] While the correspondents generally presented the stands of both sides, there was a definite tendency to accept the claims of the religious camp.

CHAPTER 7

UNIFORM EDUCATION
IN THE IMMIGRANT CAMPS
AND THE RELIGIOUS
WORKERS STREAM

The Frumkin Commission's investigation focused primarily on the education of children in the immigrant camps. However, the Commission also examined educational activity in other immigrant settlements, particularly in the *moshavim* settled entirely by new immigrants. As we have seen, responsibility for education in the immigrant camps lay with the Culture Department of the Ministry of Education and Culture, directed by Nahum Levin. The nature of the education provided in the immigrant *moshavim*, on the other hand, was not determined by the staff of the Ministry of Education and Culture but rather by people from the various settlement movements—primarily those of Tnu'at Hamoshavim (the Moshav Movement), which was affiliated with the Histadrut and to which some 80 percent of the immigrant *moshavim* belonged at the beginning of 1950. Tnu'at Hamoshavim did not allow the presence of any educational framework other than the Workers Stream. When the settlers pressed their demand for religious education, the Educational Center of the Histadrut decided that this would be provided through the Religious Workers Stream. This chapter will explore the system of uniform education operated in the camps by the Culture Department and elaborate upon the Religious Workers Stream, especially the manner of its operation in the immigrant *moshavim*.

Uniform Education in the Immigrant Camps

During the first months of Israel's existence, when it was engaged in the War of Independence and other difficult struggles, there appears to have been no initiative from above to create any special educational frameworks for immigrant children. To a large extent, in the wake of the difficulties involved in establishing the educational system in the state's early days, the special problems involved in providing these children with education were largely ignored. The Culture Department picked up this challenge at its own initiative, but from the very beginning of its activity it was given certain backing, which gradually increased, by senior personnel in the Jewish Agency and the government. The staff of this department, which took upon itself the great educational task of caring for immigrant children, was increasingly considered the government body responsible for the educational frameworks for the new immigrants.

Already in March 1948, Nahum Levin, director of the Culture Department, which was then part of the Va'ad Haleumi, first responded to the pressures of residents in one of the immigrant camps in Hadera. Thus two months before the establishment of Israel, he began to establish a special educational system with a uniform curriculum for the children of immigrants. The initial steps taken in Hadera brought in their wake the establishment of an entire network of uniform education in the immigrant camps, which grew and expanded as the number of immigrants flowing to these camps increased. By the end of 1948, when there were about 25,000 people in the camps, there was still very little organized educational activity involving immigrant children. The main educational institutions—which were called "transitional schools" and provided a uniform education—were established when the flow of immigrants greatly increased during 1949. The Ministry of Education and Culture was only officially established in March 1949. With its establishment, Levin was provided with a large staff that assisted him in the enormous task of providing education in the immigrant camps.

Who was Nahum Levin, and what views did he hold? Levin, a member of Mapai, had already been involved in the cultural absorption of immigrants in the 1930s, and from then on he was one of the senior officials of the Culture Department of the Va'ad Haleumi. He was among the leading figures involved in absorbing the Fifth Aliya (the wave of immigration from Germany and Central Europe that began in 1933, after the Nazi rise to power), organizing courses in the Hebrew language and Zionist cultural activities for these immigrants.[1] At the end of the 1930s, there was a tendency to appoint him "chief commissar" of the German press being published at that time in Eretz Israel, but this elicited strong protest among the immigrants from Germany, and the idea was never implemented.[2] Levin adhered to a Zionist-Socialist worldview, and he was convinced that all of those who came to Israel should be educated in this spirit.

To exemplify Levin's worldview, the following passage has been selected from a radio talk he gave on the "Greeting the Sabbath Program" on 14 June 1946:

> The sanctity of the Sabbath flows from the sanctity of labor as a true basis of true life. We are a working nation, a nation that builds and creates values. In this fact lies the root of the Torah. . . . "Jerusalem was only destroyed because they profaned therein the Sabbath." Let us remember this! . . . The Sabbath will return "the hearts of the fathers to the children and the hearts of the children to the fathers." . . . The generation of the rebirth of the nation in its own land will be built upon [a foundation of] both the past and the future.[3]

In this passage as well as in Levin's articles and writings, what stands out is an effort to integrate old and new and to create a new nation and a new reality in Eretz Israel based upon the traditions of Judaism. In personal notes in his notebook after the publication of the Frumkin Commission Report, he wrote:

> What is the great power of the period of renascence from a national viewpoint, its uttermost secret? My answer is: We have freed the biblical verses from their rhetoric and restored their substantive and concrete contents. . . . "Six days you shall work"; "And you shall love . . ."; "Justice, justice you shall pursue"; and "You shall proclaim freedom throughout the land, to all the inhabitants thereof," have become the basis of a worldview, which we attempt to realize in the working settlements and in the labor movement generally. . . . This great experiment was accompanied by much cultural-social and moral tension. . . . This tension is what has safeguarded us and our enterprise.[4]

Levin was convinced that the Labor movement and those people in the labor-oriented settlements were the continuators of the biblical heroes, and that the Bible was a suitable means for Zionist patriotic education and for instilling socialist values.[5]

Levin and his colleagues attempted to realize their worldview by shaping the educational system for which they had assumed responsibility. They created a system that intended to educate immigrant children in the spirit of the Zionist ethos of pioneering and settlement on the land that was prevalent in the country during the pre-state and early state periods. Unlike the general educational system, in which parents could choose from among four educational streams with different educational ideals (the General Stream, the Workers Stream, the Hamizrachi Stream, and the Agudat Israel Stream), immigrants in the camps were not given a choice regarding their children's education. Rather, a uniform system of education was in effect forced upon them, which only minimally took into account the positive attitude of the majority of the immigrants toward Jewish religion and tradition.

In justifying uniform education to the Frumkin Commission, Levin gave a series of reasons that necessitated educating the immigrants in this way and why they should not be allowed to choose among the streams: (1) "They are not ready for them, they do not understand, they are disgruntled, conditions there are terrible, and *Kulturkampf* should be left out of the camps; (2) There is a constant turnover of children in the camps; (3) lack of residential space; (4) lack of budget; (5) From a simple pedagogic viewpoint: what can be given to these children in this framework during the course of the three hours that the teachers give voluntarily?"[6] The reasons given by Levin combined legitimate and false claims. At the time he testified before the Commission, most of the teachers in the camps were no longer volunteers. Moreover, the average daily number of hours of instruction was generally more than three. True, there were severe problems caused by lack of financing and space, but the turnover rate in the camps was far lower than it had been earlier. Levin referred to the immigrants in a tone of superiority and paternalism and did not regard them as an integral part of the state's citizens. He ignored the rights that stemmed from their being citizens, including those incorporated in the Compulsory Education Law (passed in September 1949), which enabled parents to choose from among the various educational streams. According to Levin, the immigrants only had the right to uniform education.

In a closed meeting of the Mapai leadership, Levin was more frank. He expressed there his opinion concerning his own role and that of his staff in the education of immigrant children: "All of the camps are flooded today with *yeshiva* students. . . . They represent *the powers of darkness in the country*. They will not educate these children and youth to a life of pioneering or to go to the Negev. The struggle here is *a struggle for the character of the immigrants*"[7] (emphasis added). As far as Levin was concerned, he was engaged in a struggle on the central front—the sociopolitical front that would determine the future character of the country: "*This is a battle* not about religion, but for political influence over the immigrants *and the future image of the State of Israel*"[8] (emphasis added). It was clear to him and to his colleagues that the only way to build the land was not the one advocated by *yeshiva* students, who shunned labor and involvement in settlement but by Zionist pioneers, who acted in the spirit of the Labor movement and identified with its values.

The Culture Department carefully selected the teachers and instructors in the immigrant camps with the objective of transmitting its own values to the immigrants. Generally speaking—as far as possible—it chose persons who had an affinity for the Labor movement (including religious people who were affiliated with the religious labor movements). In a discussion conducted in the Mapai Central Committee, Raphael Basch related:

> We have taken certain steps under the leadership of our members, in cooperation with the Culture Department of the government, to train

a group of youth leaders intended for tasks within the camps. . . . Thus far two seminars have been conducted for this purpose. The "Young Guard" [of Mapai] also lent a hand in finding instructors for the seminar. . . . There is a very strange situation in the camps, because the instructors are members of Mapai, while the teachers come from the religious streams.[9]

Ultra-Orthodox non-Zionists were generally not even allowed to enter the immigant camps. Only at a closed meeting of the leadership of the Mapai Knesset faction did Levin admit as much: "These circles [the ultra-Orthodox] wish to penetrate into the camps. We prevented them, and this angered them."[10]

In practice, guidance from above by the Culture Department regarding work in the field was minimal and primarily limited to the first year: on the whole, it limited itself to selecting staff members and determining who would or would not be permitted to enter the camps. During the initial period, almost every teacher in every immigrant camp taught according to a program of studies determined and adapted by himself. There was little centralized supervision by the supervisors of the Culture Department. Only at the end of 1949 did the Department distribute a more binding, uniform program to the "transitional schools," entitled "Headings for a Study Program."[11] The introduction reveals something of the Department's outlook:

> The spiritual absorption of the child begins on the day he arrives at the camp. This is done . . . by providing him with knowledge of the language; but not by mere acquisition of the language, for from it and through it one also imparts to the child *values which are inalienable possessions of the nation that is coming into being in the country.* . . . These values create a closer affinity between the immigrant child and his new environment, and arouse in his soul a sense of the homeland. Knowledge of the language and knowledge of the homeland are elements of the first order of importance for the immigrant child, and they determine the basic elements of the curriculum of the school for immigrant children in the camps.[12] (emphasis added)

Under the heading "Subjects of Study," those subjects that "are linked to the goals of the school," the following are enumerated:

> One *must devote particular attention to language and knowledge of the homeland and the nation* (i.e., geography of the homeland, Bible). The number of subjects of general knowledge will of necessity be limited: they will be taught arithmetic, general geography, gardening, handicrafts, and physical education. . . . Even in the lower classes one must integrate knowledge of the *history of Zionism and the pioneering movement.* . . . One *must implant in the immigrant children a love for physical*

labor in general, and agricultural labor in particular.... There should be many hikes and trips. . . . In the religious classes that exist in some camps, in accordance with the needs of the place, special attention is to be given to sacred studies. . . . In all other matters, the same arrangements apply to the religious classes as to the rest of the school.[13] (emphasis added)

These instructions to the teachers in the immigrant camps reflect the overall worldview that the Culture Department wished to instill in the children. The pedagogical objective was to draw the immigrant children closer to accepting the Zionist revolution and the image of the "new man" that it wished to create: healthy, erect, physically developed, with a love of country and labor (preferably tilling the soil), and identifying spiritually with those historical times in which the Land of Israel was settled, in the age of the Patriarchs and in the period of Zionist waves of immigration.[14] This program did allow for some consideration of the inclinations of religious people, first and foremost of those for whose children religious classes had been introduced in a number of the camps (mostly Yemenite children). However, even with regard to the religious children it was explicitly stated that "the same arrangements apply . . . as to the rest of the school."

Special Youth Camps

One of the more intensive educational frameworks planned by the Culture Department was special educational camps for Yemenite youth. Youngsters were brought to these camps and separated from their families for several weeks or, in some cases, even a few months. Hadassa Lipmanowitz (later District Judge Hadassa Ben-Ito), who was responsible for these camps, testified before the Frumkin Commission that a budget had been allotted for the establishment of three camps for some 700 youngsters: 200 from Rosh Ha'ayin, 250 from the Ein-Shemer immigrant camp, and 200 to 250 from Pardessiya. The youths were initially sent to their parents' homes on the Sabbath, but later a special educational program was conducted on the Sabbath as well. However, she claimed, "A strict order was given in all the camps, as well as to the youth movements whose representatives came to the camps, that they were not to violate the Sabbath nor transgress any religious law."[15]

The written pedagogical and instructional program produced by the Culture Department for use in those camps clearly reflected the same educational worldview that the department wished to instill in the immigrant children (including the Yemenites who, as mentioned, were considered by all religious).[16] Under the heading "Goals of the Camps," one reads: "The purpose of the [youth] camps is to prepare the youth living in the Yemenite immigrant camps in Rosh Ha'ayin, Pardessiya, and Ein-Shemer for their future in the country. *Education in the spirit of the principles of our national renascence and the building of the homeland"* (emphasis added). In the section dealing with Bible instruction, we read: "To instruct the youth in the traditional method to which they are accustomed—in the *heder*,* in the *Talmud Torah*—in the books of the Pentateuch." On the other hand, statements made further on contradict what is stated earlier and clearly elucidate the tendencies toward "re-education," to which we have already alluded:

> The Bible is to be explained and presented . . . *in terms of those elements of the Land of Israel that interest us today.* It has the power to provide much concrete knowledge concerning the country and to serve as an important background for Israeli education. . . . One must transform what is related and described there into a living panorama of the People of Israel in its land, and emphasize the elements conveying knowledge of the country, its nature, and all that is contained therein[17] (emphasis added).

The program concludes with various suggestions for "discussions" concerning "the history of the culture of labor" and "laborers and labor in the Land of Israel."[18] Among the objectives listed in the more detailed section intended for the teacher were: "Acquaintance with the Hebrew laborers in the Land of Israel. Physical labor as a basis for the building of the Land. Self-labor and mutual help." A note states that: "It is important to conduct a series of talks on physical labor, which may induce raising the value of labor and the importance of the working person. Thus will be achieved educational goals whose value is enhanced—to the extent that they are accompanied by examples of physical labor." The educational tendency in the youth camps was obvious: to acclimatize the youth from Yemen as quickly as possible to the new Israeli milieu and culture. The program evinced a certain willingness to continue traditional religious studies, but these too were directed to achieving the objective—which David Ben-Gurion was in the habit of emphasizing—of turning the Bible (and only the Bible) into a means for educating "the new Israeli man."

One should emphasize the naive faith and goodwill that underlay the establishment of the youth villages. Unlike what one might imagine, there was no intention to "brainwash" or indoctrinate, such as was common in similar educational camps set up at various times by totalitarian regimes. The only intention was to "advance" Yemenite youth, to adjust these children as quickly as possible to the new Israeli reality—and the parents sent their sons and daughters, of their own free will, to separate youth camps. Libelous pamphlets dealing with that period, which are published to this very day, violently denounced the youth camps. Thus,

Figure 7.1 Youth movement member forcibly cuts sidelocks of Yemenite boy. Cover of *On the Talons of Eagles* (Bnai Brak: Torat Avot Organization, 1988).

for example, in *On the Talons of Eagles* (a play on the name of Operation "On Wings of Eagles"), we read:

> What is the meaning of a youth camp? . . . It was a catastrophe, deliberately intended to destroy the religious element in the souls of Yemenite youngsters. Young boys and girls from the kibbutzim of Hashomer Hatzair [in fact, members of Hashomer Hatzair did not particularly predominate in the camps—author], in provocative and lewd dress, set out in lascivious dances before the eyes of the young Yemenite boys and girls (among whom there were also married women), who had been educated to modesty and purity of character. Things which they regarded as [cardinal sins, for which] "one should choose death rather than violate them," were trampled down before their eyes with cries of laughter and light-headedness. Social pressure was applied by the youth leaders to encourage the Yemenite children to participate in the singing and dancing. And indeed, many of them could not withstand the social pressure, the contempt shown to those who refused, and temptation. Promises regarding prayer and Torah study were not fulfilled, and in their place there was exhortation to cut off *payot* and throw off the yoke of religion. All this while challenging the parents and their "old-fashioned laws."[19]

This is a distorted and an exaggerated portrayal. Research has made it clear that there was no preconceived program on the part of those who planned the youth camps to undermine religious elements. We accept the conclusions of the Frumkin Commission to the effect that there was a tendency among the planners to hasten the socialization of the immigrants to the new reality they faced in Eretz Israel, but no special pressure was applied to have them participate in singing, dancing, and so on—and needless to say, they did not engage in "lascivious dances." Everything was strictly puritanical, marked by the innocence that characterized pioneering Eretz Israel in the late 1940s. I accept the testimony of Hadassa Lipmanowitz, who told us that she herself came from a religious family, was educated in the Ma'ale religious school in Jerusalem, and respected the values of religion and tradition. More than she and many of her friends intended to encourage people to become nonreligious, they believed in the values of modernization and the Labor movement, and they wished to speedily impart them to the new immigrants.[20]

THE RELIGIOUS WORKERS STREAM

The Religious Workers Stream—founded by Haoved Hadati, the Religious Workers party, headed by Dr. Yeshayahu Leibowitz—was one of the means by which the Histadrut hoped to attract the maximum number of new immigrants.[21]

This was explicitly stated in internal discussions among the Histadrut leadership. Thus, for example, MK Israel Guri said at a plenary session of the Histadrut's Education Center: "The nature of [this] aliya is such that it is not always possible to act legitimately. . . . There is a religious tendency among these immigrants which the Hamizrachi Stream has exploited. If there is actual registration for schools, the Religious Stream will benefit from it."[22] The solution, he believed, was to expand the religious Histadrut framework (i.e., to encourage the Religious Workers Stream). In a discussion conducted by the Central Committee of the Histadrut, Israel Yeshayahu, himself of Yemenite origin, told his listeners that they must get used to the idea that there would now be tens of thousands of truly religious members in the Histadrut, and that the Histadrut membership at large must be prepared for this contingency.[23] At another discussion, this time in the Mapai Bureau, Yeshayahu was even more purposeful: "Though it is useless to think that we can provide religious needs, we must not forget that this is a respectable means by which to gain control of the immigrants. No matter how much we explain the burning issues of the state, the Yemenites will be more concerned about a rabbi or a ritual slaughterer than about a major political or economic issue."[24] In his opinion, the development of a religious educational system was important to the Yemenite immigrants, but it also was a "tool" (to use his term) for control of the immigrants.

The Religious Workers Stream was one of the offshoots that served to expand the Workers Stream, particularly in the immigrant *moshavim*. And indeed, the Workers Stream did grow considerably during the period of the Great Aliya: it increased by 39 percent from the period 1948–1949 to 1949–1950, and by another 58.8 percent from the period 1949–1950 to 1950–1951.[25] With the establishment of Israel, the Workers Stream accounted for only about a quarter of the schools, and it was the second largest educational system. Within three years it had doubled in strength to become the largest one, with nearly half of the total number of schools in the entire country.[26] The major reason for its growth was the great increase in the number of labor agricultural settlements, particularly of immigrant *moshavim*, in many of which schools belonging to the Religious Workers Stream were established: in 1948, there were only eleven schools; in the summer of 1949, sixteen schools; in the summer of 1950, thirty-six schools; and one year later, fifty-three schools. The number of pupils enrolled in the Religious Workers Stream increased in those years from several hundred to approximately 4,500.[27]

The unique content of education in the Religious Workers Stream evolved only gradually. For a long period of time, each teacher in each school decided in practice how to integrate the Jewish religious worldview with a socialistic outlook. Only in March 1949 did the pedagogic committee of the Histadrut's Education Center—most of whose members were secular—authorize a "supplementary program for Jewish studies." More detailed programs for some of the subjects studied, or those dealing with how to teach the holidays, developed in the Religious Workers Stream only toward the end of 1951.[28] One program that sheds light on the unique nature of this educational stream, *From Passover to Shavuot* (Pentecost), was prepared by Moshe Etz-Hayyim, a leading figure in the Religious Workers Stream. In a typical passage, Etz-Hayyim attempted to combine Jewish tradition with a socialist worldview. In describing the period between Passover and Shavuot, he wrote:

> It comes as no surprise that workers throughout the world, who everywhere await their liberation, are also influenced by the radiance of Israel's Torah and its vital relevance to every generation, which by the Exodus from Egypt also led to freedom from enslavement. For all the persecuted and oppressed, and for every human being, the day for demonstrating their unity and their aspiration to freedom and equality was fixed during this period of time [i.e., the first of May]: for the world heard [the message] of 12,000 pairs of Rabbi Akiva's disciples, all of whom died during this period of time [between Passover and Shavuot; Tractate *Yevamot* 62b], and by their lives and deaths sanctified the teaching of their great Rabbi.

This combination of Jewish sources and the universal traditions of labor movements may seem rather artificial and perhaps somewhat forced; nevertheless, in those days, there were those who accepted it. Others hoped that devout Jews would in this way also be brought to accept socialist ideals.

The Religious Workers Stream had to struggle for its existence within the Histadrut. In mid-October 1949, Binyamin Frankel, chairman of the Education Committee of Haoved Hadati, addressed a special secret circular letter to people in other religious parties, asking them to intervene concerning the issue of religious education in the Histadrut. He claimed that 95 percent of the immigrants arriving during the past few months were religious Jews—a somewhat exaggerated statement, but correct in principle—and that most of them had been absorbed by Histadrut organizations. According to Frankel, "Until now, Haoved Hadati has succeeded, by intense struggle and by means of various tactics, such as strikes, and by stormy inquiries . . . to assure religious education in about a quarter of the immigrant *moshavim*." But now this movement was in great financial difficulty and faced a severe shortage of religious teachers and educators. He called upon the religious parties to help Haoved Hadati with its difficulties and thereby to help save religious families from a nonreligious education for their children.[29] Frankel's call, evidently issued with the agreement of his colleagues in the leadership of Haoved Hadati, went unanswered. Haoved Hadati had to contend single-handedly with anti-religious coercion in the Histadrut, and particularly in Tnu'at Hamoshavim.

Numerous letters of complaint to Histadrut institutions bear witness to Haoved Hadati's campaign to safeguard the religiosity of new immigrants. Some letters cited severe examples while using the bluntest language, thus reflecting the great distress of religious circles at that time. Dr. Yeshayahu Leibowitz, for example, complained of anti-religious coercion in Kfar Lifta near Jeruslaem. He claimed that the local instructor explicitly threatened the new immigrants, that should they insist upon religious education, they would be penalized in terms of provision of food, clothing, and jobs. He concluded his letter with the statement: "The institutions responsible for the Histadrut ... must know the true situation; that *the first buds of an inquisitory-Yevsektsiya* approach of hatred towards the Jewish religion and its repression* are sprouting in certain places in the Histadrut"[30] (emphasis added).

We conclude our discussion of the role of the Religious Workers Stream by pointing to the ambivalence with which it was treated in the Histadrut. On the one hand, the Histadrut leadership saw it as a tool to "control" large sectors among the new immigrants. On the other hand, there were in reality numerous cases of interference with whatever religious education was provided under the aegis of the Labor movement. In his testimony before the Frumkin Commission, Dr. Leibowitz testified:

> I came into contact with the new immigrants in a number of the new
> *moshavim....* I found that the local instructors used threats against the
> new settlers ... encouraging them towards a certain tendency in edu-
> cation.... The decision of the Histadrut Executive that obligates the
> provision of religious education for those settlers who request it ... ex-
> ists and is affirmed by the central institutions of the Histadrut, but
> there are many who violate it among those acting locally in its name.
> There is interference and subtle forms of obscuring and hiding [it], and
> at times recourse is also had to coarse and brutal means of threats and
> coercion. We are forced to put up a fight in each and every place.[31]

One might add that Dr. Leibowitz's testimony, the evidence of an insider, had a decisive influence upon the commission of inquiry.

Religious leadership of all shades, from all of the other religious parties, along with the religious press, severely criticized the Religious Workers Stream and Haoved Hadati. The latter was viewed as a reformist and liberal group that did the bidding of its masters in Mapam and Mapai. Hapoel Hamizrachi leader and government minister Moshe Shapira claimed in the Knesset: "Haoved Hadati is unfortunately no more than a camouflage and not a serious body."[32] Y. M. Levin, the leader of Agudat Israel and also a government minister, stated: "It is well known that Haoved Hadati is only a front and does not even have the courage to react to acts that are committed and are opposed to religion."[33] The extremely ultra-Orthodox *Neturei Karta,** of course, leveled the most biting criticism of all, arguing that Haoved Hadati was "an openly reformist faction of Histadrut members, one that publicly calls for 'religious reforms' . . . a faction that is unable to tolerate the continued observance of the law of *halitza*,* that openly demands the acceptance of *women as witnesses*,* etc. [This is] the faction that prided itself for its protest against the Foreign Ministry when it exempted religious staff members from engaging in urgent diplomatic activity on the Sabbath."[34]

This sharp criticism was shared by some representatives of the immigrants themselves. Thus, for example, the spokesman for the Yemenite Union wrote with great severity to the minister of education and culture:

> One who chooses it [the Religious Workers Stream] deceives himself, for in practice he is choosing the Workers Stream, which is explicitly defined as being secular. We consider this stream to be extremely secular. . . . We are convinced that the religiosity of the schools belonging to the religious sub-stream of the Workers Stream is highly questionable and is only temporary, until the Yemenite immigrant is absorbed. Then the mask will be removed, and it will become apparent that these are regular schools of the Workers Stream. . . . We believe that the education provided for Yemenite Jewish children must be religious, and that this may only be done in one of the two religious streams recognized by law, namely, that of Hamizrachi or Agudat Israel.[35]

Testifying before the Frumkin Commission, Dr. Leibowitz repeatedly emphasized that the Religious Workers Stream was in no way partner to the educational activities in the immigrant camps. He claimed:

> I am unable to testify concerning matters in the camps as an eyewitness. I have not visited the camps. . . . During recent months, there have been both official declarations and public information concerning the religious education provided by the Workers Stream in the camps. . . . I wish to state . . . [that] the Committee for Religious Education that is part of the Education Center [of the Histadrut], which is formally responsible for religious education and is composed of members of Haoved Hadati, is not a partner to any educational activity in the camps.[36]

Indeed, almost all of the efforts of the Religious Workers Stream were centered in other immigrant settlements, primarily the *moshavim* and immigrant neighborhoods in cities and villages. Some of those involved testified before the Frumkin Commission and greatly influenced it.

CHAPTER 8

POLITICAL DEVELOPMENTS DURING THE COURSE OF THE COMMISSION'S INVESTIGATION

Already in late 1949, even before relations with the religious parties had become strained, Mapai attempted to have Mapam join the coalition government. One reason for this initiative was to reduce its absolute dependence upon members of the Religious Front.[1] Coalition negotiations with Mapam dragged on for about four months, far longer than anticipated, finally collapsing in the late winter of 1950.[2] During January 1950, Mapai also considered the possibility of widening the coalition by adding the right-wing General Zionist party. It conducted extensive negotiations with that party, which also finally failed about the same time.[3]

Early that winter, David Ben-Gurion also had hopes for yet another coalition option, which could be created as the result of a possible split within the Religious Front. Clandestine contacts were conducted with the socialist element within the Religious Front—Hapoel Hamizrachi and Poalei Agudat Israel—in the hope of influencing their leaders to create a religious "satellite party" to Mapai.[4] *Internal Information Newsletter No. 3* of "Lamifne," a faction of Hapoel Hamizrachi, reported on its meeting with Ben-Gurion, noting inter alia that the exchange of views also touched upon the question of uniting all of the workers in Israel and the role to be played by religious laborers in this effort. But these contacts also proved fruitless, and the government's survival remained dependent upon Mapai's relations with all components of the Religious Front.

During those months in which Mapai had no other coalition alternative, it was forced to compromise with the Religious Front, which applied pressure and threatened to undermine the government's parliamentary basis, particularly with regard to internal matters—the economy and education. Parallel to the establishment of the Frumkin Commission, the government set up a ministerial committee to examine various proposals regarding religious education for the children in the immigrant camps. Surprisingly, members of the religious parties did not attack the continuation of "soul snatching" in the educational system in the country as a whole, being satisfied with the limited share they received out of all of the schools. Even assignment of the majority of the children in the care of Youth Aliya to nonreligious kibbutzim and schools did not generally seem to bother the leaders of the Religious Front; in any event, they exerted far less pressure over this issue than they had a few years earlier, at the time of the "Teheran Children" episode. In both of these matters—their share of schools throughout the country and Youth Aliya—the Religious Front did not pose ultimatums, directing its attention primarily to the problem of uniform education in the immigrant camps.

The ministerial committee appointed by the government to examine issues relating to religion, including education in the immigrant camps, was composed of five of its members: Zalman Shazar (chairman, Mapai), David Remez (Mapai), Bechor Shalom Shitrit (Sephardic Party), Yitzhak Meir Levin (Agudat Israel), and Moshe Shapira (Hapoel Hamizrachi).[5] The commission considered two main options concerning education in the camps: (1) To conduct a poll among all parents in the camps to decide in which schools (i.e., which educational streams) their children would study; (2) The establishment of uniform religious schools in the religious immigrant camps, to be administered by a committee of supervisors representing all religious groups. The committee had difficulty coming to a decision, which reflected the uncertainty of the Religious Front and Mapai regarding what was preferable from the viewpoint of each party.[6]

Early in February 1950, Moshe Shapira, representing the Religious Front, met with Minister of Education and Culture Shazar, who represented Mapai. Surprisingly, the two of them arrived at an agreement to resolve the dispute over education in the immigrant camps. This agreement entailed considerable concession on the part of Shazar: he agreed that *religious education would be provided for all children under age seventeen who had come to Israel from all of the Oriental countries*. The concession made by Shapira was that representatives of Mapai and the Religious Front would *jointly* organize and supervise the religious education in the camps.

The leadership of the Mapai Knesset Faction, in opposition to Ben-Gurion's view, refused to approve Shazar's approach. As we have already seen, party policy on various religious issues was as a whole far less yielding and compromising than that represented by Shazar and Ben-Gurion. On 15 February 1950, Mapai Secretary Z. Aharonowitz (Aranne) wrote to its representatives in the government:

> a. On 26 January 1950, an authoritative meeting of the party was held with the participation of Z. Shazar, D. Remez, and D. Ben-Gurion, devoted to the issue of education in the camps.
>
> b. Decisions were adopted at this meeting following a tense, comprehensive, and exhaustive discussion.[7]
>
> c. At the meeting of the Knesset Faction executive held on 12 February of this year with the participation of E. Kaplan, D. Remez, and Z. Shazar, it was made clear that the negotiations with the Religious Front were conducted by our comrades in a manner that was not consistent with decisions that had been adopted by the party.

In this letter, Aharonowitz added his own view: "I am obliged to state this time that prevention of a crisis in the relations with the Religious Front cannot come at the price of a severe internal crisis within the party, one that will erupt if an agreement is made with the Religious Front contrary to party decisions."[8] Thus when the proposed agreement was brought to a vote in the ministerial committee, all three secular ministers (the two from Mapai—including Shazar—and Shitrit of the Sephardic Party, who in practice received his instructions from Mapai) voted against it. This time the Mapai ministers agreed to yield only in the case of Yemenite children, insisting on conducting a poll among the parents of children from all other Oriental communities.

During February, the Religious Front took more rapid action on the issue of the education of immigrant children, a result of increased pressure from two groups—rabbis throughout Israel and large groups of new immigrants in the camps, primarily from among the Yemenite immigrants. The rabbis closed ranks behind the two chief rabbis, and a conference of some 200 of them from all over the country passed forcefully phrased resolutions that it "adopted unanimously while standing" on the subject of children and youth who had been snatched away for "heretical education."[9] There was much unrest among the immigrants as well, and in a few days, severe riots broke out in two immigrant camps (in the Yemenite camps in Ein-Shemer on 14 February 1950, and in Beit Lid three days later). In reporting at length to the Knesset, Police Minister Bechor Shitrit said that thousands of people had been incited, described violent clashes with officials and the police, and told of injuries and arrests. The minister stated: "In these two places there was a religious background [to the incidents], that is, they were made to believe as though persons wanted to make them violate their religion, to feed them non-kosher meat." Shitrit blamed everything on false incitement by several *yeshiva* students. During that same Knesset debate, Immigration Minister Moshe Shapira also referred to the disturbances—but his position, of course, was exactly the opposite. He complained that "only 230 Yemenite children out of 1,200 study Torah," claiming that "one very simple fact is clear to me: these camps are operated by officials who do not understand the language of these people, who do not understand their spirit, and are possibly also opposed to their spirit. In my opinion, this must be clarified not only in the present debate here, but by the committee on education [i.e., the Frumkin Commission] appointed by the government." Not surprisingly, the addresses of the two ministers elicited an interjection by MK Yohanan Bader of Herut: "Are both of them from the same government, or is one in the opposition and one in the coalition? Their manner of speech is entirely different, and one contradicts the other."[10]

The rejection by Mapai of the Shazar-Shapira agreement led the Religious Front to intensify its threats to break up the coalition government.[11] Meanwhile, religious circles abroad also increased their pressure, strengthening those religious leaders who refused to give in to Ben-Gurion and his colleagues.[12] As an intermediate step, prior to a final decision to quit the government, the religious ministers decided to boycott its meetings until the issue of education in the camps would be resolved.

While the religious cabinet ministers protested and demonstratively excused themselves from its meetings, numerous discussions were held within their own parties about how far they should go in pressuring Mapai. Should they really quit the coalition if efforts on behalf of religious education in the camps were not successful? Would leaving the coalition benefit the interests of the religious public in Israel, or would it likely be detrimental to them? There were some—particularly from the largest party, Hapoel Hamizrachi—who argued that such a step would be very harmful to the religious public and that membership of religious persons in the government would ensure that the laws of *Kashrut* would be observed and civil marriages would not be performed in Israel. Others, predominantly members of Hamizrachi, Poalei Agudat Israel, and Agudat Israel, demanded that the religious parties quit the government.[13]

At this time Ben-Gurion lay ill,[14] but the increasing pressure over the immigrant issue led him to decide on personal involvement and to send a "private fact-finding committee" to the camps. He chose two IDF officers who were among his closest confidants—Col. Aharon Hoter-Yishai and his military attaché, Lt. Col. Nehemia Argov—and sent them to Beit Lid and Ein-Shemer to investigate the problems in these camps. After receiving their report, he wrote to Rabbi Y. L. Fishman (Maimon) and Rabbi Y. M. Levin, the two Religious Front ministers with whom he was on closest terms:

> I have sent a committee of Army officers to two camps, and have learned that there is no basis to the stories about use of force and coer-

cion or cutting off of *payot*. Though this committee was not a substitute for the governmental commission of inquiry, in view of the violent incidents which have erupted in the two camps I felt myself obligated in the interim to clarify the situation insofar as possible. As for the substance of the issue: the accusation that an attempt is being made to "smother" religious education in the camps or elsewhere is absolutely groundless.

He concluded the letter with a statement that in principle he was opposed to "all anti-religious coercion and injury (just as, I believe, there must not be any religious coercion)." Ben-Gurion promised that he would personally intervene and raise certain proposals concerning educational arrangements in the camps at a meeting of the government.[15]

At this stage Immigration Minister Moshe Shapira suggested a new compromise solution: (1) that all Yemenite children receive religious education, either of Hamizrachi or Agudat Israel; (2) that all other immigrants be given a choice between religious or secular education. Shapira's proposal contained a component that to this day seems problematic—possibly even unreasonable—from a religious standpoint: how was it possible that the religious parties, which were then united in the Religious Front, were prepared *to forego religious education for members of all of the other Oriental communities*, insisting only upon such education for the Yemenites? There are those who argue that the Yemenites were more zealous regarding religion than the other Oriental communities, coming as they did from a more isolated country and that was not at an advanced stage of modernization. Furthermore, they argue that even among the Oriental communities there were many who agreed to, and at times even preferred, secular education. For those holding this view, this was a possible explanation for the religious parties' agreement to compromise regarding the education of the other communities.

While basically correct, we believe this is an inadequate explanation. We would assert that had most immigrant parents from Morocco, Libya, Tunisia, and so forth been given a free choice between religious and general education—assuming that both were on the same level from the point of pedagogy and content—*most* would have preferred a traditional religious education for their children. Undoubtedly, this episode points to the severe contradiction between religious principles and political reality in which a religious party is likely to find itself. It is noteworthy that at that very time the Sephardic Chief Rabbi of Israel, Rabbi Ben-Zion Ouziel, appeared before the Religious Front Knesset faction and spoke to its members on the problems faced by the Jews of Libya, Morocco, and Iraq (i.e., communities where many of the members at that time filled the immigrant camps). Rabbi Ouziel repeatedly stressed that "these communities are dedicated to a life based on Torah and the commandments just like the Yemenite Jews and are very diligent about religious education for their children."[16] Though Rabbi Ouziel asked the Religious Front to mount a campaign on behalf of religious education for all of those communities, the Religious Front leaders evidently did not feel that they were obligated by the statements and requests of the Chief Rabbi of Israel. They were prepared to compromise—and finally did compromise—with Mapai on the provision of religious education for the Yemenite children alone.

Shapira's proposal involved defining religious education as that provided by Hamizrachi or Agudat Israel, while secular education meant that of the Workers Stream or General Stream. Defining the Workers Stream as exclusively secular evoked severe opposition within Mapai. Ben-Gurion was at the forefront of those who insisted that "the Histadrut will maintain a type of religious school *within* its school system"[17] (emphasis in original). In his letter to the two religious cabinet ministers whom he admired, Ben-Gurion wrote: "It is unthinkable that the state would deflect religious children away from their faith . . . [but] religious education should not be exclusively associated with education [provided by] one *party* or another. Religion—even for a free-thinking Jew like me—is a sublime thing. . . . When one transforms religion into *a political axe to grind*, it becomes destructive and also dangerous"[18] (emphasis in original). This, in fact, is the beginning of the firm policy adopted by Ben-Gurion, who refused to forego the Religious Workers Stream (actually, he refused to forego influence upon the religious new immigrants) which, almost a year later, in February 1951, led to the resignation of the government and to new elections in July 1951.

We have put the cart before the horse and shall now return to the stage at which the government was boycotted by its religious members. Immediately upon recovering from his illness, Ben-Gurion vehemently condemned this step and led the government to decide that "a minister who refuses to participate in meetings of the government will not be allowed to be a member thereof."[19] This ultimatum brought the religious ministers back to the next government meeting, but meanwhile the dispute came up for debate in the Knesset on 21 February. Ben-Gurion tried to put the Religious Front on the defendant's block, arguing that its members had "violated their coalition responsibility." As for the Shazar-Shapira agreement, he claimed that education was important to all, and that "[this matter] could not be arranged by means of an agreement between two [people]." In replying to Ben-Gurion on behalf of the Religious Front, Minister Shapira and MK Pinkas used extremely moderate language, emphasizing that of course education was a matter that "touches upon the very soul of the nation," and that they sensed that procrastination was being practiced concerning this critical issue.[20] Following these exchanges between Mapai and the Religious Front, and notwithstanding the disagreements within the government, its representatives in the Knesset united to reject the proposal coming from the opposition benches that the issue of education in the camps be reviewed by the Knesset.

This is further proof that the two parties strove first and foremost to preserve the integrity of their coalition government.

At the next government meeting, convened on 22 February, representatives of all parties were present. It was decided there, quite simply, that there could no longer be any differentiation between the immigrant camps and the rest of the country, and that in every camp a poll would be conducted among the parents by which they could choose from among the four different educational streams. The intention of the Mapai ministers—who pushed through this decision—was that the parents also could choose religious education provided by the Histadrut (i.e., the Religious Workers Stream). At that government session Mapai did not yet know that all of the religious bodies—including Haoved Hadati, which operated the religious educational system of the Histadrut—had on that very day joined forces to sign an agreement calling for a "uniform religious stream" in the immigrant camps. *Ha'aretz* reported that "the agreement concerning uniform religious education came as a surprise to Mapai," while *Davar* quoted some as saying that this was "the sharpest political maneuver in the history of the state."[21] At a meeting of the Central Committee of the Histadrut, Pinhas Lubianiker (Lavon) admitted: "From the viewpoint of the Histadrut, a very serious mishap has taken place with regard to Haoved Hadati."[22] He accused the leaders of Haoved Hadati of disloyalty to Mapai and expressed his anger that they had reached an agreement with the religious parties outside of the Histadrut.

In the wake of the agreement calling for uniform religious education, Mapai had second thoughts about leaving the choice of school to the parents. At an internal discussion conducted by the Central Committee of the Histadrut, in the presence of other members, Lubianiker (Lavon) said: "The composition of the camps is about 80 percent immigrants from the Oriental communities. If they confront one united religious front, which will be opposed by the heretics [secularists] of the Right and the Left, we are liable to reach a situation . . . in which the overwhelming majority of education in the camps will be in the hands of Hamizrachi. I therefore greatly fear the results of such a poll." MK Yizhar Smilansky (the author S. Yizhar) opposed conducting any poll whatsoever in the immigrant camps, convinced that Mapai would gain nothing by that. He argued that even should the Workers Stream be victorious in the poll, it lacked sufficient teachers capable of teaching in the immigrant camps. Yizhar's solution was "to already begin abroad . . . even before they immigrate. We need to immunize the people against the propaganda horror stories, to give them inoculations for spiritual resistance, just as we inoculate them to physically resist all kinds of diseases." Mordecai Surkis likewise opposed conducting a survey in the camps, adding that "there will be no effect to the appearance of Ben-Nahum[23] when compared with appearances by Rabbis Ouziel or Herzog." Most of the speakers advocated adopting the proposal of the Progressive Party for uniform education throughout the country, suggesting that it be applied initially in the immigrant camps.[24]

At the same time, there were those in the Religious Front who also were not overly pleased with the idea of a parental poll and thus were reluctant to conduct it. At a meeting of the World Center of Hamizrachi, fear was expressed "of losing large percentages because of the pressure and coercion of the Histadrut."[25] Others feared that "people from the Left might 'involve' the inhabitants of the camps by telling them that their education is state education, while ours is partisan."[26] Minister M. Shapira observed that he would not take the results of the survey for granted, since "the Yemenites are cowards."[27]

At the time the government had decided to conduct a parental poll, and both sides—Mapai and the Religious Front—were at work trying to annul that decision, responsibility for the Ministry of Education and Culture was temporarily transferred to Minister of Transportation David Remez. This was allegedly due to Shazar's illness, but the real reason was his overall lack of ability to fill the role of minister of education. We have already noted that throughout his term in office— and particularly during periods of crisis—Shazar exhibited obvious organizational ineptitude, so that Ben-Gurion saw no other solution but to replace him temporarily, and thereafter to oust him permanently from the government.[28] Several days after his temporary appointment, during the course of a discussion in the Knesset, David Remez admitted that a way to avoid a parental poll in the camps seemed possible.[29] This was on 6 February, only one day before the date that had been designated by the government for the poll. Meanwhile, contacts between Mapai and the Religious Front had become more intense, with the intention of proposing alternative solutions to the poll.

On 14 March a new agreement was reached between the Religious Front and Mapai—one that was adopted by the government and approved by the Knesset on that very same day, with sixty-two voting in favor, an absolute majority of the house. The Knesset resolution stipulated that: (1) responsibility for education in the camps would be transferred from the Culture Department to the Education Division of the Ministry of Education and Culture; (2) education provided in the Yemenite camps would be religious, under the supervision of a committee of four religious supervisors representing the four different streams that would determine the program of study, appoint the instructors, teachers, principals, and supervisors, and oversee study arrangements; (3) in the other camps there would be separate transition classes for each of the two educational tendencies, one of which would be religious. The director of the Education Division and the four chief supervisors would determine enrollment arrangements for the different classes.[30] During the Knesset debate, the agreement was strongly criticized by members of the opposition. Particularly vehement attacks came from Mapam, whose representatives argued that the working class would be the main victim of this agreement.

MK Ya'akov Hazan, one of the leaders of Mapam, complained that it reflected a posture of "bowing one's head" before the religious element in the population, adding: "As far as we are concerned, the world of religion is a world in decline, a world that belongs to the past." Regarding the Yemenites, he demanded "that the same norms be applied to them as to all other immigrants: that in their camps too there would be uniform classes, divided into religious and secular ones in accordance with the wishes of the parents."[31] MK Hanan Rubin of Mapam argued that "the government statement is in blatant contradiction to clause 10 of the Compulsory Education Law. The government knows this, and for that reason proposed amending the law."[32] MK Aharon Zisling, another representative of Mapam, said that the Workers Stream had been dealt a blow, and that "the Yemenite immigrants are differentiated from the rest of Israel, the education of their children being given over to one single religious authority without asking the parents' opinion."[33]

The General Zionists also protested the agreement. One of their Knesset members, Israel Rokah, declared: "My ear is very sensitive to the name 'Yemenites'— and I heard this name in the government's statement. I firmly oppose [the idea] that the statement by the government should refer to one tribe, called the Yemenites, which has been set apart from the general public. Why are they different from others? . . . If there are arrangements that are good for the Austrians and the Poles, they should also be good for the Yemenites."[34] The opposition's claims, as noted above, were rejected, and the Knesset approved the agreement between Mapai and the Religious Front by an absolute majority of its members.

The agreement also contained two additional clauses that had been agreed upon but were labeled "confidential, not for publication." These were:

> a. In order to facilitate and ensure an appropriate educational atmosphere, the two educational streams [the religious and general] and those classes belonging to each of them will be housed in separate buildings (or operate in two shifts);
>
> b. The government will appoint a ministerial committee comprising four members, one of whom will be the minister of education, with equal representation for both parties, which will discuss and rule regarding every problem or complaint submitted to it in connection with the educational arrangements in the camps, and it will appoint the four supervisors.

The decision not to publicize these clauses derived out of fear of Mapam's criticism and, perhaps no less, fear of anti-religious elements within Mapai itself.[35]

Only one day after the compromise agreement between Mapai and the Religious Front was concluded, relations between them were once again threatened. About half of the members of the Mapai Knesset faction voted in favor of

Mapam's proposal that thousands of immigrant children be removed from the camps and transferred to Youth Aliya institutions in agricultural settlements (nearly all of which were secular). Had this motion been passed, the fundamental dispute between Mapai and the religious parties over education would have once more burst out into the open.[36] However, it was voted down by a majority of 35 to 29. This vote indicated that many people in Mapai did not accept the compromise agreement with the religious parties, and that on all issues relating to religion there were many who were very close to the policy of Mapam.[37]

About a month after the agreement between Mapai and the religious parties was signed, the latter began to claim that its stipulations were not being carried out. Moreover, some religious circles argued that the state of religious education in the immigrant camps had even deteriorated in comparison to the period prior to the agreement. An editorial in She'arim, for example, claimed that the Culture Department still dominated the camps, that religious teachers had not been appointed in the Yemenite camps, while in the other camps teachers had not been appointed for either of the two trends, and that some of the religious teachers who had been employed by the Culture Department in March 1950 had been fired.[38] About that time word spread throughout the country concerning "the Amka Incident" which, as we have seen,[39] was to become for religious circles a symbol of how Tnu'at Hamoshavim related to the establishment of non-Histadrut religious schools in the immigrant moshavim.

Mapam, of course, put forward opposing claims, complaining of religious coercion, emphasizing Mapai's "clericalism," and stressing that religious circles were dictating the character of Israel. Their newspaper, Al Hamishmar, came out with bold headlines: "Schools in the camps of Yemenite immigrants have been reduced to the level of dark hadarim"; "Teachers with years of experience and talent were fired in the middle of the year and replaced by yeshiva students lacking any pedagogic training";[40] "If you grow a beard and payot you can be a teacher in the camps."[41] The intention of these headlines was clear: to portray Mapai as groveling before and surrendering to "the forces of darkness."

The report of the Frumkin Commission was submitted to the government on 9 May 1950, against the backdrop of the situation described above. At the time it was presented, the agreement contracted between Mapai and the religious parties in mid-March had not yet been implemented in all of the immigrant camps. The report only assisted in implementing some clauses of the agreement, primarily that the Culture Department would cease all educational activity among immigrant children. Moreover, it did not substantially lessen the tension between the Histadrut parties and the Religious Front. Finally, the report did not at all influence the nature of education provided in the immigrant camps.

CHAPTER 9

THE CULTURE DEPARTMENT'S OBJECTIONS TO THE COMMISSION'S CONCLUSIONS

The Frumkin Commission placed full responsibility for the faulty educational aspects of the absorption of immigrants and acts of anti-religious coercion that it found in the immigrant camps upon the Department for Language Instruction and Educational Absorption among the Immigrants,[1] directed by Nahum Levin. As a result, Levin and two of his staff, Yehiel Aharon Aldema and Zippora Zehavi, were found culpable and were forced to resign from their positions. Other officials of the Ministry of Education and Culture, first and foremost the incumbent minister Zalman Shazar, were not held responsible. The administrative apparatus of the Ministry of Education and Culture was likewise exonerated, because "it was still in the process of being organized and structured, and lacked any [bureaucratic] tradition and experience."[2] Shazar was not found responsible, because "for much of the time during which these matters developed he was ill and was prevented from [giving the matter] his personal and fundamental treatment."[3]

I believe that the Frumkin Commission chose the easy way out when deciding who to blame or not to blame for the serious acts it uncovered. Shazar's personal responsibility, notwithstanding his prolonged absences from office, was clearly established during the Commission's investigation. It found that over many months, Shazar had refused to transfer responsibility for the education of immigrant children to the Education Division, which dealt with the education of all other children in Israel, and it was he who decided—in the summer of 1949—that they would continue to be subject to the uniform educational frameworks of the Culture Department. In other words, it was the minister who personally decided on the administrative procedures, the educational staff, and the type of education to be provided in the immigrant camps, and it was he who refused to respond to the repeated requests—including those by Culture Department officials—that changes be introduced. Moreover, even after the appointment of the Commission, Shazar himself examined the situation in the field and reported to the public that there was nothing to the complaints voiced by religious groups, and that political considerations lay behind the "libels."[4]

The Frumkin Commission rightfully placed responsibility upon "its primary source—the government as a whole, that bears collective responsibility for all matters of state, including education of the immigrants."[5] Nevertheless, it also should have criticized Prime Minister David Ben-Gurion more sharply. It was a mistake to totally exonerate the prime minister from all responsibility for the absorption of immigrant children. True, as we have seen, Ben-Gurion's personal viewpoint differed from the majority of his colleagues. He alone among the leaders of Mapai clearly recognized the great injustice that had been done, above all to the new immigrants themselves, and the heavy price that the state and the Labor movement would be likely to pay for this at a later period of time. Nevertheless, Ben-Gurion intervened too little. On only a few isolated occasions did he attempt to convince his colleagues to refrain from the methods of coercion and pressure that they had adopted. But even these attempts were limited to verbal reprimands; he did not take sufficient steps to ensure that all legal and judicial means be applied against those performing (in his words) "violent robbery."

The Commission preferred to place the blame on one senior official and two members of his staff. The entire Jewish Agency apparatus that administered the absorption of immigrants, headed by Giora Josephtal, was barely mentioned in the report. Of all the directors of immigrant camps, only one took the trouble to testify before the Frumkin Commission, while all of the others received no mention in its deliberations. As for the numerous staff employed in the camps—most of whom held outlooks similar to Levin and his workers—no one was charged with attempting to "adjust" immigrant children to the new Zionist ethos. In practice, only a few individual members of the Culture Department's staff were blamed.

Nahum Levin was shocked by the fact that the Frumkin Commission accused primarily himself and his department. He was convinced that he was an authentic representative of the veteran Labor movement in Eretz Israel, and as such was deserving of nothing but praise—from the Commission as well as the general public—for his tireless efforts to educate the new generation of immigrants. He recorded some harsh reactions to the Commission's report in his personal notebook. The two things that most disturbed him were the terrible injustice carried out against the pioneering spirit, which he believed he represented, and the moral wrong that he was convinced had been committed against him and his staff. He wrote in his notebook:

> *An attack has been mounted against a pioneering enterprise.* The reliance upon witnesses for the prosecution and the refusal to listen to our witnesses. A double catastrophe has taken place here: a) The very person in whom I believed so deeply and whom I saw not only as a representative of the most glorious period but also as the spokesman of conscience (for otherwise it would have been impossible for this person to represent either this or any other period)—it was precisely he who did me such evil [it is not clear to whom Levin was referring: Ben-Gurion, Shazar, or perhaps Ben-Zvi?—author]; b) A terrible injustice has been done to the path that one represents.[6]

In an outline, which seems to be the draft of a letter to Ben-Gurion, he wrote:

> 1. I would have preferred had we met. . . . I hope that I shall still be given the chance to do so.
>
> 2. *The public aspect:* The attack . . . [is directed against] the Culture Department, the Absorption Department, the Education Center. . . . The [Culture] Department carries the burden of the blame, and this is *a legal injustice.* . . . Teaching Histadrut [principles is seen as] a crime. . . . *What is the real reason? The struggle is over the character of this wave of immigration and its control.* . . . [They] [i.e., the religious circles] understood that "uniformity" means the new, pioneering Eretz Israel, etc., etc., and they understand that without a scandal it [i.e., their plans to thwart it] wouldn't be achieved.
>
> 3. *The personal aspect:* It is serious from the ethical viewpoint. . . . I did not resign . . . except over the radio [Levin evidently heard of his "resignation" in a radio broadcast—author]. . . . The minister or Avrekh [a reference to Yeshayahu Avrekh, who served at the time as director general of the Ministry of Education] should resign. . . . Why should the branch that I planted be severed? Rehabilitation. [An] ethical requisite and a requirement of justice . . . and immediate appointment . . . [as] *the representative of Israel for cultural relations with the Diaspora and as the prime minister's advisor on cultural activity within the nation,* until such time as the matter is clarified.[7] (emphases in original)

Levin's anticipation of total rejection of the report, his full rehabilitation, and his own rise in the ranks were not to be realized. Even though Ben-Gurion opposed the report, as we shall see below, he was unable to ignore it completely, as Levin had wished.

The dozens of staff personnel who worked with Levin in the Culture Department also expressed their resentment over the report. They demanded that a "new and meticulous investigation"[8] be conducted and declared a thirty-six-hour strike to give more force to their demand. Employees of the Culture Department chose a committee that published a pamphlet, distributed in dozens of copies, stating the staff's objections to the report.[9] At a press conference convened by members of the Culture Department to contradict the Commission's report and to cast doubt upon the validity of its conclusions, their spokesman, Yosef Shaked, presented a series of arguments. He first raised certain extenuating circumstances which, in his opinion, explained why the Commission had erred in its conclusions: "The camps are 'terra incognita,' requiring time and effort to learn its problems"—and, of course, such time was not available to the Commission. Or: "The camps are . . . like a boiling pot," and it is therefore difficult to fathom their nature. Shaked then went on to categorically state that the Commission's conclusions were the outcome of "the government's desire to clear itself of the accusations leveled against it, that it is creating a 'police state' [an accusation repeated by both left- and right-wing opposition circles], forcing its representatives to bypass the truth and produce a 'scapegoat'—the employees of the department." What lies behind these statements is the assumption—mistaken, of course—that the content of the report was dictated by the government, with the members of the Commission merely acting as its emissaries.

Shaked's final arguments were the most significant: "The work of the commission was conducted in an atmosphere of suspicion and stormy propaganda, and the committee was evidently unconsciously influenced by this atmosphere." Shaked argued that the Commission was confronted with false evidence, "primitive testimonies," and testimonies that distorted the facts. There is some truth to these claims: there was a climate of public opinion that did affect the Commission, which also was presented with one-sided and exaggerated testimony that at times was formulated as generalizations, but all of this was insufficient to completely reject its conclusions, as suggested by the personnel of the Culture Department.[10]

The objections of the Culture Department's staff received full backing from the Labor movement newspapers (but not the rest of the press). Thus, for example, an editorial in *Davar* (the Histadrut daily) declared:

> In its report, the commission of inquiry made extremely weighty accusations, in effect directing its accusations against all the employees of the Culture Department. It is this generalization that gives ethical and substantive authority to the demand for a reexamination of the issue,

because . . . the entire staff of the Culture Department is not an unknown and anonymous public. It is well known throughout the country, as are its activities. Its approach towards cultural activity in the
country is also known, as is its attitude towards the values of the Jewish heritage and activity among immigrants, as well as its viewpoint on
cultural and educational activities among immigrants who are rooted in
the values of this heritage and in religious life. If this group has been
portrayed as it was in this report, then one needs to examine not only
that group, but also—first and foremost—the report itself. . . . True, this
is not a usual demand in regard to such a commission of investigation
. . . but the accusations regarding the employees of the Culture Department contained in this report are so serious—reflecting not only
upon this group of people but also upon the entire community—that
any challenge of its conclusions . . . is justified. . . . One cannot deny the
right of appeal against such a verdict.[11]

Mapai's newspaper, *Hador*, was even more severe. It argued in an editorial that
the Frumkin Commission Report had concluded that employees of the Culture
Department had supposedly imposed "anti-religious terror upon masses of religious people," and that "according to this report, it follows that the employees of
the Culture Department of the government of Israel are lowly sadists . . . fright-
eningly wicked . . . foolish and primitive people lacking in all pedagogic sense, who
imagine that by means of terror and violence it would be possible to bring about
within a few weeks a cultural revolution that requires generations." The same editorial noted that Culture Department employees had applied an extremely harsh
epithet to the report, calling it "The Protocols of the Elders of Edom."[12] Nevertheless, the conclusion of *Hador*'s editors is similar to *Davar*'s: "to demand that the
government find an appropriate way to reexamine the subject."[13] In its editorial,
the Mapam daily, *Al Hamishmar*, attacked not only the report and the religious circles but above all leveled its criticism against Mapai:

> The objective of the commission of investigation . . . is to justify, in
> considered and moderate language, the aspiration of members of the
> religious priesthood in Israel to dominate immigrant children in the
> camps. . . . The report was written by a commission which was
> neither public nor parliamentary, the large majority of whose mem-
> bers represent the ruling classes. . . . It is a document that sets out to
> confirm the basic axiom that encouragement and support is given in
> the State of Israel and by the Government of Israel to the domineer-
> ing tendencies of religious circles who do not hesitate to use religion
> as a means for political and bourgeois class domination in the State
> of Israel.[14]

Certain leading public figures also condemned the report and came out in defense of the Culture Department staff. In an open letter to Nahum Levin, Dr. Giora Josephtal, director of the Absorption Department of the Jewish Agency, and his deputy, Dr. Hayyim Yahil, wrote:

> We are emotionally constrained to express to you in these very days our admiration and gratitude for your efforts and those of your colleagues. ... It is very distressing that such an honorable commission, in terms of its composition and reliability, should have been so influenced by the claims of one side as to ignore the overall conditions in which immigration is being absorbed. This is so only because the commission was subject to the public and psychological pressure applied by numerous witnesses for the prosecution [i.e., those who supported claims by the Religious Front], and did not know how to seek information from other circles as well. ... We well know that without a staff of workers motivated by a pioneering will ... the sounds of the Hebrew language would not have been heard in their tents [of the immigrants]. ... We note with much distress that even the most responsible people and groups have not yet given the subject of absorption serious thought, and they tend to a division of labor by which one party will bear the burden of absorption, while others will suffice with pointing to shortcomings and casting aspersions on those who bear the burden.[15]

Various private individuals also sensed a need to support Nahum Levin and his colleagues. Thus Ephraim Tsoref—at the time a veteran teacher in the Hamizrachi Stream, a biblical commentator, and an author who was one of the religious persons working with Levin in the Culture Department—published an emotional plea to the Knesset and the government. He testified that, "Levin's relations with religious and traditional people in general were definitely positive and sincere." Tsoref blamed "those who from the outset did not turn over the entire matter of education in the camps to the authority of the Education Division with its various streams, which have the [necessary] pedagogic and administrative apparatus and are experienced." In other words, he too blamed the minister of education and culture and the ministry's senior staff rather than the Culture Department, which merely filled a vacuum that had been created.[16] Dr. Shaul Levin, a leading figure in the General Stream of education, who a few years later would serve as head of the Department of Education and Culture of the Tel Aviv Municipality, wrote to Nahum Levin: "The moment I heard the news concerning the great injustice that had been done to you, I was seized by an intense feeling that gives me no rest—that a scandalous thing has been done here, and that a scapegoat had to be found for the mistakes of others." Ephraim Shmueli, of the Haifa School and Kindergarten Teachers Seminary, wrote to Levin: "I too was hurt by this ruling. While I do not know all the details, I cannot imagine that you have done wrong, and to such a degree. I am certain that this is a case of religious persecution and am astounded at the opinions of several of the judges." These complaints were directed primarily against Gad Frumkin and Izhak Ben-Zvi.[17]

As we have seen, the report placed a strong emphasis on the responsibility of the Culture Department's staff. In practice, almost all members of the veteran Yishuv who had been involved in the absorption of the Great Aliya—certainly the secular among them who belonged to the Labor movement and bore the major burden of integration—strove to achieve the same goal as did the Culture Department: to acculturate the immigrants as rapidly as possible to the norms and patterns of the utopian image of the new Israeli pioneer. Thus camp directors, doctors, nurses, instructors, and even the cooks and maintenance personnel in the immigrant camps all adhered to the same educational policy. At times they influenced the new immigrants no less than did the teachers. Though the Frumkin Commission Report did refer to people who fulfilled various tasks in the immigrant camps—personnel representing the Jewish Agency, government offices, and social movements—it still placed all responsibility for the "melting pot" approach, which was a predominant concept among most of the society engaged in absorbing the new immigrants, upon a certain specifically defined group, which is why employees of the Culture Department were particularly offended by the report and why the labor parties and their press came so staunchly to their defense.

We have already mentioned that the Frumkin Commission Report referred to educational activity in the immigrant villages as well, but in its conclusions the members did not elaborate upon the educational approaches practiced there.[18] One may assume that they did not think they would be capable of bringing about fundamental changes in the patterns of activity of Tnu'at Hamoshavim, or of changing the system of quotas that in those days determined the movement and party with which each *moshav* would be affiliated. The quota system also automatically determined the educational stream to which the school in each *moshav* would belong, and the Commission related only to that issue. Most of the *moshavim* were affiliated with Mapai, while only in a few cases were they connected to the *moshav* movements of Hapoel Hamizrachi, Poalei Agudat Israel, or others.[19] MK Shoshana Persitz claimed in a debate in the Knesset on 13 February 1951, on the basis of information provided by Minister of Education and Culture David Remez, that of the ninety-two *moshavim* whose population included school-age children, sixty belonged to Tnu'at Hamoshavim, twenty-one to Hapoel Hamizrachi, four to Poalei Agudat Israel, four to Haoved Hatzioni (the Labor movement affiliated with the Progressive Party), and two to Herut, while only one was not politically affiliated. In the majority of the *moshavim*, the Commission noted that, "The impression gained by the commission [from whence that impression?—author] was that only in places where new immigrants alone resided, if they were within the framework of Histadrut Haovdim [i.e., *moshavim* belonging to Tnu'at Hamoshavim], did they succeed in introducing religious education within the framework of the Workers Stream." The Commission quoted Dr. Y. Leibowitz, who told it of the decision by the Histadrut Executive to provide religious education in those *moshavim* whose settlers requested it, adding that in practice, "There are those who violate it among those acting locally in its [i.e., the Histadrut's] name. Those who dominate the place are the instructors."[20] All in all, what happened in each *moshav* was largely determined by the personality and worldview of the local instructor, who generally came from one of the veteran *moshavim*. His attitude to religion and Jewish tradition very much influenced the entire nature of cultural-spiritual absorption in the *moshav* for which he was responsible.

Despite their knowledge of the facts, the authors of the report did not put any blame on the teachers and instructors of Tnu'at Hamoshavim, who were no less zealous than employees of the Culture Department in their attempts to "assimilate" immigrants to the norms of the Labor movement. They were not blamed as a movement, nor were any of them accused personally, as were Levin, Aldema, and Zehavi. On this count as well, members of the Culture Department felt that they had been treated unfairly.

AN UNPUBLISHED REACTION

One of the senior workers in the Culture Department was Hadassa Lipmanowitz, at that time director of the department's Youth Office, later to become District Judge Hadassa Ben-Ito. It was she who initiated and established the youth clubs in the immigrant camps and special camps for Yemenite youth. While conducting research for this book, I met with her, and she provided me with some thoughts that she had set down in writing after the submission of the Frumkin Commission Report.[21] As these were not intended for publication, and since Lipmanowitz was even then a person of independent opinion, albeit a Mapai supporter, there is some historic significance to her contemporary reaction to the accusations leveled against the staff of the Culture Department. I cite here a number of passages from her paper:

> The episode relating to education in the camps greatly agitated public opinion of all persuasions in the country, and it was difficult to find anyone connected to the press or in public life who did not participate in the debates surrounding this issue. Yet precisely because of the extensive debates and discussions, the political aspect of the problem stood out very strongly, while many were blind to its substantive facet.
> . . . For many, the entire debate revolved around a theoretical polemic between Mapai and the Religious Front . . . and since I am especially

close to the problems of youth in these camps . . . I will touch in particular upon this problem.

Upon its immigration to Israel, the Yemenite community as a whole took a giant step forward. This revolution, expressed so concretely in the form of people who were transferred directly from camel's back to modern airplanes, was also manifested in spiritual values. Just as we could not allow the Yemenites to accustom themselves to all the varied forms of transportation that had been in use from the time when people rode only on camels and donkeys until the invention of the airplane, so could we not agree that educating them to the spiritual and social values customary in Israel could extend over many generations.

It was clear to all that the Yemenite community was essentially a religious one, that its very essence as a community marked by nationalism and love of Israel stemmed from the religious values which its members had preserved for many years. It was clear to all who presumed to engage in the education of these youngsters that the educational revolution would have to be effected with full respect for religion and tradition—and not by its refutation and the creation of conflicts; in full reliance upon their faith and their customs, [coupled with] a desire to present them with new values—and not by uprooting positive values that are accepted by the entire community; by having new branches sprout from the tree upon which they are sitting—and not by pulling up its roots. The youth leaders sent to the camps by the Ministry of Education and Culture were educated and trained in this spirit.

The Yemenites themselves . . . related to this project [she refers here to the special youth camps established by the Culture Department—author] extremely favorably. . . . They viewed with favor the appearance on the scene of youth leaders and teachers who collected young boys and girls in a youth camp where they engaged in teaching and guidance. . . . Many queued up to register their children for the camps and personally signed the registration forms. The "council of sages" in one of the camps even issued a special broadsheet recommending that youth be sent to the special camps.

It soon became apparent that these youngsters, despite their being so primitive and lacking in education, had great potential. . . . Immediately upon the commencement of work it seemed that it would not be long before an important element would be added to the ranks of the pioneers and builders of the country.

But it was not long before this felicitous work drew fire. . . . There were those who feared that this success would be to its detriment. There were those who thought that it was not good that these youths should see the light, that they should leave the close confines of superstitious beliefs and backwardness; there were those who thought that the Yemenite community ought to be preserved like an ancient museum piece, that it must not advance. . . . And some people began a campaign of defamation the likes of which had never been seen before, and did not hesitate to use the most destructive means.

The Yemenites began to learn a new chapter in citizenship: they learned that authority is not authority, that a director is not a director, and that a policeman is not a policeman. They learned that one is only considered a good citizen if one breaks the law, if one rises up and demonstrates, throws stones at the directors of camps, denigrates teachers and instructors, conducts hunger strikes and riots—and all this, in the name of lofty values, of holy aims. All this to defend the spirit of ancient Israel, which the evil-doers want to eliminate and destroy.

Sometimes one stops and thinks: are there really Jews in this land who can do such things and whose hands do not tremble, whose conscience does not torment them? . . . Are the future of the young Yemenite boy and girl and the difficulties of absorption they undergo so worthless that they should thus be sacrificed upon the altar of political expediency? Shall they indeed be crushed by the wheels of political rivalry between the parties?

Hadassa Lipmanowitz, an innocent, idealistic young woman, cast all responsibility for the "episode of the camps" upon the politicians, especially those from religious circles. Nevertheless, as we have already seen, things were not quite that simple.

Despite her claim that the Culture Department aspired to a revolution that would take place "with full respect for religion and tradition," we have seen that at the time its personnel did not always behave in this manner. The waves of immigration were enormous, the burden of absorption was tremendous, and the dominant outlook was that the immigrants should be "upgraded" socially and spiritually and integrated as soon as possible into "the ranks of the pioneers and the builders of the country." Lipmanowitz's claim that the youth leaders and instructors were educated and trained in a spirit of respect for Jewish religious tradition does not wholly reflect the true situation in those days. It was very difficult to find instructors and teachers, for the thousands of children in the camps required many such persons, while the salaries and conditions offered to them were minimal. Thus almost anyone willing to do so was engaged. Training courses for the instructors lasted only a few days, and the nature of the education provided was in practice determined by the selection of those who would engage in it. The majority of the instructors chosen were secular, and the dominant worldview in their surroundings was unilateral: that the world of religion and tradition was in decline, to be replaced by the values of a new, enlightened world. This belief was ipso facto also transmitted to the immigrants in the camp. It was in rejection of this worldview that Yemenites demonstrated, went on strike, and protested—and not merely as "puppets" who were led to use methods of protest that were alien and remote to them.

Nevertheless, Hadassa Lipmanowitz was correct when she wrote harshly that the Yemenites also were a tool manipulated by both secular and religious politicians. Indeed, there were many people from the religious parties who sought to engage in the selfsame activity of "reeducation" of the immigrants, albeit not to the values of the labor movement but to their own worldview—that of European, or sometimes anti-Zionist, Orthodoxy. Among the religious community as well there were those whose only interest was to preserve Yemenite traditions and prevent their separation from their spiritual roots; among those circles too, partisan interests often took precedence over an educational struggle conducted on principle and in all innocence.

There can be no debate about the consequences of the struggle. Hadassa Lipmanowitz was once more correct in foreseeing that the Yemenites (and members of other communities) would pay dearly for the mistakes made in their spiritual absorption, and for the political struggles between religious and secular elements, which only exacerbated the errors. The Yemenites paid dearly, because those absorbing them were unacquainted with these immigrants' spiritual world.

In March 1950 a decision was made to abolish the special camps for youth from Yemen. Lipmanowitz vigorously opposed this decision and as a final means appealed directly to Ben-Gurion. According to her oral testimony, Ben-Gurion received her for an interview and listened to her with great patience, but he finally told her (as she recollects): "We must compromise. We cannot begin civil wars here. We have external enemies, we are in a state of war, we are creating a state, we must avoid a *Kulturkampf.*" Ben-Gurion reiterated that the youth villages must be closed down as soon as possible.[22]

Immediately following that conversation—apparently only a few days before the submission of the Frumkin Report—Lipmanowitz resigned and left the Culture Department. Despite the decisions made by the authorities, the system of taking immigrant children out of their homes and transferring them to youth camps was not entirely discontinued. Such camps continued to be supervised by two persons who had worked under Lipmanowitz, Bezalel Drori and Baruch Burman.[23] In an incisive discussion conducted among Mapai activists in December 1950, a few weeks after the losses sustained by Mapai in the elections to the municipalities and local councils, one of the party leaders still asked: "Why don't we tell the government that it should at this moment establish twenty large institutions, with 500 youngsters in each institution, and take 10,000 immigrant children and place them in these educational institutions where they should stay for two to three years, until they reach the age of seventeen or eighteen? This is the only way to assure that these youngsters will thereafter join the labor movement."[24]

Many years later, Judge Ben-Ito said of that period: "The camps were 'extraterritorial.' They weren't part of the State of Israel. . . . Everything was conducted there differently. . . . People there did not control their own destiny. . . . Everything was mixed up. It was something like an emergency ward . . . everything happened quickly and by chance . . . not by plan." As for the repeated accusations of anti-religious coercion during that period, she argued firmly: "There were mistakes. . . . Perhaps we should have been more conscious of tradition, perhaps we needed to be more aware that it was impossible to change everything all at once. . . . All kinds of errors were committed when the state was established. . . . But we were not part of some satanic scheme to entice Jewish children away from their religious beliefs. . . . This is certainly not true and it is a libel . . . like the libel of the 'Protocols of the Elders of Zion.' People do not combat it strongly enough, and so it becomes part of history."[25]

CHAPTER 10

REACTIONS TO
THE FRUMKIN REPORT

GOVERNMENT, KNESSET,
HISTADRUT

The Frumkin Report was presented to the government on 9 May 1950. Over a month later, on 19 June, a brief debate was conducted in the Knesset on motions for the agenda presented by MKs Feige Ilanit of Mapam and Meir Grabovski (Argov) of Mapai, both of whom sharply criticized the report and its conclusions. Their criticism was indicative of the great confusion evoked by the report within Labor movement circles. Ilanit clarified the position of her party, which had from the outset opposed the commission of inquiry, arguing that "even a cursory reading of the commission's conclusions indicates that it failed to carry out the task with which it was charged." She categorically declared that "no one will believe that *payot* were deliberately and systematically cut off," and she demanded, on behalf of the hundreds of employees of the Culture Department, that a new investigation be conducted that "will bring the truth to light!"[1]

In his address to the Knesset, Grabovski declared that this was "one of the severest and most serious issues . . . this is a moral issue for the State of Israel." He concurred in the demand made by religious circles that the report be distributed among the Knesset members, claiming that he had only seen parts of it (he evidently read other sections in the press, primarily that of the religious parties). Grabovski warned that, "Tomorrow the conclusions will be sent to all parts of the world—[and] all of us will be blamed for these acts, as a result of carelessly formulated conclusions."

He stated that the highest authority lay with the government and the Knesset rather than with the commission, which was no more than a commission of inquiry, emphasizing that, "The commission cannot issue a final judgment, because such a final judgment may only be reached by the Government of Israel or the Knesset."[2] Unlike Ilanit, Grabovski did not call for the appointment a new commission of inquiry but reiterated that implementation of the report depended first and foremost upon the government. It would appear that Mapai had decided at the time not to wage an all-out campaign against the report, thinking that the easiest and wisest strategy was simply to bypass it or sweep it under the carpet.

That, indeed, was the tenor of Prime Minister David Ben-Gurion's reply to the members who tabled the motions. He declared: "This was only a commission of inquiry that obligates no one. It merely clarifies matters and presents conclusions." He made clear the government's (in practice, his own) attitude to the report:

> The government did not endorse the report of the commission, due to differences of opinion regarding this matter. It did, however, accept the commission's conclusions "in general." That is, it did not approve each and every detail, because there were certain conclusions that were not at all within the mandate of the commission. The government is not committed to every detail of the conclusions, but only endorsed them in general.

It is not clear from his remarks exactly which details were endorsed by the government and precisely what it intended to change as a result of the report's conclusions. Moreover, Ben-Gurion informed the Knesset that, based upon his independent investigation of affairs in the immigrant camps, executed by "reliable and upright" army officers, he had reached the conclusion that "a sacred task . . . particularly among the children of the immigrants" was being carried out in the camps.[3]

During that initial Knesset debate on the Frumkin Commission's conclusions, one of the Commission's members, MK Elmaleh, asked for the floor, complaining that members of the Commission had been called "perverters of justice," and that he wished to "defend the honor of my colleagues who for three months investigated and labored." The Speaker refused to give him the floor. At the end of that brief debate, MK Pinkas' proposal to not vote on the report until the members of the Knesset received and read it was passed. The Knesset debate on the report was thus put off through the joint initiative of Mapai and the Religious Front—and it never took place. This technical postponement was convenient for Mapai, since the party had not adopted a coherent stand vis-à-vis the report.[4] The postponement also was convenient for the Religious Front because, from its point of view, the crisis had ended when the agreement had been reached on 15 March. A mere three months after the last crisis, the religious parties were not yet ready for a new one. The Knesset would only deal with the report again in the course of other discussions, in October 1950 and February 1951, during a new government crisis that erupted between the Religious Front and Mapai.

Ben-Gurion nevertheless did not entirely let up on the Frumkin Report, continuing to campaign against its conclusions in other ways. In a personal letter to attorney Ya'akov Shimshon Shapira, written on 7 July 1950, he expressed his opinion regarding the Commission's conclusions and the process of legal investigation that led up to them. Among other things, he wrote:

> A reading of the report by itself arouses much astonishment. One finds therein hearsay testimony, prejudice towards witnesses of a certain type, the opposite attitude towards witnesses of another type, as well as a great gap between the report and the conclusions. For this reason the government refused to endorse the report, but only its conclusions; and even these, only in general terms, because the commission went beyond its mandate.

Ben-Gurion asked Shapira to conduct "an analysis of the report in light of all the evidence" and to help him refute the report from a legal standpoint.[5]

Shapira responded with a long and detailed opinion, which he ended with the observation that, given the shortcomings of the report enumerated throughout his considered opinion, "these . . . are sufficient, in my opinion, to disqualify the report and its conclusions. I believe that any legal forum which you might petition . . . would rule that they ought to be rejected and put aside."[6] Ben-Gurion conveyed Shapira's opinion to Attorney-General Haim Cohn. In his reply to Ben-Gurion, dated 19 February 1951, Cohn advised against disseminating Shapira's legal opinion. In view of the government's statement that it accepted the Commission's conclusions in general, which in practice approved the dismissal of Levin and two of his staff, nothing more could be done. The attorney-general wrote: "Although the government did not explicitly declare that it accepted the validity of everything stated in the report by the commission of inquiry, it acted on the basis of this report in practice, and acceptance by deed and action is treated even more strictly than verbal [acceptance]."[7]

Ben-Gurion did not argue with Cohn but continued with his own tactic of ignoring the report. He deliberately hid behind the vague formula of accepting the conclusions of the report "in general" as justification for not giving specific instructions to the teachers and instructors in the immigrant camps to change their pattern of behavior. In practice, apart from the firing of three people, nothing had changed.

Even though the Frumkin Report confirmed the claims of the Religious Front, the latter's political leadership displayed great weakness. For pragmatic reasons, and fearing that "stretching the rope" too tightly might harm their cause, a moderate reaction was presented to the public. These leaders made do with the written report of the Frumkin Commission and never discussed the demand raised by MK Pinkas in an internal discussion to "force the government to come to conclusions."[8] In late July they had in effect accepted the opinion of MK Eliahu Mazor, who said: "We have the conclusions of the commission of inquiry. It is best . . . that there be no discussion of them, but the matter should be raised again after two months."[9] They decided to simultaneously continue to follow up what was being done in the camps and to finance the Hever Hape'ilim (lit., "a group of activists"), the group of people from the *yeshivot* that was active in bringing religious study and observance to the immigrant camps and *ma'abarot*.[10]

THE "INCIDENT" AT NES-TZIONA

Early in July 1950 *Hatzofe* published the text of a formal letter of the Workers Council of Nes-Tziona, signed by its secretary, that read as follows:

> Dear comrade,
> It has come to our attention that you have registered your child in a school belonging to the Agudat Israel (Hamizrachi) Stream. We assume that this was done in error. You are therefore asked to immediately ask the registration officer in the local council to transfer your child to the Workers Stream. If you do not do so immediately, we shall consider your membership in the Histadrut as subject to question.[11]

The contents of this letter, typed on official Histadrut stationery and signed by one of its functionaries, were most serious. The letter contained an implied threat of being expelled from Kuppat Holim (the mutual health benefit fund), denial of the right to buy in the Histadrut marketing network, and so on, should parents not send their children to the Workers Stream school. This time the threats were delivered in writing and aimed at both new immigrants and veteran settlers in the country. The religious groups protested vehemently, and the Central Committee of the Histadrut was forced to discuss this case.[12]

The meeting was opened by Histadrut Secretary Pinhas Lubianiker, who attempted to play down the letter's significance: "As a rule we adhere to this policy [of noncoercion in religious matters], but there is no rule without an exception, and among the hundreds of workers who are engaged in this activity there is occasionally a foolish zealot, one who thinks that if he wins over a few more children for the Workers Stream this will save the Histadrut." To Lubianiker, then, this case was exceptional, and he claimed that parents were not being pressured to register their children in the Histadrut educational system. P. Bendori, representing Mapam, continued along the same line, arguing: "Any pressure regarding choice of [educational] stream is unethical. . . . I regret, however, that in certain spots and areas . . . there is a kind of 'conspiracy of innuendos.'" Exceptionally firm opposition to the stance of his colleagues from Mapai and Mapam was expressed by Yohanan Cohen, the representative of Haoved Hatzioni (affiliated with the Progressive Party):

> The real situation is much more severe than in the Nes-Tziona episode. . . . There are dozens of facts indicating coercion of conscience and economic pressure being applied on Histadrut members in relation to education. . . . I have in my possession no little evidence proving that the secretaries of the workers councils and of the labor exchanges commit acts of coercion of conscience with regard to registration in the Workers Stream. I wish to ask the comrades here, whom I believe to be truly shocked and sincerely interested in preserving the purity of the Histadrut's mode of operation, whether it is enough for them to conduct a trial just for the record, as if to fulfill an obligation, or whether they wish to uproot from the source phenomena of "balkanization" in our public life?

Lubianiker concluded the debate without acceding to Cohen's call for an investigation of coercion in education, only stating in a general manner that every case brought to the attention of the Histadrut's Executive Committee would be turned over to its Committee of Review to investigate and draw conclusions. It is presumed that an investigation was never conducted.

The discussion in the Histadrut's Central Committee, conducted more than a month after the Frumkin Report was made public, indicated that the policy of the Labor parties had not fundamentally changed as a result of its publication. Moreover, since no participant in that meeting mentioned the report, one may assume that until that discussion many of those present had not bothered to familiarize themselves with it. Only the representative of Haoved Hatzioni, whose party opposed the Workers Stream, dared to protest against the legal and ethical injustices committed by representatives of the Histadrut in the field, but his remarks were effectively silenced.

THE GOVERNMENT CRISIS OF OCTOBER 1950

The period of political calm between secular and religious parties was an extremely brief one. A new crisis erupted at the beginning of October 1950 between Mapai and the Religious Front. The pretext this time was economic policy and

Ben-Gurion's intention to carry out personnel changes in certain government offices, in addition to a few matters related to religion.[13] This serious crisis continued for about a month, after which the breach between the two parties was healed once more, and an old-new government was presented to the Knesset. In the midst of this period of crisis, a harsh debate was conducted in the Knesset concerning religious and anti-religious coercion, with each side castigating the other. Representatives of the Religious Front leveled pained accusations. They repeated the assertions made by the Frumkin Commission, claiming that in practice the report had resulted in no improvement of the situation. Zerah Warhaftig spoke of anti-religious coercion that was being constantly repeated: "The crisis continues. We have placed one patch upon another, but we patched over one spot, and a tear appeared elsewhere." He argued that during Shazar's term as minister of education, for about a year and a half, "hundreds and thousands of children were denied the opportunity of receiving a religious education."[14] A. H. Shaag, a member of the Frumkin Commission, argued that the government had not fulfilled its obligation in relation to the Jewish religion, and that the Religious Front had suffered and bitterly continued to bear the burden out of a sense of responsibility. "We kept silent . . . for the sake of the great task which has been placed upon our generation [i.e., the establishment of Israel]." He claimed that the religious parties had never pressed for religious coercion in the private realm; all they ever demanded related to the public realm. Almost apologetically, he cried: "The public realm belongs to all of us. All we ask is: Allow us to breathe the air; we cannot breathe otherwise. Thus we are made!"[15]

Ben-Gurion responded to the accusations of the religious parties. He noted that from his personal observations, the younger generation was becoming increasingly irreligious, because "such is the human spirit. And this is also happening in our land." Throwing off religion is part of a natural process that will inevitably grow. He argued that the Religious Front forced religious law upon individuals: "MK Shaag, whose every appearance in the Knesset elicits only respect, cannot make matters so easy for himself by saying that since he is not allowed to eat non-kosher meat while others may eat kosher, therefore the state must prohibit non-kosher meat by force of a state law." Ben-Gurion warned the leaders of the religious parties: "[You] will cause much harm to religion and incite large sectors of the public against religious persons."[16] His warning was clearly understood. Religious circles sensed a growing public resentment against the extortion they practiced and against what the public considered to be hypocrisy on the part of religious people.[17]

At the same time, to lend strength to their claims, religious circles referred repeatedly to the Frumkin Commission report. Minister of the Interior Moshe Shapira told the Knesset: "There is a report . . . [that] lies here before you. You certainly did not bother to read it." Ben-Gurion immediately responded with the interjection: "This report was not endorsed by the government." Shapira replied:

"That, mister prime minister, is also a very sad episode. Is that how we will educate our public to respect reports commissioned by our government, just because someone is not pleased with them?"[18] Minister of Welfare Y. M. Levin, of Agudat Israel, who also referred to the report, told the Knesset members:

> Following the release of the report . . . I proposed the adoption of far-reaching conclusions so as to avoid the possibility that events would repeat themselves in the future, but nothing was done. The fact that one of the central guilty figures, Mr. Y. A. Aldema, was promoted to a better position, does not exactly demonstrate to the public that coercion in religious matters is forbidden—and such acts are spreading throughout the entire state.[19]

This debate once again reflected attempts by the religious circles to emphasize the importance of the Commission's report and those of Ben-Gurion and his party colleagues to downplay its importance.

The government crisis was exacerbated following the Knesset debate of 17 October, reaching its peak when Ben-Gurion notified President Chaim Weizmann of his resignation, which automatically entailed the dismantling of his government. (In effect, he continued to head an interim government, and a new one was formed before elections were called.) Some participants in an internal Mapai consultation concerning the new governmental crisis called for a decision to hold new elections immediately, while others still believed that a renewed compromise should be sought with the religious parties, and that any such compromise would be more favorable to Mapai than an election campaign or any other possible coalition government. Outstanding among those who repeatedly called for an end to the coalition with the religious parties was Pinhas Lubianiker, who claimed that most of the religious demands ought to be rejected a priori. His presentation of the demands being made by the Religious Front was somewhat exaggerated. According to him these included the appointment of one of their members as director of the Division for Religious Education in the Ministry of Education, a ban on all public transportation on the Sabbath and on the use of tractors and plows in the kibbutzim on the Sabbath, and separate army units for religious recruits. Lubianiker was willing to concede on the specific issue of a religious director for religious education.[20] A leading spokesman of those calling for a compromise with the religious public was Transport Minister David Remez, who immediately upon the conclusion of the government crisis was appointed minister of education and culture.

In internal consultations of the Religious Front leadership during the coalition crisis, MK Pinkas adopted an uncompromising stance against Ben-Gurion and his party.[21] He firmly demanded that they leave the coalition with Mapai and cause new elections to be held. One may assume that his position was influenced by his wish to be appointed minister of trade and industry, which had been frustrated by Mapai. Throughout this fortnight Pinkas and his colleagues in the Hamizrachi faction—with the exception of Rabbi Maimon, the seventy-five-year-old leader of the movement, who was Pinkas' rival—tried to lead the entire Religious Front toward a more extreme and uncompromising policy vis-à-vis Mapai. However, in the final analysis, they accepted the stand that "'In the open the sword shall bereave, and in the chambers shall be terror' [Deut 32:25]—out in the open [i.e., outside the government] is worse!"[22] The "Front" decided to make an effort to preserve its unity and remain in the government.

The crisis came to an end in late October 1950 with a renewed coalition agreement. When both sides announced the old-new government coalition, both religious and secular circles believed that victory was theirs. In an editorial on 31 October, *Ha'aretz* asserted that Ben-Gurion had in effect succeeded in implementing his original program, and that the Religious Front had only gained generally phrased repetitions of old declarations. On that very same day, Agudat Israel's daily, *Hamodi'a*, appeared with a banner headline: "The Agreement to End the Crisis: A Great Achievement for Ultra-Orthodox Jewry." The news item that followed the headline reported that six significant demands of the religious parties had been accepted, including the appointment of a religious person as director of the Division for Religious Education in the Ministry of Education. With hindsight it can be said that there can be no doubt that this last detail, whose significance many in Mapai failed to properly understand at the time, greatly influenced the activity of the Ministry of Education from those days until the present.

On one point there is no debate: the crisis ended with the replacement of Minister of Education Zalman Shazar. The prime minister informed the Knesset that the reason for the change was "a special mission . . . a major assignment involving contemporary Jewry" imposed upon Shazar by the government, the details of which could not yet be made public.[23] There is no doubt that Shazar was forced to pay the price of the disorder that reigned in the educational system throughout the period of his ministry, and that he also paid—albeit much later—the price of the report and conclusions submitted by the Frumkin Commission. Authority for education was transferred to David Remez due to his experience in that field and his organizational skill.

ANOTHER INCIDENT—
EDUCATION OF CHILDREN FROM IRAQ

Among those who abstained during the vote of confidence in the new government at the end of October 1950 was MK Pinkas. He was the most active figure within the Religious Front regarding the issue of anti-religious coercion in the im-

migrant camps, and it was he who exerted the greatest influence for the appointment of the commission of inquiry. As we have already intimated, in October
1950, Pinkas aspired to be appointed a government minister, but his hopes were
dashed; this fact also influenced the way he voted when the Knesset confirmed the
government. In a newspaper article he gave other reasons for his abstention, arguing among other things that the religious public had come to realize that promises
of the government and the Knesset did not ensure that there would in fact be a
real campaign against acts of coercion. He wrote that it was not enough to receive
undertakings from the government and the Knesset without also ensuring the
manner of their implementation, adding that he was not convinced that the government would honor its commitments.[24]

About three weeks after the vote of confidence in the government, Pinkas
brought up a new case in which the rights of religious immigrants had been im-
paired. This time, he told the Knesset, the case involved 1,300 immigrant children
from Iraq, "nearly all of whom were transferred to kibbutzim of Mapam, of
Hashomer Hatzair, with only a small and negligible number—perhaps ten in all—
being placed in religious settlements. This was done without determining the religious practice and milieu which had existed in the homes of these children's
parents prior to their immigration to Israel."[25] Pinkas' motion was struck from the
Knesset's agenda at the suggestion of Mapai, and all other members of the Religious Front passed over the incident in silence. Pinkas' timing made no sense from
the political point of view, as the breach between Mapai and the Religious Front
had been healed only a few days earlier.[26]

This case of a Knesset member who raised the episode of the children from
Iraq and the fact that it was so quickly removed from the public agenda—even by
his religious colleagues—indicate that acts of anti-religious coercion toward new
immigrants were also considered political ammunition. The truth is that this
episode dropped out of public attention in the blink of an eye, leaving barely any
traces. In retrospect, it is clear that the reason for this state of affairs was that the
Religious Front leadership could not afford to engage in a new, stubborn battle
against secular coercion less than one month after its previous campaign had come
to an end.

COMPLAINTS OF ANTI-RELIGIOUS COERCION
BY ARMY OFFICERS AND SOLDIERS

During the unusually harsh and snowy winter of 1950–1951, the armed forces
were mobilized to help the immigrants in the settlements and the *ma'abarot*. They
were primarily involved in transporting goods, laying down access roads, and providing sanitation, cleaning, plumbing, medical help, and so on. However, soldiers

also were sent to institutions for youth and children where they exerted considerable educational influence upon the new immigrants. In this case, too, representatives of the Religious Front protested. The religious press published various news reports and articles claiming that the army's objective was "to win over the *ma'abarot* for the secular camp . . . and to cause Jews to abandon their religion."[27]

Again, it was MK Pinkas of Hamizrachi who was the first to raise the issue in the Knesset. Pinkas told the members of an army commander who preached to adults against having large families and complained that the army was exerting a negative influence over children and youth: "The army, which wants to help, destroys the souls of these children."[28] Pinkas was not alone; other leading members of the Religious Front held similar views. To sum up one of the consultations in the government concerning this issue, it was decided that the minister of welfare, the minister of education, and the IDF chief of staff would conduct a joint visit to those *ma'abarot* in which the IDF was active. After their visit, complaints doubled. Minister Y. M. Levin reported to his colleagues: "The behavior of the male and female soldiers in the *ma'abarot* is reprehensible . . . it exerts a very bad influence on the Yemenites."[29]

Particularly severe complaints were lodged regarding the behavior of the army in the *ma'abara* at Jassir. These were discussed by the government and led to the appointment of Minister of Labor Golda Meir and Minister of Welfare Y. M. Levin as a "commitee to investigate the behavior of the Army in the Jassir *ma'abara.*" The pair conducted an on-site investigation on 20 December 1950. They found that an army physician had given orders to cut off *payot* and beards, that an army commander had spoken against having large families, that Yemenite women had been forcibly stripped of their clothing because the soldiers were conducting a general disinfection, and more.[30] As a result of their investigation, the ministers concluded, in part:

> The Chief of Staff must explain to the soldiers in the camps the nature of the Yemenite Jews and their sensitivity in matters of religion and modesty; to order that they refrain from all conversations regarding matters of religion, must issue an order to refrain from discussing matters of religious belief, and prohibit them from attempting to influence in any way the religious outlook of the residents of the *ma'abarot*, whether adults or children. Concerning disinfection performed on the bodies of the people, an order is to be issued, and scrupulously implemented, that only [female] nurses or soldiers or women civilians be allowed to perform disinfection of women and girls.[31]

Despite this, Minister of Welfare Levin claimed that, "Even after the end of the investigation the soldiers continue to publicly behave offensively in matters of modesty."[32]

Another military matter that aroused opposition in all religious circles—even the more moderate ones—was the activity of the Gadna (*Gedudei Noar*, Youth Corps), particularly the program that brought hundreds of youths from the *ma'abarot* to special educational camps. They repeatedly demanded the establishment of separate religious units within the Gadna, or at least that those youths coming to the Gadna from religious families would receive religious training by religious commanders.[33]

Even the outcry about anti-religious coercion conducted by the army did not lead to a government crisis. Ben-Gurion took pains to investigate a few cases, appointed investigating officers, and he succeeded in convincing the Religious Front that there was not adequate cause for breaking up the government coalition. Orders issued by the IDF command and applied to all of the IDF, which required commanders and soldiers to adhere strictly to the laws of *kashrut*, Sabbath observance, and so on, solved the problem in the Gadna. Ben-Gurion firmly opposed the division of the Gadna into secular and religious corps.

EDUCATING CHILDREN IN THE *MA'ABAROT*— ANOTHER INCIDENT

The problematic relations between secular and religious Jews and their mutual distrust emerged anew from time to time. At the end of 1950, another controversy erupted between Mapai and the Religious Front, once again over the education of immigrant children. This time, it would seem that Mapai's leaders took into account that the controversy could lead to the breakup of the government coalition and to early elections, so they were not inclined to compromise. The subject of this controversy was seemingly a formal one: Mapai refused to apply to children in the *ma'abarot* the arrangements that had been agreed upon with the religious parties in March 1950 regarding children in the immigrant camps. Formally, Mapai was in the right, since the agreement had specifically mentioned only immigrant camps. However, it should be noted that in those days the term *ma'abarot* was not yet in use; in practice, it was only about two months after the agreement, in May 1950, that some of the immigrant camps began to be called *ma'abarot*.[34] Thus beyond formal legalities, there was an obvious injustice being committed by Mapai and a complete renunciation of its agreement with the Religious Front on what education would be provided to immigrant children.

The first one who foresaw that Mapai would try to renege on the agreement was Dr. Ephraim Elimelekh Urbach, then director of the Section for Education in the Immigrant Camps. In a letter that he had already addressed to Minister of the Interior M. Shapira in the summer of 1950, he warned that the new term *ma'abarot*, and the insistence upon its use, "in effect abrogates all arrangements concerning matters of education in the camps that were decided upon by the Knesset." Dr. Urbach asked the ministerial committee appointed to review education in the camps to seriously tackle this issue.[35] When he realized that the ministerial committee also was biding its time in resolving the controversy, he submitted his resignation to Dr. Ben-Yehuda, director of the Education Division of the Ministry of Education. Part of his letter of resignation read: "So long as it has not been decided that the arrangements made by the Knesset with regard to the camps are to be applied in every settlement of new immigrants, no matter what form it may take, I consider this to be a Sisyphean task, and my participation in it a transgression."[36] The religious members of the government tried to induce Mapai to change its stance and simultaneously pressured Urbach to not leave his post. About two months later, Mapai seemingly agreed to concede, but Dr. Urbach no longer placed any trust in these concessions, and he resigned from his position.

The following are the main points of the new agreement between Mapai and the religious parties adopted in mid-September 1950:

1. In all camps whose inhabitants have not left, even if they have become permanent or transitional camps, the same educational arrangements shall continue during the 1950/51 school year as were in effect during the 1949/50 school year.

2. In all *ma'abarot* whose inhabitants are exclusively Yemenites, a joint religious school shall be opened in the 1950/51 school year, to be placed under the supervision of the committee of four religious supervisors.

3. In every other *ma'abara* three schools may be established: a joint religious school of Hamizrachi and Agudat Israel, a school of the General Stream, and one of the Workers Stream. Any child who was registered in one of the camps in a religious school during 1949/50 will not be required to register again. All others will be required to register anew, and to declare which stream they prefer.[37]

In practice, both sides wished to preserve their coalition—and so once again made concessions to each other. First, Mapai agreed to apply most of the arrangements of the March 1950 agreement for another year. Second, Mapai reiterated its agreement that all Yemenite immigrant children would receive a religious education and that a "joint religious school" would be established in the Yemenite *ma'abarot* (under four supervisors—one from each educational stream—all religious persons). The religious parties, for their part, were once again forced to agree to a formal arrangement that recognized the validity of all streams of religious education—including the Religious Workers Stream—in all *ma'abarot*, except those inhabited by Yemenites alone.

Urbach's suspicions, that Mapai would continue to not respect the right to religious education of children in the immigrant camps, proved to be justified. During the implementation of the new agreement, from mid-September 1950 on, there were again numerous disagreements over definitions: What is meant by a *ma'abara* whose residents were exclusively Yemenites? And what is "every other *ma'abara*"? Along with the disagreements, it was obvious that, in the field, the secular officials and politicians in various locales refused to compromise with the religious residents. More and more accomplished facts were created in the various settlements by local functionaries, and more and more schools of the Workers Stream were opened.[38] On 6 December 1950, Etzion and Deutsch, who were responsible, respectively, for the educational streams of Hamizrachi and Agudat Israel in the Ministry of Education, claimed in a letter to the minister of education that the agreement concerning education in the *ma'abarot* was "completely lacking in content," and that not a single school had been opened in accordance with its stipulations.[39]

On 11 December Dr. Yosef Burg addressed the Knesset on this issue on behalf of the Religious Front:

> The Jews in the *ma'abarot* [after having moved there from the immigrant camps] remain the same Jews! And if about 70 percent-80 percent of the Jews in the camps have declared that they want religious education for their children, what has changed in these Jews, who are loyal to tradition and who also today follow tradition and observe the commandments—has something changed in them after they left the camps? Why can we not provide them, in another place, with the same religious education for their children which they requested earlier in the camps?[40]

A week later the same argument was repeated by another representative of the Religious Front in the Knesset, MK E. Mazor: "It is no secret that the coercive regime of the camps has been transferred to the *ma'abarot*."[41] At that time, the claims were presented in relatively minor tones, and one may assume that there were still many within the religious parties who were reluctant to strain relations with Mapai too much.

This is the point at which we should return to Ben-Gurion's stand. Following a consultation in Mapai concerning education in the *ma'abarot*, he noted in his diary: "There is lack of understanding among us as to the true meaning of freedom—for freedom only exists where the government assures freedom to its opponents and not only to itself, and there is inadequate understanding of the problem of religion and of religious Jews."[42] It seems that once again the approach of the party's leader differed from the majority of its members: he did not seek the frontal confrontations toward which his colleagues were pushing, either regarding religious issues in general or those relating to religious education for children of the *ma'abarot* in particular.

The person who decided that he could no longer remain silent on the subject of religious education in the *ma'abarot* was the elderly leader of Hamizrachi, Rabbi Yehuda L. Fishman (Maimon), a close friend of Ben-Gurion. Early in January 1951, he suddenly announced his resignation from the government, the reason given, as formulated by Ben-Gurion in his diary, "once more religious education and coercion."[43] Ben-Gurion recorded there what he had heard from his assistant, Ya'akov Herzog: Rabbi Maimon had told him that "he is afraid that when he appears in the next world, he will be asked why he didn't prevent the apostasy of Yemenite children."[44]

On 6 January 1951, in a lengthy letter to Z. Aharonowitz, then secretary of Mapai, Ben-Gurion referred to the new aliya and the subject of religion, again arguing that, "The party has failed by adopting its stubborn approach to the problem of education. . . . We are likely to fail, if we have not already done so, because of our rigid approach to the issue of religion and religious people in the State of Israel."[45]

Ben-Gurion tried to convince Rabbi Maimon not to resign from the government. On 7 January he paid him a visit in his home, promising that "the *ma'abarot* will be treated like the immigrant camps."[46] However, upon returning to the meeting of the Mapai Knesset faction, Ben-Gurion found his colleagues unwilling to agree to what he had promised Rabbi Maimon. He once again realized that the members of his party were opposed to a policy of compromise with the religious parties, and he continued to grasp at a technical argument—that the agreement with the religious bloc pertained only to the "immigrant camps."

Why did Mapai refuse to come to an arrangement in the *ma'abarot* similar to that which they had contracted in relation to the immigrant camps? What was the difference between the camps and the *ma'abarot* from the viewpoint of Mapai's members? Why were they prepared to go all the way, even to the point of breaking up the coalition, precisely on this issue? It would seem that there were a number of reasons:

1. In a survey conducted in the immigrant camps, most of the immigrants requested that their children be educated within a religious framework. There were those in Mapai who feared that in the transfer to the *ma'abarot* they would lose control of most of the children.[47]

2. The camps were run by Jewish Agency personnel. While Mapai did have a considerable degree of influence in the camps, it was not as absolute as that in the *ma'abarot*. There were many staff members in the camps who also were party members, but the framework there as a whole was not exclusively par-

tisan. Control of the *ma'abarot*, in contrast, was divided according to a key of allocation among the various parties. Most were under the aegis of the Labor parties, who tended to the needs of their inhabitants in all areas: employment, medical services, distribution of foodstuffs and other supplies, and cultural and educational services. It was only natural that there were those in Mapai who were convinced that there should be an absolute majority of parents in "their" *ma'abarot* who would "choose" the Workers Stream.

3. The repeated pressure applied by the Religious Front, which each time cropped up in a different place, elicited much criticism among the Mapai leaders, many of whom felt that they were facing constant extortion. Moreover, many Mapai members had the feeling—which increased with time— that pressure by religious elements also was the outcome of sharp rivalries among the different parties in the Religious Front and competition for public attention from various personalities within that shaky "Front." In other words, many in Mapai were convinced that the religious pressures were not exclusively motivated by a sincere and pure faith, and for that reason alone.

4. Throughout this period, left-wing Mapam was breathing down Mapai's neck. Mapai was accused of being "pragmatist" and "reformist," of constantly yielding to the religious parties, thereby contributing to the establishment of a "clericalist state." We have already noted that there were many in Mapai who were close in outlook to their rivals in Mapam regarding issues of religion and state. Many of the younger members, particularly those from settlement movements and intellectual circles, wanted the party to adopt a more strongly secularist position with less consideration shown in matters of religion or toward the religious public in general. A willingness to compromise, a tendency that was much easier for Ben-Gurion and his colleagues immediately after the establishment of Israel, became ever more difficult as Mapai's public standing weakened and as it was presented to the public as a party that did not adhere to pioneering principles and ideologies.

5. The religious parties did not enjoy the same domestic and foreign public support regarding the issue of education in the *ma'abarot* as they had during the struggle over the nature of education in the immigrant camps. At that time it was Mapai that sought to make the camps "extra-territorial," demanding that the educational system in the camps be different from that prevailing throughout the rest of the country. This stance—difficult to explain to anyone holding democratic principles—was then subject to severe criticism. Mapai's position this time was the very opposite: it demanded that the *ma'abarot* be treated just like everywhere else in the country. In the controversy over education in the *ma'abarot*, it was specifically the religious parties

that demanded that different educational rules be applied in the *ma'abarot*—and this time it was they who found it difficult to justify their stance to the advocates of equality and democracy.

6. The major point contested by Mapai and the religious parties was no longer whether to provide the new immigrants with a religious education or a uniform secular education. The issue, rather, was whether all religious education needed to be subject to the monopoly of Hamizrachi and Agudat Israel. Members of Mapai—including those among them who were positively inclined toward Jewish tradition—argued that the demand of the religious bloc for religious party-controlled education was no more than a camouflage for their real objective—to win the immigrants over to their own parties. It was primarily regarding this last point of controversy—the right of the Labor movement to provide religious education that combined religious and pioneering values—that they were no longer willing to compromise. On this point Mapai and Mapam were of one mind, and this also was the stand adopted by Ben-Gurion. They were willing to face a coalition crisis over the right of the Religious Workers Stream to exist. From the viewpoint of Ben-Gurion, if Mapai and the Histadrut were to be prevented from providing religious education, that would be tantamount to saying that they were not universal organizations open to all, for then the religious public would be unable to become part of them. Ben-Gurion and his colleagues were unwilling to concede this principle.

THE GOVERNMENT CRISIS OF FEBRUARY 1951

At the beginning of 1951, Ben-Gurion began to tire of the continuously shaky relations with the Religious Front. He hoped that new elections would provide him with a sufficient majority that would enable him and Mapai to be less dependent upon other parties and necessitate fewer struggles with them. At that time economic conditions in Israel also began to improve somewhat. The first grant-in-aid funds began to arrive from the United States Administration, and greater sums started flowing in from American Jewry.[48] In mid-January Ben-Gurion deliberately exacerbated relations with the religious parties, firmly opposing their demand to monopolize the absorption of religious new immigrants.

On 15 January 1951, following a meeting of the ministerial committee on education, Ben-Gurion wrote in his diary: "The cat is out of the bag. The debate is not over religious education for religious children, but as to whether Hamizrachi and the Aguda [Agudat Israel] are the exclusive guardians of religion or whether other religious Jews can also be entrusted with religion and religious education."[49] In other words, Ben-Gurion joined in full combat against the Religious Front parties over the right of the Histadrut to provide religious education—that is, he was prepared to fight for the recognition and existence of the Religious Workers Stream. The next day, in a conversation with Rabbi Y. M. Levin, Ben-Gurion told him that he was unwilling to continue "in a condition of internal grumbling and accusations" with the religious parties, whose members made a habit of "profiteering in religion."[50] On 17 January, at a meeting of Mapai's Political Committee, Ben-Gurion stated that, "One must conform not only with the law but also to integrity. Integrity requires that we provide the Yemenite immigrants [including those who left the immigrant camps for the *ma'abarot* and the *moshavim*] with a religious education." True to his own stand, he continued: "It is clear that religious education is not necessarily that of Hamizrachi or the Aguda."[51] On 28 January he wrote in his diary: "The state is obligated towards the Yemenites—to give their children a religious education. We do not have any obligation towards Hamizrachi or the Aguda to give them guardianship over the Yemenites. It may be that the coalition will break up because of this."[52]

On 6 February Ben-Gurion assembled the coalition party factions in the Knesset to inform them that the decisions of the government concerning education were final, and that there would be no change in them during the term of the present government. He added: "I am not enthusiastic about elections . . . but if the choice is between elections and constant contemptuous treatment of the government and undermining its direct mission . . . I prefer elections."[53]

On 7 February, Ben-Gurion's confidant, Ya'akov Herzog, suggested a novel solution to the crisis: Mapai would agree that responsibility for education of religious children of the new aliya would be assigned exclusively to the religious Labor parties, namely, Hapoel Hamizrachi and Poalei Agudat Israel. He considered this proposal another way of combining religious and labor values. Ben-Gurion also strongly opposed this proposal: "The fair demand is that of religious education for religious Jews . . . there is no need for the guardianship by parties. . . . I agree to the growth of Hapoel Hamizrachi and Poalei Agudat Israel, but the immigrants are not sheep to be divided up among the parties."[54]

On 12 February the matter was raised in the Knesset. Following three lengthy days of debate, the government fell in a Knesset vote on the issue of education, leading to elections that were ultimately held on 30 July 1951. The first speaker in the Knesset debate was a Mapai member representing Tnu'at Hamoshavim, MK Ami Assaf. By no coincidence, he once more brought up the Frumkin Report, which had been released some eight months earlier, attacking it vehemently. He claimed that the Commission had been one-sided:

> The report . . . did an injustice to people. . . . People were accused and found guilty without cause. . . . This commission of inquiry gave different weight, from the outset, to different testimonies, depending

upon who was testifying. . . . The commission, which was chaired by a
man who had been a supreme court justice in this country and should
have been acquainted with proper investigative procedures, used a very
peculiar method of investigation: it published the testimony of people
who testified, not as [firsthand] witnesses who saw and heard, but in
the name of some other person. . . . An injustice has been done to persons who worked to the best of their ability. There is no doubt that
there were also errors committed in their work, but the commission has
failed severely.[55]

MK Beba Idelson, also of Mapai, similarly criticized the Frumkin Report: "With
all my admiration for the people who served on the commission, and despite my
conviction that they acted to the best of their ability and their will—I cannot accept their conclusions."[56] Another Mapai participant in the same debate, former
Minister of Education and Culture Zalman Shazar, expressed views, which we
have already encountered as being his and Ben-Gurion's, and attacked "a certain
person" who had appropriated to himself the authority to declare: "This is religious [education] and this is non-religious [education] and all the rest are unfit."
Shazar stated that the great growth in the Religious Workers Stream came about
because labor and Jewish tradition constituted the two pillars of the new aliya.
He added: "This aliya seeks its way . . . this silent flock that is groping and seeking knows what it needs: it needs partnership with the labor movement in the
country, and it needs religious education."[57] A fourth Mapai speaker, Professor
Ben-Zion Dinaburg (Dinur), who in October 1951 would be appointed minister of education and culture, told his religious listeners that "every migration from
one country to another involves the destruction of a part of the tradition." He
added that there is a certain influence of the "climate of freedom" in Israel, and
that "life [he was evidently referring to modernity] also has its influence in the
area of religion." According to Dinaburg, "The very assumption that religious
education cannot be provided except by Hamizrachi or Agudat Israel is of itself
religious coercion."[58]

Needless to say, Mapam representatives in the Knesset also attacked the
Frumkin Commission Report. Aharon Zisling called it a miscarriage of justice,
demanding that it be referred back to the government and that a parliamentary
commission be appointed to investigate its accuracy.[59] Feige Ilanit asserted that
"the injustice [done] to the culture workers in the camps [is none other than] . . .
coalition bribery."[60]

The representatives of the Religious Front mounted a counterattack against
the left-wing parties, although they still hoped—even at the last moment—to
avoid an absolute crisis.[61] Minister M. Shapira saw in the educational crisis "a
symptom of a disease in the body of the state" and complained of those mem-

bers of the Knesset who, rather than hoping (to quote the Psalms) that "may evildoers disappear from the land," prayed "may members of the commission disappear from the land." As for the matter at hand, education in the camps or in the *ma'abarot*, he told the Mapai members that they were grasping at a technicality in order to transfer religious children to nonreligious education. He called Haoved Hadati "merely a camouflage."[62] Minister Y. M. Levin claimed that in practice nothing had changed fundamentally following the Frumkin Report. "Even in those places where the commission of inquiry has denounced the acts of coercion that were committed there, education continues as it was before the investigation, and nothing has been corrected." Moreover, "a number of those persons who are primarily responsible and should have been put on trial were promoted."[63]

MK Pinkas dropped a "bomb," whose implications were only understood several months later (except by MK Ben-Zvi, who made the same proposal on that very same day). He suggested, as a sort of compromise and as a means of putting an end to controversies over education, that the Knesset discuss a proposal for "state education with two frameworks enjoying equal privileges and equal status, the one—religious, the second—different."[64] This represented a substantial change in the position of the religious political leadership, most of whom had until then argued that from their viewpoint there was no alternative to the educational streams. The first religious leader to call, in internal consultations, for the abolition of the streams in education and the institution of a system of state education was MK Moshe Unna.[65] Pinkas' proposal was a follow-up to Unna's article, but before this position had formally been approved by the Religious Front.

Representatives of the right-wing parties attacked both the Left and the Religious Front. MK Shoshana Persitz of the General Zionists argued that Mapai was turning contol over the immigrants to the parties and the Histadrut, and that there was in this "something frightening and horrifying, something that smells of the Middle Ages." On the other hand, she stated that the Religious Front would in the future be accountable for demanding partisan religious education and opposing separate state religious education.[66] MK Shmuel Katz of Herut likewise stated that, "The introduction of politics into education, the introduction of politics into religion . . . is a two-edged sword. . . . There is one and only one way . . . uniform state education, in which religious education will find its appropriate and suitable place."[67]

The debate was summed up by Minister of Education and Culture David Remez and Prime Minister David Ben-Gurion. Remez reiterated party policy, that "it was not for the sake of conflict with the Religious Front that this stream [i.e, the Religious Workers Stream] came into being . . . but because we seek a true path for the ingathering of the exiles."[68] Ben-Gurion spoke at length, combining principled positions with pragmatic ones. His response to the Knesset debate on the Frumkin Commission was evasive:

> The government has not charged me with the task of explaining why we did not accept the report. I will only say that we did not accept the report and that we, of course, had good reasons for not doing so. We only accepted its conclusions, and even those only in a general form. ... Even a commission of inquiry may be criticized, and one may not exempt the commission from criticism by arguing that it is a governmental commission. Even the government itself may be criticized.

As for the essential disagreement with the religious parties, Ben-Gurion stated: "Religious parties do not represent Judaism. We do not acknowledge their right to represent authentic Judaism ... any more than we do." He quoted some of his favorite verses from the Psalms: "Who shall ascend the hill of the Lord, and who shall stand in His holy place? He that has clean hands and a pure heart, that has not lifted up his soul to vanity nor sworn deceitfully" [Ps. 24:3–4]. These verses, he added, contained one of the definitions of Judaism—that the distinction between those with clean hands and a pure heart and those of the opposite qualities indicates who is closer to God and who deserves to ascend to His holy place. At this point he remarked cynically to the leaders of the religious parties: "I know some people in the Religious Front who fit this definition from the Psalms, but I'm not sure they would swear that all the members of the Front are deserving of that definition." As for Mapai's principal demand—recognition of the Religious Workers Stream—Ben-Gurion firmly reiterated his views: "None of us needs the confirmation of his neighbor that he is a Jew. We are Jews like you. We are no worse than you. We are no less involved than you in the Jewish past and in Jewish roots, but we are different from many of you." In concluding the debate, he declared:

> The decisions of the government regarding the subject of education in the *ma'abarot* and in the immigrant settlements are final with respect to this government. The government has reached a final decision in this matter. It is not prepared, and will not allow itself, to continue the discussion of this issue indefinitely.

He added that he would see the voting on the education issue as a vote of confidence or no confidence in his government.

The government fell, with forty-nine votes opposing it: those of Mapam and the majority of the members of the right-wing and religious parties. Only forty-two Knesset members supported the government. Mapam, in effect, by its overall criticism of Mapai and its voting, which led to the fall of the government, also sealed the fate of the Religious Workers Stream, which its members supported in principle.

The day after the vote in the Knesset *Ma'ariv* appeared with a report under the headline: "Desire for Domination Caused the Crisis—but Opinions Are Divided as to the Question: Whose Desire?"[69] The religious parties and Mapai leveled the very same accusations at each other. Both sides would appear to have been right, that the leaders of both parties primarily thought in terms of increasing their own electoral power.

It is interesting to note that four days after the fall of the government—for which the reason given in public was the struggle for the Religious Workers Stream's right to exist—Ben-Gurion summoned Dr. Moshe Etz-Hayyim, the supervisor responsible for schools of that stream, and asked him to explain precisely what was being taught in its schools, how many pupils it encompassed, and the extent to which members of the Histadrut and the settlement movements assisted or interfered with its activities.[70] The significance of this fact is that Ben-Gurion's adoption of a stand in principle preceded his acquaintance with the actual situation in the field: he learned the details of the Religious Workers Stream only after he had already decided in principle that his movement should struggle to support its existence.

On 20 February, less than a week after the vote of no confidence, Ben-Gurion had already written a lengthy letter, marked "Confidential," to the Mapai Central Committee, with practical suggestions about how to prepare for elections. In this letter he noted:

> Even though the Religious Front was the immediate cause of the crisis, I do not assume that the dispute with members of the Front will occupy a central or important place in the political polemic. We need to present the people with the choice as we see it: rule by the Right (Bernstein—Begin—Pinkas) or a pioneering government. The enemy is the Right—not religion. We need to denounce the Right, which utilizes religion as a camouflage for its rightist, reactionary plans. But there is no need to become either opposers of religion or defenders of religion.[71]

This letter indicates that, notwithstanding Ben-Gurion's principled position— that he and his colleagues were no less "religious" than the leaders of the Religious Front and were therefore entitled to operate a workers' religious system of education and participate in efforts to absorb religious new immigrants—he did not wish religion to become a central issue in the forthcoming election campaign. As we have seen, Ben-Gurion hoped that the positions he adopted would gradually filter down and influence the public.

During the spring of 1951 Mapai prepared its party platform for the elections to the Second Knesset. In view of the report of the Frumkin Commission and the "soul snatching" that it uncovered, as well as, of course, the ideological disputes between Mapai and Mapam, which had become much sharper, and increased partisanship within the Workers Stream, it is not surprising that this time the party platform called for the abolition of partisan streams of education. Clause 16 states:

> Mapai sees a need for *state education* for all children in Israel, to be based upon the following principles:
>
> A. Party domination of education will be totally abolished. Schools will be subject exclusively to the authority of the state Ministry of Education.
>
> B. There will be a fixed minimum of obligatory studies incumbent upon all elementary schools.
>
> C. A fundamental aspect of all elementary schools will be education for labor and a pioneering life.
>
> D. Every group of parents which wishes to do so will have the right of defining by itself the character of education, providing that it does not detract from the minimum obligatory studies determined by the state.
>
> E. Children of religious parents will be assured [that they may practice] a religious way of life in the schools.[72] (emphasis in original)

The person responsible for implementing the party platform in respect to education was the new minister of education and culture, Prof. Ben-Zion Dinaburg (Dinur), who assumed office on 7 October 1951, following the elections. In August 1953, after the General Zionists had already joined the government, the State Education Law was introduced in the Knesset. As is well known, this law only abolished the secular streams in education (and in practice only the Workers Stream). Mapai's decision to not abolish the streams affiliated with the religious parties may have been indirectly connected to the report of the Frumkin Commission and the continuous tension over education with those parties. In any event, it is clear that following publication of the Commission's findings, it was more difficult for Mapai to interfere with or exert influence on religious matters in general and issues related to the religious parties and religious education in particular.

CHAPTER 11

COMMENTS ON THE PROCEDURES
AND CONCLUSIONS OF
THE FRUMKIN COMMISSION

The Frumkin Commission was one of the first governmental commissions of inquiry appointed in the State of Israel. At that time, the principles that today govern the conduct of such commissions had not yet been formulated. Even the members of the government who were party to the decision to appoint the Commission seem not to have been fully aware of the extent to which it was to be a judicial investigating committee or a public, political commission. Its composition reflected this ambiguity: there were four representatives from political parties, but the Commission was chaired by a nonpartisan former Supreme Court justice.

It is believed that the composition of the Commission was reasonably balanced, notwithstanding the severe criticism to which it was subjected at the time, and the outcome of its inquiry could not have been predicted strictly on the basis of its composition. It is nevertheless true that all members of the Commission shared a common aspiration to bring secularist and religious Jews closer together. It was established precisely to uncover certain acts and facts that undermined relations between these two publics, to attempt to deal with these facts, and to try to strengthen relations between the two groups.

The first meeting of the Frumkin Commission convened on 25 January 1950, and its conclusions were presented to the government on the 9th of May. In the course of its work, it conducted thirty-three sessions and heard 101 witnesses

(some of them testifying for several sessions).[1] Several of its sessions were devoted to visits to immigrant camps at Ein-Shemer, Beit Lid, Rosh Ha'ayin, and
Beer Ya'akov.

INVESTIGATION PROCEDURES OF
THE FRUMKIN COMMISSION

The procedures of investigation adopted by the Commission were not the objective methods customarily applied in judicial investigation. The Commission did
not attempt to corroborate subjective testimonies by other sources, nor did it
cross-examine witnesses, whose testimony was—generally speaking—accepted at
face value, even when accusations against specific individuals were involved. It did
not examine each accusation in detail, nor did it allow the accused the elementary
right of defending themselves against such accusations. Given this, it is believed
that criticism of the investigation procedures of the Frumkin Commission—
raised by Ben-Gurion and his colleagues in Mapai, by Nahum Levin and his staff,
and by Mapam, as well as by persons from center and the right-wing parties—was
justified. One may assume that there were several reasons that led the commission
to act as it did:

1. Since this was, as noted, one of the first commissions of inquiry appointed
in the State of Israel, there was not yet sufficient experience with commissions that meticulously adhered to legal procedures of examination and
evidence.

2. The Commission evidently wished to conclude its work rapidly, sensing
that were it to insist upon strict procedures and meticulous proceedings, the
entire situation it was investigating would in the meantime change, and the
immigrant camps would disappear. (Indeed, as of May 1950, the immigrant
camps began to be transformed into *ma'abarot*, more or less at the time the
Commission's report was submitted.)

3. The Commission was primarily interested in questions of principle and
did not presume to relate in excessive detail to specific matters.

Though most of the witnesses were called to testify upon the initiative of the
Commission itself, the religious camp was the more active of the two, and it had
the Commission call upon its people to testify. About two-thirds of the witnesses
were religious people—political and religious leaders, teachers, persons active in
religious public affairs, and new immigrants. The secular community—first and
foremost members of the left-wing parties, Mapai and Mapam—seems to have

taken the Commission less seriously and barely initiated calling witnesses of its own accord. Even those who did testify—such as Minister of Education and Culture Zalman Shazar and Nahum Levin—did not realize how crucial their testimony would be, affecting opinion for many years to come on the manner in which their institutions and movements had operated.

More than it examined specific cases and complaints regarding certain persons, the Commission discussed the principles that should underlie the education of immigrant children. In its conclusions, it condemned the anti-religious coercion practiced in the immigrant camps. Based on archival documentation and all of the testimonies presented to it, we may conclude today that apparently the Commission was correct on this point, and that its general conclusions were well founded.

THE FRUMKIN COMMISSION'S FUNDAMENTAL REJECTION OF THE "MELTING POT" THEORY

"Melting pot" was one of the most widespread slogans in Israel during the period of the Great Aliya. This slogan—adopted by the government as its overriding policy—implied an aspiration to cut the new immigrants off from all elements that were unique to their specific countries of origin and their old traditions, and to create in Israel a new, uniform Hebrew-Israeli culture of a predominantly European character. As we have seen, intensive and painful steps were taken to implement the "melting pot" policy, including uniform education in the immigrant camps. The Frumkin Commission rejected the "melting pot" concept in principle and directed its major criticism against the approach that sought to "adapt" all new immigrants as fast as possible to the "new Israeli milieu." It likewise took exception to the distinction made by the Ministry of Education between the "uniform education" provided to immigrant children and the four different educational streams—from which parents could choose—available to all other children in Israel. The Commission's five members were the first to protest against giving immigrant camps an "extra-territorial status" and strove to help the immigrants preserve their traditions. The Commission also opposed the concept of "adjustment of the [immigrant] children to the Israeli milieu," so widely accepted in broad sectors of Israeli society, stating categorically that there were "serious breaches of religious education in the camps." It further declared that "it was a fatal error to relegate the education of children in the camps in general, and of those from the Oriental countries in particular, especially those from Yemen, Tripolitania, and Morocco,"[2] to the Culture Department.

Israeli sociologist Moshe Lissak wrote: "At the height of the asymmetrical encounter between the veterans and the new immigrants, many mistakes were committed—whether by force of circumstance or as a result of ignorance, cold-heartedness, prejudice, or adherence to petty bureaucratic rules—which more than once undermined the basic norms of traditional communities."[3] The Commission's members—already in 1950—were among the first to recognize these truths. Great courage was required to make such claims at that time, and the Frumkin Commission Report influenced the gradual adaptation of that policy.

The Frumkin Commission, it would seem, formulated its conclusions in an even-handed manner. The campaign of left-wing elements against religion, it declared, was not "a goal in itself" but also criticized the desire of those circles to hasten the "desired process of adjustment." The report rejected the accusations that religious circles had leveled, using terms such as "inquisition" and "genocide," but also criticized those persons in the Labor movement who intended to prepare the immigrants and their children for membership in the Histadrut and left-wing parties.

What the Frumkin Commission Report came out against was primarily the approach adopted by the people working in the immigrant camps toward those who had come from Islamic countries. It declared that it was a basic error to expect these immigrants to measure up to the same standards that the staff members demanded of themselves or expected of immigrants from Europe.[4] The report expressed a considerable degree of empathy toward the Oriental immigrants, empathy that was lacking among many Israeli leaders and those engaged in the absorption of immigrants at that time. I believe that this stand can be attributed in particular to two members of the Commission: Izhak Ben-Zvi and Abraham Elmaleh. The family background of Justice Gad Frumkin also may have led him to be more sympathetic toward the Yemenite immigrants.[5]

Specific Accusations Made by the Frumkin Commission

A distinction should be made between just and correct conclusions and those whose formulations are open to criticism. The conclusions regarding the composition of the teaching staff in the immigrant camps were justified[6]—a listing of the teachers in the immigrant camps and their previous background indicates that this was not a team appropriate for the education of children, and certainly not children from Muslim countries who came from religious homes. Similarly, the Commission was correct in noting that the teachers and instructors were not sufficiently sensitive about observance of the Sabbath, and there were even cases in which they interfered with prayers.[7] Many of the secular instructors themselves in the camps—and these were not necessarily those employed by the Culture Department—did not observe the Sabbath or attend prayer, and thus they did not take care to observe traditional practices in the presence of the immigrants. It should be reiterated that employees of the Culture Department accounted for only a small part of the manpower that was engaged in absorption. Other religion-related problems—such as an insufficient number of synagogues, ritual baths, and Torah scrolls—suggest that it was unjust to put the entire blame for all problems encountered in the process of the spiritual (as opposed to the physical) absorption of the immigrants on the staff of Levin's department.

Notwithstanding the fact that the Commission was correct in noting an over-all anti-religious atmosphere, it seems to have erred in concluding that cutting off *payot* and interfering with religious studies were methodic.[8] This formulation is questionable and would appear, upon examination of the records of the Commission's sessions, to be completely unproven. Whose "method"? All teachers employed by the Culture Department, all camp directors and instructors, or the political leadership of the Labor parties? The Commission's investigation proved, at most, that there were numerous incidents in which there was obstruction of religious studies and dozens of cases in which *payot* were deliberately cut off. The term *methodic* is too unequivocal, suggesting a deliberately organized system of interference with and disturbance of the religious lifestyle, an accusation that remains to be proven, at least insofar as may be determined from the documentation and the Commission's records. As we have seen, many of the secular teachers consciously or unconsciously attempted to draw their students toward their own lifestyle, but one cannot speak of a coercive "method." Many attempted to hastily inculcate the immigrant children with their own "Israeliness," and this was often done in a manner insensitive to the wishes of the immigrants themselves, but there was no deliberate planning and execution of the cutting off of *payot* in all immigrant camps. The records of the Frumkin Commission—which in its report referred primarily to two "*payot*-cutting campaigns," namely, in Ein-Shemer and Beit Lid under the supervision of Yehiel Aharon Aldema and Zippora Zehavi—did not give sufficient consideration to the formulation of this grave accusation against the entire staff of the Culture Department active in the immigrant camps.

What emerges from oral and written testimony is that many Yemenite Jews changed their religious lifestyle of their own initiative when they arrived in Israel, without the help of any "methodical"cutting off of *payot* by the veteran population. Thus, for example, the head of the Department of Yemenite Jews of Hapoel Hamizrachi, Rabbi Y. Meshorer (himself a Yemenite Jew), reported to his party that he had visited a village of Yemenite immigrants—this prior to the activity of Nahum Levin and his staff in the immigrant camps—and was greatly pained to see the spiritual and religious decline among the members of his community. He claimed that the residents of this village, all of whom had been accustomed to praying in Yemen, had stopped attending the synagogue, and that many families had even ceased praying in their homes.[9] This report is dated on the eve of Rosh

Hashana 5708 (i.e, late September 1947), however, I believe that there is no real difference between the behavior of these immigrants in Kfar Yavetz and what happened to immigrants from Yemen a year later. Based on testimony, it would appear that cessation of prayer—which occurred as part of the process of adjustment to life in the State of Israel—was in many cases accompanied by cutting off *payot*. Moreover, many of the Yemenite immigrants who maintained their religious Orthodoxy and their attachment to religious frameworks also cut off their *payot*. We may accept the testimony of H. Zadok, one involved in the absorption of Yemenite immigrants, who stated that even without the influence of instructors and teachers, a considerable number of the "younger immigrants . . . hastened to resemble, at least externally, their brethren and veteran [Israeli] relatives, and began . . . to cut off their *payot*."[10]

Prof. Mordecai Breuer, then editor of *She'arim* and a leader of Poalei Agudat Israel, related in oral testimony[11] that some religious circles made propagandist use of the cutting off of *payot* to evoke connotations from the Holocaust period. According to his account, which also is implied in other studies, while religious circles opposed the entire sysem of anti-religious coercion practiced by Labor movement circles, they did not intend to accuse them specifically of cutting off *payot*. True, there were cases in which *payot* were deliberately cut off, but the generalization that accused educators and instructors coming from the Labor movement of systematically removing the *payot* of Yemenite children was just another anti-Zionist myth deliberately cultivated by ultra-Orthodox anti-Zionist groups. The myth of cutting off *payot* was a convenient one for a public propaganda campaign. It found willing listeners both in Israel and abroad, and it is the myth that to a great extent survives to this day and is nurtured by certain circles.[12] Actually, it was the practice of young Yemenite boys to cut off their *payot* when they studied in the religious frameworks of Hamizrachi, or even Agudat Israel.[13] Even Agudat Israel leader Y. M. Levin and Ashkenazic Chief Rabbi Isser Yehuda Unterman, in their testimony before the Frumkin Commission, stated that, "It is not the *payot* that are important." They repeatedly argued that "one can be a religious Jew without *payot*, and a non-religious Jew with *payot*."[14] Notwithstanding these testimonies, it nevertheless seems that to this very day, certain ultra-Orthodox circles use the myth of cutting off *payot* in their anti-secular propaganda and as a means to attack Zionist circles.

In summation, we can say that the removal of *payot* was part of the process of coming to resemble the absorbing society as a whole—both its secular and religious elements, for even the majority of the latter refrained, as a rule, from growing *payot*. True, there were certain cases of forcible removal of *payot* and of encouraging Yemenite children to cut off their *payot*, but this was not "methodic" and certainly not directed "from above." There were at best local initiatives of various people who came into contact with immigrants, and not specifically—

certainly not solely—by staff members of the Culture Department. Frequently the Yemenite children themselves decided to remove their *payot*. Only rarely were there deliberate "campaigns," and these were related to genuine health problems (lice, ringworm, and so on). The Frumkin Commission noted the statement made by Aldema, from the camp at Ein-Shemer, that Dr. Klein, the medical doctor responsible for the camps, told him that 64 percent of the Yemenite children suffered from ringworm, and that it was necessary to shave their heads.[15] In the report submitted to the 23rd Zionist Congress, the Youth Aliya Department contended that *about half* of the first Yemenite children who were referred to the department suffered from ringworm, and that they were forced to shave their heads and send them for special medical treatment, including X rays.[16] Firsthand evidence of the withholding of food or other forceful coercive measures adopted against children who refused to cut off their *payot* is not available, though such cases may have occurred here and there.

The Commission's Stand Concerning the Controversy between Secularists and the Religious

It is believed that the Commission erred in giving evaluations and "grades" to the various political movements. It was mistaken when it wrote, in its conclusions, that the "passions aroused in religious circles were indeed innocently sincere and only for the sake of Heaven, in order to strengthen religious sentiment among the immigrants."[17] True, a diametrically opposed formulation also is found on that same page: "The wish to strengthen the religious parties and to weaken the influence of other parties upon these immigrants was not lacking,"[18] but it does not negate the earlier statement. Some of the statements of the Frumkin Commission were not phrased with the care and accuracy expected of a governmental commission of inquiry.

In order to point to the lack of innocent sincerity among the religious parties, it is sufficient to quote from statements made in public by Minister Moshe Shapira, leader of Hapoel Hamizrachi, at his party's convention. It is obvious that he himself admitted his movement's desire to grow in strength and Hapoel Hamizrachi's policy of marshaling its membership to win over the immigrants:

> The aliya in the near future . . . this is a great multitude which will change the character of the country . . . I have begun to believe that the day is not far off when religious Jewry will be the majority in the country. . . . We must mobilize ourselves in order to attain our goal, which is the creation of a Jewish religious majority in the country, and this majority shall surely emerge, with God's help, in the not too distant future.[19]

Nor is this testimony unique, for there are many similar ones. Various religious circles hoped to change the demographic ratio between religious and nonreligious Jews and to refashion the principles upon which the state was founded. Leftist groups naturally feared this and struggled to counter such a change.

As noted on several instances, the majority of those engaged in the absorption of the Great Aliya belonged to left-wing parties. In their efforts to absorb the new wave of immigration, they played a role much greater than their relative numbers within the veteran community warranted. Many were salaried employees of the bodies involved in immigrant absorption, while others engaged in this effort as volunteers, with great dedication. There is no doubt that the left-wing parties are today paying the price of their efforts: the collective memory of those absorbed holds them accountable for the the process of absorption. This judgment seems to be based partly upon historical facts, some of which were cited by the Frumkin Commission, but also upon others that were greatly exaggerated by religious and ultra-Orthodox circles and have become fixed in public consciousness. Though the Frumkin Report declared that "it should be noted that a heavy burden was placed upon the workers [of the Culture Department], under quite difficult conditions, and they acted with considerable dedication in their overall objective,"[20] this aspect seems to have been forgotten. The Labor movement, which bore the brunt of the absorption of the Great Aliya, has in the long run paid a high price for its efforts.

On the Personal Responsibility Assigned by the Commission

The first draft of the Frumkin Commission Report, apparently prepared by Gad Frumkin himself, included the following sentence: "The commission was not required to determine the guilty parties, or those responsible for these activities; nevertheless, the commission deemed that it would be remiss in its duties were it not to also cite its conclusions with regard to this important point."[21] Though this sentence was omitted from the final version of the report, the Commission did state quite clearly "who is responsible."[22]

Despite the fact that in dealing with personal accusations the Commission did not follow established legal procdure, in practice it did issue several verdicts against individuals. It imposed "direct responsibility" upon Nahum Levin, and it specificallly condemned the cultural coordinator at the Ein-Shemer camp, Y. A. Aldema, and Z. Zehavi, an instructor in the youth camp at Beit Lid. The specific mention in the report of these three by name led in effect to their dismissal and influenced the future employment of all staff members of the Culture Department.[23] Since the Commission did not give these three—especially the last two—the opportunity to defend themselves against specific accusations, it would seem that this judgment involved a miscarriage of justice. The injustice was even greater, because this was a case of a governmental commission of inquiry whose decisions were not subject to appeal. It should be noted, however, that Mapai officials compensated these three for the injustice that had been done to them by finding them alternative senior positions.

As has been shown, the three paid the price for a general norm common to most of the veteran community and to those active in the absorption of the Great Aliya. Nevertheless, they also paid the price for their own deeds. One may assume that among the factors that determined the fate of Aldema was the arrogant tone of his testimony before the Frumkin Commission. In this testimony, he recounted a number of coarse experiences from his work in Ein-Shemer.

> I saw the following scene with my own eyes: a Yemenite barber stands with a razor in one hand and a whetstone in the other. He spits and sharpens the razor, wipes it off on the back of the child, and begins cutting. This is simply like the inquisition. Why did I suggest bringing in a barber from Pardes Hanna? Because there are Moroccan immigrants there who, by contrast with this one, are truly modern.

This description is an example of the gross generalizations, regarding both Jews from Yemen and Morocco, that are unacceptable when coming from one who bore responsibility for culture in the immigrant camps. Aldema related a second experience to the Commission, again creating unacceptable stereotypes by the example he chose: "A [Yemenite] school-teacher stands with a strap in his hand, teaching the children. Suddenly he sticks his five fingers in his nose and wipes his hand, again on the back of a child. I was in such a state that I could have killed him." He concluded his testimony by saying: "There are such nuances that an outsider cannot understand. After all, I must be in contact with them twenty-four hours a day."[24] The Commission, which resolved to censure him, in practice decided to relieve him of this responsibility. Nevertheless, only shortly afterward, the educational coordinator of the Histadrut appointed Aldema as principal of a Workers Stream school in another immigrant center, Migdal Gad. On 11 June 1950, D. Z. Pinkas submitted a parliamentary query to the minister of education and culture following Aldema's new appointment. Minister of Education and Culture David Remez replied in the Knesset exactly half a year later, saying, "The appointment of Mr. Aldema as principal of the school of the Workers Stream in Migdal Gad and his resignation from his previous assignment occurred about two months before the government discussed this matter, and he has since served in his new position, where he has earned recognition and admiration." This was a clear cover-up for Aldema and his colleagues in the Culture Department and a definite affront to the religious public.[25]

Zippora Zehavi was likewise dismissed, probably due to her forthright testimony and following her own unequivocal admission to the Commission concerning the "campaign" to cut off *payot* of Yemenite children, which she herself carried out. She explicitly told the Commission, "I cut off all the hair of all of the boys. [They] were infected with lice and they also had ringworm, which is an extremely contagious disease. It was impossible to allow it in the camp." To Justice Frumkin's question: "Was a check made to see if it was possible to remove them by means of comb and brush?" she replied: "Who would do it? The parents turned the children over to me, and no one took an interest in them." When asked if she cut the hair of the girls, she replied: "No. I didn't cut their hair. . . . They comb their hair. They try to find a comb somewhere or other, but the little boys completely neglect themselves." It should be noted that Zippora Zehavi herself came from a Yemenite family that had immigrated to the Land of Israel in the late nineteenth century. She wished to quickly direct the new immigrants from Yemen toward the cultural milieu of which she was a part, and because of this the Commission called for her dismissal.[26]

THE COMMISSION AND POLITICAL RESPONSIBILITY

The Frumkin Commission was the first governmental commission of inquiry in Israel to impose responsibility upon the "administrative level" while exempting the "political echelons" from all responsibility. It is a well-known fact that since then the State of Israel has witnessed a number of investigations by state commissions of inquiry, including two relating to wars. The Agranat Commission, appointed in the wake of the Yom Kippur War, was sharply criticized for refraining from making "personal recommendations" regarding the political leadership. In contrast, the Kahan Commission, set up to investigate the massacre carried out by Christian Arabs against Muslim Arabs in the Sabra and Shatilla refugee camps in Beirut during the Lebanon War, earned plaudits from many in Israel and throughout the world after it fixed ministerial responsibility upon Defense Minister Ariel Sharon and recommended that "the minister of defense ought by rights to reach appropriate personal conclusions from the shortcomings displayed in the execution of his duty."[27]

While the Frumkin Commission did not deal with questions related to wartime, it should be noted, regretfully, that this was the first commission of inquiry in Israel that so clearly covered up for those on the political level, possibly establishing thereby a norm for the future. The Commission, as we have seen, assigned primary blame for all of the shortcomings or failures of immigrant education upon three individuals, employees of the Culture Department, thereby leading directly to their dismissal. Nevertheless, it should be stressed that during Israel's early years the "melting pot" policy was widely accepted and supported by the veteran Israeli public, and these three were merely loyal devotees of that norm. They actually only performed what was being preached by the leaders of the Labor movement—albeit at times they may have done so with excessive fervor.

Regarding Minister of Education and Culture Zalman Shazar, who was the superior of Levin and his colleagues, and who guided the policy of "uniform education" implemented by the Culture Department in the immigrant camps, the Frumkin Commission to a large extent covered up for him, exonerating him from responsibility for the anti-religious coercion practiced by employees of his ministry, since "for a considerable period of time during the development of these events [he] was ill, and was therefore unable to give [the issue] his personal and fundamental attention"[28]—a state of affairs that was true for only a few weeks. This cover-up does not seem to have been justified: Shazar was not sufficiently aware of what was going on in his ministry, and he did not act in a way that befitted a minister within the system for which he was responsible.

There seems little doubt that the Commission treated Shazar with respect and handled him with kid gloves. It did not impose upon him "personal responsibility" for what was done in the immigrant camps, nor did it use the term *ministerial responsibility*, which holds a government minister accountable even when he has no knowledge of the specific acts or errors performed by those serving under him.[29]

In the present case, Nahum Levin himself felt that education of immigrant children was not being handled correctly, and he repeatedly requested—including a direct appeal to Shazar—that responsibility for such education be transferred from his department to the Education Division, and that these children receive the same education as all others in Israel. He received no reply from the minister and the senior officials of the Ministry of Education and Culture, who bore personal responsibility for Levin's efforts, were fully aware of them, and gave them their full backing.

Some five months after the publication of the Frumkin Commission Report, Ben-Gurion and other senior members of Mapai realized that there was no alternative but to replace Shazar. He was removed from office—something that the Frumkin Commission was not daring enough to recommend—and David Remez was appointed in his stead. There can be no doubt that if in many respects the Frumkin Commission will be remembered by future generations as a significant, courageous commission, in its decisions regarding the degree of responsibility of elected public officials its image will be of a commission that protected senior public figures and practiced whitewashing.

Izhak Ben-Zvi's Appendix to the Frumkin Commission Report

Izhak Ben-Zvi decided to go beyond contemporary political-social issues, appending to the Commission's report a learned historical study, "On the History of the Jews in Yemen and North Africa."[30] Ben-Zvi took advantage of the report to try influence the public to become better acquainted with the Oriental Jewish communities, hoping in this manner to change accepted historiosophic viewpoints toward these groups.

Regarding Yemenite Jewry, Ben-Zvi emphasized the antiquity of Jewish settlement in the Arabian peninsula in general and in Yemen in particular. He stressed Yemenite Jews' great religious devotion and the fact that all attempts by Muslims, as well as a few by Christians, to assimilate them had ended in complete failure. "The Jews of Yemen remained a living tribe of the Jewish nation, a branch which did not wither and was not dispersed in the course of generations."[31] Ben-Zvi outlined the age-old ties of the Yemenite community to the Land of Israel and took pains to present the strong Redemptionist expectations of this community, which characterized it throughout the centuries.

According to Ben-Zvi, most Jewish children in Yemen "studied Torah and prayer and were educated to observe the commandments. They never attended any school other than the traditional *heder* . . . [apart from] a feeble attempt by the Alliance [Israélite Universelle] at the beginning of the twentieth century."[32] Thus he provided learned documentation for a position toward which all members of the Frumkin Commission tended—that Yemenite children in Israel should continue to receive religious education.

Ben-Zvi's historical description of the Jews of North Africa likewise emphasized the antiquity of Jewish settlement in those countries, the military prowess of the Jews (and converts to Judaism) against the Muslim Arabs, and the harsh edicts and disasters that the Jews suffered in various periods as well as times of relative peace and calm that they enjoyed. Ben-Zvi, wishing to combat the prejudices against the Jews of North Africa that were then developing (such as those expressed in Arye Gelblum's series of articles in *Ha'aretz*—see Chapter 3), emphasized the many immigrants from North Africa who had already come to the Land of Israel "many generations ago," during the Mameluke and Ottoman periods. He stressed that the main group, "the *Ma'araviim* [Maghrebites, literally "Westerners," a term used to denote the Jews of the Maghreb or Northwest Africa], held together the Jewish communities in Jerusalem and Safed and later in Haifa, Tiberias, and Jaffa."[33] This exposition was intended to enhance the pride of North African Jews in their own community as well as to create a more positive image of Oriental Jewry among Ashkenazic readers.

In an attempt to explain "the source of those social phenomena in our generation that must be dealt with and corrected,"[34] Ben-Zvi wrote of the various pressures and temptations that had been applied upon North African Jewry—pressures by Muslim rulers and the temptations of French culture. He also attempted to explain more fully the processes of secularization that had been the lot of the Jews in Libya, Morocco, Tunisia, and Algeria, as opposed to the closed society and religious devotion that characterized the Jews of Yemen. One may assume that he did so in order to further clarify the different attitudes toward members of the various communities in relation to education in the immigrant camps.

Ben-Zvi's appendix sought to add an additional dimension to the report of the Frumkin Commission and to convert it into an objective report, with a certain scholarly, academic aura. Nevertheless, in all discussions of the report, I have never encountered any quotations from the appendix, and it would appear that few people read it, learned something from it, or derived from it the conclusions that Ben-Zvi had hoped to impart.

SUMMATION

Notwithstanding the justified criticism of the Frumkin Commission and its methods of operation, this was a courageous public commission that had the intrepidity to arrive at daring conclusions—particularly given the public and social conditions of the time. In particular, the three secular members of the Commission—Justice Gad Frumkin, MK Avraham Elmaleh, and MK Izhak Ben-Zvi—dared to depart from the accepted line at that time within the veteran community in Israel and to attack fundamental values of the dominant secular society of those days. Perhaps most daring of all was Ben-Zvi, a longtime member of Mapai who, it will be recalled, informed his party comrades at the outset of the Commission's work that he would not cover up any acts nor hide facts.[35] It could be that the courage he displayed in this context further contributed to recognition by the public leadership in Israel of his unique moral qualities. This may have influenced his election as the second president of the State of Israel in December 1952 (an election of which David Ben-Gurion was the chief initiator).

The Frumkin Commission was successful in the short run, in that it helped maintain the coalition government for another year. In the long run, however, the Commission, upon whom many pinned hopes that it would help achieve a compromise between religious and secular Jews in Israel, essentially scrutinized each of

the groups through a magnifying glass, thereby enhancing the polarization between them. The facts uncovered by the Frumkin Commission and the unwillingness to deal with them only deepened the chasm between the secular and religious
Jews and, in the long run, caused great damage to the delicate fabric of relations
within Israeli Jewish society.

The conclusions of the Frumkin Commission increased public criticism of the
system of ideological streams of education. They influenced the policy then being
broached both within Mapai and the Religious Front, particularly from mid-1950,
which called for the division of state education into two separate educational systems: one secular and the other religious. Religious circles understood—partly as a
result of the Commission's report—that they had to mount firmer efforts for education that would, as far as possible, be connected to and dependent upon their parties. As a result of increasing mutual distrust, future political crises between the two
camps were inevitable. It is no coincidence that Israel's first elected government
found it difficult to function, and in the final analysis it fell precisely over the issues
of education and the shaping of the new Israeli society.

"Soul snatching" in education was indicative of the character of Israeli society and of the basic problems of the new Jewish state during its early years. Acts
of coercion, violent pressures, the withholding of food and medical services, and
other harsh means described in the introduction to the Frumkin Commission Report all characterized the birth pangs of Israeli democracy. The members of the
Frumkin Commission were among the first elected representatives to warn against
anti-democratic "acts of violent robbery"—to use Ben-Gurion's phrase. The very
fact that the government was prepared to appoint such a commission and the great
courage exhibited by its members in collectively formulating their conclusions are
evidence that already during its first years, there was an openness and a willingness
within the State of Israel to improve and advance its democratic system of government. In retrospect, one may state today that the Frumkin Commission made
a substantive contribution to the transformation of the state from a *demoktatura*—
to quote the witty double entendre of poet Yonatan Ratosh, which may be ren-
dered roughly as "democtatorship"—to a true democracy, one of the enlightened
democracies of the world.

CHAPTER 12

THE DECISION TO INTRODUCE
A STATE EDUCATIONAL
SYSTEM (1953)

Though the Frumkin Commission Report did enable Israel's first elected government, led by Prime Minister Ben-Gurion, to survive for almost another year, in the end the coalition between Mapai and the Religious Front was dissolved due to a controversy over the character of education in the State of Israel. On 15 February 1951, the government fell when the Knesset passed a motion of no confidence. A few days later, a date—30 July—was set for the elections to the Second Knesset.

Already on the eve of these elections the Mapai leadership had decided to abolish the system of partisan streams of education and to introduce in its stead a state educational system. However, for various reasons, this decision was implemented only in 1953.[1] While the Frumkin Commission Report greatly influenced the shape that the state educational system would take, it was not a central element in bringing about that decision. As I will show, it did play a central role, however, in the decision to enable two partisan religious streams to continue within the new framework: the "state religious educational system" (which everyone knew would in effect not truly be a state system but would continue to be influenced by the religious Zionist parties, a direct continuation of the Hamizrachi Stream) and *Hinuch Azma'i* ("Independent Education," a new name for the Agudat Israel Stream).

ABOLITION OF THE SECULAR EDUCATIONAL STREAMS

There were three major reasons that led the Mapai leadership to dissolve the Workers Stream and the General Stream and to introduce a general (secular) system of state education.

First there was the enormous growth of the Workers Stream, which gave rise to expectations among Mapai leaders that the educational content of that stream would predominate in the general (i.e., nonreligious) educational system. It should be noted that most of the increased enrollment in the Workers Stream was the result of the absorption within its schools of three-fifths of the children of immigrants between 1948 and 1953, some of them—as we have seen—having been given no choice. As a result, the Workers Stream had grown by 150 percent between the 1948–49 and 1951–52 school year. Its share of the entire school population increased from 27.3 percent upon the establishment of Israel to 37.3 percent three years later, becoming the largest educational stream in the country.[2]

Second, the decision was influenced by public opinion, especially pressure exerted by the new immigrants themselves, who now accounted for about half of the population of Israel. They tired of the narrow party considerations and the constant "soul snatching" in the educational system. Public pressure increased after the publication of the Frumkin Commission Report, and the facts that it brought to light, and also because of the difficult economic situation.

One teacher, who was actively involved in the Teachers Union, had this to say about the school system, his opinion echoing that of many others:

> [Under the system of educational streams], some schools are established in small settlements which are unable to properly support even one school. One puts up "signs" and erects skeleton schools that lack equipment and pedagogic materials, and at times even trained teachers. The manner in which competition is conducted between the streams, accompanied by vulgar propaganda that every civilized person abhors, penetrates every single home, tarnishes the respected status of education, strikes at the very souls of the children, encourages much hatred and anger among the teachers, and fouls the educational environment throughout the entire state.[3]

Third, an important motive that led to the abolishment of the secular streams was the widening split within the Israeli Left, especially between Mapai and Mapam. An increasing number of members of Mapai, which showed growing signs of orientation toward the West and the United States, began to fear that educators who belonged to Mapam were too submissive to Stalin and

Stalinism and were leading Israeli youth toward "Russian apostasy," to quote Ben-Gurion.[4]

Differences between Mapai and Mapam had become more intense against the backdrop of the Cold War during the late 1940s and early 1950s, particularly after the outbreak of the Korean War in 1950. The decreasing support of Israel by the USSR and its increased anti-Zionist and anti-Jewish activity (beginning in late 1948 and early 1949), on the one hand, and Israel's growing orientation toward the United States and American economic aid to the new state, on the other hand, also greatly influenced relations between the two parties. For Mapam's leaders, the USSR was a "second homeland."[5] There were even extremists among them who expressed hope to see the Red Army gain control of the Middle East,[6] some going so far as to claim that "the Russian Army is not a foreign army."[7] Even MK Israel Galili, leader of Ahdut Ha'avoda,[8] part of Mapam's "right wing," declared: "We shall never fight the USSR . . . the USSR does not subjugate [other] nations."[9] The formation of Israel's first government in March 1949, after the elections to the First Knesset, without the participation of Mapam led to a fierce split in the Histradrut, a schism in the kibbutz movement, and harsh quarrels within left-wing families, resulting in many divorces. As noted, this rivalry in the Israeli Left was a weighty consideration that led Mapai to decide that the Workers Stream must be abolished.

After the second elections, in July 1951, Ben-Gurion once again formed a government in October without Mapam. When he presented his government to the Knesset for confirmation, he announced that the minister of education would be Mapai member Professor Ben-Zion Dinur (then sixty-eight years old), who was known to be a staunch adherent of a state educational system. Ben-Gurion declared that the government's basic guidelines included a program to abolish educational streams and introduce a system of state education. He would later write that he considered this declaration a "historic moment":

> There are few days that can compete in importance and greatness for Jewish history with the 14th of May 1948—the day on which the state was declared. However, it is fitting that the day on which the Government of Israel declared state education [8 October 1951] also be recorded in our history: the removal of education from the authority of the parties and its transfer to the authority of the state is a decisive step towards the establishment of the state [on firm foundations] and the unification of the nation.[10]

Ben-Gurion's phraseology was an exaggeration: the government decided to abolish only the two secular educational streams (the Workers Stream and the General

Stream). The State Education Law passed by the Knesset on 12 August 1953, left intact the two partisan religious streams and the connection of the religious parties to religious education.[11]

WHY WERE THE RELIGIOUS STREAMS NOT ABOLISHED?

In the elections conducted in July 1951, Mapai (led by Ben-Gurion) received 37 percent of the votes, or 45 of the 120 seats in the Knesset. But even such a great electoral victory necessitated the formation of a coalition government. Mapai had two alternatives: either to renew the pact with the religious parties that contested the elections in four separate lists and together lost one mandate, their representation dropping from sixteen to fifteen, or to come to an agreement with the largest right-wing party, the General Zionists, which greatly increased its parliamentary strength, voting in twenty members to the Second Knesset compared with only seven in the first, thus becoming the second largest party and an alternative to Mapai.

Mapai first tried to reach a coalition agreement with the General Zionists. However, fundamental differences of opinion cropped up during the negotiations, particularly on economic and social issues, as the General Zionists demanded that the leading socialist party must agree to foster a capitalist economy and encourage private initiative. After negotiating for a few weeks, the Mapai leadership decided to turn once again to the religious parties whose demands seemed to be "lower," limited to the realm of education. Contemporary leading personalities in Mapai believed that whatever concessions they made on this issue constituted the lowest possible price that Mapai would have had to pay to any other party.[12]

We have seen that elections to the Second Knesset were conducted after a bitter controversy between Mapai and the Religious Front, centering mostly on whether the religious parties would continue to monopolize religious education in Israel. In these elections Hapoel Hamizrachi won eight seats, Hamizrachi, two, Agudat Israel, two, and Poalei Agudat Israel, three. Hapoel Hamizrachi, now the largest religious party, raised three demands during the coalition negotiations: (1) that religious-Zionist education would be under its sole supervision in a separate division of religious education directed by its members; (2) that the 100 schools of the Religious Workers Stream, which had been established at the initiative of the Histadrut, be transferred to its division; (3) that its *haredi*[*13] opponents be allowed to retain an educational stream, which would be completely separate from the religious Zionists.

Ben-Gurion at first rejected their demands. He was especially opposed to having two types of religious education—religious-Zionist and *haredi* non-

Zionist. He did not put up much of a fight over the Religious Workers Stream, which had been one of the causes of the crisis with the Religious Front. His first reply to Hapoel Hamizrachi was: "Two [religious educational systems financed by the state]—no. I agree to one religious system in which you can teach anything you wish."[14] However, somewhat later he explained to his colleagues in Mapai that he wished to form a government coalition with a Jewish majority in the Knesset and did not want to rely upon the votes of Arab Knesset members. (At that time there were only two Arab MKs, who were in any case completely subservient to Ben-Gurion.) Therefore, he informed his party that he was forced to add to his coalition not only Hapoel Hamizrachi and Hamizrachi but also Agudat Israel and Poalei Agudat Israel. He asserted that it would be necessary to submit to the major demand of the ultra-Orthodox parties—that there be two separate religious educational systems—and he convinced a majority of the Mapai leadership that this was a minimalist demand, which Mapai had no choice but to accept.[15]

There is no doubt that the conflicts over education during Israel's early years, along with the facts exposed by the Frumkin Commission, greatly exhausted Mapai's leading members. They undermined the ability to resist the establishment of separate religious educational systems. Furthermore, after the report of the commission of inquiry appointed by the government, Mapai could no longer deny the fact that when secular persons were responsible for religious educational institutions—as was the case with the Religious Workers Stream—there was no real care shown for the basic values of Judaism.

THE INDEPENDENT EDUCATIONAL SYSTEM OF AGUDAT ISRAEL

The State Education Law of 1953 authorized the establishment of the "state general educational system" and the "state religious educational system" and also recognized the existence of a third one, the "independent educational system of Agudat Israel," but stated that the State of Israel would provide it with only partial financial support.[16]

The decision to grant recognition to the independent system was passed by the government by a majority of only one vote and would not have passed at all without the appreciable pressure applied by the leaders of the religious-Zionist parties.[17] The government decision was presented to the Knesset, which ratified it, granting the Agudat Israel schools the status of "exempted institutions."[18] Government financial support for the 1953–54 school year was set at 60 percent of their budget. Over the years, government support has increased to 100 percent (and even more!) of their budget.[19] Furthermore, what began as one independent system of education has been transformed over the years into a conglomerate of educational networks that is subordinate to various and opposing *haredi* groups.

State recognition and massive financial support of the independent educational system have led to a proliferation of diverse systems of *haredi* education. All of them together—and there are fifteen variants[20]—have increased from about 5,000 children in 1948 to about 200,000 as the twentieth century drew to a close. In 1948, they accounted for 5 percent of the elementary school age population, while in 1997, they had more than doubled that percentage to 12.7. On the basis of data that he collected, the minister of education, in 1997, Prof. Amnon Rubinstein, apprehensively surmised that should the present demographic patterns prevail, within twenty years *haredi* children would account for about one-third of elementary school pupils. He claimed that in time, "Non-Orthodox Jewish Zionist culture will be professed by a constantly decreasing minority."[21]

Even after the decision was made to supply state financing for the independent educational system, Agudat Israel did not allow the Ministry of Education and Culture to intervene at all in setting the curriculum in its schools. Though the State Education Law authorizes the minister of education to force upon non-state educational institutions recognized by the state a curriculum that would account for 75 percent of class time, in effect already during the first year after the law was enacted it was decided not to enforce it upon the *haredi* schools.[22] When professional staff members of the ministry protested, they were silenced by the politicians.[23]

On many occasions the *haredim* proudly spoke of their independence, not hesitating to flaunt it publicly. In most cases they admitted that they received the promised financial support from the state but stressed that every educational issue "whether small or big is decided [only] by the Council of Torah Sages or whoever is authorized by the council."[24]

In 1978, on the occasion of the twenty-fifth anniversary of the establishment of the independent educational system, Israel Spiegel, the editor of Agudat Israel's daily newspaper *Hamodi'a*, wrote that the agreement reached in 1953 was a clear victory of the *haredim* over Ben-Gurion and his colleagues. He detailed the step-by-step development of the independent educational system and related that the Agudat Israel leadership negotiated with Mapai with "faked moderation," requesting that they be granted "only Yavne and its sages."[25] He argued that since they focused on one issue alone, asking nothing of Mapai but an independent educational system, their victory was complete. "To this very day there are many in the secular camp who bitterly complain: Why did they give in to them? Why did they let them have it? And why did they give them, the weak and downtrodden, what they staunchly refused to give to powerful elements in the secular camp, those who with great anger fought against the abolishment of the Workers Stream?"[26]

Spiegel's assertion that many in the secular camp, especially in its left wing, believed that Ben-Gurion and his colleagues erred twice—once when they abolished the Workers Stream and again when they permitted the partisan educational system affiliated with Agudat Israel to continue to operate—turned out to be quite true. Some see that decision as the stock from which evil sprouted—the major element that led to the end of education in pioneering values in Israel, and one of the important reasons for the rising power of the *haredim* in the country at the turn of the twenty-first century. The feeling, shared by many, that the *haredim* are the subject of favoritism and that they alone operate an educational system without any intervention by state authorities, increased especially after the establishment of the Shas political party in 1983 and the decision to permit it to establish its own educational institutions under the title Ma'ayan Hahinuch Hatorani (The Fountain of Torah Education). That feeling became more intense when Shas became the third largest party in Israel, and even more when the realization sunk in that this was a party that could greatly influence basic issues related to the future of Israel, such as the fate of governments or fateful decisions in the peace process with the Palestinians.

YESHIVOT IN ISRAEL

When the State of Israel was established in 1948, only a few thousand young men studied in *yeshivot*, the absolute majority of them in Ashkenazic *haredi* institutions. The number of Sephardic students, both in the religious-Zionist *yeshivot* and in the *haredi* ones, was very small—no more than several hundred. All in all, there were only several dozen *yeshivot* in the country in 1948, most of them belonging to the *haredim*. Various estimates place the number of students age thirteen and up in these institutions in 1948 at about 5,000.[27]

It was then, while the War of Independence was still being fought, that the arrangement began by which Prime Minister Ben-Gurion exempted about 400 *yeshiva* students from service in the IDF (formally, they received only a deferment).[28] This exemption (extended to many more men over the years) and the condition that whoever wished to extend his deferment must not seek employment and must prove that "the Torah is his profession" led to a great increase in the number of students in the *haredi yeshivot*. Moreover, the extremely high rate of natural increase of the *haredi* community, along with the many economic benefits they received, led to more and more *haredi* youngsters enrolling in the *yeshivot*.

The immediate result of this situation was that in 1965 there were more than 300 *yeshivot* in Israel with over 15,000 students. Five years later, the numbers were approximately 500 and 20,000, respectively. After the Likud party came to power in 1977, the number of students in *yeshivot* greatly increased. By the early 1990s, there were already more than 1,600 *yeshivot*, in which about 100,000 persons studied, about half of them ages thirteen to eighteen, while the others were older, some of them having reached old age.[29] At the beginning of 2000, almost 200,000 persons were registered as students in the *yeshivot*. As we shall see in the next chapter, due to the rise of Shas, many of those enrolled in *haredi yeshivot* were now members of the Oriental communities.

CHAPTER 13

SHAS—THE PARTY WHOSE ROOTS
LIE IN THE ANTI-RELIGIOUS COERCION
OF ISRAEL'S FIRST YEARS

Whoever wishes to know from whence Shas developed must study the Frumkin Commission Report. I argue that the roots of this party lie in the period of the Great Aliya (from May 1948 to late 1951),[1] and that they are intimately connected to similar traumas of immigration absorption that continued throughout the first two decades of Israel's existence.

As noted earlier in this book, during these first three and a half years, an average of 10,000 to 30,000 immigrants entered Israel a month, about half coming from Islamic countries, with an absolute majority of the latter arriving from Iraq and Yemen. During the next three years, there was a great decline in immigration: only 24,369 arrived in 1952, 11,326 in 1953, and 18,370 in 1954. Immigration on a large scale was renewed during the next three years, when about 170,000 Jews came to Israel (mostly from North Africa): 37,478 in 1955, 56,234 in 1956, and 71,224 in 1957, and once again between 1960 and 1964 when the organized immigration of Moroccan Jews brought around 100,000 to Israel (about the same number as all immigrants from Morocco between 1948 and 1960).[2] The conceptions that underlay immigration absorption in the first years of the state did not change to any great extent during these latter waves of renewed immigration. The state's leaders and much of the public still put their trust in the Zionist-secular "melting pot."

The shock of absorption in Israel suffered by immigrants from Muslim countries led to several social reactions, and a few political ones. All of this happened long before the creation of Shas. We shall briefly survey some of the religious-*haredi* reactions, as well as a few political-ethnic ones, from the 1950s to the 1980s.

In 1950, a group of *haredim* banded together, calling themselves Hever Pe'ilei Hamahane Hatorati (Group of Activists of the Religious Camp), or simply, Hever Hape'ilim (Group of Activists). Their objective was to lead the new immigrants, particularly those of the Oriental communities, toward religious education, whether of the Hamizrachi or Agudat Israel Stream. Though it has undergone various changes over the years, Hever Hape'ilim still exists today. Its achievements during Israel's early years were rather marginal, succeeding in transferring only a few hundred pupils to religious educational institutions.[3] However, from the broader viewpoint, and with historical perspective, there is no doubt that the hard core of the several hundreds of Hever Hape'ilim members amassed a potency that constantly increased. Furthermore, many of the youngsters of the Oriental communities, whom the Hever succeeded in bringing to *haredi yeshovot*, were among the founders of Shas in 1980.[4]

During that same year, simultaneously with the establishment of Hever Hape'ilim, a group of more extremist *haredim* organized itself, planning to adopt violent measures against the state authorities. Theirs was an even wider program than Hever Hape'ilim's, not only to defend religion but to impose observance of the laws of the Torah and of *halakha** by the use of force. In April 1950, in the Porat Yosef Yeshiva, one sector of this group created a terrorist underground that called itself Brit Hakanaim (The Union of Zealots).[5] Its leaders were Yehuda Rieder, Eliahu Raful, and Mordechai Eliahu. Brit Hakanaim numbered a few dozen young members. Among their terrorist acts they set afire cars whose owners drove on the Sabbath, placed incendiary bombs in football fields where games were played on the Sabbath, and burned down butcher shops that sold non-kosher meat. The underground was exposed by the Israel security services when it was planning to throw a dummy bomb into the Knesset to frighten its members during a debate on military conscription of women and as its members were planning to set fire to military records in the Jerusalem conscription office. Most members of the underground who were arrested were put on trial, and a few of them were sentenced to prison terms.

It is worthwhile to quote a passage from a statement by Mordechai Eliahu who, years later, between 1983 and 1991, was to be the Sephardic Chief Rabbi, and after terminating his term in that office became the spiritual mentor of the National Religious Party.[6] During his trial in 1950, he said: "While still a student at the Porat Yosef Yeshiva I heard first reports about the educational condition of immigrant children in the immigrant camps. . . . I could not suffer such licentious behavior. . . . I believed that we could impose behavior based on the Torah in the state by means of an underground. . . . I understood that words [alone] would not help."[7]

After Brit Hakanaim was disbanded, *haredi* activity against what they called "anti-religious coercion" returned to accepted democratic norms: many demonstrations, leaflets, forceful speeches, and so on. For three decades—from the 1950s to the 1970s—there were dozens of confrontations by *haredi* circles, particularly of Ashkenazim, with the police and the armed forces. They were mainly concentrated in Jerusalem and turned on various forms of the desecration of the Sabbath, or other transgressions of the *halakha*, such as mixed bathing in swimming pools, the performance of autopsies, and more. All such confrontations—with the exception of one case that resulted in a death[8]—ended with, at most, some slightly wounded persons.

In the mid-1950s, leading Sephardic rabbis warned new immigrants of the anti-religious coercion being practiced in Israel. One leaflet, written by these rabbis and distributed among the immigrants from North Africa, who were then arriving in large numbers in Israel, contained the following, inter alia:

> Know that many of the new immigrants who came from Morocco were unaware [of the danger] and fell [into the clutches of those responsible for the immigrant *moshavim*], and now they are biting their fingers, for their sons no longer belong to them, the sons are already violating the Sabbath, eat non-kosher food, and have divested themselves of all the splendor of Judaism. All this happened because they did not ask or try to ascertain where they were being taken, and who would be their instructors. Therefore, we have come to warn you that you too may not stumble, and before you go to any *moshav* you must investigate and find out if there is a synagogue, a ritual bath for women, a real religious school [i.e., not one of the Religious Workers Stream], and only then should you go. Know that here in our holy land no one is forced into apostasy if one knows how to avoid falling into the hands of the hypocrites who deceive the immigrants and lead them to fall into the snare that they have laid for them.[9]

The leaflet was signed by Rabbis David Sabbah, Yeuda Zedaka, and Nissim Kedouri. The youngest of the signatories was Rabbi Ovadia Yosef, then thirty-five.[10]

This warning, and other similar ones, had no real effect. During Israel's first and second decades, many immigrants from the Oriental countries continued to settle in *moshavim* that lacked suitable frameworks for religious life and education.

In many cases, once the new immigrants reached their new homes they discovered that there was no provision for their religious needs. Families from Morocco and Tunisia, who in 1956 reached Moshav Shefer (near Meron, in the vicinity of Safed), complained: "We cannot [stand it] here in the *moshav*. . . . Teachers and instructors are waging a war against religion. . . . [We] want a religious [lifestyle]. We wish that our sons study Torah and that the teachers [be]

God-fearing, like back home in Morocco."[11] Other Moroccan immigrants who were brought to Moshav Sde-David in the Lachish region wrote to Minister of Education and Culture Zalman Aranne: "We are all religious and want religious education. In the Diaspora, too, we were all religious and immigrated to Israel in order to keep the Torah and its commandments. . . . Send us immediately envoys to investigate the situation here and to enroll [children for religious education]."[12] Another case is the complaint of immigrants in the Yeruham *ma'abara* against the "*ma'abara* director" Muchnik, a member of Mapai from Nahalal, who informed them: "There will be no religious school here, for I am the father of this place, and the muscles in my arm are the mother."[13] Or take the case of the well-known Jerusalem physician, Sh. Shereshevsky, who claimed that "the authorities responsible for immigration and absorption send immigrants to settlements where pigs are raised. They help out in raising the pigs, work in the pigsties, and eat pork."[14] There are many similar complaints, the majority coming from development towns and immigrant *moshvim*. Furthermore, many immigrant families were forced to send their children—primarily through the agency of Youth Aliya—to secular educational institutions and kibbutzim. There were not enough religious settlements and educational institutions to absorb all children coming from traditionalist and religious families.

Internal documentation produced in government circles indicates that even at the beginning of Israel's second decade, official policy, especially that adhered to by the Mapai leadership, was no less flexible or more empathic toward the religious public. Take, for example, a confidential letter from Minister of Education and Culture Zalman Aranne to Prime Minister David Ben-Gurion, evidence of an even more rigid anti-religious policy. The letter was written in anticipation of the elections that were to be held on 3 November 1959, and with the expectation that coalition negotiations would once more have to be conducted between Mapai and the religious-Zionist parties. Aranne warned the prime minister that in no case should he succumb to the demands of the religious parties nor agree to state funding of religious high schools (the State Education Law of 1953 sanctioned such support only for elementary schools). Aranne wrote: "It is unthinkable that the state will be able to establish two networks of high schools [it is quite enough that there is one network, the secular one]. . . . If the state laws on education apply for the moment only to elementary schools, we should refrain from mounting the path of agreements or laws that will also apply the [negative] decree of two trends [general state education and religious state education] to the high schools that will be built by the state." Despite informing the prime minister that fifteen to twenty high schools would be established in the near future in development towns, most of whose population were religious and traditionalist people who had come from North Africa, Aranne asserted: "The curriculum, the appointment of teachers and the like, cannot, under any circumstances, in any way, and in any place be under the authority of the Division for Religious Education."[15] In the final tally, Ben-Gurion had no choice but to disregard Aranne's opinion, but the fact remains that this was the outlook of Israel's fourth minister of education and culture. Aranne, one of the most powerful members of Mapai, did not recognize the right of religious parents to decide the character of the education their children would receive, and his policy—at least up until 1959—did not take into account the needs of the religious public.[16]

A social confrontation, known as the "Wadi Salib riots," erupted between Sephardim and Ashkenazim in July 1959.[17] The riots—which included attacks upon public institutions, setting fire to shops, and sharp clashes with the police—broke out primarily against an ethnic-economic backdrop, but they also were an expression of an abysmal hatred of the veteran Ashkenazic establishment. The riots spread from one slum in Haifa to several development towns (Migdal Ha'emek, Beer Sheba, Acre, Kiryat Shemona, and Beit-Shean). They were one of the first serious blows to the veteran absorbing establishment. Though Mapai did try, after the riots, to dampen the tense emotions between Oriental and Ashkenazic Jews—especially through some benefits for the development towns and members of the Oriental ethnic communities[18]—unrest among the latter continued unabated.

Elections to the Fourth Knesset were held in November 1959, just a few months after the riots. A small group of leaders of the "Wadi Salib riots" tried to exploit their public effect by running for the Knesset in a list called "Union of North-African Immigrants." They were unsuccessful: the "Union" received only 0.8 percent of the votes, not enough to seat even one member in the Knesset. In later elections as well—those of 1961, 1965, 1969, 1974, and 1977—the attempts by ethnic-communal lists to be elected to the Knesset proved unsuccessful.

The first significant success of an ethnic-communal party came only in 1981. MK Aharon Abuhatzeira, who a few months previously had seceded from the National Religious Party, created a new party that he called Tnu'at Masoret Israel (Movement for Tradition in Israel, known in short as "Tami").[19] Abuhatzeira, the scion of a renowned family of rabbis in Morocco, had just finished serving three months of works for the public benefit to which a court had sentenced him for theft and fraud. For the first time in about thirty years, ever since parties of Yemenites and Sephardic Jews placed a few members in the First and Second Knesset, a Sephardic ethnic-communal party won three seats. However, in 1984, when the party's list stood for election a second time, it managed to return only one member and began to disintegrate.[20]

We may sum up and say that until the 1980s all attempts to exploit ethnic-communal tension and to transform it into social and political power were short-lived. The *haredi* camp also was small and divided. Only from the middle of the fourth decade of the State of Israel did Shas—a *haredi* and an ethnic-communal party—succeed in becoming a force to be reckoned with in Israeli society.

SHAS' SUCCESS IN VARIOUS ELECTION CAMPAIGNS

Rabbi Ovadia Yosef is the founding father of Shas (its full title, Hitahdut Se-
faradim Shomrei Torah, means Union of Torah-Observant Sephardim). He was
one of the leading rabbis who already during the first decade of Israel struggled to
counter the "secularization" of the new immigrants, and he has not let up since.
Three decades later, he was the mainstay of a political party.

Though Shas arose only in the 1980s, as we have already intimated, its roots
and justification should be sought in the traumatic experiences undergone by Oriental Jews during their absorption by the Zionist establishment in Israel in the
1950s and 1960s. It adopted as its slogan "to return the glory to its pristine condition" (i.e., to reinstate the glory of Oriental Jewry, which had been trampled under
by the veteran establishment in Israel). The movement's leaders declared that their
major objective was to encourage *mizrahiut*, literally "Orientalism," by which they
meant the traditions and lifestyle of the Oriental Jewish communities and the
restoration of religion. They called upon Oriental Jews to embrace anew their traditional roots and ethnic-communal culture.

Rabbi Ovadia Yosef is one of the greatest sages of our times.[21] In 1983, he
decided to back the proposal to establish Shas, an idea then broached by several
young Sephardic men, including Arye Deri.[22] There were two major reasons that
led Rabbi Yosef to adopt this step. First, as we have seen, was the harsh impression
left upon him by the process of absorbing Jews from the Oriental countries, and
his strong belief that the splendor of Oriental Jewry must be restored. Second, he
had taken his ousting in March 1983 from the office of Sephardic Chief Rabbi,
which he had filled for ten years, as a personal insult.[23] It was precisely then that
he decided that the only way to advance the Oriental Jews and strengthen their
religious convictions was by the creation of a center of political power.

The first elections in which Shas participated, with the encouragement of
Rabbi Yosef, were the municipal ones conducted in 1983. Political analysts were
surprised when the Shas list in Jerusalem made a commendable achievement in its
first public campaign, receiving over 11,000 votes and three mandates on the
Jerusalem Municipal Council. It also made significant gains in Bnai Brak (four
seats) and Tiberias (15 percent of the votes).

On 23 July 1984, Shas competed for the first time in a national election (to
the Eleventh Knesset), receiving about 64,000 votes that entitled it to four seats.
However, soon after the elections, it became clear that, due to the Israeli parliamentary system, Shas' achievement was much greater: it could tip the balance between the left- and right-wing blocs, and the formation of a coalition government
was greatly dependent upon it. The left-wing bloc, along with the Arab parties,
won 60 of the Knesset's 120 seats (with 44 going to the Labor Party and its leftist
"Alliance," and the other 16 divided among another 6 parties), while the right-

wing parties, along with the religious ones (including Shas) received the other 60 (41 to the Likud party and 19 divided among 7 others). After exhausting coalition negotiations that dragged on for more than two months, a "national union government" was formed in September, headed by Yitzhak Shamir (Likud) and Shimon Peres (Labor Party), who were to fill the role of prime minister in rotation. Shas played a central role in this government, and its representative, Rabbi Yitzhak Peretz, was appointed minister of the interior.[24]

Member of Knesset Yitzhak Navon (Labor Party) was appointed minister of education and culture in the "national union government." With the support of the two large parties and the agreement of the minister of education and culture, state recognition was granted to a new educational stream, that of Shas (known as Ma'ayan Hahinuch Hatorani). Simultaneously, the government—with the backing of the two largest parties—allocated considerable state funding for Shas' extracurricular programs: youth clubs, religious lessons for the general public, celebrations to mark the New Moon (the first day of each month), special gatherings for women, trips to sites throughout the country, and more. Other funds were specially earmarked for day nurseries, clubs for the retired, and other social welfare activities. Shas' educational system began operation in the 1984/85 school year, at first with the enrollment of only several hundred pupils. Over the years it expanded, though at a slower rate than Shas itself: in 2000, it educated about 20,000 pupils in elementary schools and a few thousand children in its kindergartens. Despite the growth of Ma'ayan Hahinuch Hatorani, in 2000 only about 10 percent of those who voted for Shas in the elections of 1999 sent their children to its schools.

The second national elections in which Shas participated were those for the Twelfth Knesset, held on 11 November 1988. Once more there was a political standoff: the right-wing bloc and the religious parties (with the exception of Shas) voted in fifty-nine members, while the left-wing bloc and the Arab parties accounted for fifty-five. Shas, with its six members, became the third largest party in the Knesset and once more could tip the balance of power to whichever side it wished.[25] The major right-wing party, Likud, had forty seats, while the Labor Party received thirty-nine. Shas received 107,709 votes, 4.7 percent of the qualified ballots.[26]

Under pressure from Shas, a right-wing government was formed in December 1988, headed by Likud leader Yitzhak Shamir. This time Shas received two portfolios in the new government: the Ministry of the Interior and the Ministry of Immigrant Absorption. Shas, however, did not cease raising additional demands. In March 1990, hoping to receive more from the Labor Party, Arye Deri of Shas concluded a sort of *Putsch* with Shimon Peres of the Labor Party (that came to be known in Israeli politics by the term coined by Yitzhak Rabin, "the stinking subterfuge"). They agreed on certain benefits that Shas would receive if it

toppled the Shamir government and formed a new one, with Peres as prime minister. This *Putsch* was foiled at the last moment upon the instructions of Rabbi
Eliezer Menahem Shach, head of the Poniewiec Yeshiva. On 13 March 1990,
Shamir deposed Peres, who had conspired against him, as a result of which all
other Labor Party ministers resigned. A new government with Shamir as prime
minister was formed and confirmed by the Knesset in June of that year. Shas remained within the coalition, which continued to function for another two years
until the next general elections.

In those elections, conducted on 23 June 1992, the Zionist left-wing parties
received fifty-six seats (forty-four went to the Labor Party and twelve to Meretz).
However, along with the five Communist and Arab members, this bloc had an absolute majority of sixty-one. The right wing, which had split up prior to the elections, dropped to only forty-three seats (thirty-two of the Likud, eight of Zomet,
and three of Moledet).[27] All of the religious parties together won sixteen seats,
six of them by Shas, which received almost 130,000 votes (4.9 percent of the qualified ballots). Yitzhak Rabin, the Labor Party's candidate for the office of prime
minister, invited two rival parties to join his coalition: secular Meretz, led by Shulamit Aloni, and *haredi* Shas, led by Arye Deri. Despite its severe rivalry with
Meretz, Shas opted for membership in the government, knowing full well that in
this way it would further shore up the economic foundations of its institutions.

Just before the formation of his government, Rabin sent a written obligation
to Rabbi Ovadia Yosef: "The Jewish heritage is what preserved the People of Israel throughout all of its wanderings and exiles, and I am obligated to safeguard
the mutual tie and relationship between the State of Israel and the heritage of Israel." He then went on to promise the spiritual mentor of Shas: "Preservation of
national unity mandates tolerance and the creation of conditions for living together in a spirit of mutual respect, and [this objective] will guide me in acting to
prevent polarization and anything that will offend the feelings of those faithful to
Judaism. I am aware, honored rabbi, of your sincere, deep-hearted concern for the
education of all Jewish children in the spirit of Jewish values, and I make my
solemn promise to you that the government and the Ministry of Education and
Culture will continue the policy of imparting these values in their entirety."[28]
However, Rabin and his government—particularly Shulamit Aloni, who served as
minister of education and culture—did not fulfill the promises given Rabbi Yosef.
Tolerance and mutual respect were not qualities that characterized the new coalition government. The very opposite was true—within a few months, polarization
between secular and religious Jews reached new heights, leading to many disputes
between them. This led, inter alia, to a situation in which Aloni, who did not hesitate to come out with anti-religious provocative statements, was forced to resign
from the Ministry of Education and Culture in May 1993. At the same time,
pressure was increasingly applied upon Prime Minister Rabin from the Left to fire

Minister of the Interior Deri because of the criminal investigation being conducted against him. Rabin, however, put off taking this step. His overriding objective at this time was to sign the Oslo Accords with the Palestinians in September 1993, and he feared that deposing Deri would make it difficult for him to win a majority vote in the Knesset on the Accords.

On 4 November 1995, about two years after the signing of the Oslo Accords, Rabin was assassinated by a right-wing extremist. Until the next elections, held about half a year later, Shimon Peres was Interim Prime Minister.

In the May 1996 elections, Israel for the first time went to the polls under a dual election system: direct election of the prime minister, with simultaneous elections to the Knesset based on proportional representation. Likud leader Benjamin Netanyahu and Labor Party leader Shimon Peres ran against each other in the direct elections for the office of prime minister. Netanyahu won with only a very small majority: 50.6 percent of the qualified ballots (his majority among Jewish voters only was much greater). The Likud won thirty-two Knesset seats. Shas made a surprising gain—influenced no doubt by a reaction to the criminal accusations leveled against its leader, Deri: 251,988 votes that accounted for 8.5 percent and gave the party ten seats in the Knesset. Prime Minister-elect Netanyahu realized that only with Shas in his coalition could he form a government having a majority (of 68 members) in the Knesset.[29]

Despite its majority, the Netanyahu government did not last out its term of office. Toward the end of 1998, it was obvious to all that its end was fast approaching. The two largest parties agreed to hold elections in May 1999. This time, the opponents in the direct elections for prime minister were Ehud Barak (who headed a bloc called Yisrael Ahat, "One Israel," made up of the domineering Labor Party and two smaller ones, Gesher and Meimad) and Benjamin Netanyahu (who was proclaimed to be the candidate of the Right). Barak won an overwhelming victory, receiving 56.08 percent of the qualified votes. The two large parties, however, lost much of their representation in the Knesset, with Yisrael Ahat receiving twenty-six seats and the Likud only nineteen. To the surprise of many "political experts" who had prophesied a decline for Shas, that party won seventeen seats, just two less than the Likud, which until the elections had been the ruling party. It is noteworthy that in 1999, about 430,000 persons voted for Shas, seven times more than it had received in the first elections in which it had participated. Various analyses of voting patterns have shown that 1 of every 4 Oriental Jews holding the franchise voted for Shas. Furthermore, in municipal elections also held that very year, Shas won some great victories, particularly in several development towns.[30]

Political analysts who have studied the rise of Shas' political power emphasize how, in the face of declining ideological commitment in the secular-liberal sectors of Israeli society, Shas raised the banners of a return to religion and nationalism.[31]

There is no doubt that Shas is restoring to its voters—the majority of whom are members of the Oriental ethnic communities—a renewed pride in their Sephardic heritage and a sense that they are now being compensated for what happened to their parents and families at the time of their immigration to Israel and during the process of their absorption into the new state.

CHAPTER 14

SUMMING UP:
ISRAEL—FROM "MELTING POT"
TO PLURALISTIC STATE

As we have seen throughout this book, during the first years of the State of Israel the socialist-Zionist ideology was predominant, with its main educational objective to forge a new "Jewish pioneer" type. The hegemony of the left wing also was obvious in the political sphere: a majority of the 120 members of the First Knesset belonged to the two large labor parties—forty-six to Mapai and nineteen to Mapam. In addition, there were also five Communist MKs. Until 1953, during Israel's first five years of existence, these two parties provided a system of labor-oriented education (in schools of the Workers Stream), and in all of these institutions they proudly flew the red flag (in most of them side by side with Israel's blue and white flag), especially on festive occasions. Despite differences of outlook within the leftist camp, these two parties shared a common utopian vision: to transform Israel into an egalitarian state of *halutzim* (pioneers). In their view, the kibbutz movement was exemplary, something to be emulated by all. The "kibbutznik" from the Valley of Jezreel (the region in which many of the first kibbutzim developed) was the ultimate model for the educational system. It is not by chance that the kibbutz movement, which in 1949 accounted for only 6 percent of the population of Israel, had twenty-six members in the First Knesset, more than four times its relative weight in the country.

It is noteworthy that leaders of Center and religious parties—and even some right-wing leaders—in effect accepted the socialist-Zionist vision. They, too, held in great esteem the agricultural settlements, their pioneering members, and those who lived along the borders of Israel and considered them "the salt of the earth."

Thus during the Knesset debate on the Military Service Law (September 1949), when Prime Minister Ben-Gurion proposed that all soldiers, male or female, be obligated to spend a year of service on a kibbutz or a *moshav* in order to enhance their "pioneering abilities,"[1] no member of the Knesset voted against that initiative. Only some of the religious MKs abstained, this in protest against the prime minister's intention to conscript women, as well as men. The pioneering vision—of which the "Everest, " to use Ben-Gurion's term, was the kibbutz movement—was, in effect, accepted by the vast majority of the young state's leaders. Exceptions to the rule were opponents on the fringes of society: the *haredim* (who were not counted as part of the Zionist *yishuv* and were thought to be *galutiim*—a derogative adjective indicating that they still thought and acted like oppressed Jews in the Diaspora), and some belonging to the right wing (and also were the target of disparaging epithets such as "bourgeoisie," "capitalists," "speculators," and more). Opponents of the dominating labor vision of society were, at most, 20 percent of the Jewish population. Their influence in politics and public life was insignificant.

In contrast, the State of Israel, half a century later, has become a state without one domineering vision. At the turn of the twenty-first century, various publics in Israel, belonging to diverse movements and political parties, have different dreams and often opposing aspirations. There are those who dream of "a state for its citizens," while others yearn for "a state based on *halakha*" (Jewish law); there are those who emphasize Oriental Jewish culture, while others prefer that of Russia or the United States; and there are those for whom Jerusalem (and the Temple Mount) and what it stands for is uppermost in their minds, while others prefer a "Tel Aviv lifestyle." Israeli society is split into subdivisions, and often relationships between these splinter groups and the mutual stereotypes they hold of the "others" lead to much tension.

The population of Israel in 2000 numbered about 6,400,000. Almost 5,000,000 were Jews, about 1,200,000 Arabs (mostly Muslims, but with minority groups of Christians, Druze, Cherkessians, and others), and another 200,000 or so who cannot be classified by religious affiliation, many new immigrants from the former Soviet Union. Sociologists tend to enumerate five rifts within Israeli society: (1) first and foremost is the rift between Jews and Arabs, one that has greatly intensified as a result of the ongoing conflict between Israel and the Palestinians; (2) between the poor and the rich, a rift that greatly expanded with the growing gap in income during the last two decades of the twentieth century; (3) between old-timers and new immigrants (in this case, referring to the million or so who immigrated during the last decade from the former Soviet Union and Ethiopia); (4) between *haredi*-religious communities and secular Jews; (5) between those who belong to the Oriental ethnic communities and those who originally came from Europe, or the descendants of these two groups. The problematics presented by these rifts are even more intense, because there is a high degree of correlation among the last four enumerated above, all of which apply only to the Jewish population of Israel.

The Frumkin Commission Report and my analysis of it point to the deepest roots of the last two of these rifts.

On the basis of the facts presented in this book, I would assert that in opposition to widely held conceptions—primarily among large groups of secular Israelis—conflicts between religious and secular Jews in Israel have not become more numerous during the past few years. Why, then, do so many feel that this is the deepest schism in Israeli society? It is my humble opinion that the major reason giving rise to a sense of frustration by the secular community is the fact that it is no longer the sole holder of power in Israeli society. For the past quarter of a century, secular hegemony, whether of the left or the right, is no longer exclusive; it is now conditioned. Since 1977, as we have seen, the religious-Zionists and the *haredim* can tip the balance of power. Furthermore, many secular Jews are pessimistic about the future. They sense that the increase in *haredi* strength—manifested in a much higher birthrate, which of itself means a growing percentage of *haredi* children in the educational system and adult voters in the electorate—will in a few years lead to the creation of a religious-fundamentalist state, in which basic issues will be decided by the "Torah sages."

It is difficult to deny the fears of the anxious in both camps. However, there is at least one bright spot in the developing reality of Israel: aggressive, anti-democratic processes of anti-religious coercion, such as that which occurred in the early years of statehood, the likes of which we have met throughout this book, are no longer possible today. The fiery Zionist "melting pot" that was intended to produce a monolithic Israeli public—and in the process left many scalding burns on the Israeli body politic—is no longer. The process of "Israelization" and the serious cases of anti-religious coercion described here, even though some were committed in good faith and with good intentions, are no longer possible.

Furthermore, the "democratic dictatorship" of one party and the dominance of one movement—under the charismatic leadership of David Ben-Gurion, who determined much of the course of events in Israel during its first two decades—are a thing of the past. Today, Israeli society is much more pluralistic, and the government is much less centralist. Moreover, Israel's legal system will today not permit cases of coercion such as were prevalent in the state's early years. The media, too, the defenders of democracy throughout the entire Western world, are much less dependent than in the past upon political parties and movements and are much more aggressive in cases in which civilian rights have been infringed upon.

The origins of another rift, between Ashkenazim and Sephardim in Israel, have been highlighted in this book. As I have shown, about 80 percent of the Jews in the Land of Israel were Ashkenazim prior to the establishment of Israel. As a result of the great waves of immigration of Jews from Oriental countries in the 1950s and 1960s, the latter today account for almost 50 percent of the Jewish population. I believe that without awareness of the difficult absorption processes documented here, especially those undergone by Oriental Jews, it is difficult to understand what lies behind the anger that many of them and their descendants still bear toward Ashkenazim in general and left-wing Ashkenazic politicians in particular. However, it also should be noted—in opposition to what is often stressed—that relationships between the two communities have greatly improved throughout the more than half a century of Israel's existence.

During the early years of the state, all of the democratic government frameworks were "Europe centered"[2]: there was an absolute majority of Ashkenazim in the Knesset, in the court system, and first and foremost in the government (with a scattering of a few representatives from the Oriental Jewish communities). Furthermore, when in the 1950s an Oriental Jew was made a member of the government, it was obvious to all that he would be appointed to the Ministry of Posts, or the Ministry of Police, commonly accepted as second-rate ministries. During the first two decades, it did not cross anyone's mind that a member of an Oriental Jewish community could be president of the State of Israel, or its prime minister, foreign minister, minister of the interior, minister of education and culture, or minister of defense. Moreover, in those years there were very few Oriental Jews among the upper echelons in academic institutions, in the army, in industrial and economic circles, or in any other elitist group. The few who were part of these leadership groups came mostly from old Sephardic families whose forefathers had emigrated to the Land of Israel decades and even centuries earlier. True, Ben-Gurion did like to say that he aspired to the day when there would be a "Yemenite [IDF] Chief of Staff," but it was universally believed that this was a far-off dream, and that even if it should come true some day, it would be in the very distant future.

Things have changed for the better, especially during the past three decades. At the turn of the millennium, the presidency of Israel, all government ministries (with the exception of the prime minister's office), the chief of staff, and other high posts have all been filled at one time or another by members of the Oriental Jewish communities. An appointment of an Oriental Jew to a leading position is so common that it is no longer unique. Today there are so many Oriental Jews in high positions in Israel that one does not even know their communal origins. One reason little attention is paid to ethnic origins is that among second- and third-generation Israelis, there is much "intermarriage" among various ethnic communities, so these couples and their children can no longer identify themselves along ethnic-communal lines. Almost half of the couples in the past few years have "intermarried."

Two political movements were the prime contributors to the constantly increasing integration of Oriental Jews into the highest levels of Israeli society. The first, in the 1960s and 1970s, was the Likud party; later, from the 1980s onward, the overriding influence in this direction was exerted by Shas. The process by which Israeli society freed itself from the hegemony of the Labor movement was closely connected to its parallel extrication from Europe-centered (i.e., Ashkenazic) domination. More and more Oriental Jews were elected to fill public office, at first on the municipal level (such as David Levy, Moshe Katzav, Meir Shitreet, David Magen, and others) and then on the senior national level, as members of the Knesset, government ministers, and even state president.

The meteoric rise of Shas greatly contributed to the influence wielded by the new Israeli leadership that emerged from the ranks of Oriental Jewry. These young public figures, especially those elected into office by Shas, have become quite prominent in Israeli society. At least part of the Israeli public is not at ease with a situation in which fateful decisions are entrusted to these leaders, some of whom suddenly appeared on the scene without their merit having been tested in previous positions of responsibility. Furthermore, this sector of the public cannot see how democracy can be maintained when one of Shas' attributes is blind obedience to the instructions of Rabbi Ovadia Yosef.

This book has described a period in the history of the State of Israel in which there was an intensive attempt to create educational and cultural uniformity, as the Frumkin Commission Report has clearly shown. That attempt, as we have seen, has failed (at least in part). Contemporary reality is exactly the opposite: cultural pluralism has obviously won the day. Today, the questions asked are: What is common to the various sectors that comprise Israeli society? What is the minimum of uniform values that should be imparted to those diverse sectors? In recent years, immigrants are no longer required to adopt Hebrew names, to speak Hebrew with an "Israeli" accent, to dress in an "Israeli" fashion, to read a Hebrew newspaper, to study Zionist history, and more.[3] Moreover, even the laws enacted by the Knesset, which stipulate that all educational systems that receive financial support from the state must have a minimum of "Israeli content," are not enforced. The political strength of minority groups deters the majority from trying to force upon them minimal cultural values such as one language, a common historical infrastructure, and so on. What will happen to the Israeli infrastructure?

It is my opinion that the conclusion that Israeli society must draw from "the melting pot days" should not be headlong flight in the exact opposite direction—toward educational systems that do not have a minimum in common. The lesson to be learned from the extreme "pressure cooker" of the 1950s must not be "every man unto himself." Israeli society should not only see to the needs of the individuals and minority groups that comprise it, it also must care for what holds it together.

The difficult issue facing Israel in the sphere of education and culture, as well as in other areas, is how, as much as possible, to take the middle road. The problem, in other words, is how to combine what outwardly seem to be opposites: education to Zionist ideals with favorable sentiments toward the Diaspora and the heritage of the Diaspora; encouragement of "Israelism" with a positive relationship to ethnic roots; promotion of modern, Western values with an attitude of respect toward religion; and encouragement of scientific thinking with study of the traditions of the past.

At the outset of the twenty-first century, the State of Israel must repeatedly ask itself how it can put into practice, in a contemporary, educational-cultural milieu, the dialectic saying of Rabbi Nahman of Braslav: "I traverse a very ancient path, yet— and at the very same time—I am treading along a completely new road."

NOTES

NOTES TO INTRODUCTION

1. I will be using this word throughout the book to refer to the prime minister and his ministers, who together form "the government." The term cabinet has in recent decades been used in Israel to designate a smaller body, comprising a few members of the government, and generally dealing only with security matters.

2. See Ben-Gurion's remarks at a meeting of the Mapai faction in the Knesset, along with additional members of Mapai, 26 January 1950, MA. The citations from the writ of appointment are from the opening page of the Frumkin Commission Report. All references to this report are to the original mimeographed version, which is available only in archives. The relevant page numbers in the text of the report are given, followed by page numbers (in square brackets) of the English translation in the present volume.

3. Deleted is an appended study by Izhak Ben-Zvi, a member of the Commission, on the Oriental Jewish communities, which is today outdated.

4. Quotations are from chapter 6 of the Frumkin Commission Report.

5. See *Eleven Years of Absorption...* (Tel Aviv: Division for Publications and Statistics of the Absorption Department of the Jewish Agency for Israel, 1959), 7.

6. According to the testimony of Dr. Giora Josephtal, head of the Absorption Department of the Jewish Agency, in January 1950, 76 percent of the inhabitants of the camps belonged to the Oriental communities, and it was anticipated that this percentage would increase. See Meeting of Mapai Knesset Faction, 26 January 1950, MA.

7. *Ha'aretz*, December 1996–January 1997.

Notes to Chapter 1

1. Tuvia Friling argues that it was believed then that it would be possible to save thousands of children—and there were even some who thought that tens of thousands could be rescued in this manner. See T. Friling, "David Ben Gurion...," Ph.D. dissertation, Hebrew University of Jerusalem, 1990, 78.

2. Minutes of Mapai Executive Committee, 9 December 1942, MA.

3. Ibid., 23 December 1942.

4. See *Ha'aretz*, 19 February 1943.

5. Details of the institutions to which the children were transferred are in B. Z. Tomer, *Red and White...* (Jerusalem: Hasifriyya Hatzionit, 1972).

6. Jewish Agency Executive, 7 December 1942 and 17 January 1943, CZA; cf. Friling, "David Ben-Gurion," 80. Pressure was brought to bear through the Polish government-in-exile in London and the British Mandatory government.

7. Report of the Committee to Clarify Complaints Regarding the Care of Refugees and Children in Teheran, CZA, S26/1243. The report contains handwritten emendations of the sharper formulations of the committee. Cf. *Davar*, 17 August 1943.

8. According to *Davar*, which summarized "a precis of a comprehensive report submitted by Miss Henrietta Szold to the Jewish Agency Executive regarding the Teheran Children," 19 May 1943.

9. This information was attributed to Henrietta Szold in *Davar*, 11 June 1943.

10. Concerning tension over this issue within the religious public see Geula Bat-Yehuda, *The Life and Times of Rabbi Maimon* (Jerusalem: Mossad Harav Kook, 1979), 492–93; M. Schoenfeld, ed., *The Teheran Children Accuse* (Jerusalem: Agudat Israel, 1943); Ada Schein, "The Incident of the 'Teheran Children,'" Master's thesis, Hebrew University of Jerusalem, 1991, 217 ff.

11. Friling, "David Ben-Gurion," 93–96; cf. M. Friedman, "The Chronicle of the Status-Quo," in *Transition from "Yishuv" to State* (Haifa: Haifa University, 1990), 54.

12. *Davar*, 19 May 1943; M. Schoenfeld of Agudat Israel argues that only 32 children "were sent . . . to Torah institutions," Schoenfeld, *The Teheran Children Accuse*, unnumbered opening pages.

13. *Hatzofe*, 20 May 1943.

14. Ibid.

15. Friling, "David Ben-Gurion," 95–96.

16. Records of meetings of Ben-Gurion, Gruenbaum, and Kaplan with Chief Rabbis Herzog and Ouziel, 24 June 1943, BGA.

17. Correspondence Files, 2 July 1943, BGA.

18. Records of meetings: Ben Gurion's remarks at the meeting with the Chief Rabbis, 24 June 1943, BGA.

19. Records of meetings, 26 June 1943, BGA.

20. A. Surasky, *History of Religious Education* . . . (Bnai Brak: Or Hahayyim, 1967), 169. This, of course, is just one example of many.

21. Ibid.

22. Ibid.,166.

23. Leib Yaffe, a friend of Shmuel Yavnieli (who was instrumental in bringing Yemenite immigrants in 1912) wrote to him in that year: "Greetings to you from the Yemenites who came to us thanks to your influence . . . . The farm at Kinneret left a harsh impression upon the Yemenites, for they are unable to comprehend Judaism without religious practices. This reality destroyed their vision of the Land of Israel." M. Tabib relates that when one asked a Yemenite: "Are you already a pioneer?" the sense of the question was "Have you already abandoned religion?" These examples are from Y. Tzurieli, *Education and Society* . . . (Jerusalem: Academon, 1990), 3–7.

24. From Yemen, 236 immigrants arrived in 1942; 2,419 in 1943; and 1,788 in 1944. See D. Levitan, "The Immigration of Yemenite Jews ...," *Afikim* 95–96 (September 1990): 39–48.

25. Editorial in *Hatzofe*, 15 February 1944.

26. *Kol Yisrael*, 11 November 1943.

27. *Hatzofe*, 25 January 1944.

28. *Kol Yisrael*, 27 January 1944.

29. *Hatzofe*, 10 February 1944, "Inquisition" will be encountered again, with greater intensity, in the late 1940s.

30. Ibid.

31. Ibid., 15 February 1944.

32. *Kol Yisrael*, 17 February 1944.

33. *Hatzofe*, 24 February 1944.

34. *Kol Yisrael*, 24 February 1944.

35. Referring to Yemenite immigrant children who were brought to Kibbutz Alonim, *Hatzofe*, 1 March 1944.

36. Ibid., 2 March 1944.

37. *Kol Yisrael*, 9 March 1944.

38. Ben-Gurion's Office Files, CZA, S44/297.

39. Ben-Gurion to Rabbi Berlin, 12 April 1944, Correspondence Files, BGA.

40. Z. Maimon to Y. Rabinowitz, 12 April 1944, Ben-Gurion's Office Files, CZA, S44/297.

41. CZA, S6/1472.

42. H. Zadok, *Out of Distress* . . . (Tel Aviv: [the author], 1990), 525.

NOTES TO CHAPTER 2

1. Figures from U. O. Schmelz, "Mass Immigration . . .", *Pe'amim* 39 (1989): 21.

2. M. Sicron, "Mass Immigration . . .", in *Immigrants and Transit Camps* (Jerusalem: Yad Izhak Ben-Zvi, 1986), 31ff.

3. See *Israel Government Yearbook, 1950* (Jerusalem: Government Printer, 1950), 305.

4. For the definition of this concept, see Hanna Yablonka, "The Absorption of Holocaust Survivors . . .", Introduction, Ph.D. dissertation, Hebrew University of Jerusalem, 1990.

5. Schmelz, "Mass Immigration": 21.

6. Meeting of Mapai Knesset Faction, 26 January 1950, MA.

7. Schmelz, "Mass Immigration": 29.

8. It is impossible to supply exact figures, due to the haphazard nature of statistical recording in those days. The minister of education and culture himself admitted as much at the meeting of the Mapai Knesset Faction on 5 July 1949, when he said: "To this day there are no decent statistics in Israel. Among all areas of state activity, what is most deficient among us is statistics." See MA.

9. Ministry of Education, ISA796/*Gimel*, File 1215.

10. L. Eshkol, *In the Agonies of Settlement* (Tel Aviv: Am Oved, 1962), 223.

NOTES TO CHAPTER 3

1. For details, see *Survey of Immigration* . . . (Jerusalem: Jewish Agency, 1950), 32. This was a report submitted by the Immigration Department of the Jewish Agency to its General Council. In November 1948, permission was granted for the immigration of 5,500 Jews from Yemen who had been kept in a camp in Aden since 1945, and their transfer to Israel was completed by March 1949. In May 1949 the Imam of Yemen allowed all Jews living in his country to leave. See *Report Submitted to the 23rd Zionist Congress* (Hebrew; Jerusalem: Jewish Agency, 1951), 191, 208–09; Schmelz, "Mass Immigration": 23.

2. See, for example, H. Lufban, *A Man Goes Out to His Brethren* (Tel Aviv: Am Oved, 1967), 153: "They are apathetic to bread and are thirsting for religious teachings." Or, for another example, I. Yeshayahu, *Alone and Together* . . . (Tel Aviv: The Center for Culture and Education of the Histadrut, 1990), 176: "They not only observe the tradition and the religious commandments but also spend much time contemplating Torah, when they go and come, when they sit and walk about, so that at times they are more absorbed with matters of the spirit than they are with material matters and daily life."

3. Giora Josephtal, at the meeting of the Mapai Knesset Faction, 26 January 1950, MA.

4. Yeshayahu, *Alone and Together* . . ., 174.

5. For details of the waves of immigration from Yemen from the late nineteenth century on and their impact upon the Yishuv, see D. Levitan, "The Magic Carpet . . .," Master's thesis, Bar-Ilan University, Ramat Gan, 1983, passim; see also: M. Sicron, *Immigration to Israel 1948–1953* (Jerusalem: The Falk Institute, 1957), 14–20.

6. Giora Josephtal told the Mapai Council, which convened on 21–22 May 1949, that "There are among them [the non-Ashkenazic immigrants] certain sectors, who already have their own active leaders, such as for example the Yemenites and the Bulgarians." See MA.

7. Ben-Gurion's preference for Yemenite immigrants is well known. Note the advice he was given by his colleagues when visiting army bases—to inquire about members of other ethnic communities as well, and not only Yemenites: "Ben-Gurion's confidants pointed out to him that he must cease in this, because he was arousing jealousy . . . . He altered slightly the formulation of the question, and would ask 'Who here is not an Ashkenazi?'. . . But it was patently clear that he was looking for Yemenites." Oral testimony of Israel Yeshayahu, 8 February 1978, BGRC. For Josephtal's attitude, see Lufban, *A Man Goes Out . . .*, 142–43: "Giora . . . holds a special affection for the Yemenite immigration which steadily increases the deeper his acquaintance with it." On the general attitude of admiration and respect for the Yemenite community see Y. Press, *Ethnic-Communal Relations in Israel* (Tel Aviv: Sifriat Po'alim, 1976), 54–56.

8. On this subject, see Vicki Shiran (Ben-Nathan), "The Damning Label . . .," Master's thesis, Tel Aviv University, 1978, 103–05.

9. For a discussion of the Yemenite lists to the Elected Assembly and the Knesset, see Hanna Herzog, *Political Ethnicity . . .* (Efal: Yad Tabenkin, 1986), 34–75.

10. See the meeting of the Mapai Secretariat on 4 May 1950, MA. The minutes of the Mapai Bureau meeting of 26 April 1950 note that the number of members to be "jumped over" was only fourteen. See also MA.

11. The letter is evidently from 26 December 1949, ISA, Prime Minister's Office, 5543/3631/*Gimel*. A copy is in the Yemenite Immigrants file, ARZBI. Incidentally, Rabbi Yitzhari later left Hapoel Hamizrachi, complaining that the religious party disdained him and other members of his community. See Herzog, *Political Ethnicity*, 63.

12. *Knesset Debates*, vol. II, 1041–42, session of 18 July 1949.

13. There are, of course, many testimonies relating to the religiosity of the Jews of Libya. One of the most interesting written ones is the diary of a training camp (*hakhshara*) of Hakibbutz Hameuhad in Tripoli compiled by Y. Guetta. It contains many passages reflecting the attempts by members of the *hakhshara* to counter rumors in the city to the effect that they were not religious—rumors that threatened the very existence of the camp. See B. Z. Rubin, ed., *Echoes from the Diary* (Jerusalem: Association for the Heritage of Libyan Jewry, 1988), esp. pp. 142, 144, and 152 .On religious education in Libya and the beginnings of secularization and modernization, see Sh. Sela, *Education among the Jewish Communities of Libya* (Nahalal: Yad Eliezer Yaffe, 1987); Y. Arnon, "The 'Hehalutz' Movement in Tripoli . . .," *Pe'amim* 44 (Summer 1990): 132–57.

14. According to B. Duvdevani, "Chapters in the Aliyah of Libyan Jewry," in *Libyan Jewry . . .* (Tel Aviv: Committee of Libyan Communities in Israel, 1960), 310.

15. A. Raccah, ed., *From an Ancient Diaspora* (Tel Aviv: Association of Libyan Immigrants in Israel, 1983), 36.

16. Duvdevani, "Aliyah of Libyan Jewry," 310.

17. On this periodical, see Raccah, *From an Ancient Diaspora*, 188.

18. *Hayyenu* (Tripoli), 1: 5 (23 September 1949). A copy is in RKA.

19. *Hayyenu* 23 (26 January 1950).

20. Maimon was the only Oriental Jew to speak. There were 200 delegates to this convention, of whom only 10 percent were from Oriental countries. See *Report of the World Assembly of Mizrachi, Jerusalem 19–26 Av 5709* (Tel Aviv: Hamizrachi, 1950), 218–19.

21. Ibid., 109–10.

22. J. Maimon, "Representatives . . . ," in *Libyan Jewry . . .* (Tel Aviv: Committee of Libyan Communities in Israel, 1960), 166.

23. Ashkenazim accounted about 80 percent of the population in 1943, as were 90.4 percent of Histadrut members. See Y. Weitz, "The Attitude of Mapai . . . ," Ph.D. dissertation, Hebrew University of Jerusalem, 1988, ch. 5.

24. Schmelz, "Mass Immigration": 20.

25. The first article was published on 13 April 1949. The seventh (22 April 1949) particularly disparaged immigrants from North Africa.

26. *Ha'aretz*, 22 April 1949.

27. Ibid., 16 May 1949.

28. *Davar*, 24 June 1949.

29. ARZMHK, Education File 10/2, 1949.

30. Ibid. The letter is dated 30 December 1948.

31. According to the extant documentation, non-Zionist religious circles were even less aware of the problem until mid-1949 than were Hamizrachi circles.

32. The original letter and copies are in ARZMHK, Education File 10/2, Protocols, 5710–5711.

33. See E. Don-Yehiya, "Cooperation and Conflict between Political Camps . . . ," Ph.D. dissertation, Hebrew University of Jerusalem, 1977, 512.

34. See, e.g., M. Unna, *By Separate Paths . . .* (Alon Shevut: Yad Shapira, 1984), 136.

35. Ya'akov Yehoshua, "Shekhunot ha-Temanim," *Bama'aracha* 171 (April 1975): 10–11, 26. Cf. what Moshe Natan, a Yemenite Jew from the Ezra-Ubitzaron neighborhood in Rishon Lezion, wrote on 21 November 1950 during the municipal election campaign: "The responsibility for this [i.e., the lack of interest in the religious parties among the Yemenite immigrants] lies with the rabbinic leadership of Orthodox Jewry . . . . Had they immediately respected them and brought them into their ranks, and had their rabbis and ritual slaughterers appointed [Yemenite] rabbis and ritual slaughterers out of affection and respect, and had they not been concerned 'lest they multiply,' there would be no need today for agitation." See ARZMHK, File on Yemenite Immigrants.

36. See Tzurieli, *Education and Society*, esp. p. 75 ff.

37. A. Tabib, *Explanations to the North Africans . . .* (Tel Aviv: Center of the Association of Yemenites in the Land of Israel, 1944), 4–5; cf. Levitan, "Magic Carpet ."

38. H. Zadok, *The Yemenite Burden 1946–1951* (Holon: [the author], 1985), 151, 210. See also the letter addressed to the Central Committee of Hapoel Hamizrachi, *Get Piturin* ("Writ of Divorce"). The letter was written by 70 to 80 families from Be'er Yaakov on 26 December 1949, complaining that they were "set apart and discriminated against" by the religious parties. This and similar letters by Yemenite immigrants, complaining that the religious parties did not help them even regarding their most elementary religious needs, such as Torah scrolls, are in ARZMHK, File of Yemenite Immigrants.

39. Herzog, *Political Ethnicity*, 63.

40. Minutes of the Zionist Executive, 10 April 1949, CZA.

41. Ibid., 29 April 1949.

42. *She'arim*, 31 August 1950.

43. Based on N. Nardi, ed., *Education and Culture Annual 5711* (Jerusalem: Ministry of Education and Culture, 1952), 42.

44. *Hakol*, 31 July 1949.

45. *Report of the 18th World Convention of Hamizrachi*, 207, ARZMHK, Education File 10/2, 1949.

46. On this, see Don-Yehiya, "Cooperation and Conflict," 620.

47. ARZMHK, Education File 10/2, 1949. The four were Minister Y. M. Levin and Knesset members D. Z. Pinkas, D. Levenstein, and Z. Warhaftig.

48. Ibid.

49. *Hakol*, 27 September 1949.

50. *Hatzofe*, 25 October 1949.

51. The convention was held on 5–12 Heshvan 5710 (28 October– 4 November 1949). A protocol of the resolutions adopted is in LMA, IV424, File 2.

52. Don-Yehiya, "Cooperation and Conflict," 617.

53. Ibid., 620.

54. Minutes of the World Center of Hamizrachi, no. 22, ARZMHK.

55. See D. Tidhar, *Encyclopedia of the Pioneers and Builders of the Yishuv*, vol. XII (Tel Aviv: D. Tidhar, 1962), 4051.

56. Correspondence File, 9 December 1949, BGA; cf. *Hatzofe*, 14 December 1949.

57. For the personality and activity of Pinkas, see *The Minister Rabbi David Zvi Pinkas of Blessed Memory: The Second Anniversary of His Death* (Tel Aviv: The National Center of Hamizrachi, [1955]); cf. Unna, *By Separate Paths*, 218; Y. Rafael, *Not Easily Came the Light* (Jerusalem: Edanim, 1981), 177 .

58. Frumkin Commission Report, 19 [p. 205 in this volume].

59. Ibid., 19–20 [205–06].

60. Meetings of the Knesset Education Committee, 23 and 30 November; 7 December 1949.

61. Correspondence File, 14 December 1949, BGA.

62. That very month the government was greatly involved in other cardinal issues, both in Israel's relations with other countries and among the members of the government themselves. One of the most difficult of these was whether to transfer the seat of government, including the Knesset, to Jerusalem.This decision deliberately preceded the United Nations resolution of 7 December 1949 calling for the internationalization of Jerusalem. The policy adopted by Israel was not to the liking of Foreign Minister Moshe Sharett, who submitted his resignation to Ben-Gurion on 14 December 1949, withdrawing it at Ben-Gurion's urging. See Yemima Rosenthal, ed. *Documents on the Foreign Policy of Israel, May–December 1949* (Jerusalem: Israel State Archives, 1986), document 494, p. 726. See also U. Bialer, "Jerusalem 1949," *Cathedra* 35 (April 1985): 163–91; I. Pappé, "The Lausanne Conference," *Iyunim Bitkumat Israel* 1 (1991): 241–61.

63. Quoted from the Frumkin Commision Report, 21–22 [207–08].

64. Ibid., 23 [208–09].

65. ISA, *Het*/1208.

66. *Hakol*, 30 November 1949.

67. Ibid.

68. Ibid.

69. Ibid., 4 December 1949.

70. *She'arim*, 8 December 1949.

71. Quotation from Frumkin Commission Report, 96 [270–71].

72. Ibid., 5 [194].

73. *Ma'ariv*, January 25, 1950.

74. Correspondence File for February 1950, BGA. Most of the telegrams were composed in Hebrew in Latin characters.

75. Ibid., 1 February 1950.

76. Ibid. This telegram, dated 4 February 1950, is in English.

77. Frumkin Commission Report, 24 [210].

NOTES TO CHAPTER 4

1. This can be construed from what Minister of Education and Culture Zalman Shazar told the executive of the Mapai Knesset faction on 24 January 1950: "The commission was proposed by him [Ben-Gurion] alone, without consulting the government." See MA.

2. In a parliamentary query submitted by MK Aharon Zisling to the minister of justice following the presentation of the commission's conclusions, he complained regarding the formulation on p. 6 [195] of the Frumkin Commission Report: "Former Supreme Court Justice Gad Frumkin was appointed chairman of the commission." Among other things, Zisling complained, that "The use of this title [former Supreme Court Justice] is misleading . . . when one is in fact referring to membership in the high court of a foreign power and administration which were done away with by the War of Independence." Justice Minister Pinhas Rosen rejected this accusation. *Knesset Debates*, vol. VI, 2449–50, session of 7 August 1950.

3. Ben-Gurion to Frumkin, 30 August 1949, Correspondence Files, BGA. The letter was the final outcome of a committee charged with verifying certain accusations leveled against Frumkin. In the wake of those accusations, Justice Minister Rosen decided not to appoint him to the Supreme Court during the period of transition from British Mandate rule to the State of Israel. The committee members were Izhak Ben-Zvi, Ben-Zion Dinaburg (later Dinur), and Rabbi Meir Bar-Ilan (who died toward the end of the committee's deliberations). For documents connected to the committee see CZA, A116/174I, A116/90I.

4. On the appointment of the commission, see *The Palestine Gazette* 68 (1 June 1922): 7. A copy of the commission's report is in the personal archives of Gad Frumkin, CZA, A199/21.

5. CZA, A199/55.

6. BGRC, Department of Oral Documentation, interview conducted on 8 February 1978.

7. See, for example, Tzurieli, *Education and Society*, 43, on Ben-Zvi's assistance to Yemenite Jews who requested that their children be educated in accordance with that community's traditions.

8. Ben-Zvi was well known for his positive attitude toward religious tradition. Thus, for example, at a meeting of Mapai's Political Committee on 21 November 1950, at which the composition of the coalition in the Jerusalem Municipality was discussed, Pinhas Lavon proposed giving the mayorality to the religious parties. He enumerated the religious persons who had been chosen to the Municipal Council, describing Ben-Zvi as "semi-traditional." See MA.

9. Meeting of Mapai Knesset faction, 26 January 1950, MA.

10. Bechor Shalom Shitrit (see Biographies at the end of this book).

11. Z. Shazar at the meeting of the Mapai Knesset faction, 24 January 1950, MA.

12. See S. Barad, *History of the Zionist Movement in Tunisia* (Efal: Yad Tabenkin, 1980), 18.

13. Meeting of Mapai Knesset faction, 26 January 1950, MA.

14. See Herzog, *Political Ethnicity*, 104–08.

15. See A. Elmaleh, "Yihya Tzaram of Blessed Memory," in *Harel* . . . (Tel Aviv: [no publisher], 1962), 243 ff.

16. ISA, 7263/33/5/*Gimel.*

17. Israel Guri at the meeting of the Mapai Knesset faction, 16 January 1950, MA.

18. Records of the Frumkin Commission, first session, 25 January 1950, CZA A116/164I.

19. On 27 July 1950, on the eve of elections to the Second Knesset, *She'arim* devoted an article to the personality and biography of Kalman Kahana, describing him inter alia as "a kibbutz member who is related to and involved with nature and the land."

20. Y. Shavit et al., eds., *Lexicon of Personalities of Eretz Israel 1799–1948* (Tel Aviv: Am Oved, 1983), 268.

21. Interview with K. Kahana, 7 September 1990, copy deposited at YBZ.

22. Records of the Frumkin Commission, session of 27 February 1950, CZA, A116/164I.

23. BGRC, Department of Oral Documentation, interview conducted on 8 February 1978.

24. In the interview conducted on 7 September 1990, Kalman Kahana said: "By the appointment of Israel Yeshayahu, it was intended that he would be able to dominate the Yemenite community with regard to the commission's findings."

25. ISA, Prime Minister's Office, 5543/3631III/*Gimel.*

26. Ibid.

27. CZA, A199/23.

28. Meeting of the executive of the Mapai Knesset faction, 24 January 1950, MA.

29. Meeting of the Mapai Knesset faction, 26 January 1950, MA.

NOTES TO CHAPTER 5

1. Nathan Yanai emphasizes the consolidation of Ben-Gurion's national status with the establishment of the state. See his *Political Crises in Israel* (Jerusalem: Keter, 1982), esp. p. 55.

2. Y. Gorny, "From Zionist Ideology to Zionist Vision . . . ," in *Transition and Change* . . . (Jerusalem: Zalman Shazar Center, 1988), 336.

3. On the Gadna, see D. Dayan, *Yes, We are Youth!: The Story of the Gadna* (Tel Aviv: Ministry of Defense Pub. House, 1977); on the concept of a state youth movement, see Y. Nishri, "Plans for a State Youth Movement" in *The Youth Movements* . . . (Jerusalem: Yad Izhak Ben-Zvi, 1989), 205–10.

4. Ben-Gurion Diary, 3 April 1947, BGA.

5. D. Ben-Gurion, *Vision and Path*, vol. I (Tel Aviv: Mapai, 1951), 38–39.

6. Correspondence File, 9 January 1949, BGA.

7. "Comments by Authors at a Meeting Convened by the Prime Minister, March 27, 1949," Meetings File, BGA.

8. Meeting of the Mapai Central Committee with the Knesset faction, 23 July 1949, MA.

9. The record of this consultation—which I have been unable to find in the archives—was given to me by Professor Yaacov Shavit of Tel Aviv University, to whom I am most grateful.

10. D. Ben-Gurion, "Uniqueness and Destiny," Introduction to *Israel Government Year Book, 5711, [1950/51]* (Jerusalem: Government Printer, 1951), vii–xxx; cf. also D. Ben-Gurion, *Stars and Dust* (Ramat Gan: Masada, 1976), 26.

11. In addressing the Knesset, Ben-Gurion stated quite simply: "Throwing off religious beliefs is imbued in man's spirit." *Knesset Debates*, vol. VII, 36, session of 17 October 1950.

12. D. Ben-Gurion, *From Class to Nation* (Tel Aviv: Am Oved, 1974), 62.

13. D. Ben-Gurion, "Uniqueness and Destiny," in *Vision and Path*, vol. II, 41.

14. On this subject see I. Kolatt, "Ben-Gurion and his Generation," *Skirah Hodshit* 34:1 (March 1987), esp. the section "Ben-Gurion's Statist Approach."

15. Ben-Gurion's statism has been the subject of much study. Some went so far as to accuse him of tending to Bolshevism. See, for example, A. Shapira, "Berl, Tabenkin, and Ben-Gurion," *Zemanim* 27–28 (spring 1988): 80–97. Others are more cautious about using this label, such as Y. Gorny, "The Historical Roots . . . ," in *David Ben-Gurion As a Labor Leader* (Tel Aviv: Am Oved, 1988), 88–89. I would accept the formulation of M. Lissak "The Creation of Organizational Frameworks . . . ," in *David Ben-Gurion As a Labor Leader* (Tel Aviv: Am Oved, 1988), 117: "During the 1950s . . . his intellectual climate was characterized by statist tendencies"; cf. P. Y. Medding, "Ben-Gurion: Democratic Political Leadership and Statism," *Yahadut Zemanenu* 5 (1989): 25–49; see also N. Yanai, "Ben-Gurion's Concept of *Mamlahtiut*," *Jewish Political Studies Review* 1 (1989): 151–77. The latter two claim that Ben-Gurion distanced himself from the statist approach.

16. In 1949 there were 26 Knesset Members from Mapai, Mapam, and Ahdut Ha'avodah who were members of kibbutzim. See B. Kanari, "The Kibbutz Movement . . . ," in *Transition . . .* (Haifa: Haifa University, 1990), 187–97.

17. Meeting of Mapai members with Ben-Gurion in the Prime Minister's Office, 8 April 1949, MA.

18. Meeting of Mapai Knesset faction, 26 January 1950, MA.

19. Shapira, "Berl, Tabenkin and Ben-Gurion": 96; cf. Y. Gorny, "The Utopian Starting Point . . . ," *Mibifnim* 49 (1987–88), esp. pp. 263–65.

20. His remarks made on 8 April 1949, published in Ben-Gurion, *Vision and Path*, vol. II, 98.

21. Meetings File, 27 March 1949, BGA. For the elitist approach toward the immigrants as expressed in Ben-Gurion's meetings with writers, see M. Keren, *Ben-Gurion and the Intellectuals . . .* (DeKalb, Ill.: Northwestern Illinois University Press, 1983), 124–26.

22. Lissak "The Creation of Organizational Frameworks," 114.

23. Ben-Gurion Diary, 23 September 1949, BGA.

24. Ben-Gurion, *Vision and Path*, vol. II, 181. See also his remarks addressed to "pioneers in the Western countries," ibid., 277–80.

25. Ben-Gurion to Yigael Yadin, 27 November 1950, Correspondence File, BGA.

26. Ibid.

27. Ben-Gurion's formula was as follows: "For myself, the donning of phylacteries seems extraneous, but for him—for that Jew who has just arrived—it is one of his principles. . . . We need to relate . . . to phylacteries with respect." Meeting of Mapai Knesset faction, 26 January 1950, MA.

28. Ibid.

29. Ibid.

30. Meeting of Mapai Knesset faction and others, 19 February 1950, MA.

31. Dr. Yosef Burg, in an interview conducted on 15 March 1991, claimed that Ben-Gurion told him: "You are Catholics. The Oriental communities are Protestants." See YBZ.

32. Meeting of Mapai Knesset faction, 26 January 1950, MA.

33. Amka became "a symbol of the state and its governmental regime"—thus a headline in *Hakol*, 2 June 1950. The writer even suggests that the symbol of the state be "a picture of an abandoned village, underneath which is written the word Amka." See also *Hatzofe*, 10 May 1950; *Haboker*, 8 June 1950.

34. *Knesset Debates*, vol. V, 1723, session of 14 August 1950.

35. Meeting of Mapai Secretariat, 1 June 1950, MA.

36. *Knesset Debates*, vol. V, 1723, session of 14 August 1950.

37. Meeting of Mapai Political Committee, 31 December 1950, MA.

38. See E. Sprinzak, *Everyone Does As He Sees Fit* (Tel Aviv: Sifriat Po'alim, 1986), esp. p. 80 on the nonlegalism of the 1950s.

39. See M. Michalson, *The Nahal* (The IDF in its Strength: Encyclopedia of the Armed Forces and Defense, vol. IV) (Tel Aviv: Reshafim, 1981), 26, about a special course for commanders in which 140 immigrants from Yemen participated. See also *Maslul: A Weekly for Yemenite and Oriental Immigrants* 1:14 (26 July 1951), which reports about a meeting of 120 Yemenite leaders with Ben-Gurion. At that meeting, "he expressed his sorrow that there are no Yemenite commanders in the IDF, and besought all the members of the delegation to assist in finding suitable youngsters to participate in appropriate officer training courses."

40. Meeting of Mapai Secretariat, 1 June 1950, MA.

41. D. Ben-Gurion, *The Restored State of Israel*, vol. I (Tel Aviv: Am Oved, 1969), 432–33.

NOTES TO CHAPTER 6

1. All quotes are from an article published in Mapam's daily newspaper, "The Life of the State and the Laws of Religion" (Hebrew), *Al Hamishmar*, 28 January 1949.

2. Y. Bankover, in his introductory remarks to the Mapam Council, 5–6 March 1950, AHH, Section 13/*Yod*, Container 3, File 4.

3. Decisions of the Mapam Council, 25–28 November 1949, GHA, *Kaf*-290, File 2.

4. Bankover (above, n. 2).

5. See, for example, the report of Menahem (no family name given) concerning efforts among the Oriental communities, presented to a meeting of the Mapam Secretariat on 2 January 1950, AHH, Section *Yod*, Container 1, File 6.

6. Meeting of the secretariat of *Hakibbutz Ha'artzi*,* 5 May 1950, GHA.

7. In a similar context see Y. Douer, "The Development of the Gordonia-Maccabi Hatzair Movement . . . ," in *The Gordonia Movement in Tunisia* (Ramat Efal: Yad Tabenkin, 1990), 67, who warned his colleagues in the kibbutz movement that one must honor one's obligations regarding religious matters: "I heard of the bitter experience and of the failures of the Dror movement, which promised members of its *gar'inim* [settlement groups] that it would fulfill these two needs [Sabbath observance and kosher food] and did not honor the commitments."

8. See minutes of the meetings of the Political Committee of Mapam on 19 and 26 January 1950, GHA, 66.90 (A).

9. Remarks by Y. Bankover, Mapam Council, 5–6 March 1950, AHH, Section 13/*Yod*, Container 3, File 4.

10. Remarks of M. Ya'ari, ibid.

11. These claims were made notwithstanding the fact that the majority of children in those days studied in schools that were affiliated with the Right or the Center. During the 1948/49 school year the General Stream—which was associated with the Right and the Center, especially with the General Zionists—accounted for 43.8 percent of all of the pupils in Israel. At that same time, the Workers Stream—supported by the Left—had only 29.3 percent of the pupils, while the Hamizrachi Stream had 20.9 percent and Agudat Israel, 5.5 percent. Within two years the relative strength of the two largest streams was completely reversed: in 1950/51 the General Stream became the second largest, with 32.7 percent of the pupils, while 37.3 percent of them were enrolled in schools of the Workers Stream. These data are based upon N. Nardi, ed., *The Education and Culture Annual 5711*, 214.

12. On the relative strength of these parties during the early days of the state, see P. Y. Medding, *The Founding of Israeli Democracy* (New York: Oxford University Press, 1990), 241.

13. *Debates of the Provisional State Council*, vol. II, session of 15 December 1948.

14. Ibid., session of 23 December 1948.

15. *Ha'aretz*, 26 July 1949.

16. *Knesset Debates*, vol. II, 1153, session of 26 July 1949.

17. Ibid., 1659, session of 12 September 1949.

18. Editorial in *Herut*, 19 September 1949.

19. See, for example, the proposal of Y. Shapira, *Ha'aretz*, 19 October 1949.

20. *Knesset Debates*, vol. VI, 888, session of 28 February 1950.

21. *Herut*, 7 March 1950.

22. See, for example, a report in *Herut*, 13 February 1950, of "terrible kidnappings and use of force" in the educational system, consisting entirely of details of acts that affected the General Stream in education.

23. *Ha'aretz*, 16 January 1950.

NOTES TO CHAPTER 7

1. Y. Gelber, *New Homeland* (Jerusalem: Yad Izhak Ben-Zvi, 1990), 296–313.

2. Ibid., 313.

3. Prime Minister's Office, 5543/3631III/*Gimel*, ISA.

4. Levin's personal notebook was deposited in the Central Archives for the History of the Jewish People, Jerusalem, P 161.

5. Levin was not the only one to hold this opinion. On the role of the Bible in the educational system of the workers' movement see, for example, A. Shapira, "The Religious Motifs of the Eretz Israel Labor Movement," in *Reshafim* . . . (Tel Aviv: Tel Aviv University, 1991), 166–67.

6. Frumkin Commission Report, 38–39 [221].

7. Meeting of Mapai Knesset faction, 26 January 1950, MA.

8. Meeting of the Executive of the Mapai Knesset faction, 24 January 1950, MA.

9. Meeting of Mapai Central Committee, 2 March 1950, MA.

10. Meeting of the Executive of the Mapai Knesset faction, 24 January 1950, MA.

11. The program is dated Kislev 5710 (November–December 1949), Prime Minister's Office, 5543/3631/*Gimel*, ISA.

12. Ibid., 8.

13. Ibid., 10-11.

14. The Zionist ethos of the "the new Jewish man" has been the subject of much study. See, for example, G. Shaked, "'From the Sea? On the Image . . . ," *Mehkerei Yerushlayim be-Sifrut Ivrit* 9 (1986): 7–22.

15. Records of the 15th session of the Frumkin Commission, 6 March 1950, CZA A116/164I.

16. *Youth Camps for Yemenite Immigrants* (Hebrew), published by the Culture Department, copy in ISA, 5543/3631/*Gimel.*

17. Ibid., 7.

18. Ibid., 14.

19. *On the Talons of Eagles* (Bnai Brak: Torat Avot Organization, 1988), 9.

20. Hadassa Lipmanowitz (Ben-Ito) told us: "For me Eretz Israel was a tremendous revolution, but not in the anti-religious sense . . . . I grew up in a very religious home . . . . My parents always voted for Hapoel Hamizrachi, but they were never party members in Israel . . . . In those days the labor settlements, 'one *dunam* after another' [a slogan of the Jewish National Fund for land acquisition], settlement along the borders, and all those things—that was Eretz Israel . . . . This was the Zionist ethos . . . . It wasn't anti-religious . . . . It has no connection with being anti-religious." Interview conducted on 15 April 1991, YBZ.

21. On the beginnings of the Religious Workers Stream, its history and its demise, see Z. Zameret, "The Religious Workers Stream . . . ," in *Reshafim* (Tel Aviv: Tel Aviv University, 1991), 121–54.

22. Meeting of the Plenum of the Histadrut Education Center, 6 December 1948, LMA, IV215, File 24.

23. Minutes of the Central Committee of the Histadrut, 19 February 1950, LMA.

24. Minutes of Mapai Bureau, 30 November 1950, MA.

25. Nardi, *The Education and Culture Annual 5711*, vol. I, 214.

26. Ibid.

27. M. Etz-Hayyim, "A Brief History of the Religious Workers Stream" (Hebrew), LMA, IV215, File 1139.

28. The programs are found, inter alia, in ARZMHK, Ha'oved Hadati file.

29. A copy is in ARZMHK, Education File 10/2, Protocols, Miscellanea, 5710–5711.

30. LMA, IV208, Temporary File 5497.

31. Frumkin Commission Report, 29–30 [213–14].

32. *Knesset Debates*, vol. VIII, 1043.

33. Ibid., 1051–52.

34. *Tear Off the Mask* (Hebrew), a pamphlet published by Neturei Karta, Jerusalem, 1950.

35. Letter to Minister of Education and Culture David Remez, 16 January 1951; copy in ISA, Prime Minister's Office, 5543/5/*Gimel.* While the letter is from a later period, there is no doubt that many Yemenite immigrants also would have agreed with its contents the previous year.

36. Records of the Frumkin Commission, session of 7 March 1950, CZA A116/164I.

NOTES TO CHAPTER 8

1. Zalman Shazar was of the opinon that the attempt to widen the coalition was the cause of strained relations with the Religious Front and the reason it decided to "organize a crusade of religious people." See the meeting of the executive of the Mapai Knesset faction, 24 January 1950, MA.

2. See the meeting of Mapai Secretariat with the Knesset faction, 12 March 1950, where an explanation was presented about why, from the Mapai viewpoint, the four-month long negotiations with Mapam failed.

3. For the contacts conducted by Mapai at the very time in which the Frumkin Commission was appointed, see, for example, *Ha'aretz*, 19 January 1950: "Serious contacts by Ben-Gurion for a new coalition with the General Zionists and Mapam." About three and a half months later, Ben-Gurion still wrote in his diary about his contacts with representatives of the General Zionists. See Ben-Gurion Diary, 27 April 1950, BGA.

4. See ibid., 24 January 1950: "My proposal to Shapira: Hapoel Hamizrachi will unite with Poalei Agudat Israel, to become a subsidiary party of Mapai. They will later join the Histadrut if conditions are suitable—we will see in another year. They will identify [with Mapai] on social and political issues and will be given all possible encouragement in receiving the religious immigrants [into their ranks], their education and settlement." In his diary entry for 29 January 1950, there is mention of another meeting with Moshe Shapira, and on 31 January of one with the leaders of Hapoel Hamizrachi's "Lamifne" faction.

5. The committee was appointed at the meeting of the government on 17 January 1950.

6. Concerning the reluctance of the religious parties, see Don-Yehiya, "Cooperation and Conflict," 637–40. On the indecision in Mapai, see especially the meeting of the Mapai Knesset faction, 26 January 1950, MA.

7. The tension at the meeting was primarily between Remez and Ben-Gurion. In oral testimony, Golda Meir claimed that Ben-Gurion wished to see Remez out of the government. See BGA, Institute of Oral Documentation.

8. Copy of the letter in Correspondence File, BGA.

9. The quotations are from a report in *Hatzofe*, 8 February 1950.

10. *Knesset Debates*, vol. IV, 855–56, session of 27 February 1950.

11. On 16 February 1950 *Ha'aretz* reported that the three religious ministers threatened to resign from the government if the Shazar-Shapira agreement was not approved.

12. See, for example, the telegram from "representatives of all the religious organizations and circles in America" to Ben-Gurion, dated 16 February 1950, Correspondence File, BGA.

13. See World Center of Hamizrachi, Protocols, 26–27 Shevat 5710 [14–15 February 1950]; cf. Don-Yehiya, "Cooperation and Conflict," 647–53.

14. From the 9th to the 19th of February 1950.

15. Ben-Gurion to Rabbis Maimon and Levin, 20 February 1950, Correspondence File, BGA.

16. *Ha'aretz*, 20 February 1950.

17. Ben-Gurion to Z. Aharonowitz, 19 February 1950, Correspondence File, BGA.

18. Ben-Gurion to Rabbis Maimon and Levin, 20 February 1950, ibid.

19. *Ha'aretz*, 22 February 1950.

20. *Knesset Debates*, vol. IV, 831–33, session of 21 February 1950. The quotation is from Shapira, ibid., 831.

21. *Davar*, 23 February 1950.

22. Meeting of the Histadrut Central Committee, 3 March 1950, LMA.

23. Moshe Ben-Nahum was one of the Haoved Hadati activists who remained in the movement after Dr. Leibowitz and several other senior members resigned in the wake of Mapai pressure upon them to repudiate the agreement regarding uniform religious education in the camps.

24. Meeting of the Histadrut Central Committee, 3 March 1950, LMA. See also similar formulations in the meeting of the Mapai Central Committee with its Knesset faction, 5 March 1950, MA.

25. B. Cohen at the meeting of the World Center of Hamizrachi, 6 Shevat 5710 [24 January 1950], ARZBI. These discussions took place about a month before the agreement for uniform religious education in the camps was signed.

26. Remarks of Michael Hayyim Hazani, meeting of the World Center of Hamizrachi, 29 Teveth 5710 [18 January 1950].

27. Meeting of the World Center of Hamizrachi, 7 Shevat 5710 [25 January 1950].

28. *Hatzofe* reported on Shazar's one-month absence on 13 February 1950. In October, Shazar was removed from the government, and David Remez was formally appointed minister of education and culture in his stead.

29. *Ha'aretz*, 7 March 1950.

30. *Knesset Debates*, vol. IV, 1015, session of 14 March 1950.

31. Ibid., 1012.

32. Ibid., 1018.

33. Ibid., 1026.

34. Ibid., 1020.

35. See Don-Yehiya, "Cooperation and Conflict," 669–70.

36. *Ha'aretz*, 16 March 1950.

37. At a meeting of the Mapai Secretariat on 12 March 1950, Aharonowitz reported on the progress in the coalition negotiations with Mapam. He notified the participants that an agreement in writing had been reached between the two parties regarding matters of religion, which advocated "prevention of the domination of religious people over the life of

the state and matters of education; freedom to strive for a secular lifestyle; freedom to vote [without party constraints] on all matters pertaining to freedom of conscience, such as civil marriage, public transportation on the Sabbath, import of non-kosher meat, taxes for religious purposes, etc." On 23 March, *She'arim* informed its readers of the close agreement between Mapai and Mapam regarding religious matters in the course of their coalition negotiations. Its editorial argued: "Mapai is double-faced. [It exhibits] a kind of 'dual loyalty' which is no less dangerous—at least in matters which are vital to us—than that of its stepsister, Mapam."

38. *She'arim*, 13 April 1950.

39. See Chapter 5, p. 56. See also *Hatzofe*, 10 May 1950, and material in ISA, Prime Minister's Office, Files 5543/3631 III/*Gimel* and 5543/6/*Gimel*.

40. *Al Hamishmar*, 10 May 1950.

41. Ibid., 15 May 1950.

NOTES TO CHAPTER 9

1. The official title of the department that was commonly known as the Culture Department, the title used throughout this book.

2. Frumkin Commission Report, 115 [289].

3. Ibid.

4. See the lengthy report in *Davar*, 16 January 1950, and the editorial that followed on 18 January.

5. Frumkin Commission Report, 115 [289].

6. CAHJP, P161.

7. Ibid.

8. See *Davar*, 15 June 1950.

9. ISA, Prime Minister's Office, 43/5558/3885/*Gimel*.

10. See the report of the press conference, *Davar*, 15 June 1950.

11. *Davar*, 18 June 1950.

12. A play on the notorious and libelous *Protocols of the Elders of Zion*.

13. *Hador*, 15 June 1950.

14. *Al Hamishmar*, 14 June 1950.

15. *Al Hamishmar*, 20 June 1950.

16. CAHJP, P161.

17. Ibid.

18. All incidents in the *moshavim* are summarized in the Frumkin Commission Report, 71–76 [250–54].

19. For Tnu'at Hamoshavim after the establishment of Israel, see D. Weintraub, M. Lissak, and Y. Azmon, *Moshava, Kibbutz and Moshav* . . . (Ithaca, N.Y. and London: Cornell University Press, 1969), 265–72.

20. Frumkin Commission Report, 75 [253].

21. We met on 15 April 1991. My deep gratitude to Judge Ben-Ito for the amicable conversation and her edifying testimony. My thanks also to Dr. Nana Sagi of the Project for Oral Documentation at the Institute for Contemporary Jewry of the Hebrew University in Jerusalem for her great assistance in conducting this and numerous other interviews relating to this period. The recorded interview forms part of a project concerning the Great Aliya at Yad Izhak Ben-Zvi in Jerusalem.

22. Interview, 15 April 1991, YBZ.

23. The survey, dated 10 October 1950, concerning the youth camp at Pardes Hanna, where some ninety boys and girls stayed at the "Central Preparatory Ulpan" (a special framework for the study of Hebrew) prior to their transfer to labor settlements. See ISA, Ministry of Education and Culture, 781/12/1/1/*Gimel*.

24. Mapai party discussion, 14 December 1950, MA. The speaker quoted was Arye Bahir.

25. Interview, 15 April 1991, YBZ.

NOTES TO CHAPTER 10

1. *Knesset Debates*, vol. V, 1759–60.

2. Ibid., 1760–61.

3. Ibid., 1761–62.

4. Joint meeting of the Mapai Knesset Faction and Mapai Secretariat 19 June 1950, MA.

5. Correspondence Files, 7 July 1950, BGA.

6. ISA, Prime Minister's Office, 5543/4a/*Gimel*.

7. Ibid., letter from 19 February 1951.

8. Executive of the Religious Front, 11 Menahem Av 5710, 25 July 1950, ARZBI, Symposium 3.

9. Ibid.

10. Ibid., 30 July 1950.

11. *Hatzofe*, July 1950.

12. Meeting of the Central Committtee of the Histadrut, 6 July 1950, LMA.

13. On 27 October 1950, *Ha'aretz* claimed in an editorial: "The Religious Front initiated the crisis over economic issues and went on to an entirely different area: demands in the realms of religion and education."

14. *Knesset Debates*, vol. VII, 11–12, session of 17 October 1950.

15. Ibid., 31.

16. Ibid., 36.

17. It was about this time that news of smuggling for the black market became public knowledge. In an internal discussion of the Executive of the Religious Front, concern was voiced that, "There are many crimes committed by secular Jews, and yet there is such strong incitement precisely against religious Jews. . . . The atmosphere is being poisoned. . . . The situation of the religious Jew in his own state is like that of Jews in the Diaspora, where the guilt of the individual is applied to many." Remarks by MK Zerah Warhaftig, Executive of the Religious Front, 11 Av 5710, 25 July 1950, ARZBI, Symposium 3.

18. *Knesset Debates*, vol. VII, 42, session of 17 October 1950.

19. Ibid., 44. After Aldema was dismissed, he was appointed principal of a school in Migdal Gad (Ashkelon).

20. See meeting of the Mapai Central Committee, 22 October 1950, MA.

21. In discussions within the Religious Front Knesset faction, Pinkas was the most outspoken. On 1 Marheshvan 5711 (12 October 1950), he said: "If Hamizrachi will not leave the government, I will quit the Knesset . . . they are destroying us from the religious aspect." On 12 Marheshvan (23 October), he stated: "Mapai takes for itself every good portion in the state and disposseses all the others. The state stands before an abyss, and there is no certainty that we can maintain ourselves for even one day if such a policy continues in the state for another half a year." See ARZBI, Symposium 4.

22. MK Zerah Warhaftig, meeting of the Religious Front faction, 1 Marheshvan 5711 (12 October 1950), ibid.

23. *Knesset Debates*, vol. VII, 102, session of 30 October 1950.

24. *Ha'aretz*, November 9, 1950.

25. *Knesset Debates*, vol. VII, 274, session of 20 November 1950.

26. On 5 October 1950, that is, even before the coalition crisis erupted, *Ma'ariv* already reported that the transfer of 950 Iraqi children to Mapam kibbutzim had been discussed in a consultation held in the home of Chief Rabbi Herzog. Likewise, Agudat Israel's *Hamodi'a* reported that very day regarding 1,300 Iraqi children "who have already been forced into apostasy."

27. *Hatzofe*, 1 December 1950.

28. *Knesset Debates*, vol. VII, 483, session of 18 December 1950.

29. Meeting of the Religious Front, 9 Teveth 5711 (18 December 1950), ARZBI, Symposium 4.

30. On the investigation, see ISA, *Peh*/16/703.

31. Ibid.

32. Ibid.

33. See, for example, the remarks of MK Genachowski, *Knesset Debates*, vol. VII, 510–11, session of 19 December 1950.

34. Don-Yehiya writes: "One receives the impression that in establishing the *ma'abarot* the Jewish Agency officials actively cooperated with the representatives of the Workers Stream . . . . It may be that the timing and pace of establishing *ma'abarot* was also to a large extent determined by the influence of Workers Stream interests." See "Cooperation and Conflict," 682.

35. Letter of 11 July 1950, ISA, Ministry of Education, 796/*Gimel*, File 1215.

36. The letter is dated 25 July 1950, ibid.

37. ISA, Ministry of Education, 796/*Gimel*, File 1209; cf. Don-Yehiya, "Cooperation and Conflict," 686.

38. In 5710 (1949/50), 111 special schools were opened for immigrant children, of which seventy-two belonged to the Workers Stream. Of the 7,106 children in schools for immigrant children, 5,477 (77 percent) were enrolled in the Workers Stream. See data of the Ministry of Education, ISA, Ministry of Educaton, 796/*Gimel*, File 1214.

39. ISA, Ministry of Education, 796/*Gimel*, File 1102.

40. *Knesset Debates*, vol. VII, 411, session of 11 December 1950.

41. Ibid., 487, session of 18 December 1950.

42. Ben-Gurion Diary, 31 December 1950, BGA.

43. Ibid., 3 January 1951.

44. Ibid., 5 January 1951.

45. Correspondence Files, 6 January 1951, BGA.

46. *Hatzofe*, 8 January 1951; *Haboker*, 8 January 1951.

47. Don-Yehiya, "Cooperation and Conflict," 758.

48. H. Barkai, *The Beginnings of the Israeli Economy* (Jerusalem: Mossad Bialik, 1990), 57–59.

49. Ben-Gurion Diary, 15 January 1951, BGA.

50. Ibid., 16 January 1951.

51. Ibid., 17 January 1951.

52. Ibid., 28 January 1951.

53. Quoted from a letter to Pinhas Rosen, Correspondence Files, 19 February 1951, BGA. Meir Argov reported this meeting to the Mapai Knesset faction on 7 February. See MA.

54. Ben-Gurion Diary, 7 February 1951, BGA.

55. *Knesset Debates*, vol. VIII, I, 1039–40, session of 12 February 1951.

56. Ibid., 1079, session of 13 February 1951.

57. Ibid., 1072–73, ibid.

58. Ibid., 1082–83, ibid.

59. Ibid., 1044–48, session of 12 February 1951.

60. Ibid., 1066, session of 13 February 1951.

61. On 15 January 1951 *Ma'ariv* reported that efforts had been continuing for a long time to prevent the final split.

62. *Knesset Debates*, vol. VIII, 1040–44, session of 12 February 1951.

63. Ibid., 1049–52, ibid.

64. Ibid., 1084, session of 13 February 1951.

65. See his article in *Hatzofe*, 5 May 1950.

66. *Knesset Debates*, vol.VIII, 1075-76, session of 13 February 1951.

67. Ibid., 1092, session of 14 February 1951.

68. Ibid., 1098, ibid.

69. *Ma'ariv*, 15 February 1951.

70. Ben-Gurion Diary, 18 February 1951, BGA.

71. Correspondence Files, 20 February 1951, BGA.

72. Mapai platform prior to elections of July 1951, MA.

NOTES TO CHAPTER 11

1. Frumkin Commission Report, p. 6 [195]. For the full list of witnesses, see pp. 118–22 [293–96].

2. Ibid., 113–14 [287].

3. M. Lissak, "Some Historical Perspectives on Mass Immigration in the 1950s," *Hatzionut* 14 (1989): 216.

4. Frumkin Report, 114 [288].

5. Justice Frumkin's father, Israel Dov Frumkin, was one of the public figures in Jerusalem who helped absorb the first Yemenite immigrants in the 1880s.

6. Frumkin Report, 113 [288].

7. Ibid.

8. Ibid.

9. ARZMHK, Yemenite Immigrants File.

10. Zadok, *The Yemenite Burden*, 147.

11. Interview in 1990, Oral History Division, Institute of Contemporary Jewry, Hebrew University of Jerusalem.

12. See, for example, *On the Talons of Eagles*. The book's title is an ironic play on the code name of the airlift from Yemen, "On the Wings of Eagles," (itself taken from Exod. 19:4). The jacket portrays a man wearing a blue Labor youth movement shirt cutting the

payot of a Yemenite child (see illustration above, Ch. 7). In the introduction to the book, we read: "We have attempted to present the material concisely, in part as a personal story and in part by presenting the events as well as documenation and quotations from the sources." See ibid., p. 83, for an example of a contemporary (late 1980s) effort to utilize the myth of cutting *payot*: "Under the pretext of a nurse's visit to the school to counter infection by lice, the instructors shaved the heads of all the boys, including the *'simanim'*—the curled *payot*—which are the distinctive sign of Yemenite children. Salam noticed an interesting and surprising phenomenon! While the 'barbers' did not touch the forelocks, not a single sidelock was left intact! He was wise enough to sense the deception, intended to remove the external religious signs from the Yemenite children. He asked the instructor: 'Are there no lice in the forelocks?' . . . for which he received a ringing slap on his cheek. Salam forcibly covered his *payot* and firmly refused to allow them to be cut . . . .When the meal was served, which included bread and jam, Salam was refused his portion until he removed his *payot*."

13. Rabbi Zarom, a leader of Yemenite Jewry in Israel, wrote to one of the parents who had complained about the removal of *payot*: "For you know that it is the practice among students in the Mizrachi schools to shave them off, because of the ridicule that comes from their fellow students themselves." Quoted by Tzurieli, *Education and Society*, 435.

14. Frumkin Commission Report, 17, 86 [203, 216].

15. Records of the Frumkin Commission, 28 February 1960, CZA A116/164I.

16. *Report to the 23rd Zionist Congress, Jerusalem, Av 5711* (Hebrew), 239; cf. the discussion at the meeting of the Steering Committee of the Jewish Agency and the Israeli government in Jerusalem on 18 April 1951, at which Dr. Haim Sheba testified that, "According to the estimate of the Medical School, the number of cases of ringworm in Israel has reached 9,000. It comes primarily from North Africa and Yemen." See ISA, Golda Meir Files, Steering Committee, *Gimel/7595*.

17. Frumkin Commission Report 114 [289].

18. Ibid.

19. From remarks made at the Tenth Convention of Hapoel Hamizrachi, 6–12 Heshvan 5710 (29 October–4 November 1949), ARZMHK.

20. Frumkin Commission Report, 114 [288].

21. "Draft Report, secret, for members of the commission only," CZA A116/164I.

22. Frumkin Commission Report, 115–16 [289–90].

23. The following decision was adopted by the government at its meeting of 7 June 1950: "The government notes the statement of the minister of education and culture concerning the *dismissal* of two workers, Y. A. Aldema and Zippora Zehavi, *which was effected before the presentation of the report*, *and of the resignation* of the director of the department, Nahum Levin" (emphasis added).

24. Testimony of Aldema before the Frumkin Commission, 28 February 1950, CZA A116/164I.

25. *Knesset Debates*, vol. VII, 402–03, session of 11 December 1950.

26. Testimony of Z. Zehavi before the Frumkin Commission, 28 February 1950, CZA, A116/164I.

27. [*Report of*] *the Commission of Inquiry to Investigate the Events in the Refugee Camps in Beirut* (Hebrew), Jerusalem. 1983, 122.

28. Frumkin Commission Report, 115 [289].

29. On commissions of inquiry, personal and ministerial responsibility, see Yitzhak Zamir, "The Judicial Aspect of Commissions of Inquiry," *Haperaklit*, 35 (1983–1984): 323–27; Moshe Ben-Zev, "The Political Level vs. Commissions of Inquiry: The Confrontation, the Tension, and the Fear," in *Yitzhak Kahan Memorial Volume*, ed. M. Elon et al. (Tel Aviv: Papyrus, 1989), 234–44.

30. The appendix is not included in the translation of the Frumkin Commission Report in this book.

31. Ibid., 125.

32. Ibid., 126.

33. Ibid., 130.

34. Ibid., 131.

35. Meeting of the Mapai Knesset faction, 26 January 1950, MA.

Notes to Chapter 12

1. The reasons for this delay are detailed in Z. Zameret, *Across a Narrow Bridge* . . . (Sde Boker: Ben-Gurion Research Center, 1997), 190–242.

2. Ibid., 191.

3. Z. Libai, "Concerning Uniform State Schools," *Beterem* 8 (20 July 1950): 20.

4. Ben-Gurion to the Mapai Central Forum, 10 March 1951, Correspondence Files, BGA.

5. Ya'akov Hazan, one of Mapam's leaders, in a session of the Knesset, *Knesset Debates*, vol. I, 125, session of 10 March 1949.

6. Zameret, *Across a Narrow Bridge*, 201, 318.

7. MK Moshe Erem, *Ma'ariv*, 2 September 1949.

8. At that time a faction within Mapam, but in a few years would become an independent party.

9. E. Kafkafi, *Truth or Faith* . . . (Jerusalem: Yad Izhak Ben-Zvi, 1992), 122.

10. Ben-Gurion, *Stars and Dust*, 131.

11. For a more detailed discussion see Zameret, *Across a Narrow Bridge*, 231–40.

12. That was the essence of Pinhas Lavon's statement to the Political Committee. See meeting of Mapai Political Committee, 4 September 1951, MA.

13. Literally, "fearful," that is, God-fearing. This is a connotation covering all of the ultra-Orthodox groups that do not adhere to religious Zionism.

14. Meeting of the Mapai Political Committee, 10 September 1951, MA.

15. Ibid., 28 September 1951, MA.

16. Ben-Gurion noted in his diary that when he met with Rabbi Y. M. Levin, leader of Agudat Israel, in the winter of 1953, Levin requested that "the government cover 50 percent [of the costs] of the Aguda schools, and they would raise the rest in the country and abroad." Ben-Gurion Diary, 18 February 1953, BGA.

17. Sh. Daniel, *Minister Haim Moshe Shapira* (Tel Aviv: Don Publishers, 1980), 181.

18. Institutions in which, while they are not state schools, all of those who study do so without violating the Compulsory Education Law.

19. According to the report of the Israel State Comptroller for 1998.

20. Various Hasidic communities have separate systems, such as Habad, Gur, Vizhnitz, Karlin, Satmar, Toledot Aharon, and others. Their opponents, groups of ultra-Orthodox that emerged from the Lithuanian *yeshivot*, as well as Sephardim and many others have their own autonomous systems of education, and of course, there are separate educational institutions for girls.

21. A. Rubinstein, "The Secular Hourglass," *Ha'aretz*, 8 May 1998.

22. See the testimony of Dr. Baruch Ben-Yehuda, director of the Education Divison of the Ministry of Education and Culture, before the Knesset Committee on Education and Culture, 15 March 1950, ISA, Ministry of Education, *Gimel Lamed*/1100, file 135.

23. Zameret, *Across a Narrow Bridge*, 241.

24. A. Surasky, *A History of Religious Education in the Modern Period* (Bnai Brak: Or Hahayyim, 1967), 272.

25. With the destruction of the Second Temple and Jerusalem at the hands of the Romans in 70 C.E., a group of sages, under the leadership of Rabbi Yohanan ben Zakkai, moved to the small village of Yavne, where they created the new, post-Temple world of Judaism. By using the phrase "grant us only Yavne and its sages," Agudat Israel meant "grant us a small corner of our own and we will try to create therein a new religious society."

26. I. Spiegel, *On the Highway . . .* (Jerusalem: Mashabim, 1982), 124–25.

27. L. I. Hayerushalmi, *The Domineering Yarmulke* (Tel Aviv: Hakibbutz Hameuhad, 1997), 81.

28. For five reasons of eligibility for exemption from military service, see M. Friedman, *Haredi (Ultra-Orthodox) Society: Sources, Trends, and Processes* (Jerusalem: Jerusalem Institute for Israel Studies, 1991), 55.

29. Ibid.

NOTES TO CHAPTER 13

1. N. Horowitz, in his important article "Shas and Zionism: A Historical Analysis," *Kivunim Hadashim* 2 (April 2000): 30–60, claims that the roots of Shas were already laid in the pre-state period. The seeds may have been sown then, but they germinated in the traumatic anguish of the days of the Great Aliya.

2. For immigration from Morocco see Y. Tzur, "The Ethnic-Communal Problem", in *The Second Decade* (Jerusalem: Yad Izhak Ben-Zvi, 2000), 108–13. Quoting the Central Bureau of Statistics, Tzur lists the following figures: 4,260 Moroccan Jews immigrated in 1960, 11,676 in 1961, 35,839 in 1962, 36,988 in 1963, and 15,851 in 1964.

3. This group's publications are replete with complaints that the *haredi* public is too apathetic, and that "we take no interest in our immigrant brethren . . . who remain far removed from us as we are from them . . . . True, we know of their existence, because we read the papers, but they... it may very well be that they do not even know that there is a religious Jewry in this country, and that there are Talmudei Torah and schools that are absolutely [devoted to] sacred studies, and large and famous *yeshivot*." Quoted from *Hever Hape'ilim's Report of Activities and Survey of the Condition of Religion in the Immigrant Moshavim* (Tel Aviv: Hever Hapei'lim, April-June 1955). Copy in ISA, 38–6/6291 *Gimel Lamed*.

4. Friedman, *Haredi (Ultra-Orthodox) Society*, 59–60, 177–79.

5. See I. Harel, *Security and Democracy* (Tel Aviv: Edanim, 1989), 179–82; E. Sprinzak, *Political Violence in Israel* (Jerusalem: Jerusalem Institute for Israel Studies, 1995), 34.

6. A party formed out of the union of Hamizrachi with Hapoel Hamizrachi.

7. Quoted in Sprinzak, *Political Violence*, 34.

8. Eliahu Segalov died while participating in a demonstration against traffic on the Sabbath conducted in Jerusalem in 1956.

9. Published in *Report of Activities and Survey of the Condition of Religion in the Immigrant Moshavim* (Tel Aviv: Hever Hapei'lim, April-June 1955). Copy in ISA, 38–6/6291 *Gimel Lamed*.

10. The leaflet informed its readers who the signatories were: Rabbi David Sabbah had been a rabbi and a teacher in Morocco and North Africa; Rabbi Yeuda Zedaka had been the director of the Porat Yosef Yeshiva in Jerusalem; Rabbi Nissim Kedouri was a former chief rabbi in Baghdad; Rabbi Ovadia Yosef had formerly been the head of a rabbinical court in Egypt.

11. *Hedim: Information Bulletin of Hever Hape'ilim*, 7 (Tishrei 5718) [September–October 1957]: 25.

12. A facsimile of the letter dated 14 Tammuz 5717 (13 July 1957) is reproduced in ibid.: 28.

13. *Yediot Aharonot*, 15 September 1957.

14. Quoted in E. Livne, "Until When Will Coercion of Immigrants Continue?" *Yediot Aharonot*, 31 May 1957.

15. Correspondence Files, letter of 21 October 1958, BGA.

16. On Aranne as minister of education and culture see Z. Zameret, "Aranne and Educational Policy . . ." in *The Second Decade* (Jerusalem: Yad Izhak Ben-Zvi, 2000), 61–78.

17. Much has been written about the Wadi Salib Riots. See, for example, *Report of the Public Investigation Commission concerning the Events of 9 July 1959 in Wadi Salib* (copy in the ISA), reprinted in Sh. Shetreet, *Tearful Pioneers: Studies in North African Jewry* (Tel

Aviv: Am Oved, 1991), 225–39; Tzur, "The Ethnic-Communal Problem," 102–08; R. Patai, "The Riots in Wadi Salib," *Midstream* (winter 1960): 5–14.

18. Allowances for families with many children were increased; the wages for relief work for the unemployed were raised slightly; a higher minimum number of days per month was set in which relief work would be provided; and more.

19. It is interesting that Abuhatzeira received public support from several Oriental intellectuals such as poet Erez Bitton, journalist Ben-Dror Yemini, and academics Viki Shiran and Dr. Asher Idan—all secular persons with openly declared leftist opinions. The only things they had in common with Abuhatzeira were their roots in Oriental Jewry and their belief that the Oriental ethnic communities were the subject of discrimination.

20. For Tami see: Y. Sheleg, *The New Religious Jews . . .* (Jerusalem: Keter, 2000), 76.

21. He is the author of scores of *halakhic* works, published in multi-volume series entitled *Yabi'a Omer*, *Yahve De'a* and *Hazon Ovadia*. *Halakhic* guidebooks (twenty-three in number to date!) written by his son, Rabbi Yitzhak Yosef, on the basis of his father's *halakhic* rulings, which are to be found in many Sephardic households. He was awarded the Israel Prize in 1970 for the series *Yabi'a Omer*. Among the many works that analyze his great knowledge and deep understanding of Jewish law, see: B. Lau, "The Struggle of Rabbi Ovadia Yosef," in *The Challenge of Independence . . .* (Jerusalem: Yad Izhak Ben-Zvi, 1999), 214–27.

22. The biography of Arye Deri is one of the most fascinating in Israel. To date, he has been the subject of several books and many articles. The most extensive is Y. Nir's *Arye Deri . . .* (Tel Aviv: Miskal, 1999). Though universally recognized as an exceptional genius, he went through several educational ups and downs until he began to study in some Jerusalem *yeshivot*: first in Porat Yosef (under Rabbi B. Z. Abba Shaul), then in Yeshivat Kol Ya'akov (under Rabbi Adass), and finally in Yeshivat Hevron (under Rabbi Sh. Z. Broide). It was there that he made the acquaintance of one of Rabbi Ovadia Yosef's sons and through him drew close to Rabbi Yosef, who was then the Sephardic Chief Rabbi. A few years later, out of these close relations, would arise Shas, of which Deri was one of the initiators, representing it in the government. Late in 1989, complaints were first lodged with the Israel Police accusing Deri of taking bribes and illegally transferring funds to Shas. Only in June 1990 was a police investigation begun, which continued for more than three years. In June 1993, he was formally charged with accepting bribery, fraud, breach of loyalty as a public official, and receiving something by fraud under severe circumstances. His trial dragged on for seven tiring years through various courts, concluding with his being found guilty and sentenced to three years in prison. The prison gates closed behind him on 3 September 2000.

23. A. Dayan, *The Story of Shas* (Jerusalem: Keter, 1999), 22–25.

24. Rabbi Yitzhak Peretz was born in Casablanca, Morocco. Arriving in Israel in 1950, Peretz spent some time in the religious kibbutz Tirat Zvi, afterward moving with his family to the nearby immigrant town of Beit Shean. He spent his teenage years in religious-Zionist schools, graduating from the prestigious Midrashiat No'am in Pardes Hanna. Awaiting his conscription into the Army, he studied in the "Lithuanian" Hebron Yeshiva. Though originally intending to study for only one year, he remained there for six years and was ordained as a rabbi. In 1984, he headed the Shas list in the Knesset elections and was appointed minister of the interior.

25. For details see A. Arian and M. Shamir, eds., *The Elections in Israel—1988* (Boulder, San Francisco and Oxford: Westview Press, 1990), 4.

26. Based upon G. Doron and R. Kook, "Religion and the Politics of Inclusion . . . ," in *The Elections in Israel, 1996* (Albany: State University of New York Press, 1999), 72.

27. Baruch Kimmerling emphasizes that the right-wing bloc actually received 9,057 votes more than the left wing, and that "only the fragmentation of the right wing into small parties that failed to pass the threshold needed to receive a parliamentary seat made the difference of one out of 120 parliamentary seats and Labor's victory." See B. Kimmerling, "Elections as a Battleground over Collective Identity," in *The Elections in Israel, 1996* (Albany: State University of New York Press, 1999), 31. See also his n. 9, ibid., 44. For full election results see A. Arian and M. Shamir, eds., *The Elections in Israel – 1992* (Albany: State University of New York Press, 1995), 2. On Shas in these elections see A. P. Willis, "Shas . . . ," in ibid., 121–39.

28. Rabin's letter is reproduced in facsimile in ibid., 90.

29. The distribution of these 68 seats was as follows: the Likud-Gesher-Zomet alliance, 32; Shas, 10; the National Religious Party, 9; Yisrael Be'aliya (a party of immigrants from the former Soviet Union, led by Nathan Sharansky), 7; Yahadut Hatorah (an alliance of a few Ashkenazi *haredi* parties), 4; Haderech Hashelishit (a new, Center party), 4; Moledet (a more extreme right-wing party, led by Rehavam Zeevi), 2.

30. For instance, Kiriat Malachi , 34 percent; Shelomi, 31.6 percent; Sderot, 22.6 percent; Kiriat Shemona, 22.2 percent, and more. See Sheleg, *The New Religious Jews*, 233.

31. Doron and Kook, "Religion . . . ," 80.

NOTES TO CHAPTER 14

1. See above, Chapter 5.

2. This trend did not begin with the establishment of Israel but was actually quite conventional throughout the entire twentieth century. Note, for example, what the Revisionist Zionist leader Zeev Jabotinsky (d. 1940) had to say: "We are Europeans, and we shall remain Europeans forever from the cultural viewpoint . . . . There are experts who think that we must make our accent sound more like the Arab accent. That too is but a mistake . . . . We are Europeans, and our taste in music is a European one, that of Rubinstein, Mendelssohn, and Bizet." See: O. Almog, *The Tzabar . . .* (Tel Aviv: Am Oved: 1997), 290, 153–61.

3. For these issues see, among other works, Almog, *The Tzabar*.

BOOK II

REPORT OF THE COMMISSION OF INQUIRY CONCERNING EDUCATION IN THE IMMIGRANT CAMPS*

Appointed by the Government
at its meeting of 28 Shevat 5710 (17 January 1950)

Authorized

a. to investigate all accusations concerning religious coercion in the immigrant camps;

b. to clarify the accusations published in the press and those responsible for them;

c. to examine the sources of the propaganda abroad concerning the accusations in question.

Members of the Commission:

Chairman: Gad Frumkin
Avraham Elmaleh
Izhak Ben-Zvi
Rabbi Kalman Kahana
Rabbi [Avraham] Hayyim Shaag
Secretary: Israel Yeshayahu

Jerusalem, 22 Iyyar 5710 (9 May 1950)

---

*This is a literal translation of the report, with very few explanations in brackets in the text and notes at the end of the report explaining concepts.

INTRODUCTION

APPOINTMENT, AUTHORITY, AND PROCEDURES OF THE COMMISSION

1. WHAT PRECEDED THE COMMISSION OF INQUIRY

It is difficult to determine exactly and chronologically, nor is it particularly important, how, when, and from whence came the first complaints concerning interference in matters of religion and education in the immigrant camps. It is a fact that already, during the summer of 1949, parents presented requests that religious teachers be sent to, or at least that religious classes be opened in, the camps. These requests were addressed to the Department for Language Teaching and Cultural Absorption of Immigrants, sometimes referred to simply as "The Culture Department." This department, as will become clear below, deals not only with teaching the Hebrew language and all cultural matters for adults, but also is responsible for the education of children in the camps. The demand increased with the great Yemenite wave of immigration, and from that time on there also were more frequent complaints and accusations concerning matters of religion and education, upon which we shall elaborate further on in this report. It was then that people began coming to the immigrant camps to teach Torah to the immigrants and their children, without the permission of those responsible for running the camps. These people were not well received nor offered help or encouragement but, on the contrary, they complained of serious interference, to the point [where it became necessary] to involve the police. Rabbis and religiously observant public figures began visiting the camps to determine the facts, and complaints were made to the government during the meetings and discussions with the prime minister, the minister of education and culture, and senior officials responsible for the camps. Articles and reports also began to appear in the Israeli press, and on several occasions the issue was raised in the Education and Culture Committee of the First Knesset. Matters reached their peak during the meeting of the committee on 28 December 1949, at which Mr. Pinkas made exceedingly sharp comments concerning the situation, pointing out that a serious division was likely to occur in both the government and the state—"the coalition known as the State of Israel"— if the matter was not speedily corrected. His main demand was that responsibility for education in the camps be immediately transferred from the Department for Language Teaching to the Education Division of the Ministry of Education and Culture. Some two weeks later, on 10 January 1950, the issue was raised for discussion at a government session, at which the minister of religious affairs summarized his accusations to the effect that "the children in the camps are being coerced to abandon their religion." The following day the local press gave extensive publicity to what had occurred at the government meeting, and to the threatened resignation of the ministers belonging to the Religious Front. The London *Jewish Chronicle*, in its issue of 13 January, published sensational details about this affair in general, and about the ultimatum of the religious ministers [who threatened] to quit the coalition in particular, as well as about the threat by Religious Front Knesset members to resign from the Knesset. The next day the government was informed of this in a detailed telegram from London, where the United Jewish Appeal was about to begin its activities. On 16 January the government also received telegrams signed by several religious organizations in New York, including some parallel to those belonging to the Religious Front in Israel, informing of an emergency meeting which called upon the government to "reexamine the issue of absorption of children, so as to prevent a miscarriage of justice to the children and their parents and to the foundations of religious Judaism, and in order to avoid a worldwide scandal."

At its meeting on 25 Teveth [5710] (17 January 1950), the government appointed the present commission concerning education in the immigrant camps and charged it with the following tasks:

1. to investigate all accusations concerning religious coercion in the immigrant camps;

2. to clarify the accusations published in the press and those responsible for them;

3. to examine the sources of the propaganda abroad concerning the accusations in question.

This commission, which was appointed under Clause 2 of the Commissions of Inquiry Ordinance (Chapter 21), and Clause 14(a) of the Law and Administration Ordinance, 1948, was invested with all the powers enumerated in Clause 5 of the Commissions of Inquiry Ordinance.

Former Supreme Court Justice Gad Frumkin was appointed chairman of the commission, and the following members of the First Knesset were appointed members: Avraham Elmaleh, Izhak Ben-Zvi, Kalman Kahana, and Avraham Hayyim Shaag.

The writ of appointment, issued on 23 January 1950, was published in *Reshumot*[1] on 25 January 1950, and on the same day the commission met for its first session.

2. The Commission's Procedures

The commission met for thirty-three sessions, during which it heard 101 witnesses. Most of the sessions were conducted in the prime minister's office in Jerusalem, some of them in the prime minister's office in the Kirya,[2] and a few meetings were held in Hadera and Netanya in order to make it easier to hear witnesses from those vicinities.

The commission visited the most populous camps—namely, the blocs of camps in Ein-Shemer, Beit Lid, Rosh Ha'ayin, and Beer Ya'akov.

Among the witnesses who appeared before the commission (see the Appendum at the end of this report) were Minister of Education and Culture, Mr. Sh. Z. Shazar; Minister of the Interior, Immigration, and Health, Mr. Moshe Shapira; and Minister of Welfare, Rabbi Yitzhak Meir Levin. Senior officials of the Ministry of Education and Culture who testified were the director of the Education Division, Dr. B. Ben-Yehuda; the director of the Department for Language Teaching and Cultural Absorption of Immigrants, Mr. Nahum Levin; the directress of the Youth Bureau of this department, Hadassa Lipmanowitz; and the supervisor of the Section for Torah Culture, Docent[3] [Hayyim] Lifschitz. Testimony also was heard from a number of culture coordinators, school principals, teachers, and instructors active in the camps. Since the Jewish Agency also is involved, albeit indirectly, in matters of education and culture in the camps, the acting director of the Absorption Department of the Agency, Dr. [Hayyim] Yahil, and the directors of the camps were also called upon to testify. Several of the witnesses also testified with regard to the second aspect of the commission's charge. Testimony was heard regarding this matter in particular from the director of the State Information Services, Mr. Gershon Agron, the director of the World Center of Hamizrachi, Mr. [Arye Leib] Gelman, and Rabbi Ze'ev Gold, a member of the Jewish Agency Executive.

Others who appeared before the commission included rabbis, [political] activists, and representatives of various organizations and bodies, including the representative of the Religious Front in the Knesset Education and Culture Committee, Mr. D. Z. Pinkas, and representatives of the World Center of Hamizrachi, the Va'ad Hayeshivot, the Center of Agudat Israel, the Center of Poalei Agudat Israel, and Haoved Hadati. Testimony also was heard from rabbis from among the immigrants from Yemen, North Africa, and Eastern Europe, as well as from ordinary immigrants, both adults and young persons, from among those living in the camps.

The testimonies were given under a declaration of *hen tzedek*,[4] a full stenographic record was taken of the meetings, and the chairman of the commission also recorded a summary of each session.

During tours and visits to the camps, members of the commission conversed at length with immigrants of all sorts, and with workers in the camps.

Most witnesses were summoned at the initiative of the commission itself, at times in order to clarify or supplement the testimony of witnesses who preceded them. At the outset of its work, the commission announced that anyone who wished to do so would be invited to testify, if he would apply to the commission in writing and describe the content of his testimony. Many people applied as a result of this notice, and most were invited to testify, with the exception of those whose testimony, on the basis of their notification [i.e., the written description of their intended testimony], contained nothing new or was outside of the bounds of the commission's charge. A few of the witnesses failed to appear, for reasons unknown to the commission.

3. THE ORIENTATION OF THE COMMISSION'S INVESTIGATION

From the outset, the commission saw its function as a double one: first, to examine all accusations concerning religious coercion in the camps; second, to examine the accuracy of the accusations made in the press and [to determine] who was responsible for them, as well as the sources of the propaganda campaign abroad concerning the accusations in question. The commission interpreted the first function in the broadest sense, that is, [examination of] any kind of coercion involving religion and education, whether intended to impose religious education upon the pupils against their will or that of their parents, or the opposite—coercive means and pressure to prevent and limit [the provision of] religious education for those who wished it or were accustomed to it.

The commission undertook to fulfill both tasks simultaneously. With regard to the first function, it also operated in a dual fashion—clarification of the general background and examination of concrete facts.

CHAPTER 1

THE GENERAL BACKGROUND

The commission notes with satisfaction that the government presented it with the fullest opportunity to conduct the investigation and did not withhold from the commission any material or information it needed. Following a conversation with the prime minister, the commission's chairman invited two ministers to appear before the commission to report on how matters had unfolded in terms of the two approaches or evaluations expressed by members of the government, for it was impossible to ignore the fact that it was precisely these opposing outlooks which had led to the investigation of the issue. The two government ministers were Minister of Education and Culture Mr. Sh. Z. Shazar, responsible for education in the camps, and Minister of the Interior, Immigration, and Health, Mr. M. Shapira, who reflects the views of those government ministers belonging to the Religious Front.

A. THE OPINION OF THE GOVERNMENT MINISTERS

1. The Minister of Education and Culture

Minister Shazar began his remarks before the commission with the request that it should not view him or the minister of the interior as two opposing camps, even though they differed in their evaluations, but rather as representatives of the government, all of whose members had chosen this commission, and all of whose members wished to establish the truth.

He testified before the commission that when he was told of what had been reported by D. Z. Pinkas, representative of the Religious Front, to the Knesset's Education and Culture Committee, "the information was hair raising!" When he received the stenographic record of the meeting of that committee, this during the period of his illness, he realized that, "Even if only a smattering of these things were true, it is impossible that the matter should not be investigated thoroughly and be uprooted from the source." He related that at the cabinet meeting (of 21 Teveth 5710—10 January) the reports were formulated as extremely serious accusations. He quoted from the record of that meeting what was said by Minister Rabbi Maimon: "We make the accusation that the children in the immigrant camps are forced to attend Histadrut schools, are forced to violate their religion, are forced not to put on *tefillin* [phylacteries],[1] [and] are forced to cut off their *payot*. A rabbi who, after much effort, was induced to come to the camp was asked to remove his skull cap."

We quote below several passages from the testimony of Minister Shazar:

> These things were said before an important body and by an important person. They are carefully phrased. There are some generalizations: "to violate their religion" is a general concept. But they also assumed more concrete form: "They are forced not to put on *tefillin*" [and] "they are forced to cut off their *payot*." We need to check this out. There were also complaints by parents against teachers whom they asked to provide religious education but did not do so.

The minister reported that he had gone to see things for himself. He did not manage to see them in all of the camps. He sent people from his office to visit the other places and reported the results of his investigation: in the place where it was alleged that *payot* had been cut off (Beit Lid), not a single person was found to support the accusation that there had been such a policy. There were those who claimed that such things had happened, but only by order of the doctor who was responsible for hygiene in that place, whose instructions were: "In every case in which the nurse comes across a contagious skin or hair ailment, it will be necessary to cut the hair without consideration of religious arguments. This haircut must include the *payot*, because otherwise we will not be able to overcome this contagion." In the same place he also saw "seven girls whose hair had been cut off, and who wept bitterly." There were about twelve children whose hair needed to be cut off for this reason, and they were presently (at the time of his visit) being brought from Ein-Shemer to Hadera for radiation [treatment]. "This was the basis for the policy of cutting off *payot*; perhaps you will manage to clarify it further, but this is what I have arrived at. Regarding a prohibition against putting on *tefillin*, I did not discover anything of that type in any place."

As for the claim that the rabbis were allegedly not allowed to teach Torah, the minister said: "I was in that camp (Beit Lid), and I spoke with the Yemenite teacher who told me that there are about thirty 'synagogue tents.' In all of these places every opportunity is provided any teacher or *mori*[2] who wishes to teach there."

In his testimony, the minister of education elaborated upon "the second factor which led to the need for investigation, that with its outbreak there broke out an extensive, well-organized, and widespread protest movement abroad."

After quoting telegrams that had been received from London and America, which shall be dealt with later, he said:

> I think that such a large alliance and a call for a great protest rally against the Government of Israel and against the educational arrangements within the camp did not emerge of its own. Since the creation of the State of Israel, this is the first action, the first organized protest among the Jewish public throughout the world against the Government of Israel. This is the first time that action has been organized abroad against the Israeli government with the intention of protesting. Anyone who is familiar with such matters and with sentiments in America knows the meaning of such a "meeting," for we were in the habit of holding such "meetings" against Hitler, against the edicts limiting aliya, and against [British Foreign Minister Ernest] Bevin.[3] This is the first time since the state has come into being that such action has been organized against the State of Israel in such a harsh manner. There is something strange about this; in any event, we are not used to it. Even if we assume that certain negative deeds were done and that some things must be changed, even if there are things that need to be corrected in the camps and one government minister needs to persuade another government minister that things should be done differently, we have not yet gotten used to such action and did not imagine that there was need for such acts, and that such influence needs to be applied by mobilizing forces against the Government of Israel, and this beyond the boundaries of the [authority of the] Government of Israel.
>
> When confronted by this fact, we found it very strange and asked, first of all: How did it come about, and is this the way in which mutual influence should be applied? This matter should be examined, and it is your task to determine how this whole movement came about. Even if all the complaints are justified and deserving to be heard, that is the responsibility of the government and of the Knesset [something to be clarified] among us, and the matter need not be passed abroad and come to us from abroad. This issue interested the government. The government cannot examine these things; this must be done by a governmental commission. The question is whether this is the path that should be followed, or whether there is no need for it, and concerning

whom and against whom we must make these claims. That is the assumption, even if these accusations prove to be correct.

I want to show you the different manner in which the same things are said in different places and in different times. When Pinkas proposed in November, for the first time, that we take care of education in the camps, he claimed before the Committee on Education [and Culture] that the instructors engaged in this work are lacking in training and do not know how to conduct these activities; they do not have enough time, and it turns out that there are many children who go without education. Therefore, he said, we must speedily do it. Nothing was said at that time about religious coercion, about cutting off *payot*, or about forcing people to violate their religion. That was in November. At the time he spoke only of children who were not receiving proper education and that they should be transferred to the Education Division. In December, when the matter was closer at hand and it was necessary to organize a wide movement to create public opinion regarding the issue of education in the camps, Pinkas came to the [Knesset] Committee on Education, and this time his claims were: inquisition, genocide, forced violation of religion, spiritual coercion and, even more than all these, destruction of a people's culture. He claimed that these cultural instructors [instructors of the Culture Department] were destroying Jewish culture within the camps. He said these things after the International Treaty for Preserving National Cultures had been adopted, and as a result of this.

I see the major importance of this commission in that it will put an end to such statements. If everyone begins turning to the Diaspora, it will be like a return to the period of the [pre-State] Va'ad Haleumi,[4] in the worst possible sense. A state cannot tolerate such a thing. My view of politics is that we may argue among ourselves, but we must not bring the Diaspora into our concerns, particularly not in the religious sphere.

But no less important than this is the matter of educational arrangements in the camps. This is a question that interests me and interests the commission, because that was why it was appointed. This is a political matter of the first order for the destiny of the state and its ability to develop.

2. The Minister of the Interior, Immigration, and Health

Minister Shapira also concurred with the opinion that all wished to arrive at the real truth of the matter and he referred the commission to sources from which it could receive details concerning the facts and actions that were done. He did not agree that the propaganda abroad had been organized. He claimed that, "We live here in a glass house and for what is done here to be known abroad there is no need to send telegrams or messages." "One can very easily check who conducted this propaganda. One only needs to ask the Postal Service to provide us with copies of the telegrams which were sent regarding this matter. In my opinion, now that we control all the state services, that is the simplest and easiest method. I imagine that the archives of the Post Office will be available to the commission, and then you can examine the matter in depth." Concerning the organization of the Religious Bloc in the United States and the calling of a rally in Manhattan, the witness said: "The Religious Front in America was not established in connection with this matter. It has already existed for some time and was not established in order to launch accusations against the State of Israel." He repeated to the commission what he had said at the government meeting: "I feel that in order to enable religious children and religious Jews to live in a religious manner, as they are accustomed and wish to do, they cannot be educated by non-religious teachers, educators, and instructors"; "It is inconceivable that the youth leaders of Hanoar Haoved or Mapam's youth [movement][5] can educate the Yemenites to [live by] the Torah and [to observe] the commandments." If such a situation exists, "there was in my opinion a serious intention to divert these children from their religion and from knowledge of their Creator." It is not possible, he added, "that a secular Jew, who prominently displays this [trait] in his daily life and in all his behavior, on weekdays and on the Sabbath, can be the educator or instructor of a community such as the Yemenite community. Whoever did this sins towards the community and towards the state."

He went on to say:

> The camps are not hermetically sealed off. Many Jews visit there, including Jews from overseas. These Jews hear the immigrants' complaints about the economic situation, but also about the spiritual situation. Rabbi Levin showed the government—he will certainly bring it up here as well—a letter from a rabbi who visited the camp, saw conditions there, and asked: "Is such a thing possible?"
>
> There was thus no need to specially organize propaganda abroad, because the acts, in my opinion, are the best propaganda. Apparently there were certain things done that aroused public opinion abroad. The Jews in America are very close to us spiritually, far more so than the physical distance [would indicate]. They are very perturbed by everything that happens here. If they hear that an entire religious community is living in camps where the instructors and teachers are mostly secular, this obviously arouses apprehension that there is a specific intention here.
>
> If someone tries to convince me that all intentions here were without ulterior motive, only in order to educate these youngsters according to the tradition of their forefathers, this would only be in order

to distort reality and the truth. I believe that we must allow the Yemenites to live their lives as they wish. I think that the best way is to be less involved in their spiritual life. They have rabbis, they are Jews like us, they are imbued with a deep Jewish feeling of their own, [a sense of] how a Jew ought to be.

In my opinion, what happened was no accident but [reflected] a certain approach, how to save this youth and this Jewry from ultra-Orthodox Judaism. Certain acts were perpetrated which, in my opinion, if you succeed in uncovering them, you will see them just as we do as base relationships that have no place in an orderly state and among decent people. I am not one of those who seek sins, but I belong to those who wish that he who has sinned be punished, otherwise I do not know how we can live in this state.

Among themselves, Jews need to know how to respect one another, the religious sensibilities of the other person, and the social sensitivities of the other, but with an attitude of respect. What we have seen here is the opposite of respect, and I would not wish this [to be the case].

3. The Minister of Welfare

Another member of the government, Minister of Welfare Rabbi Y. M. Levin, added his own testimony before the commission to his colleagues'. Several quotations from this are cited below:

> I returned to Israel several weeks ago. While abroad, I participated in several public gatherings and cited our accomplishments. I explained abroad that there is no religious coercion here, and the fact that we participate in the government also is an accomplishment. Though I did hear about the beginning of events in the camps, I did not want to listen to the rumors because I was involved in explaining to American Jewry that the Israeli government is doing more on behalf of religion than [that of] any other country. I must state that when I returned here I was very disappointed, and I conveyed my disappointment to the prime minister. Of course, I cannot take upon myself responsibility for everything [about which I will testify], for I wasn't here. However, from all that I have heard I am forced to the conclusion that there is some basis to these rumors, and that scare tactics and threats were used in the camps. I also want to comment with regard to the propaganda being conducted in the camps, for it is important. There was a propaganda campaign carried on in the camps to the effect that the entire matter of religion and tradition [is something] characteristic of the Diaspora, and that here in Israel there is a better substitute for religion, and that religion is already superfluous. As far as I am concerned, I am almost certain that there was such propaganda.

If these things are not correct, then those who disseminate this slander should be punished, but if there is a basis for this information, this evil must be uprooted from the source. You need [try to] think like a religious Jew. We have been waiting for Redemption for two thousand years. We, the religious Jews, believe that religion and Torah are the very essence of our lives; we believe that in the Diaspora a Jew cannot live as he is supposed to live, and that only in this country can one ascend spiritually. This is a very serious issue; it is not a matter of joining or not joining a government coalition.

We do not wish to sever the Jewish people into two nations. If here in Israel there will be persuasion and coercion of religious people, if religious people will not be able to be free like others, this will cause a deep split within the Jewish people which we will afterwards be unable to bridge. We are a young state, we have just now come into existence, and we confront difficult problems that increase from day to day. We religious Jews would prefer a uniform education, for we are one people and have one Torah. We must be careful, because everything we have accomplished can be destroyed by our own hands. There is no room here for obfuscating things: we must uproot the evil from the roots. We must have the courage to investigate, and to punish those who are guilty, this through a joint effort. These rumors and reports make a bad impression overseas. We must acknowledge that we are living in a democratic country. We are not like Russia [i.e., the USSR], where nobody knows what goes on inside it. Everything that is done here, everything said in the Knesset, every minute detail—all is known in the Jewish and non-Jewish world. There are correspondents and there is radio, and people make a major issue out of every little thing. Nothing can be covered up, and obfuscation won't help. That is what I wanted to say about the matter in general.

Almost everybody now admits that there are presently non-religious educators in the camps of the Yemenite Jews and those of Jews from Oriental countries, in which the immigrants are religious. Clearly, one cannot educate children against one's own feelings and consciousness. If the teacher is not religious, he in any case cannot educate towards a religious life. There is a great difference between religious and non-religious teachers, even in regard to neutral subjects and sciences. Secular influence can be felt in any sphere. As for the youth, it is clear that Hanoar Haoved and the entire social milieu can influence the Yemenite youngsters and view these matters through eyes that have never seen such things. It is clear that they are having a good effect upon them in material matters—this makes an influence. The result is that immigrant youth is also influenced regarding religious matters.

People have spoken to me about the matter of *payot*, etc. It is not the *payot* that are important: one can be a religious Jew without *payot*, and a non-religious Jew with *payot*. But when Mr. Shazar testified that they don't cut the children's hair, that it only happened once, etc., I considered this to be a case of some degree of covering up. I met many children who told me that they cut their *payot*, and not for health reasons, because they cut only the *payot* but left the forelocks. If they claim that this was done for health reasons, then why, I ask, didn't they cut the hair of the girls as well? There are many children whose *payot* alone were cut off. Rabbi Cahanmann of Zichron Meir relates that he heard children who study in his institution say, during the Blessing after Meals: "May the All-Merciful take vengeance for us, may the All-Merciful punish Zippora." He thought this to be a Yemenite custom, because they were Yemenite children. But it turned out that Zippora was the instructor who cut off their *payot*. One must not cover up this matter, and one must not say that it was done for health reasons.

Rabbi Levin concluded his testimony, saying:

I think that you have a historical role [to play]. I believe the day will come when even non-religious Jews will thank us for standing guard and protecting religion in the State of Israel. The whole world looks upon us as a young state which has been resurrected. We must be very careful and ensure that there be no coercion regarding religion. If the Yemenite tribe, which awaited Redemption for two thousand years, came here, it should be allowed to live here as it wishes.

B. TESTIMONY OF DEPARTMENT HEADS, PUBLIC PERSONALITIES, AND ORGANIZATIONS

Following the testimony of the three government ministers, the commission continued to hear testimony concerning the general background of the issue of education in the camps. It first heard personalities and representatives of those organizations which had raised complaints and accusations against those responsible for education in the camps, and then those against whom the accusations were directed.

1. Religious Front Members of the First Knesset's Education Committee

Knesset Member D. Z. Pinkas saw the crux of the problem in the necessity of transferring responsibility for education in the camps to the Education Division. The purpose of his testimony was to demonstrate that the scandalous events concerning education in the camps did not arise in one day but were preceded by lengthy developments.

> So long as there were not many children in the camps, education was handled by the Culture Department, first of the Va'ad Haleumi and afterwards of the government's Ministry of Education and Culture. . . . Mr. Nahum Levin, who heads this department, though he is not its director, brought to the camps a vulgar type of culture—female dancers and singers—presenting this as Israeli culture. After the Ministry of Education was established, I approached Minister of Education Mr. Shazar and drew his attention to this matter. He replied: "I've already heard about this, I have abolished the whole business, and now in camps they are already dealing with Jewish culture."

After the passage of the Compulsory Education Law, Mr. Pinkas was of the opinion that education of children in the camps should be provided by the Education Division and within the framework of the above-mentioned law, since the camps are an inseparable part of the State of Israel. He demanded this at a session of the Knesset Committee on Education conducted on 23 Heshvan 5710 (15 November 1949). At that session he stated that there are between 10,000 and 15,000 school-age children in the camps and no regular educational care of these children. Mr. Pinkas cited the response of the Director of the Education Division, Dr. B. Ben-Yehuda, as recorded in the protocol of that same meeting, from which it emerged that he too agreed that education must be made the responsibility of the Education Division:

> There is a fairly large blemish in the matter of which Mr. Pinkas spoke—the issue of the camps. Thus far, education of the children in the camps was not the responsibility of the Ministry of Education. I cannot say exactly how the matter developed. Last year, when we began to open schools in abandoned villages, the need was so great that we were pleased that they freed us to turn our attention to other matters. The Jewish Agency, on the other hand, saw the camps as a kind of continuation of the Diaspora, as if a person's aliya[6] to the Land of Israel began only after he left the camps; hence they took [responsibility for] the camps upon themselves. Since people were not in the camps for such a lengthy period of time, it also didn't present such a big problem. Meanwhile, the situation has changed: the period during which immigrants remain in the camps has grown longer, and there are immigrants who stay there for six–seven months. There is also another factor that one should bear in mind: until now, those who came to the camps had few children, so that this wasn't such a great problem; the problem concerned mostly

kindergarten children, there not being such a great problem in relation to schoolchildren. Those coming to the camps today have many
children, and the problem increases from day to day. We have learned
that the children in the camps are being cared for in some fashion.
But this is more care through recreation centers than through
schools, and from an educational viewpoint this is not a proper
arrangement. The Division is prepared to assume responsibility for
the education of the children in the camps. In my last meetings with
the minister I also raised this question and he confirmed that education in the camps would be transferred to the Education Division,
like [that in] all other schools. In a very few days we shall meet with
the representative of the Jewish Agency and begin to open schools
for immigrant children in the camps as well. We hope that within a
short period of time education in the camps will also be transferred
to the Education Division, so the children will receive good—or
poor—education, but the same as that received by the immigrant
children in all of the abandoned villages. Of course, if we handle education in the camps as well, registration will be conducted there as
well, and we will open schools there as is customary everywhere, according to the same rules and the same procedures as in all other
schools for immigrant children in Israel.

Mr. Pinkas also cited sections from the minutes of the meetings of the Knesset Committee on Education of 2 Kislev 5710 (23 November 1949), 9 Kislev 5710
(30 November 1949), and 16 Kislev 5710 (7 December1949) to show that he had
not desisted from this issue, and that at every session he related new facts and new
difficulties in the camps, such as the signing of declarations by thousands of parents that they wished to register their children in the Workers Stream.

At the session of 8 Teveth 5710 (28 December 1949), he submitted a parliamentary query to the Committee on Education, which we quote here in full because it marked a sharp turning point in the controversy concerning education in
the camps, particularly after this query was widely publicized in Israel and abroad.
The following is the text:

I deeply regret that I must express great anger. At several sessions of
the Committee on Education, I asked what the Ministry of Education
intends to do in order to have education in the camps operated by the
Education Division. Already at the previous session I heard from Dr.
Ben-Yehuda that all preparations were being made and that this would
soon be implemented. If Dr. Ben-Yehuda will confirm this even today,
that things are being done, I would be satisfied, but according to the information I have some things are being done there that should not be
done. [The information is] that an institution known as the Absorp-

tion Committee—which is under the responsibility of Mr. Nahum Levin, acting director of the Culture Department in the Ministry of Education and Culture—has decided not to transfer responsibility for education in the camps to the Education Division but continues itself to operate it. I hear that the Education Division, which is directed by Dr. Ben-Yehuda, has not yet done that which is necessary to place education in the camps under the authority of the Education Division, and that they continue to carry on there something that resembles education, through the agency of a body headed by Mr. Levin. I do not want to give a personal evaluation of Mr. Levin, whether his own training is adequate for him to head an operation of this type. I can only state, according to the information in my possession, that what is being done in the immigrant camps, to use the mildest possible language, may be termed coercion of conscience and inquisition against the Jewish religion. This man employs dozens of teachers and chases away, even by use of the police, religious teachers who come to work with him. I know that there are destructive acts being perpetrated against the Jewish religion. I claim that there has never before been such a state of coercion and exploitation of the unfortunate situation of the people in the camps. An attempt is being made to make them abandon their religion and their beliefs.

The day before yesterday the Treaty against Genocide was discussed in the Knesset. I claim, with full responsibility, that the activity of Mr. Nahum Levin and his associates is cultural and religious murder and that if this matter does not cease immediately, the coalition known as the State of Israel will fall apart at the seams. At this moment I represent the Religious Front and I declare that we shall launch a civil war, a truly bloody war, if this does not stop immediately. I demand that the minister of education and culture give orders immediately to cease the activity of this body, and to accept responsibility for education [in the camps] in accordance with the [Compulsory] Education Law. True, I was bitterly disappointed by the minister of education who at the outset of his term in office became a law violator when he dispersed the Executive Committee, and I am disappointed that he continues to transgress the law by allowing this ongoing violation of the Education Law, which established [educational] streams and stated that the Education Division will be responsible for the education of children in Israel. I ask: Are the camps outside the State of Israel? Did someone give the minister of education the authority to turn over the education of tens of thousands of children to a person who engages in the destruction of Jewish religion, the cutting off of *payot*, economic pressure, threats of denial of work and of the arrangement of housing? These are the means which are used to pressure parents to allow their children to receive an education that is contrary to their religion and their beliefs.

I propose the appointment of a commission of inquiry with the participation of several members of the Committee on Education, and I am prepared to bring before this commission dozens of witnesses who will testify to what is being done within the camps. I will demand the punishment of those who violate the law and prevent the government from applying the Education Law in the camps, as it is applied throughout the State of Israel. We will not remain silent, we will appeal to public opinion in Israel and in the entire world. Were the Poles, for example, to do to us what Mr. Nahum Levin is doing to us under the aegis of the minister of education, we would raise a great commotion. I never imagined that there could be such a rebellion against the law by people who are charged with its enforcement. I cannot demand more than that education be administered according to the Education Law: the existence of [educational] streams and freedom of registration. I think that it was the duty of Dr. Ben-Yehuda—director of the Education Division—to alert the Knesset Committee on Education after he was unsuccessful in carrying out what he needed to do, and to say: either they are hindering me, or I received other instructions, or I hold a different view. About six weeks have already passed since I heard Dr. Ben-Yehuda's statement that education in the camps is being transferred to the Education Division. Is he unable, over the course of six weeks, to carry out something which he has obligated himself to do, or is this a case of unwillingness? There is one fundamental principle necessary for any possibility of joint life and shared responsibility in this state—freedom of conscience in the education of children. What the Histadrut is doing in this matter is the application of a rule that we believed to belong to the Middle Ages, or to a period near in time to it. This is expressed in an old Latin adage: "He who rules also determines the religion of those he rules," the king decides the religion to which his subjects adhere. I accuse the Histadrut of attempting to apply this rule in our times. The people who do this are acting according to its instructions, and I am prepared to prove that they are also receiving payment from the Histadrut.

It is my intention that a commission of inquiry be appointed, and I wish to present it with all the facts. I offer my services as a member of this commission of inquiry, and I hope that there will be other members who will be prepared to join it. I will demand punishment of those who violate the law.

From the continuation of Mr. Pinkas' testimony, it emerges that according to his proposal the Knesset Committee [on Education] decided to appoint an investigating commission composed of the following members: Devora Netzer, Esther Raziel-Naor, Rahel Cohen, Yizhar Smilanksky, Mr. Pinkas, and Mrs. Persitz as chairperson. The investigating committee met for one session, on 12 Teveth 5710

(1 January 1950), and decided not to examine itself the material which had been submitted by Mr. Pinkas but to request the Ministry of Education to investigate the facts which he [Pinkas] had brought when making the accusations. The material was passed on to the Ministry of Education, and the investigating commission did not continue in its activity.

Regarding the question of propaganda overseas, Mr. Pinkas responded to questions raised by members of the commission:

> These acts were published in the press many weeks after we brought them to the attention of the state's authoritative bodies. We began to complain regarding this issue on 15 November, but until the beginning of January there was no publicity in the newspapers concerning this matter. Weeks passed without the matter coming to the attention of the public, yet the government did nothing to correct the situation. After the news was publicized here, it of course was also transferred to the Diaspora. I—and I emphasize this—never made any appeal to any place, neither directly nor indirectly, concerning our complaints. I had the opportunity to see some of the "jargon" [Yiddish] press in America, and I saw that they were full of [reports on] this subject, but all this was from correspondents here and through news agencies.

After quoting an exchange of telegrams with the Religious Front (to which we will refer further on in this report) and copies of which have been attached to the files of the commission, the witness continued:

> There was another telephone conversation. A day before the rally I was called, to my great surprise, by the head of the Religious Bloc in America. He phoned me from America, told me that next day they were holding a rally, and asked me whether I had received the telegram and whether I had replied, and also whether the other people who had been asked to communicate had done so. I said that I would do what I could and would ask the others. I know that Rabbi Herzog replied, [and] I know that Rabbi Maimon sent them a telegram giving a negative reply to their request and advising them not to assemble—but the rally took place nevertheless.
>
> I mention this because Mr. Ben-Gurion asked me who had misled the Religious Bloc in America. He considered their telegram to be a mistake on their part. I said that they had been led into such a failure by the Ministry of Education in Israel, which does things that call for such a reaction, and if this is a failure then it is our failure. One thing is clear to me: everything done in Israel is widely publicized in the Diaspora, and there is nothing new in this. I recently visited America, and I saw the tremendous reaction to every little thing done in Israel.

To the question of the chairman as to whether the response abroad was organized from here, Mr. Pinkas replied:

> No! Absolutely not! In any event, there was no appeal initiated on the part of the Religious Front. There was some action on my part after Rabbi [David] Lifschitz, Chairman of the Religious Bloc in America, told me over the telephone that Hamizrachi in America did not want to participate in this rally for reasons that are beyond my understanding, and he thought that they need to be told that they must do so, and after I heard that Rabbi Maimon had sent them a telegram that they shouldn't participate, believing this to be an expression of anti-Zionism—I wired that in my opinion they ought to participate.

Neither Minister Shapira, Minister Levin, or Mr. Pinkas, were able to provide any information based on investigations they had made but referred us to sources from which it would be possible to obtain direct information concerning facts and deeds. Representatives of the World Center of Hamizrachi and of the Va'ad Hayeshivot did likewise. Even though representatives of the latter two groups were able to testify about that to which they had been eyewitnesses or about personal impressions from visits to the camps, the commission did not rely upon their testimony alone in order to come to conclusions but insofar as possible sought firsthand testimony of people who were able to tell of things involving themselves. Much help in locating these sources was received by the commission, in particular from Rabbi Goldberg, who had himself visited several of the camps, and in the wake of his clear testimony, it was possible to arrive at an examination of the facts.

2. Va'ad Hayeshivot

Va'ad Hayeshivot is, as was explained to the commission by representatives of this body, an umbrella organization uniting a large number—according to them, more than sixty—of *yeshivot*.[7] These include some of the oldest *yeshivot* in the country, such as Etz Hayyim, as well as those which had been transferred to the country from abroad, such as those of Poniewiec, Mir, and so on. The organization as a whole is known as Va'ad Hayeshivot and is headed by the [Ashkenazic] Chief Rabbi of the Land of Israel, Rabbi Herzog.

Mr. [i.e., Rabbi Baruch Pinhas] Goldberg, supervisor of the Talmud Torahs[8] of Va'ad Hayeshivot, recounted the beginning of the group's activities in the camps:

> During the month of Shevat 5709 [31 January–1 March 1949] we were approached by immigrants from the camps and those active around the camps, asking us to come to their help by providing reli-

gious teachers and also to send them ritual objects. The reason they came with this request was that, first of all, there are many camps without any teachers at all, and the children there do not receive any education. Secondly, in several camps in which there are already teachers the teachers are not religious, while the majority of the immigrants in those places were religious and did not want to send their children to the schools in the immigrant community centers. They appealed to Va'ad Hayeshivot, as an institution that supports the establishment of religious educational institutions in Israel, to also provide help to the immigrant camps. Of course, initially we did not want to get involved in this. We asked them to turn to the director of the camp or to the director of the Culture Department and ask them to see to this. When we learned of the reply received to the request they had made of the director of the camp, who answered that this was not his responsibility, that he was not at all involved in education and [that this area] is [the responsibility] of the Culture Department; and after receiving reports that they had appealed to the cultural coordinator and also to the Culture Department in Tel Aviv, asking them to send religious teachers, but had been turned down, we felt it incumbent upon us to come to their help. We started to help, not by sending teachers directly from Va'ad Hayeshivot, but by helping those activists who were handling such matters and who sent teachers to instruct the children in the camps. We helped the activists, among whom were several new immigrants from the camps themselves, with regard to ritual objects and by providing a budget for religious teachers.

As requests increased to send teachers, and also ritual objects, to the camps, we turned to these activists who asked for our help and told them that we were prepared to provide them with aid only after they would apply directly to the Culture Department and its director, Mr. Nahum Levin, requesting in writing, in a letter signed by the immigrants from each camp, to provide them with teachers. If the Culture Department would not help them, then we would weigh the provision of such help. We changed the order [of things], because we originally thought that they were only talking about one or five teachers, but they later requested that we send several teachers to each camp, and we also heard that the directors and staffs of the camps objected to this, and we did not want to get involved in a dispute with them. We received reports that they were not allowing the teachers there to teach the children.

During the months of Sivan–Tammuz [June–July 1949] (we had begun in Shevat [February]), we heard disturbing reports regarding the educational situation in the camps and the manner in which the religious teachers were received in the camps, something which we had not at all expected. We thought that religious teachers had not been sent to the camps only due to lack of budget or because of a lack of organization; but then we heard that religious teachers had come, asked to be allowed to enter the camps, and were refused permission. On the contrary: they were told that they had no permission to enter the camps, and even after they entered the synagogue to teach the children, [the officials] objected to this.

After several important persons, including renowned rabbis, appealed to us to assume this task, to send teachers, we decided that I myself would visit the camps and see the general condition of education, and the situation in general, after religious teachers had been sent with our help, though not directly by us. I began to visit the camps.

At this stage, Mr. Goldberg cited a number of facts which will be discussed later.

3. The World Center of Hamizrachi

In order to add another aspect to this general background, we cite here a passage from the testimony of representatives from the World Center of Hamizrachi, Mr. [Yeshayahu] Bernstein and Rabbi Bezalel Cohen:

Our material includes two facts that do not pertain to the camps but rather to the general background and to members of the government, [specifically] to two highly respected members of the government of Israel: Minister of Culture Mr. Shazar, and the prime minister. The first fact is that we met with Mr. Shazar in his office on 25 Elul [5709; 19 September 1949]. Among other things we discussed, we brought to his attention complaints concerning cases of coercion, pressure, and police intervention. Present at this meeting were the two of us, Mr. Pinkas and [MK Zerah] Warhaftig. He [Shazar] said that he would investigate this, and we relied upon his investigation. However, by the end of Teveth [mid-January 1950] there had not yet been any investigation, neither by himself nor by his ministry. I can justify his own lack of activity, because he was ill in the interim for an extended period of time, albeit even during that time there was contact between himself and the Ministry of Education. I assert that had the investigation been conducted in due time, it would have been possible to avoid much suffering regarding this matter. It was this attitude of belittling that contributed a great deal to the way in which things developed thereafter.

We met with the prime minister on 23 Kislev 5710 (14 December 1949) and presented him with a memorandum containing the demands of Hamizrachi concerning education, a comprehensive memorandum. Present at this meeting were the two of us, Pinkas, Warhaftig, and Mr. [Rabbi Arye Leib] Gelman. At that meeting we presented him with a memorandum about Hamizrachi's demands concerning education, and cited two facts from a letter of the representative of

Haoved Hadati[9] in Tarshiha[10] (or, according to the Hebrew name, Me'ona) and Lifta (Mei Naftoah).[11]

We brought these two facts to the attention of the prime minister. During the course of this meeting, I recorded the following statement by Mr. Ben-Gurion: "If there is any coercion of the immigrants, it must be stopped; that is an obligation of the government. Both the Jewish Agency and the government must make sure of that. I will investigate the facts mentioned in your memorandum about Tarshiha and Lifta: I will investigate both in the party and at the site. Such acts must be uprooted from the source!" I regret to say that we have no information regarding such an investigation of this matter or of any conclusions [drawn].

Elsewhere, Mr. Bernstein said:

> Our main claim is that this entire matter is essentially one of coercion. These people are under government pressure, and they sense themselves as being under pressure. Our main conclusion is that we ask for the general obstacle to be removed! That is, placing responsibility for the education and culture of religious people in the hands of those who are not religious. This is the original sin.[12] We would not have reached such a state had approval not been given from above.

Several of the witnesses also touched upon the problem of education in the work villages and immigrant settlements. Although these problems were beyond the scope of the mandate given [to the commission], the commission found it proper, in order to clarify the situation, to relate also to claims regarding coercion and pressure in educational matters in these places, insofar as these involved facts pertaining to the first educational arrangements, shortly after the departure of those who had been living in the immigrant camps.

4. Haoved Hadati

The testimony of the representative of Haoved Hadati dealt primarily with immigrant settlements. Since it touched upon certain facts, these will be presented elsewhere in the report. However, it is worthwhile citing here the following passage from the testimony of Dr. [Yeshayahu] Leibowitz:

> I came into contact with the new immigrants in several of the new *moshavim*[13] and in several workers' villages. I was in the environs of Jerusalem, in Lifta, in Malha, as well as in the settlements of the northern Sharon [Plain] and in Ein-Ayala. As noted by other colleagues, I too found that the local instructors used threats against the new settlers,

who had just left the camps, mostly members of the Oriental communities, encouraging them towards a certain tendency in education.

The general impression we gathered regarding the question of the state of education in the work villages and in the new workers' *moshavim* was that the decision of the Histadrut Executive that obligates the provision of religious education for those settlers who request it for their children exists and is affirmed by the central institutions of the Histadrut, but there are many who violate it among those acting locally in its name. There is interference and subtle forms of obscuring and hiding [it], and at times recourse is also had to coarse and brutal means of threats and coercion. We are forced to put up a fight in each and every place.

5. Rabbi Unterman

In order to have access to primary sources for the investigation of certain facts and events which took place, we also asked for the testimony of the Chief Rabbi of Jaffa and Tel Aviv, Rabbi [Isser Yehuda] Unterman, who had visited the camps of Beit Lid VII, Ein-Shemer, Mahane Israel, and Rosh Ha'ayin. The commission also asked [other] eyewitnesses about the facts cited by the rabbi. We bring here several passages from his testimony concerning conditions found by the rabbi and his colleagues in their visits to the camps.

> In Mahane Israel I met after *Minha*[14] in the synagogue some of the immigrants from Poland, Romania, etc.; when I asked about their condition, they immediately began a series of complaints about the educational situation. "We cannot educate our children to live by the Torah and observe the commandments, as we did even during war time." We questioned them, and they told us that there is a school, but the school is not only non-religious, it is not even neutral. . . . Thereafter we went to see the [camp] director, and sat with him for about an hour. The director spoke with us pleasantly and respectfully, and he seemed to agree with us. I said that in the days of the Czar the synagogue served as a fortress in which [Jews] found refuge, whereas here they had a person removed from the camp with his hands tied behind his back (see below, chapter on "Facts").[15] I added: these same people whom you relate to as "criminals" are teachers of Torah. He replied that he had to travel to Tel Aviv. I was sure that he had agreed with us. A day or two later I heard that he had apparently returned from Tel Aviv with other instructions, because they again came and expelled the children from the house [that had served as a school], hung a lock [on the door], and notified that families would be housed in this building.
>
> After that we were in the Yemenite Ein-Shemer Camp I and heard the same things, only more extensively. Not only is there no reli-

gious school, but there were rumors abroad that they draw children to the cinema, they take boys and girls to dances, and they [the children] rebel against their parents. One [of the immigrants] complained of great immodesty among the young girls. There are some who are married and were modest, and suddenly they dance in immodest dress, and this arouses very grave fear in their hearts.

I wanted to know the general trend of events, and not the specific case of an individual sinner. We went to see the director, [Mr.] Trachtenberg, and went to the synagogue with two Yemenite rabbis, Alchech and Yihya Nahum. The Yemenites know and admire him. I asked them to help us understand what the Yemenites want. In the synagogue we found a temporary religious court which resolves various disputes. The public started to shout; with difficulty we managed to quiet them, Rabbi Yihya Nahum speaking to them in their own dialect. The director who stood next to me was angry: "He is not allowed to speak that way." I said to him: "Why? He isn't inciting them to rebel. He is just telling them what we also tell new immigrants: that they should observe the commandments!" I said that, for example, this is a free country, and that one is allowed—although I personally may not like it—to walk around in short trousers, and that Jews who came with *payot* are allowed to go about wearing *payot*. They said that they are lacking books—we sent them. They asked for a holy ark, and we sent them. . . . Among the complaints that I heard from the public was that the children who go to the cinema or listen to the radio on the Sabbath become irreligious.

Rabbi Unterman then recounted his conversation with Mr. Nahum Levin:

When I returned I invited Nahum Levin, and also with me were Rabbi Ochs (the director of Moria) and Hayyim Okin of the Beit Ya'akov school. An interesting conversation developed between us, and he said that his aim is in particular to ensure that people receive that which unites the country—in brief, rhetoric, but I did not find that he was really prepared or willing to give these Jews religious freedom.

Rabbi Unterman told of his conversation with Mr. Levin concerning the youth camps:

Youngsters aged 13–14 are in the greatest danger, and it is possible to completely destroy their world [of beliefs and customs]. Mr. Levin showed us a curriculum with 4 hours of Bible study, and Rabbi Ochs said that this is too little; moreover, the question is what they study during the other hours. Then there was another question: Who will teach the Bible? I came from England, where the Catholics do not allow the Protestants to teach their children religious subjects. All the more so we cannot allow teachers who are not at all religious to teach our children Torah. We argued, and agreed to meet again, but we did not meet. Our feeling was that this Jew's view of education is that the study pattern must be fashioned only according to his wishes, like a factory all of whose implements are fashioned in one style.

We spoke shortly about the subject of *payot*. The public was in an uproar about the cutting off of *payot*, but for me educational arrangements are far more important.

6. Director of the Department for Language Teaching and Cultural Absorption among Immigrants of the Ministry of Education and Culture

Mr. Nahum Levin, director of the Department for Language Teaching and Cultural Absorption among Immigrants, testified before the commission during the course of four sessions.

Mr. Levin's position and title require some clarification. Mr. Nahum Levin referred to himself as "Director (or Acting Director) of the Culture Department of the Ministry of Education and Culture." His official title, as provided to us by the Ministry of Education, was "Director of the Department for Language Teaching and Cultural Absorption among Immigrants." Indeed, the major effort of this department, as became clear from the testimony of the department's regional supervisor, Dr. E. Lubrani, is carried out in the camps, although there also are some activities in the cities. The Ministry of Education and Culture has apparently not yet established a full-fledged department to deal with all cultural affairs throughout the country, in all of their varieties and aspects, parallel to the Education Division. It should be noted that according to the testimony of the director of the Education Division, which shall be dealt with below, there is no contact between this division and the department headed by Mr. Levin. It also became clear from the testimony of the supervisor of the Torah Section of the Ministry of Education and Culture, Docent Lifschitz, that there is no substantive contact between the department dealing with matters of culture for the immigrants and the Torah Section, directed by Rabbi [Avraham] Hen. The commission saw fit to note these facts, since all educational matters in the camps are in the hands of the department headed by Mr. Levin.

At the beginning of his testimony, Mr. Levin lodged a vociferous protest, referring to Mr. Pinkas' statement before the Knesset Committee on Education and Culture, which included accusations lodged against him and his colleagues regarding "cultural and religious murder, inquisition against religion, forcefully making observant children abandon their religion and their beliefs." He then proceeded to describe the way in which things developed in the camps. He told of the great difficulties he had encountered when suddenly, with the creation of the state and the expansion of the camps, he was confronted by the problem of providing education for hundreds and thousands of children, without sufficient preparation and without any appropriate apparatus for this task. Under these conditions, he saw his main task as "providing the children in the camps with that which unites, and not with that which rips the nation to pieces." He stressed that, "Our primary success during this generation is the Israeli spiritual fortitude as forged anew here, the miracle that has occurred, the common denominator." He described Israeli strength as relying upon three main passions: "I speak of passions, not of ordinary inclinations or longings, not of lip service; passions that are imprinted in the blood of this people: a passion for the love of freedom, a passion for labor, and a passion for the love of man. . . . This is the great reason that the Hebrew nation has survived, for itself and for others. . . . We concentrated all of our very essence on the third passion—the passion for the love of man. . . . These are three sublime passions, and the Hebrew genius created them here in the Land [of Israel]. . . . The power of this spiritual strength is capable of uniting us all, it may serve as a spiritual basis for the entire nation."

After relating his experiences in the refugee camps abroad,[16] he said:

> I understood that we would encounter first of all a tremendous problem of immigration absorption, and that this will be the entire substance of the State of Israel. I feared this greatly, because I had the privilege of becoming acquainted with the masses who would come here. I got to know them there and I knew the great difficulty involved in their absorption. . . . These are brokenhearted masses, lacking faith in man after all they have undergone. Whether an individual was himself in a concentration camp or whether he was far removed from the concentration camp, the concentration camp left its mark upon all of those who are coming here. Even those who lived in North Africa felt it [i.e., the concentration camp] and feared it. But even worse, they lack faith in themselves. This great tragedy led to very strange results: on the one hand there are very pious Jews—and on the other hand there are those who are pious in their irreligiosity; that is to say, they are irreligious to the point of religiosity. . . . Of course, this is more evident in someone who was in Dachau and less so in someone who came from Yugoslavia. . . . We said to ourselves, let us find a way to approach these Jews, how to awaken in them first of all faith in us. We knew that there are only two things that, if we possess them, we may be able to overcome this psychological difficulty: first of all, love of Israel. . . . that they believe in us, in the simple sense of the word, that we desire their well-being. . . . We said [to ourselves] that we will shape the state . . . and prevent spiritual struggle and *Kulturkampf*, for to the best of our knowledge and our understanding, they are not yet ready for this. We will not give them that which divides, we will not come to them divided, and we will not come to them in order to divide.

Mr. Levin claimed that, "The masses of immigrants gratefully and with great satisfaction received the work of his department, both in the camps and in the immigrant settlements," adding:

> We said that this concrete project which we are operating—culture cen-
> ters, teaching the Hebrew language, lectures, artistic events—all these
> are capable of drawing people together; likewise group singing and
> choirs. But the concrete project is not enough of itself, and we said that
> we must bring the immigrants and the veterans closer together, insofar
> as possible. So this summer we undertook a wonderful project: We ap-
> proached the youth movements and told them that we wanted them all
> to come together—from Hashomer Hatzair through Young Agudat Is-
> rael—to the youth camps, where they would act together and present
> what is common to all to the youth in the camps. For weeks I met with
> the youth movements and conducted negotiations. It wasn't so simple, it
> wasn't so much the religious [movements] which were reluctant, but
> Hashomer Hatzair, who said they could not do that. I told them that if
> they were unable to do it this way, they wouldn't participate in this proj-
> ect. We must work out an organized, common program and together
> bring the message of the Land of Israel to the youth in the camps. In
> the end, everyone agreed. There were joint meetings under the auspices
> of the Youth Branch of the Ministry of Defense, and representatives of
> all the youth movements participated. Participating in this project were
> Hashomer Hatzair, Hatenu'a Hameuhedet,[17] Hatzofim [Girl and Boy
> Scouts], Bnai Akiva,[18] Ezra,[19] and Young Agudat Israel. About 400
> young boys and girls went out to three camps, or more correctly to three
> blocs of camps—in Pardes Hanna, in Beit Lid, and in Beer Ya'akov—
> and were active there for a whole month.

As for the role played by religious people in state cultural activities in the immigrant camps, Mr. Levin cited several names and figures, stating that during
Teveth 5710 (December 1949–January 1950) there were, among the 157 teachers
in the camps, 77 religious ones—that is, nearly 50 percent.

> When asked what is the criterion of religiosity or non-religiosity, he
> replied: Our questionnaire does not include any question as to whether
> the candidate is religious or non-religious—just as there is no question
> as to whom (i.e., to which party?) the candidate belongs. The depart-
> ment's Selection Committee charged with hiring culture instructors
> has received from me very detailed and strict instructions not to exam-
> ine the candidates except in terms of their personal and pedagogic
> qualifications. I mention the personal aspect first because, in line with
> what I told you at yesterday's session, this aspect is far more determi-
> native and decisive, even more so than the professional aspect.

When the storm erupted, and we nevertheless wanted to know, and the minister also asked me to inform him what the situation was—while warning me very strictly not to do so by means of a circular letter, because it is not in accordance with our policy and our norms to ask a teacher whether or not he is religious—we asked the principals of our schools to inquire of each member whether he is religious or not. Religious means that he observes the practical commandments, prays, observes the Sabbath, and all those things which are known as being characteristic of a religious person. When a person declares himself to be religious, I have no reason to doubt him.

During the year 5709 [1948–1949], we provided 9,400 Passover *Haggadot*,[20] 2,300 Scrolls of Esther,[21] 502 Bibles, 142 prayer books, 128 copies of the Mishna,[22] 67 sets of the Talmud, 87 copies of *Kitzur Shulhan Arukh*[23] and *Hayyei Adam*,[24] 51 Hasidic works of moral instruction, 230 *Selihoth*.[25] And this we certainly did out of the "desire to make the immigrants abandon their religion and their beliefs" and as "destroyers of Jewish culture."

I state here with full responsibility, and as a person testifying under oath, that to the best of my understanding and my consciousness, this storm comes from outside! Someone was interested in stirring up the camps and the state.

So long as there was no incitement from outside and the camps were not flooded with propagandists, the religious persons on our team were an integral part of the totality of the staff, and they performed their work faithfully. Happily, notwithstanding outside pressures, most of them even today remain loyal to our goals and our task, and continue to work out of a sense of solidarity with their non-religious colleagues. If they are called upon [to testify], they will even tell the truth regarding the "coercion" and "inquisition." Certainly, as religious people they would themselves wish that things were better from the religious viewpoint, that the camp would be more religious, etc. But it is clear that we are not a religious institution, we are not the Chief Rabbinate. We follow the middle path, and I spoke yesterday of this path. These colleagues can testify whether there was coercion here and whether people were forced to abandon religion or their beliefs. For in the final analysis, it is of this that we are accused, and it is regarding these accusations that you must pass judgment, and not as to whether or not we allowed Va'ad Hayeshivot to open schools. Regarding the latter question, there is no need for a commission: I will openly admit that we did not let them do so. I have not denied this, I do not deny it, and I never will deny it. We will not allow them or others to do so, even if they be very respected and important in the state.

Turning to the history of the children's centers (i.e., schools in the camps), Mr. Levin related that the issue of children in the camps was first raised in March

1948. Prior to that, there were no children in the camps. The first children—thirty-four in number—were brought to the centers in Hadera. When the [camp] coordinator approached him, he replied that this was neither his concern, his authority, nor his task, and that he also did not have any funds for this work. The witness eventually turned to the head of the Education Committee in Hadera and the latter, after some persuasion, expressed willingness to accept them, [in exchange for] payment of one pound per child per month and money for additional equipment. Since he [Levin] did not have any finances, he turned to Dr. Josephtal, but he did not respond because the situation of the Absorption Department also was difficult. And thus he began, under the pressure of events and the demands of the parents, to gather the children together for a few lessons. This was initially done through the volunteer work of teachers who taught the evening classes. As the number of camps grew, the number of children also increased, and there were more children's centers. With the appointment of the minister of education and culture to his present position, the witness appealed to him, both orally and in writing. He cited a letter from 21 Tammuz 5709 (18 July 1949):

> Within the framework of our limited budget for cultural and language activities in the immigrant houses [i.e., community centers], we are unable to operate the children's centers (transitory schools) in the immigrant houses in a proper manner. We have always considered the education of children in the immigrant houses to be the concern of the Education Division, and we have only taken this burden upon ourselves because we could not bear seeing the anguish of the children and their parents. On several occasions we have expressed our view on this matter to the directorate of the Education Division, and we now ask you to relieve us of this task, that is outside the scope of our activity and for whose implementation we don't have the appropriate means.
>
> The reply was dated 22 Av (17 August): "The subject which you raised is extremely serious and requires fundamental clarification. And indeed, take note that at one of your next meetings with the minister of education this question should be raised for thorough discussion. For the time being, no change will be made, of course, in the work arrangements among the children and the youth, and your activities will continue as previously."
>
> We again addressed him on 3 Kislev (21 November), arguing that "the education of children does not fall under the definition of the tasks of our department, and it has neither the funds nor the means required to deal thoroughly with this profession. We have only done so to meet an urgent need, which no one was meeting. The maintenance of the children's centers weighs heavily upon our limited budget, [which is intended] for activities among adults and youth. . . . I would be grate-

ful if you would inform me when the above-mentioned transfer, which has already been agreed upon in principle, will be carried out."

Mr. Levin continued his testimony:

I want to state clearly that until today I continue to request the transfer of the children's centers to the Education Division, and to this very day I believe that this matter must be transferred to the Education Division.

So long as the children's centers were the responsibility of the Culture Department, I could only act to the best of my national and personal understanding and conscience as a human being, this before the minister had been appointed. After he was appointed—in accordance with the policy that was approved by him, this policy being that "the uniformity of the children's centers in the camps must be strictly safeguarded," and this for the following reasons:

A. One should not apply [educational] streams to these people, who are living in the terrible conditions of the camps (because they are not ready for them, they do not understand, they are disgruntled, conditions are terrible, and *Kulturkampf* should be left out of the camps: they will have enough time to learn about this once they leave the camps. That is what we told ourselves).

B. There is a constant turnover of children in the camps.

C. Lack of residential space.

D. Lack of budget.

E. From a simple pedagogic viewpoint, what can be given to these children within this framework, during the course of the three hours that the teachers give voluntarily, apart from a little Hebrew, a little geography of the country, a little hiking, and some Hebrew songs?!

F. Most of those teaching the children also teach the adults. The children's center, since it was anyway in our hands, became in every camp—and I think it is good that we did this—the bright spot of the camp, influencing all cultural activity in the camp.

We therefore opposed the introduction of [educational] streams and did everything possible to prevent their introduction.

Nevertheless, we did recognize the religious problem that confronted us. Insofar as there were requests on the part of parents, from inside and without outside pressure, to open religious classes for their children—we opened them, but within the children's center and not outside it.

At the beginning of 1949 we were approached by a representative of the Workers Stream who requested permission to open classes for children of the workers, for the Workers Stream, in the camps. We conducted one conversation with him, albeit a lengthy one—but only one! During that conversation I attempted, to the best of my power, my understanding, and my conscience, to explain to them that they should not do this, and that if they do it, we will fight them—because we have no way of opening such classes. To my great sorrow, the religious circles did not behave in that manner, especially those who operated on behalf of Va'ad Hayeshivot, who were primarily those engaged in this "great work," carried out clandestinely, of signing up parents and setting them against our culture centers. We tell them: if you have teachers and we will have the budget, we will refer your teachers to the Selection Committee, and those who are qualified will be accepted; and indeed, many of them were accepted. On the one hand, they sent teachers to the Selection Committee, and on the other hand, they operated clandestinely. This same Rabbi Goldberg (whom I shall mention further on), came to me many times and I spoke with him. On the other hand, he would visit the camps, he and his emissaries, in order to open classes for the children. When they proposed: if you do not have funds, allow us to teach voluntarily—I could not accept this. There are many volunteers who were willing to come to the camps. They succeeded, and in no small degree, to my great distress, in bringing division into the camps. Willingly or unwillingly, they thereby infected the camps with the poison of division and hatred among brothers—and today there is hatred among brothers in the camps!

I want to state very clearly: this activity is also anti-Zionist, for it is aimed against the free state. I will mention here one example that shocked me: Gitta Landau, who teaches a religious class in Beer Ya'akov (incidentally, this class was opened clandestinely, but nevertheless I said: for the sake of peace we will allow this class, and we did), represented the state [i.e., as a state employee] in Beer Ya'akov. When a youth club was opened there and her pupils were invited to participate in its activities, she said: My children will not go to the club house. This was in connection with the re-interment of the remains of Herzl[26] in Israel, and the plan was to conduct a joint program. She said the whole business of transferring Herzl's bones is idolatry!

At the conclusion of his testimony, Mr. Levin addressed the issue of the Yemenites, saying:

This is an issue of a unique character. I was already acquainted with this tribe earlier, but in the course of my work I became closer to it.

It is a very noble tribe, perhaps the most noble of all the Tribes of Israel. It unites heartfelt emotion, purity of soul, and manual labor. But, together with this, the Yemenite tribe is very primitive. I have never yet seen quite such primitivism. And I say in the clearest manner: there is no way for you, for us, or for the state, except to serve as a bridge between them and the State of Israel. No other way is open to us.

The question is: what is the bridge over which we may reach the Yemenites and by which they may come to us? From close familiarity with the subject, I can say that the bridge lies in the magic attraction of the state. We must not ignore the fact that all of us are foreign to them. A *yeshiva* student from Bnai Brak is no less foreign to them than any other Jew. Believe me, gentlemen, that I am speaking the truth. Only one language is known to them, desired by them, and enchants them— and that is the language of the state. They were overjoyed that they came to the State of Israel. When I appear before them, and I have done this more than once, I speak for the state. And then I do not feel any barriers between us. I say: the state as a bridge is the only bridge, a bridge that does not disappoint and which has the power to transform the Yemenites into citizens of the state.

All of our cultural activity in the Yemenite camps, and also in the children's centers established in the Yemenite camps, is of an explicitly religious character. It is a crime to hurt this tribe, which is at once noble and primitive; it is a crime to undermine the branch upon which this noble tribe sits, namely, ancient Jewish tradition. We gave much thought to this question, and whoever knows anything about educational activity will understand this soul searching. We wondered how to proceed while relying upon the tradition of generations and at the same time providing them with the rudiments of elementary enlightenment: the milieu of the state, of the Yishuv,[27] and all that constitutes the great enterprise known as the State of Israel. For in the final analysis, it is our task and that of the state not to leave each Diaspora tribe in a state of Exile, but to make it a loyal partner in the great and wonderful Israeli revolution that is taking place and whose manifestation is the State of Israel and its achievements.

7. Director of the Education Division of the Ministry of Education and Culture

Dr. Baruch Ben-Yehuda, director of the Education Division in the Ministry of Education and Culture, began his testimony by relating the history of the administration of educational matters in the country, beginning with the Education Division of the Va'ad Haleumi of Knesset Israel until the establishment of the State of Israel. [The first months of Israel] were a transitional period during which the division continued to exist as part of the Va'ad Haleumi until, in anticipation of the beginning of the 1948–49 school year, a government ministerial committee was appointed. It was then that the provisional council and the already existing division were afforded a special status, and [the latter] became known as the Education Division of the State of Israel, without belonging to any ministry. The ministerial committee, consisting of six members, appointed an administrative committee, also composed of six members representing the ministers, on which Dr. Ben-Yehuda served as the seventh—as chairman, having a deciding vote.

Upon the establishment of the permanent government, the ministerial committee was abolished, and the administrative committee and the entire educational enterprise were transferred to the Ministry of Education and Culture. This was now named the Education Division, and Dr. Ben-Yehuda was appointed its director. All other activities, which had not previously been part of the educational undertaking, remained outside of the Education Division. The intention was that all those activities that did not belong to the Education Division would be concentrated in a parallel sector—the Culture Division. "But this does not exist, for there is no director in the other half of the ministry today that can be called 'The Culture Division.'"

> To the best of my knowledge, there is no Culture Division. . . . Nahum Levin is the Director of the Department for Language Instruction to Immigrants. . . . In addition, there are the Department of Antiquities, the Department of Physical Fitness (now called the Department for Physical Culture), there has just been established a section called the Music Section, and there is also a Department for Torah Culture, and another department connected with the dictionary of Eliezer Ben-Yehuda.[28] There are many activities, but they are not united into one division.

Even after the Education Division was established, it was not [the body] which opened schools. Rather, the local authorities opened schools, with permission from the division.

The following is what the witness related concerning the opening of the first school upon the beginning of the Great Aliya:

> At the end of the [Hebrew] year 5708 [i.e., autumn 1948], there was a vacuum for some time. Immigrants arrived, and nobody approached us officially—neither the Jewish Agency nor any other body—about providing the educational needs of the immigrant children. The first unofficial call came to us from Jaffa where, I believe, the first concentration of immigrants outside of the camps was located. At that time the administrative committee still functioned. There were some complaints about its members in our ranks, why they were not seeing to the

education of the children in Jaffa. Even though we did not have any budget for such an effort, we were in any event not used to opening schools in which 100 percent of the budget was taken care of, and such a state of affairs hardly existed anywhere in Israel. We were unable to see children going about in Jaffa without receiving an education.

That was how the first school was opened in Jaffa, and the first problems arose relating to the competition between the [educational] streams regarding the opening of the schools. We immediately established regulations in order to prevent friction. We sent a special committee comprised of representatives of the four streams, together with a fifth [person] who conducted the registration. Brief, printed descriptions of the nature of each stream were prepared so as to rule out oral propaganda that might cause friction among the streams. If any parent asked, he was provided with the sheet describing the character of each stream, and everything was done calmly: four schools were opened in Jaffa. . . . Nothing was written there either about a party or about the curriculum of studies. I don't have the descriptions here, but they were roughly as follows: the Workers Stream claims to educate the child to a life of labor, a progressive social life, justice, absence of exploitation, etc.; the Hamizrachi Stream states that it educates on the basis of Torah and labor; the Agudat Israel Stream says that it educates towards strict observance of [religioius] tradition and continuation of the education of the *heder*,[29] etc. No one noted in what he differs from the other streams; likewise, no one made a point of his party affiliation. We always avoid this, and even the streams, when describing themselves, claim no political affiliation. This activity was carried out peacefully, and four schools were opened in Jaffa, with our full financing.

This case served as a precedent. Shortly thereafter, immigrants settled at various points nearby—in Yahudia, in Salame, and elsewhere—and we continued to operate in the same manner in every place. Quite a large school was opened in Jaffa. In Yahudia, for example, on the day registration opened, there were all in all 52–53 children, and these were divided among three schools that opened on the same day: a school of the General Stream—17 children; a school of the Workers Stream—17 children; a school of Hamizrachi—16 children. This fact was later used to criticize the concept of streams. But in time the schools grew, and today all three of them (and I think there is already an Agudat Israel school there as well) are much larger.

This activity continued throughout almost all of 5709 [1948–1949]. Today we already have about 150 such schools, in all places where immigrants have settled. These schools were opened upon our initiative, and are 100 percent maintained by us.

Nobody mentioned the camps because, as you know, the camps were a transient and changing phenomenon. Generally speaking, people did not remain for a long time in the camps, and the camp was a

closed-off territory of the Jewish Agency. If in the immigrant neighborhoods we took the initiative without the Jewish Agency approaching us, in the camps no one else had the right of entry. A year and a
half ago the public was silent, the Jewish Agency did not turn to us,
and there was no initiative to take care of [education in] the camps.
This may have been a mistake on someone's part, but the prevailing
view was that the immigrants did not begin to be "part of the country"
until the day they left the camps: the camp itself was still an extension
of the activity of the Jewish Agency, of the process of aliya. It didn't
occur to anyone that we needed to take care of these people.

News concerning education in the camps began to reach the Education Division at the end of last year, 1948–1949. By then, the camps
had become a more permanent phenomenon, and there were groups of
immigrants who remained in the camps for 5–6 months. Immigration
from the Oriental countries, which was blessed with many children,
began. It was then we heard reports of joint action by the Jewish
Agency and the Culture Department of the Ministry of Education and
Culture, about the opening of schools for the education of the children.
This very much surprised us: someone told us that he was in a camp and
saw a sign reading: "Children's School of the Culture Department."
People expressed their astonishment: how can it be that this school is
called a school, and the Education Division doesn't know about it?

At the outset of the 1949–1950 school year education in the
camps began to be discussed in the Education Division. Within the di-
vision there is something we called "the Department": Mr. [Avraham]
Arnon is the Chief Supervisor for the General Stream; Dr. [Raphael
Halevi] Etzion is the Chief Supervisor for the Hamizrachi Stream;
Mr. Moshe Avigal is the Chief Supervisor for the Workers Stream; and
Dr. Avraham Deutsch is the Chief Supervisor for the Agudat Israel
Stream. I serve as chairman at meetings of the Department. There is
also a secretary: [Ephraim Dov] Serlin, who is the Chief Secretary of
the Hamizrachi Stream but also serves as secretary at meetings of the
Department, that consists of the chief supervisors together with the
director of the division. In practice, the "Department" is the supreme
pedagogic and administrative-pedagogic body overseeing the entire
educational system in Israel.

At a meeting of the "Department" on 6 Tishrei [5710; 29 September 1949],
there was general agreement that the minister of education should be asked to include the education of children in the camps within the educational system, for
according to the [Compulsory] Education Law, education is [also] compulsory
for them, and that the Education Division's astonishment at the fact that the
Culture Department is dealing with schooling for the children in the camps
should be conveyed.

The witness reported that he was supposed to convey the decision of the "Department" to the minister of education and culture, but the minister took ill. Some time later, when the witness visited the minister in the hospital (at the beginning of Kislev [i.e., late November 1949]), the minister affirmed that he agreed to the transfer of these activities from the Culture Department to the Education Division.

Adjunct to the "Department" is an Absorption Committee, whose function is to deal with all questions concerning the opening of schools in immigrant neighborhoods to prevent friction between the streams. The committee consists of four members, one from each stream. In a formal sense, this is a subcommittee of the "Department," because all of its decisions require the approval of the director of the Education Division. One of its four members serves as chairman of the Absorption Committee, and the committee chose Mr. Ya'akov Halperin, who is a supervisor of the Workers Stream and is today deputy chief supervisor of that stream [to fill that role].

At a meeting of the Absorption Committee on 4 Kislev [25 November 1949], the chairman announced a decision to transfer all schools in the camps from the authority of the Culture Department to that of the Education Division. It was therefore decided:

A. To approach the Culture Department and request relevant details;

B. To open the schools in the camps in an organized and orderly manner, by conducting registration in the presence of representatives of all streams;

C. Not to open a school for a given stream unless it had at least twenty registered pupils.

The committee later added that propaganda [for the streams] was permissible from that time on. In other words, the committee thought a priori that schools would be opened under the same arrangements as everywhere else—that there would be four streams, and there would be registration.

Dr. Ben-Yehuda went on to recount:

Three days later a meeting of the "Department" was convened, and its records show that Dr. Etzion raised the question of schools in the immigrant camps and wished to proceed to the placing of the schools in the camps under the supervision of the Department. [Ya'akov] Halperin participated in that particular meeting, because Mr. Avigal was in America in the early winter, and he was his replacement. The minutes [of that meeting] record that, "Mr. Halperin notifies that the Absorption Committee has already discussed this issue and charged its secretary to obtain from the Culture Department more-or-less exact figures of the number of school-age children in the camps. After this the committee will begin practical implementation, in the accepted manner." In other words, clearly everyone thought that there would be registration for four streams. The minutes conclude: "The Department requests the Absorption Committee to execute this matter as soon as possible."

Four days later, on 11 Kislev (2 December 1949), a meeting of the Absorption Committee was held at which it was reported that "Mr. Halperin proposes that the committee begin visiting the camps." At that same meeting, it was decided that they would meet on a certain date to visit the camps in Beit Lid and in Pardes Hanna. Afterwards they were busy visiting [the camps], and there was a two-week interruption in the meetings of the Absorption Committee.

At the meeting of the Absorption Committee on 25 Kislev (16 December 1949), there was a turnabout when it was proposed that two types of schools be opened in the camps, one religious and one that does not fly the banner of religion, and that control of each camp would alternate between the two streams—religious and non-religious. That is, to avoid tension within the camp, they would decide that in one camp there would be only a religious school, and in another camp there would only be a non-religious school. Dr. Deutsch thinks that Mr. Arnon's proposal will prevent conflicts. Mr. Halperin agreed that the problem of streams should not be introduced into the camps. He saw the following possibilities: (a) The Absorption Committee will continue to maintain the schools in their present form (that is, the first possibility is to leave the schools that were already being operated by the Culture Department), and that apart from the fact that they will be transferred from one authority to another, they will undergo no change. A pedagogic committee will be appointed to supervise the methods of instruction; (b) Mr. Arnon's proposal seems acceptable to him, but here there emerges one difficulty, namely, that no stream—neither the Workers Stream nor the General Stream—will agree to take upon itself the stigma of being "non-religious"; (c) To maintain the four streams with all their attributes. In his opinion, the best alternative is to maintain the existing situation.

After this turnabout, some doubt arose as to whether there is need to conduct registration in the camps, and there were already certain probes being made towards another view.

After that, the topic was raised at a meeting of the Department, and on 6 Teveth [26 December 1949] it was agreed, at Dr. Etzion's request, that education in the camps would be one of the first items on the agenda of the next meeting. A few days later, the agenda was once more clogged, and he asked that this matter be placed on the agenda of the next meeting.

Meanwhile, at the meeting of the Absorption Committee, Mr. Halperin reiterated the same proposal he had already raised at the meeting of the Department, namely, to leave the situation in the camps unchanged. The only change would be that the schools would be transferred from one authority to another. He suggested that pedagogic supervision of the camps be entrusted to the Absorption Committee and be executed by its members or by another committee which it would appoint.

In the discussion among the members of the Absorption Committee, according to the protocol quoted by Dr. Ben-Yehuda, the representatives of Hamizrachi and Agudat Israel agreed with the proposal of the representatives of the stream to have two types of schools in each camp—religious and secular. However, the representatives of the Workers Stream and the General Stream stated that under no circumstance would they be willing to accept the designation of "non-religious." It was decided: (a) To leave the schools in their present form; (b) To notify the parents of the option to send their children to religious classes.

At a meeting of the "Department" on 13 Teveth (2 January 1950), which was supposed to confirm the decision of the Absorption Committee, Dr. Etzion appealed against that decision. Dr. Ben-Yehuda read from the minutes of that meeting:

> Arnon again suggests two blocs. Dr. Deutsch agrees, but not to joint representation. Avigal (representative of the Workers Stream) accepts two blocs, but does not agree to call them religious and non-religious. It was decided that: (a) "The parents in the camps are unable to differentiate among the four streams, and the vast majority are only able to distinguish between one bloc and another." Votes in favor of this proposal were cast by myself, Arnon, Avigal, and Dr. Deutsch, against— Dr. Etzion. (He was of the opinion that even in the camps it would be possible to have [the parents] decide about the four streams.); (b) "Conditions in the camp require allowing for two blocs." This motion was accepted unanimously, also by Dr. Etzion. On this basis the following decisions were taken: (a) Notification will be made in the camps about the transfer of schools from the Culture Division [!] to the Education Division; (b) Announcement of the closing of the existing schools for two or three days, and the opening of two new schools, one for each bloc; (c) The schools will be referred to by the following titles: (1) Transitional school under the supervision of the General Stream and the Workers Stream; (2) Transitional school under the supervision of the Hamizrachi Stream and the Agudat Israel Stream; (d) Registration will be in the two schools. That is, a poll will not be conducted, but notification will be given about the opening of two schools, and each father can come and notify [to which school] he wishes to register his son, thus avoiding a poll and propaganda [by the

streams]; (e) This will be carried out by the Absorption Committee; (f) Representatives of the Jewish Agency will be asked to act through the local committee; (g) Each bloc will decide on the issue of joint supervision, as well as about a pedagogic committee. That is, each bloc will decide if it wants joint supervision or whether the schools are to be divided on a geographic basis. This decision was adopted because Agudat Israel notified of its opposition to joint supervision with Hamizrachi; (h) Each bloc is permitted to open a school, if at least 20 children are registered. These decisions were adopted on 13 Teveth (2 January 1950).

On 22 Teveth (11 January 1950), an appeal against this decision of the Absorption Committee was lodged at the meeting of the "Department," which decided [to sanction] two schools. The minutes of that same meeting record the following:

Halperin notifies that the Absorption Committee proposes one school having religious classes, to be under the supervision of a special committee. Dr. Deutsch denies that this was the decision taken by the Absorption Committee and requests implementation of the decision of the Department—two blocs. Avigal states that, as a new person who has just now returned from America, he erred at the previous meeting and now changes his mind and asks for one school having religious classes. Dr. Etzion demands implementation of the Department's decision regarding two blocs. Dr. Deutsch reiterates that he concedes that the camp inhabitants are unable to distinguish between one stream and another, but that one does need to distinguish between religious education and secular education. A request was made to bring the matter to the decision of the minister. As chairman of the meeting, I announced that I would bring the issue before the minister for his decision, and it was agreed that a meeting would be held in which all members of the minister's Department would participate.

Concerning the meeting with the minister in Haifa on 24 Teveth [13 January 1950], Dr. Ben-Yehuda reported:

By then the minister was already in a convalescent home, and all of us went to see him. The following is the precis of the protocol (the same arguments were repeated there; I only cite the altered proposal of Mr. Arnon): "Mr. Arnon proposes a transitional school with religious classes under the supervision of the General Stream and the Workers Stream, and a transitional religious school under the supervision of the Hamizrachi and Agudat Israel streams." The conclusions of this meeting entailed a certain change. It was decided as follows: "(a) In the

Yemenite camps only one school will be established; (b) A committee will be appointed to prepare the curriculum and appoint the teachers; (c) The curriculum will be based entirely upon religious elements, and the teachers must all be God-fearing and religiously observant people; (d) The four members of the committee (referred to in section b) must all be religious and observant, one from each stream. Their appointment will require the minister's approval; (e) As for those camps in which there are European immigrants, two schools will be opened, belonging to the two blocs, in accordance with the previous decision of the Department; or three schools—a united school of the Hamizrachi and Agudat Israel, a school of the General Stream, and a school of the Workers Stream; or four schools, Mr. Avigal asked to postpone decision on this clause until the next meeting; (f) In the other camps (that is, neither of the Yemenites nor of the Europeans), the directorate of the Department will visit and gather information concerning the makeup of the people there, in order to decide whether they are similar to the type of the Yemenite camps or to that of the European immigrants."

What was new [in this decision] was that only one religious school would be opened for the Yemenites, in which all the teachers would be religiously observant and God-fearing people. These schools were to be directed by a special committee of four people representing the four streams, but all of them Orthodox: that is, not only God-fearing[30] but also religiously observant. We drew a distinction between these two concepts, because we realized that there are many religious people in all the streams, but we decided that they must also be religiously observant. Their appointment would have to be approved by the minister. On this point there was some disagreement. Dr. Etzion, who tended to accept the entire proposal, asked that they be appointed by the Chief Rabbinate. But the minister said that he does not wish to introduce an additional [decision-making] element, and he assumes responsibility for appointing people who are God-fearing and observant.

At this meeting, the minister had to decide [among the different proposals]. The summary was adopted, apart from Avigal's reservation regarding those camps in which there are European immigrants. Myself and the secretary (a member of Hamizrachi) were to visit those camps and report to the Department as to whether they were like the Yemenite camp, and if not—whether it was necessary to open there [schools of] two blocs, or three or four schools.

These in effect are the principal issues with which the Department dealt. Thereafter the matter passed out of our hands and became a public issue.

These were the main testimonies regarding the general background of the conflict over education in the camps, testimonies that emphasize the general accusations leveled by [the supporters of] both approaches. While it is preferable to postpone their final summation until we clarify concrete accusations referring to specific places and cases which also will shed light upon the general accusations, it may already be stated at this stage that the main accusation raised by those who were concerned about religious education in the camps centers around entrusting that education to the Culture Department (as it is called below for the sake of brevity, although its full name is "The Department for Language Instruction and Cultural Absorption among Immigrants in the Camps"), whose personnel was fundamentally unsuited to the needs of a religious populace. Hence, from the very outset of the conflict, there was a forceful demand on the part of the religious [camp] to transfer education from this department to the Education Division.

CHAPTER 2

THE IMMIGRANT CAMPS

Before discussing specific accusations, we need to dwell briefly upon the establishment of the immigrant camps in the State [of Israel], how they developed, and the composition [of their population] during the period dealt with by this report, particularly the camps for Yemenite immigrants, which were a central subject of the commission's investigation.

The "camps" were a new feature introduced into the country following the establishment of the State of Israel in connection with the great waves of immigration that increased from month to month.

Former British Army camps were turned into immigrant camps. Those engaged in absorbing aliya frequently note that had it not been for these large camps with facilities for housing thousands of people, who knows how it would have been possible to receive the myriads of new immigrants to Israel.

On 15 May 1948, there were seven such camps in Israel, which served as homes for the new immigrants, and the [population] concentration in them was quite low—about 7,000 people all told—and this did not deviate from the accepted norm in the immigrant houses (*batei olim*) in Israel.

However, the number of camps increased at almost the same rate as did immigration:

On 1 September 1948, there were 13 camps, inhabited by 15,000 people.

On 1 December 1948, there were 16 camps, inhabited by 21,976 people.

On 1 March 1949, there were 21 camps, inhabited by 32,745 people.

On 1 June 1949, there were 27 camps, inhabited by 63,500 people.

On 1 September 1949, there were 32 camps, inhabited by 71,323 people.

On 1 December 1949, there were 34 camps, inhabited by 78,441 people.

By 28 February 1950, the number of camps reached forty-one, in which there lived about 88,000 people.

The camps were originally intended to serve as points of transit, like the former immigrant houses, in which the immigrants would stay for a relatively short period of time until completing their medical examinations and the necessary procedures for their registration and transfer to their permanent place of absorption.

And indeed, whereas the average stay in the immigrant houses until the end of 1948 was from four to six weeks, by February 1949 it had risen to seven to ten weeks, in April 1949 the average stay was already twelve weeks, and in April 1950 the average stay in the camps had become six months or more.

During the period from 1 September 1948, until 24 April 1949, 152,000 immigrants came from European countries, as opposed to 23,000 from Oriental lands (including about 17,000 from North Africa), who accounted for about 15 percent. However, during the second half of 1949 and early 1950, the number of Oriental immigrants, particularly from Yemen, increased, so that among the 88,000 inhabitants of the camps in February 1950, 57,752 were immigrants from Oriental countries, as against 30,296 from European countries (including immigrants from Turkey and "other Asiatic lands"), or 66 percent compared to 34 percent.

The following is a detailed table relating to the Yemenite immigrants, showing the dates upon which the camps were opened, the number of inhabitants, the number of children ages 6 to 13, the number of children studying in the schools, the number of youth ages 14 to 18, and the number of participants in the youth clubs—all based on information supplied to the commission by the Absorption Department of the Jewish Agency and the Department for Language Instruction and Cultural Absorption among Immigrants.

Name of Camp	Date Opened	No. of Immigrants 2.28.50	Children Ages 6–13	No. of Children in Schools	Youth Ages 14–18	No. of Youth in Camps
Rosh Ha'ayin I	9.13.50[1]	4,976	1,181		381	
Rosh Ha'ayin II	9.27.50	5,791	1,367	1,100	326	120
Rosh Ha'ayin III	9.28.50	1,212	264		101	
Ein-Shemer I	12.25.50	5,788	1,242		342	
Ein-Shemer II	11.13.50	5,394	1,292	1,700	428	150
Ein-Shemer III	12.4.49	3,312	484		208	
Beit-Lid VII	8.27.49	5,145	1,174	500	351	50
TOTAL		31,618	7,004	3,300	2,137	320

The table indicates that less than half the children were in schools in the camps, and the same holds true in relation to the youth.

To this report is appended a survey of the history of the Jews in Yemen and in North Africa, written by Mr. Izhak Ben-Zvi, a member of the commission.[2]

CHAPTER 3

SPECIFIC ACCUSATIONS

In turning from general to specific accusations, one ought to begin with those accusations which, while relating to specific facts, also have general significance.

A. Non-Religious Teachers and Youth Leaders

There were many complaints that the vast majority of teachers and instructors, as well as the general workers in the camps, are not religious. The argument raised is that not only are non-religious educators unable to provide religious education, but that the very fact that those running the camps are non-religious influences the way of life of the immigrants. For we are talking of primitive children, youth, and adults, who in the countries of their exile were accustomed to submission and ob-sequiousness, and when they need favors of the directors tend instinctively to try to please them by following in their footsteps and accepting their lifestyle.

How much truth is there in this accusation?

The minister of education reported that out of 170 teachers and instructors, 77 are religious; furthermore, he provided the commission with a list of the religious teachers. Mr. Nahum Levin reported the same number of religious [teachers] out of a total of 157. These numbers constitute about 50 percent of all the teachers, encompassing all the camps, but even they are not proportionate to the [number of] religious persons in the camps who, according to the estimate of the commission, constitute some 70–80 percent of the total number of the immigrants. Concerning Beit Lid (VII), for example, testimony was given that out of 9 teachers, only 1 is religious. There was also testimony given that in Ein-Shemer, which shelters Yemenite immigrants alone, only 8 out of 28 male and female teachers are religious.

Hadassa Lipmanowitz testified that out of 25 instructors in the youth clubs, only 2 are religious. She explained the difficulty involved in that they appealed to all the youth movements, including Hapoel Hamizrachi and Bnai Akiva, and received no response.

Moreover, there is no standard for determining the religiosity of a given employee, and this is a matter of judgment. Mr. Nahum Levin reported that at first they had not asked a candidate about his religiosity, and only after the conflicts [over the issue of education] did they begin to question each person orally, recording him as being religious or non-religious according to his reply. While generally speaking a non-religious person is not in the habit of describing himself as being religious, one needs to exercise some reservation when such a declaration is made under circumstances which are not lacking political overtones.

Thus, for example, a certain witness appeared before the commission who felt the need to present himself as being religious, yet there were substantial grounds for the commission to relate rather skeptically to this claim.

Apart from this, some of the cultural coordinators and school principals testified that they were not asked about the religiosity of their teachers at all. One cultural coordinator who testified that he had in fact been asked to inquire as to whom among his teachers were religious admitted that one teacher who appeared in the list as being religious was not recorded as such by him. Moreover, the lists of religious teachers include five Yemenite *melamdim*[1] from Beit Lid, but without noting their names. The commission learned that Yemenite *melamdim* had indeed taught at Beit Lid for two or three weeks in the month of Tishrei [September– October 1949], but that already in Heshvan [October–November] they were no longer teaching. The list was presented to the commission [three months later] during the month of Shevat [January–February 1950].

There is indeed a serious claim made by those dealing with education in the camps that there are not enough religious teachers; it was claimed that on the whole there is a great lack of teachers, and particularly of religious teachers. Mr. Nahum Levin rejected the proposal to send *yeshiva* students to teach in the camps, for two reasons: (1) that they are not certified teachers, nor do they have pedagogic experience; (2) that if he were to accept teachers of this type, he would need to open the camps to other streams as well, thereby violating the rule of unity which he had adopted as his policy.

This explanation seems unsatisfactory to the commission, for two reasons: (1) Lack of pedagogic experience would be an important factor if all the teachers and instructors had in fact been professionally trained, and if one were speaking of giving a proper education to the children in the schools. But in a situation in which the vast majority of the employees of the department are not professional teachers, the candidates proposed by Va'ad Hayeshivot were not on a lower pedagogic level. (2) This would not involve discrimination of those who asked to open special schools of the Workers Stream or of organizations such as Hashomer Hatzair, who also wished to send their own teachers and instructors, since these bodies are adequately represented on the department's staff in the camps, in several of which there are also Histadrut houses [i.e., clubs run by the Histadrut].

Thus, for example, Mr. [Dr. Eliezer] Lubrani, director of the regional office of the Culture Department in Galilee and Samaria, who supervises all of the Yemenite immigrant camps apart from Rosh Ha'ayin, commented that "most of the workers in the camps and in our department are Histadrut members."

There was a period during which it seemed as though the problem had been resolved by means of opening religious classes, after negotiations that were conducted between Mr. Goldberg, on behalf of Va'ad Hayeshivot, and Mr. Nahum Levin, in which the latter suggested an arrangement that had previously been suggested to the Torah Section [i.e., Section for Torah Culture], namely:

> If, in the view of the administration, on the basis of the opinions of the director of the regional office, the supervisor of the Section for Torah Culture, and the local cultural coordinator, a Torah [i.e., religious] class ought to be set up in the "immigrant house," and after an examination of the needs, [then] a religious teacher should be hired for this purpose to teach all the subjects to that class, and he and his class will be part of the framework of the local children's center (transitional school) and will be subject to the arrangements and work schedule of the local department.

Even though Mr. Goldberg was not satisfied with this arrangement, and even though he insisted that a religious class be opened immediately upon the request of the parents of twenty children rather than of thirty, as is the rule, he agreed to this. Mr. Levin initially intended to implement this arrangement only after receiving the consent of the Torah Section, headed by Rabbi [Avraham] Hen. Mr. Goldberg did not want the matter to be postponed, and it was agreed between himself and Levin that a circular letter would be sent to the camps without awaiting Rabbi Hen's agreement, but if the latter should object they would reexamine the question. Mr. Goldberg was prepared to go to the camps immediately in order to organize the matter. Mr. Levin objected to this, and it was agreed that Mr. [Hayyim] Lifschitz, of the Torah Section, should go in his stead. In the final tally, the circular was not sent out and, for reasons that are not entirely clear, Mr. Lifschitz did not go to the camps; above all, the agreement was not implemented.

B. Interference with Religious Studies

In addition to the accusation that no room was found for religiously observant teachers and instructors on the department's staff, the Culture Department is accused of interfering with religious studies even in the synagogues, of constraining the activities of the local Yemenite *melamdim*, and of preventing external teachers of religious studies from entering the camps. Some of those who came were chased away, and synagogues were also locked, except during hours of worship, in order not to enable religious studies.

What is the proof for this [accusation]?

1. Ein-Shemer

Rabbi Yitzhak Yitzhak Levi, a Yemenite immigrant from Ein-Shemer, an elderly and distinguished man, moderate and balanced in his words, and who was also accepted by the director of the camp, appeared before the commission together with three associates and testified under an affirmation of truth, that "after three weeks (since the arrival of Aldema) the *melamdim* came to me and told me that Aldema was hindering them from teaching and told them: Get out, you are not fit to teach. We vigorously protested. Aldema chose nine of the *melamdim*, and told the remaining ones, five in number, to go. The nine that remained were also interfered with, and they too left, so that not one Yemenite *melamed* has remained." Rabbi Yosef David Madmon, also a Yemenite, likewise testified that Aldema said that "there is no need for Torah [studies]."

There are also the testimonies of Yehuda Rieder and Moshe Segal, teachers in the Ein-Shemer school, to the effect that when Aldema came to the camp he announced at a teachers meeting that he would not allow the *melamdim* to teach Torah and that the teachers too would not teach Torah. One teacher who was present at that meeting, Sa'adya Yarimi, whose overall testimony gave the impression of being intended to justify the administration, likewise reported that when Aldema was told that the teachers were teaching Torah, he [Aldema] said that this was not to be done so long as there were no instructions from the department. As for the stopping of Torah instruction by the Yemenite *melamdim*, Yarimi said that the intention was only to separate [between the two types of instruction]—that they would teach separately and the [regular] teachers teach separately—since "the Yemenite *melamdim* have no conception of what a school is like." When asked about this, Mr. Aldema related the difficulties he had with Yemenite *melamdim* who do not know how to behave properly and are unfit to teach, and that he had kept on nine who were better than the others. He ascribed the cessation of their teaching for a brief time to the need for repairs in the building. This explanation was not convincing.

Regarding interference with Torah study in the synagogues in that same camp, Mr. Goldberg testified that "on 22 Heshvan [14 November 1949] at noon, the director of the camp (Trachtenberg) entered the synagogue and instructed the teachers to stop the classes and to leave the place. They refused. He then sent officials to forcibly remove the pupils from the synagogue. I gave instructions to continue, and then the director assigned the synagogue [as the venue] for meetings of members of the [Rabbinic] court."

Concerning discrimination in Ein-Shemer regarding religious schools, Rabbi [Yehoshua Zelig] Diskin testified: "The Midrashiya (a religious high school in Pardes Hanna) wanted to conduct an educational, cultural, and artistic program on Tu Bishvat[2] [2 February 1950], and encountered many difficulties, whereas the youth from Kfar Vitkin had always enjoyed free access to the place."

2. Mahane Israel

Two teachers, Piltz and Schneursohn, testified that they had been sent to Mahane Israel by Va'ad Hayeshivot at the demand of parents who requested religious education, and had begun to teach in the synagogue. After they were told that there was no need to teach in the synagogue since there is a religious school, the camp guards came, twisted Piltz's hand behind his back, dragged him to the gate, placed him in a hut, and [then] removed him from the camp. When he tried to return, he was threatened with a rifle. Schneursohn too was forcibly removed. Rabbi Unterman visited the camp during this same period, and according to his testimony before the commission, spoke with the director, [Yosef] Bodniv, who promised that the matter would be taken care of. The two teachers continued to teach in the synagogue. The principal told them that they must receive authorization from the department that they are teachers. The authorization was received but, said Piltz in his testimony:

> The director of the camp refused to receive me, saying that in the camp he decides and no one else. We continued to teach and then the director came, accompanied by the camp police and officials. The officials of the camp forcibly removed the pupils and then forcibly removed me and Schneursohn from where we were teaching. I publicized what happened in *Hatzofe*. Later, when I visited Mr. Ben-Zimra, an official with responsibility in the Culture Department, he told me that it is forbidden for teachers to engage in politics, and that since I published these things I had violated that prohibition. After Rabbi Goldberg intervened with Nahum Levin, I was permitted to continue teaching, but after two days the camp guard told me that he would not allow me to enter, and that if I went in he would not be responsible for the consequences, including bloodshed.

Yitzhak Schneursohn related that after he received authorization as a teacher he was transferred to the transit camp in Pardessiya. He said that there "nobody disputes that the children are religious, but apart from myself none of the instructors are religious. I feel like a *mezuza*—a *kashrut* certificate."[3]

Rabbi Fuchs and Rabbi Dramer of Mahane Israel confirmed in their testimony that two religious teachers had been hired after they and hundreds of other religious families decided to open a religious school in the camp. The teachers began to teach in the synagogue, but then the director, Yosef Bodniv, came and gave an order to close the synagogue. Sacred books and textbooks were thrown outside, and locks were also placed on the synagogue of the Sephardim and they would open it only during prayer hours, in order to prevent study in the place, and it also happened that people came to pray and found the synagogue closed and couldn't pray. Rabbi Dramer asked:

> Under what law was the director's order issued, which does not allow religious Jews to educate their children according to their inclinations? When I was in Romania, a Communist country, I was able to maintain in my neighborhood three Talmud-Torahs and a school for girls, and every religious Jew was able to educate his children according to his wishes, while here in our own country the right of the religious Jew to educate his children as he sees fit is violated in an arbitrary and vulgar manner.

In his testimony before the commission, Mr. Bodniv, the director of the camp, confirmed that he prevented study in the synagogue. This, he said, he did in accordance with instructions and what was customary—that synagogues are closed other than at times of worship, but he had no knowledge that they found the synagogue closed at prayer times. He denies that they removed textbooks and holy books from the synagogue.

3. Athlit

In this camp the director informed the teachers who taught in two synagogues that they had no permission to continue teaching without special authorization from the Culture Department. Goldberg related in his testimony: "Meanwhile the camp's teachers from the Culture Department took over one synagogue in which one of our teachers taught, and started to give there classes in Hebrew. We had to make do with one synagogue. On 22 Heshvan (14 November 1949), the director of the Athlit camp came into the synagogue, accompanied by several officials and a policeman, and ordered the teachers to leave the place immediately and go to his office. There they were detained for about two hours. The teachers asked that they be released, but the director of the camp said that they must remain in his office until policemen would come from the Zikhron Ya'akov police to take them for questioning. On 24 Heshvan (16 November 1949), I went to the director of the camp and asked what was the reason for expelling the teachers, and he replied that he suspected that the teachers had removed several children from the camp to *yeshivot*.

4. Agrobank

In his testimony, Shaul Baranitz, a teacher in the Agrobank transit camp (near Hadera), related that the Hamizrachi Stream had received permission to open a school there and that he had been sent there as a teacher. He began to teach in the synagogue of the Ashkenazim. The next day the director of the camp, Mr. Nathan, summoned him and said that it was impossible to teach there, because someone was living in the synagogue. After lobbying with officials of the Absorption Department, they began to teach in the synagogue of the Sephardim, which was only used for worship on the Sabbaths.

> The director yelled at me, threw me out of the place, and threatened to call the police. Afterwards the director told the parents of one of my pupils: "We have already expelled the teacher of Hamizrachi, send your children to the general school." I again went to Tel Aviv, to the director of the Hamizrachi schools. Once more I received authorization. I returned to the director, and he put me off with various pretenses. In the end, I received a small, isolated place [in which to teach]. Meanwhile several children were transferred to Giv'at Olga.

5. Beer Ya'akov

The commission had received hearsay reports of interference with religious studies in the synagogue in Beer Ya'akov. During the commission's visit to the camp, the members of the commission sensed that there were people who wished to say something but refrained from speaking in front of the camp staff members. Several of these were called upon to testify before the commission in Jerusalem, and one of them, who had been a rabbi in Tunisia, an impressive looking Jew who conveyed an unmistakable impression of thorough integrity, testified:

> One day people came to me and said: Come, they want to close the synagogue. I also taught Talmud. That day there was supposed to be a circumcision. The *mohel*[4] was my son-in-law. I went and found Mordechai the carpenter there holding a lock in his hand—he is my study companion for Talmud—and he said to me: I received an order to close the synagogue in Camp III. After the conversation between us he felt

ashamed, and did not close the synagogue. Ten minutes later he returned and said: I asked the director of Camp III. He said that [this was done] because there is a school in Camp I. I asked the carpenter what he intended to do. He said, I don't know if I'm in Germany or in Russia. The next day the teachers came to the synagogue as usual and did not find any benches to sit on. They were told: the director removed them. Afterwards, before Shabbat, the benches were returned, and the day after Shabbat the two teachers returned to teach in the synagogue. When we came for the evening prayer I found the teachers sitting [on the floor] like mourners. They said: the director and Dr. Ross prevented us from teaching, they chased away the children and took the benches with the help of the police.

His colleague, a rabbi from Morocco, supplemented his remarks: "I worked hard to open the synagogue. Before that we prayed outdoors." When asked why he was careful not to speak in the camp, he said: "I thought that they might do something to us."

In his testimony, Dr. Ross confirmed that fact [closure of the synagogue], explaining that it was necessary to do so, since permission had been granted to open the synagogue in Camp III under the explicit condition that they not teach religious studies there, since there is a religious class in the synagogue in Camp II nearby. The teachers were warned to stop teaching and refused, and this was a matter of discipline—not to teach without permission, even though in the synagogue in Camp II the teacher is an Ashkenazi, and here the teachers are Tripolitans [i.e., from Libya], from the same ethnic community as the students.

This explanation speaks for itself.

6. Immigrant Houses: Ahuza, Kiryat Shmuel, Kiryat Motzkin, and Moshav Amka

In his testimony, Rabbi [Avraham Yitzhak] Winkelstein described his various experiences in these places. He arrived in Israel in the middle of Teveth 5710 (January 1950) from Poland, via France, bringing with him twenty-four orphaned children whom he had rescued from the hands of Christians.[5] The rabbi told of himself:

> I may testify that I have been devoted to this work for years. I fled from Poland with a transport of children, with whom I managed to flee on the verge of death, before my fate would be sealed in a Polish court for the sin of devoting myself to the rescue of children, and the authorities didn't manage to catch me. From France they wanted to enable me to go with the children to America, but as an Orthodox Jew and an idealist, who wishes to live in his homeland, I did not agree. Out of deep

love for my homeland I am always the first to extend blessings and comfort to the new immigrants who stand frustrated on the threshold of their new life, and explain to them that these are the trials of aliya.

In his testimony before the commission, given under an affirmation of truth, Rabbi Winkelstein recounted several of his adventures, as if to justify his persistence despite the difficulties he encountered. He said: "I have no family. I have no home. My wife is in prison." The following are some passages from his testimony:

The *beit olim* [immigrant house] in Ahuza:[6] On the basis of the requests by the religious parents we brought a teacher. On the first day of classes the director of the camp strongly reprimanded him, and he was forced to stop teaching. The parents persisted in their demand, and we brought one male and one female teacher from Haifa, collecting signatures of 50 parents to send to Nahum Levin in Tel Aviv. The director chased them away, and they taught out of doors, under the sky, until the rains began and they had to stop. Then they went into the *beit midrash* [literally, "house of study," i.e., synagogue], and the assistant director threatened that if they would not stop immediately he would call the police. I told the director that I had 50 signatures. He asked for the list in order to examine it, and that very evening he gathered all the parents who had signed the petition and threatened them that if they would continue to teach religious studies, they would be removed from the *beit olim* and no one would take care of them. All this at a time when there was not yet any other school.

Kiryat Shmuel:[7] When it became known to the [camp] administration that children were studying Torah in the house of study, it summoned the teachers and expressed strident opposition to this study, threatening to close the house of study if they continued to teach there. In this manner they frightened the male teacher and the female teacher, [threatening] that if they continued to appear in the camp they would be chased away.

Kiryat Motzkin:[8] One day the secretary of the camp appeared and announced that teaching religious subjects in the camp was prohibited. A few days later the secretary again came, with a teacher from the Education Department and a policeman, and raised a scandal during the studies. They started to chase the children out of the room, and when the children's parents came, they too were all chased out of the room.

The following is what Rabbi Winkelstein related about Amka, near Nahariya:

I was in Amka, which is near Nahariya. There we got the signatures of 64 parents and received authorization from Agudat Israel to open a school. We found a teacher from Haifa, but the [camp] director did not allow him to teach. We thought that this was simply a mistake. A few days later I came with three teachers, and the next day the director, Lukov, came and notified us that he would not let them teach. I asked him what he meant by this! For there was a permit from the government, and the Yemenites had requested this, and why was he interfering? I pleaded with him, I begged him, and he answered that if I did not stop, I would end up like De-Haan![9] He said this in the presence of witnesses. I spoke with him quietly, but all my requests that he act on our behalf were in vain. The next day, when the Yemenites sent their children to the house of study, the director, Yosef Lukov, and an official from the [camp's] grocery store came and forcibly chased the children outside. At that time I was in the house of study and I could not believe my eyes. They behaved arrogantly. I asked them to stop, but in response they wanted to beat me. The Yemenites were very angered, the children were brought back into the house of study, and they again started to teach.

That same day the Yemenites came and asked me to study Torah with them. That evening we started to study with 30 Yemenites, and at that moment shots were heard outside. An armed Ashkenazi broke into the house of study, shouting that Arabs had invaded the camp, and ordering us to lie down on the floor and put out the lights. This seemed a bit strange to me, and I thought that if Arabs have broken into the camp, why aren't we getting weapons, so that we can go out to help the camp police, or at least be able to protect ourselves? I went outside, and to my great astonishment saw that all the houses in the camp were lit up, and only the house of study was shrouded in darkness. The police and guards on the spot calmed us, saying that the whole thing was staged. It turned out that they simply wanted to scare us in order to interrupt our study of Torah.

The road leading to Amka is in poor repair, so that one can only get there by tractor. The director of the camp had instructed not to give a lift into the camp to any person who gave the impression of being a religious Jew, and even prohibited walking on the path that leads there. The teachers were forced to take a circuitous route and come in another way that passes by Arab villages, and is dangerous. To this day, that path is closed to such people.

For the acts of the type cited here, the camp directors and cultural coordinators relied upon an instruction in this matter that had been issued by the director of the Absorption Department of the Jewish Agency. And indeed, the commission was presented with a circular that was sent on 18 Kislev 5710 (9 December 1949) to the directors of all the immigrant houses in the country, reading as follows:

In order to avoid any misunderstanding, we notify you that people who have no written authorization from the Ministry of Education and Culture of the State of Israel may not engage in educational activity for children or adults in the immigrant houses.

[Signed] Dr. G. Josephtal

According to the testimony of Minister of Education Mr. Shazar, this order became necessary after the emissaries of the streams began appearing in the camps. Formally, the instruction had to be issued by Mr. Josephtal, since the camps were subject to the Jewish Agency, which [also] had an indirect interest in them due to budgetary reasons, as explained by Mr. Shazar.

Whatever may be the reason for the prohibition against teaching Torah without permission, in several camps they were very strict about the execution of this order, to the point of removing people by brute force, and even prohibiting the teaching of Torah by religious teachers from [among those living in] the place, or even by teachers who had been authorized to teach. For this there is no justification.

C. DISCRIMINATION AGAINST RELIGIOUS PEOPLE IN CONNECTION WITH ENTRANCE INTO THE CAMPS

In addition to the facts described above regarding the case in Ein-Shemer, in which visitors to the camp encountered difficulties when they were already inside the camp, the commission heard complaints from a number of witnesses who testified that obstacles were placed before people wishing to enter the camps and having the appearance of religious Jews.

Thus Mr. Goldberg testified that during his initial visits to the camps he did not encounter any difficulties, but over the course of time entrance was made more difficult, since he has a beard and *payot*. He reported an incident that he experienced on 1 Shevat 5710 (19 January 1950) in Rosh Ha'ayin. According to his account, his bag was searched and he was denied entry, despite the fact that other beardless visitors, including a *yeshiva* student who had accompanied him, were allowed to enter the camp without any difficulty.

One of the members of the absorption staff of the Jewish Agency, who has a beard, reported that on three separate occasions he was not allowed entry to the camp, when due to arrangements he had to see to at the Jewish Agency he arrived late at the camp instead of coming in the car that brought the other workers. The witness added, that despite the fact that he was told, on the third occasion, that because of a curfew he was not allowed to enter, he saw many people who had no function in the camp entering without being questioned as to the reason for their going in.

Rabbi Zadok Yitzhari, who had arrived in Israel a year earlier from Yemen, and was responsible for organizing the immigrants in the camps for [permanent] settlement on behalf of Hapoel Hamizrachi, likewise testified before the commission. The witness, whose family is still in the camp, reported that he encountered great difficulty in entering the camp, even to visit his family. He also reported incidents that happened to other people with beards who were barred from entering the camp.

D. Sanctions against Religious Teachers and Attempts to Tempt Them

The day after Mr. Aldema came to Ein-Shemer he assembled the teachers and informed them that the *melamdim* would not be allowed to continue to teach religious studies, and that the [regular] teachers also could not teach Torah, but only Hebrew, arithmetic, and Zionism. To those who argued with him he said: "Whoever does not agree to these conditions can leave the camp." Two of the teachers who were present at this meeting, Rieder and Segal, publicized this in a letter to the editor of *Hatzofe*, and thereafter the employment of one of them, Moshe Segal, was terminated. In his testimony he said that although he was not told so explicitly, they spoke primarily about the publication [of the meeting] in the newspaper, and he was informed that they were terminating his employment until the matter was clarified, without any time limitation. According to the testimony of the second signatory to the letter to *Hatzofe*, Yehuda Rieder, Aldema came to him and told him that after the business with the letter in *Hatzofe*, he could not continue to hold responsibility for the school in Camp II, and that he was not firing him only because they were friends. Some time later Mr. Aldema approached him to offer him once more a responsible position in the camp, on the condition that he [Rieder] compensate him for having written in the newspaper, and he asked Rieder—according to his testimony—to state what the compensation should be.

The explanation regarding the punishment of those two teachers was that it was not done on account of their being religious persons, but because teachers must not engage in politics or publicize events in the newspapers.

But particularly instructive was the attitude towards female religious teachers in that same Ein-Shemer camp. Five girls, last-year students at the Beit Ya'akov Seminary[10] in Jerusalem, responded to the call to make up for the lack of teachers in the camps. According to the testimony of three of them before the commission of inquiry, Yehuda Rieder asked them to teach, at Aldema's request, but once they got to Ein-Shemer they were told that teachers could only be appointed through the Culture Department. They returned to Tel Aviv and received authorization, three of them for Ein-Shemer and two for Rosh Ha'ayin. The following is a section from their testimony:

> We were housed in a room in which a female sports instructor who belonged to Mapam lived. On the first evening her [male] friends came in a wild and mocking manner to see if we would react. Several days later I found in my notebook: "Shoshana, I have set my eyes on you. You will yet hear about me." Several days later I found two additional beds in our room that had been placed there by the instructors, supposedly for officials from the electricity company. When we told Aldema, he laughed and ordered the beds removed, saying that the instructors had staged this in order to annoy us. Our parents came to visit us, they complained to Aldema, and we were promised a room by ourselves. On 27 Shevat 5710 (14 February [1950]), at midnight, the male instructors burst into our room while we were sleeping. They woke us up and started to dance in our room until one o'clock in the morning. The next day Mr. Goldberg came, and we told him what had happened. He turned to Aldema, who promised him that by 4 Adar (21 February) we would certainly have a separate room. Meanwhile the situation went from bad to worse. For example, this week the boys sat on our beds and one of them refused to get off. On 21 Adar (10 March) we submitted our resignation. When we suggested to Aldema that we bring others of our friends to replace us, he said that that was a matter for Tel Aviv. But that same day friends of our roommate from Binyamina came and were immediately accepted. While we were getting ready to leave, they moved our friends to another room, which had been empty the whole time.

And [here is] more of their testimony, even though the matter does not pertain to the subject under discussion: "Among the 30 male and female teachers in Ein-Shemer, only 8 are religious. The teachers travel on Shabbat, they light and extinguish candles on Shabbat. The children told us that one instructor asked [them] where is the Holy One blessed be He."

E. Sanctions against Children Who Studied Torah and Their Parents

In Deir-Yassin (Givat Shaul II),[11] they stopped providing lunch to those children who participated in the class of the religious teacher, Balass, who had been sent there by Va'ad Hayeshivot. There was also an attempt to remove the teacher from the camp using the police. After Mr. Goldberg complained, the children began receiving food again. The explanation they gave for not providing food was that a Compulsory Education Law had been enacted, and food could not be provided to children who violated the law. When it was pointed out that these were children studying in a religious class, they replied: That is not considered a school.

From the documents submitted to the commission, it was claimed that in Beer Ya'akov clothing was distributed to the children, but the children of the religious class did not receive any. A mother of two girls, one in the religious class and one in the general school, also asked for clothing for her child participating in the religious class, and she was turned down. This fact was not supported by direct evidence. The testimony of one teacher, Gitta Landau, who might perhaps have been able to testify directly about this, was not accepted because she refused to answer or to declare under *hen tzedek* [an affirmation of truth] that she would tell the truth. This teacher was more extreme than rabbis and leaders of her own party, Agudat Israel, who did not refrain from testifying under an "affirmation of truth."

During his visit to the Rosh Ha'ayin camp, the chairman of the commission encountered a group of six children aged 10–14, some of whom were barefoot or wearing shoes that did not fit, who complained: "We study Torah, so we don't receive clothes or shoes. The children studying in the school do get them." And indeed, during his visit to the school, not during class hours, he found a small number of children rehearsing for a play who were wearing new and properly fitting shoes. During that same visit, one religious teacher complained that wherever Torah was taught there were no benches, while in the school there were benches. When he was asked: And did you have benches in Yemen? he replied: There we had mats.

F. DISTURBANCES AND THREATS IN THE IMMIGRANT VILLAGES

The commission decided to include within the scope of its investigation the immigrant villages and immigrant neighborhoods settled by those who had left the camps, even though it did not give special attention to this problem. The commission reached this decision on the basis of an assumption that the education provided in these villages and neighborhoods was a direct outcome of the education in the immigrant camps, and that immigrant children had not changed their views or their religious or non-religious outlook when they moved to the villages.

According to Dr. Ben-Yehuda (on 30 Shevat–17 February) last year there was a consensus in the Ministry of Education that "if a certain stream notifies that a workers settlement (*moshav ovdim*) has been established belonging to a given settlement stream, no poll [of parents] will be conducted there, and the school to be opened there will be determined on the basis of the particular settlement stream involved." And such, indeed, was the practice over a period of time. Of course, this agreement does not take into account a case in which the parents specifically request the establishment of a school belonging to a different educational stream than the settlement movement to which the *moshav* belongs. This explains, therefore, what Dr. Ben-Yehuda related—that lately Israeli reality has changed and in two cases there have been requests, in *moshavim* of the Histadrut, to open religious schools: in Kfar Hagilboa the parents wanted a school of the Hamizrachi Stream, and in Amka an Agudat Israel school. It is therefore understandable why the minister of education, in his testimony on 12 Shevat (30 January), said that "also in every *moshav*, every thirty children who want to, may receive whatever [type] of education they wish."

But the commission also heard a number of testimonies from which it emerges that the freedom of choice, which in principle is required by the existence of educational streams, is not always observed in practice in the immigrant neighborhoods and in other concentrations [of immigrants] after they leave the camps. There are many complaints that those responsible for the abandoned places [i.e., abandoned Arab villages and towns] did not provide a structure for a school of the religious stream, despite the fact that the establishment of such a school there was approved by the Ministry of Education. Moreover, if a place was found for a religious school in such a settlement, it was allocated in an inappropriate site. According to the witnesses, this was done to prevent the religious school from gaining a firm foothold, so that they could meanwhile have the children register for the Workers Stream school. Such complaints were voiced by Rabbi Hayyim David Kahana, the rabbi of Migdal Gad, in connection with the opening of a Hamizrachi school in Migdal Gad; by Rabbi Moshe Glickman-Porush in connection with the opening of Agudat Israel schools in Ein Karem and in Musrara;[12] and by Mr. Moshe Schwartzman and the teacher Shaul Baranitz, in relation to the opening of a Hamizrachi school in the Agrobank transit camp. In the latter place, this was most obvious. This transit camp initially served as the site of a regular immigrant camp, only later becoming a transit camp. So long as it was an immigrant camp, there was a school of the Culture Department, as was customary in the immigrant camps. Upon the camp's change in status, the school remained on the same standing and with the same composition of classes, becoming a "*Beit Hinukh*."[13] The [only] change was that they changed the sign to read "*Beit Hinukh*" of the Workers Stream. At the same time, they put off for more than three months the allocation of a site for a Hamizrachi school, and the camp director even chased away the teacher and children from their temporary quarters in the Ashkenazic synagogue, and later in the Sephardic [synagogue].

The general impression is—as stated by the witness Dr. Yeshayahu Leibowitz—that there were subtle forms of obstruction such as obscuring [the facts] and ignoring, and at times even the use of the vulgar and brutal means of threats and coercive measures. The purpose of using these means was not only to prevent the opening of a school of the Hamizrachi Stream or the Agudat Israel Stream, but also to prevent the opening of a school of the Workers Stream having a religious tendency.

Obfuscation begins with not allowing people whose outward appearance is religious to enter the village. Such a situation was related to the commission in the testimony of Rabbis Nahum Friedman (rabbi of the synagogue in Mahane Yehuda), Yitzhak Weingarten (who teaches in the Hayyei Olam Yeshiva), and Israel Grossman (head of the Karlin Yeshiva). According to their report, they went to Mei Naftoah (Lifta) on the first day of Shevat [5710] (19 January [1950]) to encourage the Yemenites in religious practices. On the way they were met by a woman named Miriam, who presented herself as an instructor on behalf of the Jewish Agency, and with curses and abuse tried to prevent them from entering the village. She called the village coordinator, Shalom Amar, who joined in the curses and reviling, and even pushed the people. Finally there also came Yosef Shamash, a member of the local council, a Yemenite who has been in the country for a number of years, and he, apart from shouting "Enemies of the Jewish People," also threw stones at these rabbis which, so they claimed, could have endangered their lives. Thus they were prevented from entering the village.

Another example of obscuring the facts was presented in the testimony of Dr. Leibowitz, regarding Ein-Ayala: an instructor in this village [lied] to a representative of the Histadrut's Educational Center, denying that there were religious parents in the village, so as to prevent the opening of a religious school by the Workers Stream. Dr. Leibowitz reported that a delegation that later visited [the village] on behalf of the Educational Center, composed of the educational supervisor, Mr. Giladi, and Mr. Ben-Nahum of Haoved Hadati, stated that the instructor had deliberately concealed from people living there the possibility of [receiving] religious education within the framework of the Workers Stream, and lied to the first emissary of the Educational Center regarding the nature of the population and its requests.

Rabbi M. Glickman-Porush reported about other acts of interference in Ein Karem. After a school of the Agudat Israel stream was opened there in rented rooms—because, as noted above, that school did not receive a building from the abandoned property—a Jewish Agency official removed the furniture from the school. When, despite everything, the school was opened, for a number of days people lay in wait in the street for children on the way to school and brought them forcibly to the school of the Workers Stream so as in this manner to be able to empty the Agudat Israel school of pupils.

Complaints concerning threats to remove the people from their homes or their place of settlement, withholding of work, clothing, etc., were repeated numerous times. We shall cite here a few cases.

Rabbi M. Glickman-Porush testified about Malha, where there were a [male] teacher sent by Va'ad Hayeshivot and a [female] teacher sent by Beit Ya'akov. The people in charge of the place threatened the settlers that if these teachers were not removed they would themselves be expelled from the village. There were also threats that if they would not put an end to the classes with these teachers Sabbath violators would also be brought to this settlement. According to Rabbi Porush, Mr. Shalom Halevi, the regional supervisor of the Workers Stream, admitted to him that he had participated in a meeting [organized by] the Histadrut in Malha at which the settlers were warned that if they did not register their children in the Workers Stream school, they would be expelled from the place [i.e., Malha].

Rabbi Porush related another fact about Ein Karem. While registration of the children for schools was being conducted, one parent came and registered his child for the Agudat Israel Stream. A little while later he returned to the registration room, cancelled this registration, and registered his child for the Workers Stream. When asked why he changed his mind, he said that he was told outside [the building] that if he were to register his child in the school of the Agudat Israel Stream he would not get a job.

Dr. Yeshayahu Leibowitz testified that the coordinator in Lifta, Shalom Amar ("a representative of the Histadrut, who was formally appointed by the Jewish Agency"), explicitly threatened parents that should they demand religious education for their children, this would be to their detriment—whether in the area of food, of clothing, or of receiving employment.

Dr. Leibowitz claimed that he knew of other cases similar to those which he had reported, but that he only reported those of which he had firsthand knowledge and not hearsay evidence from others.

The commission gained the impression that in places where new immigrants lived that were part of the Histadrut framework, they were automatically provided with non-religious education. It was only by putting up a fight and struggling that they succeeded in introducing religious education within the framework of the Workers Stream. What lies behind this fact—according to Dr. Leibowitz—was that "though the decision of the Histadrut Executive that obligates the provision of religious education for those settlers who request it for their children by means of the Educational Center [of the Histadrut] exists and is affirmed by the central institutions of the Histadrut, there are many who violate it among those acting locally in its name. Those who dominate the place are the instructors. The instructor in each place is the sole ruler, and I think that if the Histadrut were to demand his removal—he would be removed."

This is the state of affairs with regard to religious education in the framework of the Workers Stream. However, the Histadrut institutions evidently do not recognize the right of parents living in places defined as belonging to the Histadrut to choose another educational stream—and this is opposed to the law of the state and to the interpretation given [the law] by the minister of education, as cited above.

Another case was reported by the director of the Education Division of the Ministry of Education and Culture, Dr. Ben-Yehuda. He related: "In Kfar Gilboa, the parents requested a school of the Hamizrachi Stream, and we opened such a school there. We subsequently received various reports concerning severe disputes which took place there, because they said that Tnu'at Hamoshavim[14] does not agree that a school of the Hamizrachi Stream be opened in a *moshav* belonging to Tnu'at Hamoshavim. Once I even received reports of acts of violence."

In addition, testimony was presented to the commission concerning a severe educational dispute in Amka. The disturbing facts were reported by Rabbi A. I. Winkelstein, who reported interference with the school (despite the fact that this school was authorized by the Ministry of Education as a school of the Agudat Israel Stream) by means of threats, preventing the sale of goods [to parents of children enrolled at the school] at the shop, expelling children from the school, instructions not to allow the teachers to come near the neighborhood, and similar acts of terror. The commission heard that the facts had been investigated on the spot on behalf of the Ministry of Education by the supervisors Dr. Deutsch (supervisor of the Agudat Israel Stream) and Ya'akov Halperin (supervisor of the Workers Stream), who had been asked to testify before the commission. While Dr. Deutsch was willing to testify, Mr. Halperin notified [the commission] that since they had been appointed by the minister of education, he would only be prepared to testify if the minister of education would permit him to do so. Given these circumstances, the commission decided to forego this testimony.

G. DISREGARD OF PRAYER

1. Insufficient Place for Prayer in the Camps

There were numerous complaints that in several camps there was not adequate place for worship. According to the testimony of Mr. Goldberg, there is no synagogue in Rosh Ha'ayin. There are nearly 15,000 people there, and there is not a single synagogue. The inhabitants of the camp worship in tents which they have commandeered. These tents lack benches, and there is no place in them convenient for study.

Concerning Ein-Shemer, one witness, S. Kroll, reports: "In Camp III, where there are thousands of Yemenites, there is no synagogue. This I know for certain. In Camps I and II as well there are not enough."

Concerning Beer Ya'akov, Rabbi Hafita [Hafuta] testifies: "In Camp III there was no synagogue. We have only a synagogue of the Ashkenazim."

While visiting Beit Lid, members of the commission saw the synagogue set aside for the Ashkenazim in Camps I and II, which is a small room with a tent as a passageway, and were told that both the room and the passageway are filled to capacity on Sabbaths. The Tripolitans have no place of worship, and they pray outdoors. They were not allowed to pray in the cultural center, even on Rosh Hashana [the Jewish New Year].

2. Denying Opportunity for Prayer before Classes, and Interference with Worship

Rabbi Yitzhak Yitzhak, who was mentioned previously, related in his testimony:

> Every day Aldema takes the radio outside during the time when prayers are conducted. He also took the radio outside during the first two Sabbaths of his stay in the camp. Now he doesn't take it outside on the Sabbath. But by taking the radio outside during the time for prayer, and he has a loudspeaker around his house, he disturbs the worship.

In his testimony, Minister Levin reported that the Yemenites had introduced a new "May the All-Merciful" petition in the Grace after Meals: "May the All-Merciful punish Zippora," and the commission determined the source of this innovation. Sa'adya Shar'abi, who was at the time a pupil at the youth camp in Beit Lid under the supervision of Zippora Zehavi, relates: "Once we were praying and the children sang in the dining hall. I told Zippora that it disturbs us. She said: You don't need to pray in the Land of Israel. Zippora would interfere with us during the Grace after Meals, and then we would say, 'May the All Merciful remove Zippora from among us.'" The same witness recounted: "During the time for prayers they did not let us pray. The instructor blew his whistle and said: now is the time for exercises, they did not arrange [time] for the morning prayers, and also during *Minha* they disturbed us."

H. Modesty and Morals

There were many complaints pertaining to this matter of modesty and morals. Of course, they must be examined relatively, taking into consideration the practices, way of life, customs, and mood of the immigrants from the Oriental countries, and particularly those from Yemen. Their customs of modesty seem to be exaggerated and excessive to native-born Israelis, but one may not ignore the fact that they are very punctilious about gatherings involving men and women who are not of the same family, about exposing parts of the body such as arms, legs, and knees, and so forth.

For example, the same Rabbi Yitzhak Yitzhak Levi relates:

> Aldema said that we need to organize a youth camp. We asked him, what is a youth camp. He said, children from the ages of 14 to 18. We

said, it is impossible to have boys and girls [together]. While he is learning—his evil nature is before him, and he cannot learn. He said: we shall arrange that boys and girls will be separated. He gathered together the entire camp, lecturing to them on what is a youth camp: they would pray in the morning and then go to eat, and afterwards they will go to study Torah for two hours, and then go out to work in the fields, then go to eat; after eating they will come to learn Hebrew and arithmetic for two hours, and afterwards to strengthen themselves [gain proficiency] in the other subjects. They will say the Afternoon and Evening prayers, then go to eat. In the evening they will come to learn songs. They accepted this. They brought the children to the youth camp, and then they were told, there are no rooms for boys and girls separately until they would be built, so they began to study in one room with boys on one side and girls on the other. The public, the fathers of the children, complained to the Rabbinic Court: we did not agree to this, that our children should do evil things, nor did they [the instructors] keep the rest of the agreement, there is no Torah [study] and no prayers. I went to Meir (his nephew, a teacher or instructor in the camp, who has been in the country several years), and I discussed it with him, and he said that this is untrue. I went and found that they are all in one room, [and] he took out the girls and said, in the afternoon the girls will come to study by themselves. The parents of the children said that he took them to Camp III for dancing. They said that they want no part of a youth camp. The youth camp still exists, but many of the parents have removed their children from it. Only the orphans remain.

The representatives of the World Center of Hamizrachi testify concerning dancing in the camps: "They consider dances of youths with maidens, which are the finest dances of the youth of the Land of Israel, to be an immoral act." And the representative of Agudat Israel testified: "We received reports that in the youth camps they were accustomed to dance Land of Israel dances, which in the eyes of the Yemenite immigrants were considered immoral."

It turns out that the complaints were twofold:

1. That they invite youths from the vicinity who dance folk dances that arouse the passion of the Oriental Jews;

2. That they also bring Yemenite youngsters to dances of boys and girls together.

Zippora Zehavi, who is responsible for the youth camp in Beit Lid, admits that in the evenings there was mixed dancing, boys and girls, in the youth camp under her supervision, and she did not see anything wrong in this. Mr. Trachtenberg, the director of the Ein-Shemer I camp, also found nothing wrong in the dances conducted by the youth who came from Kfar Vitkin or elsewhere, "orderly, well-behaved Land of Israel youth." Concerning these youngsters, he said:

> When these [youngsters] come to us, they come as educated youth, and if it is during the summer they wear shorts. The songs [they sing] are folk songs of the Land of Israel, songs of labor, songs of heroism; the same applies to the dancing, these are folk dances. If a *hora*[15] dance is immorality, then there was immorality. I know that thanks to the *hora* we achieved the State of Israel, and I still remember the days when I was in Gedud Ha'avoda:[16] on more than one occasion we had nothing to eat, there was malaria, and the only thing that kept our spirits up was the *hora*.

There is admittedly a considerable degree of naivete, perhaps it would be better to say superficiality, in the comparison drawn between the members of the Gedud Ha'avoda, part of the first pioneering wave of immigrants in the 1920s, people who were steeped in European culture, to the Yemenites, who brought with them other outlooks and other customs in similar matters.

The same holds true with regard to movies. The following is the statement of Rabbi Yitzhak Yitzhak Levi, the head of the Rabbinic Court in Ein-Shemer:

> There is yet another matter that is called cinema. At first they said: we want to show the public how one fights. We were pleased. After a month and a half Aldema brought a movie in which men and women embraced. Those who watched the movie at night came to me in the morning and said: This we cannot accept. I said, I will talk to Ya'akov (Trachtenberg). He said, this is not in accordance with my wishes nor is it under my control. We said, we won't keep silent. And they stopped showing the movies.

Rabbi Alchech added in his testimony: "Since the dining hall collapsed there is no cinema. I have claimed this to be a sign and a miracle, for there is no building more stable than the dining hall, and it was the only one that collapsed."

Rabbi Unterman testified:

> They draw children to the cinema, they take boys and girls to dances, and they [the children] rebel against their parents. One [of the immigrants] complained of great immodesty among the young girls. There are some who are married and were modest, and suddenly they dance in immodest dress.

I. Desecration of the Sabbath

A number of details were brought [to light] in the documents submitted to the commission concerning public desecration of the Sabbath in the camps. There was even firsthand testimony concerning this subject, enabling us to state that, particularly during the first period, there were several such cases that angered and pained those living in the camps. Mr. Goldberg, for example, tells us that in Athlith he was told that teachers smoke in public on the Sabbath, and a large number of the children who study in the school stopped coming to prayers and began to smoke cigarettes on the Sabbath. Rabbi Unterman quoted from a letter that he was given, signed by several rabbis and immigrants from Ein-Shemer, in which they wrote, among other things:

> Last Sabbath the secularists killed (i.e., beat) several people in Camp II, because they protested regarding observance of the Sabbath. They take boys and girls out to dance on the Sabbath, to play ball, to turn off electric lights, and to light gas stoves.

Rabbi Yitzhak Yitzhak Levi denied what was written in a letter signed by several Yemenite teachers and submitted to Minister of Education and Culture Mr. Shazar, which he passed on to the commission, claiming, among other things, that the Sabbath is strictly observed. He said: "This is not true; on Friday night there is laughter and dancing outdoors." Another witness, Rabbi Yihya Netanel Alchech, said: "I have never seen desecration of the Sabbath in the camp." And he went on to explain: "On the Sabbath I don't leave my home, so that I might not see how the Sabbath is desecrated."

In another testimony it is related that "a month after Aldema came to the camp a radio with a loudspeaker was brought, and it was also operated on the Sabbath. When Bar-Zimra [i.e., Ben-Zimra] visited the [camp] next day, the teacher Sabatito complained to him about this, and since then they have ceased playing it."

Several witnesses told of a Sabbath hike of campers at the youth camp in Beit Lid conducted under the leadership of the instructor Yefet Hashai. They were led to the orchard where they picked oranges. Rabbi Shar'abi relates: "The children went for a hike on the Sabbath. The children returned to the camp with oranges in their hands. I told them: that is forbidden. They said: the teacher said that it is permitted to pick."

Shaul Shar'abi, who participated in the hike, testifies:

> There was a hike on the Sabbath, and when we got to the Sabbath limit[17] I said that we cannot go any further. The instructor Yefet said:

There is no Sabbath in the Land of Israel. We continued walking to the orchard. He told the children: Pick oranges. The children didn't want to pick. He said to them: Why are you afraid? He picked first, and the children after him.

And Y. Shklar relates: "One child, the son of *Hacham*[18] Zalah, told me that the instructors deliberately took them to the orchards and told them that here in the Land of Israel there is no need to observe the Sabbath, but only in Yemen. And he told them to pick the oranges on the Sabbath."

Yefet Hashai, the instructor mentioned, while confirming the fact of the hike, said that it was inconceivable that he would pick oranges at all, and certainly not on the Sabbath, and that if there were cases of orange picking, the youngsters did so on their own initiative.

J. CUTTING OFF OF *PAYOT*

The cutting off of *payot*[19] was the subject of the testimony of many witnesses and served as the topic of several documents that were submitted to the commission. The general accusation was that both youths and adults had been forced or persuaded to cut off their *payot*. There were even cases in which *payot* were cut off despite the protests of their bearers. They talked about a "*payot* campaign" launched by Mr. Aldema upon his arrival at the Ein-Shemer camp. There were those who called this campaign the "lice campaign," because the intention was to cut off the *payot* under the pretext that the children were infected with lice or were afflicted with ringworm. One version was that Mr. Aldema said that should there be protests, "We will find excuses."

When the minister of education and culture visited the Ein-Shemer camp, he was told, as he noted at great length in his testimony recorded at the beginning of this report, that there were only isolated cases, twelve in all, in which *payot* were cut off together with the children's hair by order of Dr. Klein, since there was no other way of avoiding infection. As evidence that the removal of the hair was performed for that reason only, he was also shown seven girls whose braids were cut off for the same reason. As against this, other witnesses quoted a physician, Dr. Dushinski, who had told them of cases in which *payot* were cut off not because of infection. During their visit to Ein-Shemer, members of the commission encountered a large number of young boys without *payot* but [whose heads] were covered with hair, without any sign of illness. One of these children, Yosef Sa'id Ra'ibi, about eighteen years old, told several members of the commission: "They said: We need to shave off the *payot* of the Yemenites. I said: I will put up a fight. They said: You have to, it is permitted."

Another youth, Yosef Avraham (eighteen years old), related: "They took away my *simanim*[20] (i.e., *payot*) in Ein-Shemer; they said that it is forbidden." When these two youths were invited to testify before the commission, they were not to be found. Another youth said in the presence of the chairman of the commission and commission member Mr. Elmaleh: "One held my hand, one cut." This youth refused to give his name, saying [that this was] "out of fear." Another youngster, Yihya Yehoshua Hassan (he was the only one among these youths who spoke with the members of the commission who was located and sent to testify), said: "When I came to Israel I had *simanim*, but they were removed by the barber. He said it was because of illness." He denied what he had said in the presence of the commission members during their visit to the camp, namely, that he was told that there is no need for *payot* in Israel, adding: "We did not ask, we are afraid, let them do whatever they will do."

Rabbi Yitzhak Yitzhak testified:

> When I came to the camp I discovered that they were shaving the new immigrants. I told the Yemenites that this was forbidden. They told me that they were told that this was the law in the Land of Israel. I don't know who told them this.
>
> I went to the barber shop with Meir Levi, and we found people standing in line [waiting] to be shaved. Meir told them that they are not required to shave off their *payot*. The people dispersed and were not shaved. Last Wednesday I found an Ashkenazi barber shaving off *payot* in the barber shop. I told him: This is forbidden. He told me: The Yemenites are paying me to do this. I turned to Ya'akov, the director, and he answered: I gave no instructions for that. On Friday I came across a ten-year-old child who was walking with Yosef Kofteil and crying. His name was Shmuel Yihya Shuker. He told me that he had received from Penina[21] a slip and a shilling for him to go get a haircut. The barber shaved the hair of his head but left the *payot*. When he came to Penina she told him: That is no good, go back to the barber to have it fixed. He went back to the barber who shaved his *payot*. I went to Ya'akov, the director, and he said: Whoever wants to shave his *payot* should go to Karkur or Tel Aviv; in the camp it is forbidden. When the child came out, people told him: Why are you complaining? They didn't cut your hair against your will. Then the child went to Ya'akov, the director, and informed him that he had agreed to cut his hair.

One Yemenite, Shalom Ya'akov, also from Ein-Shemer, testified:

> On the day my nephew arrived at the camp from Lod, he was given a slip to have his hair cut. He went to the barber and told him that he

should cut his hair but not his *payot*. He was told: You don't need them;
[the barber] did it against his will, and he cried.

There is evidence that the cutting off of *payot* began in the Ein-Shemer camp
even before Aldema's arrival. It was stopped after the intervention of the Yemenite
rabbis. When Aldema came, he tried to begin doing it again. The following is the
relevant evidence. Yehuda Rieder said:

> Before Aldema came, I took children to the barber. The barber was
> himself a Yemenite and had *payot*, and he began to cut off the *payot*.
> The Ashkenazi caretaker also told him in my presence to cut off the
> children's *payot*. I asked Rabbi Yitzhak to intervene in this matter, and
> since then the barber stopped cutting off *payot*.

We have already cited previously the testimony of Rieder and Segal concerning the teachers meeting immediately after Aldema's arrival at the camp, in which
he [i.e., Rieder] related:

> Aldema also proposed bringing a barber from Pardes Hanna to begin
> the *payot* campaign. This was not done for technical reasons. Aldema
> likewise said that if they would raise complaints afterwards then they
> will say that there were lice and ringworm.

Mr. Segal testified:

> Regarding the *payot* campaign announced by Mr. Aldema at the teach-
> ers meeting, he also added that if there is an outcry they would say that
> this was needed for hygienic reasons—lice and ringworm and so forth.

In his testimony, Aldema relied upon Dr. Klein's letter, denying that there was
ever a "*payot* campaign," and that at most it was a "hair campaign."

Members of the commission encountered a similar situation in their visits
to the Rosh Ha'ayin camp. In conversations with the chairman of the commission, Shlomo Nahum (sixteen years old) related that he has been in Israel for five
months, and that when he arrived he was told: "You don't need *payot* in Israel."
Zecharia Zadok, nineteen years old, testified: "When we came they shaved us.
They said: There is no need for *simanim* in Israel; in Yemen they were necessary
because there are Arabs there." Zecharia Ben Hoter, a Yemenite teacher, when
asked why several of the children had no *payot*, said: "Stupid fools, they were
told there is no need for *payot* in Israel, and they cut them off." When asked
whether they weren't cut off because of lice, he said: "There were a very few
cases like that."

Regarding the youth camp in Beit Lid, there is testimony that Zippora Zehavi, the instructor, organized the cutting off of *payot*, and here are two direct testimonies to this effect. Shaul Shar'abi relates:

> They cut off my *payot*. Zippora, the instructor, went to Camp II, brought a barber from there, and said: Cut the children's hair. I said: Not the *payot*. Zippora said: There is no need for *payot* in the Land of Israel. They left us a small tuft of hair around the head. I saw no evidence of any lice or diseases. The whole ruckus was raised by Zippora. I told her: It's forbidden. She said: It's permitted.

Sa'adya Yehuda Avraham confirmed the story that only those who had cut their *payot* were allowed to participate in a trip to Haifa. He said the following:

> Zippora brought a barber from Camp II, and told him: Whoever wants to go on the trip must cut off his *payot*. They cut off [the *payot*] of about 50 children. I did not have hair, and they didn't cut mine—[I had] only *payot*. Zippora told me: If you don't have them cut, I'll throw you out of the room.

In her own testimony, Zippora Zehavi confirmed that she brought a barber to the camp to cut the children's hair together with the *payot*, because of ringworm and lice. There was no [medical] inspection, and there was no one to care for the healing of the skin or combing the youngsters' hair to remove the lice.

"They didn't cut the girls' hair, they cried when they wanted to cut it, but the boys didn't protest. There were children who didn't want them to cut off their *payot*, and we didn't cut them." She also denies that there were explanations or [efforts] to entice them.

Actually, the *payot* are not of such great [religious] importance. Minister Levin, for example, said that the *payot* do not determine [who is religious]. There are religious Jews without *payot*, and there are Jews with *payot* who are not religious. Rabbi Unterman expressed himself in a similar manner. But once again, the matter needs to be examined from the viewpoint of the Yemenites. For them the *payot* are regarded as *simanim*, the "signs" that distinguish between Jews and Gentiles. The directors of the camps know that the Yemenites are primitive and are unlikely to draw a distinction between less important and more important matters. Hence, there is a danger, particularly in the views of the elders of the community, that when this sign distinguishing between Israel and the nations is removed, the youngsters may think that now it makes no difference at all, and they will cease to be meticulous even about important commandments. It would have been possible to prevent this whole affair, that gave rise to so much anger and added fuel to the flames, if an instructor such as Zippora Zehavi would have considered the boys' *payot* in the same light as she saw the girls' braids. True, one cannot ignore the technical difficulties involved in shampooing their heads and combing their hair, [but] this is not sufficient reason.

Hence, one cannot escape the conclusion that there was in fact a certain intentional, systematical effort in the cutting off of *payot*, [one] that was repeated in Ein-Shemer, Rosh Ha'ayin, and Beit Lid, and certainly elsewhere as well.

Even from the viewpoint of those wishing to tear down the barriers between the Yemenite children and native-born ones, there was no reason to hasten the process immediately upon the immigrants' arrival in Israel; they could have relied upon time to do the job.

One of the children whose *payot* had been cut off, when asked by the chairman of the commission, replied: "They laughed at me in Kfar Sava so I removed my *payot* of my own free will."

K. Prohibiting Laying on of Tefillin and the Removal of Skullcaps

No proof was presented to indicate any prohibition against laying on of *tefillin*[22] or [requiring] the removal of *kippot* [skullcaps]. There were complaints about the failure to provide *tefillin*, which is an issue in its own right, but the cultural coordinators or the camp directorates are not to be blamed for this.

The same holds true for the removal of *kippot*. The complaint is that when the immigrants came off the planes they were not provided with hats or with scarves for the women.[23] But this too is something to which we cannot attribute any bad intentions, and there is no doubt that the matter was [later] rectified.

From their visits to the camps, the members of the commission gained the impression that all of the Yemenites walk about with their heads covered. This is not the case with the staff members in the camps, who walk about bare-headed, enabling the visitor to distinguish immediately between immigrants and staff.

L. The Scandal in the Ein-Shemer Camps

While the commission was engaged in conducting its investigations and intended, according to its plans, to tour the camps, it learned from the press and by means of a personal request about the riots which had occurred at the Ein-Shemer camp on Tuesday, 27 Shevat (14 February 1950). The commission therefore decided to conduct its visit to Ein-Shemer before those to other camps, and on Thursday, 29 Shevat (16 February 1950), all members of the commission set out to visit there.

In the office of the director of Camp II (who was slightly injured in the riots), there were also present at that time the director of the Absorption Department of the Jewish Agency, Dr. Josephtal, and others. Minister of Immigration and Health, Mr. Shapira, and Minister of Police, Mr. Shitrit, had left the camp a short time previously. As a result of discussing [the matter] with those present, the background of the incident, that had occurred two days earlier, became clear. This is what happened:

Two young men from a *yeshiva* in Bnai Brak had come to the camp; they were detained by the caretaker, brought to the director's office, asked to identify themselves, and refused to do so. The police were called in, and meanwhile a large crowd of Yemenites assembled outside and cried: "Bring the rabbis out to us!" When the police arrived two shots in the air were heard; some Yemenite immigrants pulled out metal tent pegs, and one policeman was injured. It is not clear which came first—the shots in the air or the pulling out of the tent pegs.

There is no disagreement among all sides involved regarding these details, neither in the informal conversation conducted in the director's office on that day, nor in the testimony collected by the commission during its sessions in the next few days; opinions differ only as to the purpose of these young men's visit. The camp director thinks that they came to incite, while one of the two young men, who testified, claims that they did not come with any intention of incitement but only to find out what was happening there, to strengthen the immigrants in their religious observance and in observing the Sabbath, and to determine whether there were any young boys who wished to join the *yeshiva* in Bnai Brak.

In the camp director's office, during the course of the conversation, there were various leaflets lying about signed by religious organizations, and at first the impression was that the young men had been caught distributing these leaflets. However, after a few questions it became clear that these flyers had already been distributed in the camp two weeks and even a month earlier, and that there was no direct connection between the distribution of the flyers and the visit of the young men.

As if to justify the detainment of the young men, it was also reported that one day earlier a certain young man had come to the camp and despite being requested by the director of Camp I to leave the camp, he remained, intending to sleep there. That night he was discovered hiding in one of the tents and was forcibly expelled by the director, who also tore his shirt. Furthermore, it was related that several days before this incident there had been a gathering of Yemenite rabbis from the vicinity at the home of the rabbi of Pardes Hanna, where they supposedly said harsh things about the government.

All this moved the camp directors to lay down more strict instructions forbidding young religious people to enter the camp. Even Dr. Josephtal, who found that all the excitement had abated very quickly and that nobody really knew what the "rabbis" had intended, drew the necessary conclusion from this incident—to insist upon a stricter check of those entering the camps and closing them to visitors who had no business there.

When Mr. [Dr.] Josephtal was asked whether, on the basis of the investigation that he and his colleagues had conducted, they concluded that these young men had incited to rebellion or the like, he said that this was the conclusion they had reached from interrogation of the staff. He claimed that the immigrants, even their rabbis, did not know what the "rabbis" had said.

From the testimony taken from people who participated in the meeting in Pardes Hanna, it became clear that there had not been the slightest denunciation of the government [there].

The police statement to the press, made on 29 Shevat (16 February) concerning the scandal in Ein-Shemer, referred to the arrest of two fifteen-year-old youngsters who had come to engage in religious propaganda. One of these two youths appeared before the commission, and is aged twenty-one. The commission was informed that the second was not much younger than the one who appeared [before it], and was in any event over the age of fifteen. The attack on the policemen took place many hours after the young men were detained in the office of the director, who unjustifiably refused to free them. There was certainly no reason for the camp directors to behave as they did towards these two young men or the other young man who had come the previous day.

Once again: with greater understanding and tact it would have been possible to prevent not only the fracas in the camp, but also the bad impression which this and similar riots make upon public opinion in Israel and abroad.

If there are those who complain of propaganda concerning educational matters in the camp—there is certainly no propaganda more harmful to the state than allowing such behavior.

There were also complaints about the police force, which allegedly behaved improperly towards the young men who were removed from the camp and taken to the police station, as well as towards the Yemenites who were detained and also brought to the police station—but investigation of this matter is beyond the authority of the commission.

M. Separation of Married Women from Their Husbands

The commission has heard reports that married women were separated from their husbands in the camps, or in any event that such young women were given support when they refused to live with their husbands.

These cases concern immature marriages. There are many such cases involving girls of a tender age who, according to the practice in Yemen, were married to older husbands.

It is redundant to say that there is a need to establish restrictions against these ancient customs and to take suitable action to prevent their repetition. It is certainly desirable to extend every possible help to these girls, to extricate them from a situation which is unhealthy in every possible sense. However, there are cases in which the directors or educational workers in the camps see only the human aspect of this matter and disregard the religious and legal aspects of such marriages which, even if they are immature marriages, are nevertheless legally valid marriages that can only be nullified by legal means.

When the members of the commission visited the Ein-Shemer camp, they were followed the entire time by one young man who didn't give them a moment's rest, stuck notes into their hands, and claimed that his wife had been stolen from him and was being incited against him.

The commission had the "wife" brought before it—and this turned out to be a girl about twelve years old who had come to Israel with her uncle and aunt, and who, we learned, was an orphan. There is a law in Yemen that turns orphans over to the guardianship of the *Imam*,[24] who exploits his authority to convert them to Islam. In order to save orphans from such conversion, a "redeemer" is sought who takes her under his wing as his wife. This is what happened in this case. However, the "redeemer" was older than the girl, and she disliked him.

The members of the commission drew the attention of the cultural coordinator to the fact that, despite the need to protect the child, he cannot act arbitrarily. If the child had been living with her husband, he could not forcibly remove her; however, since the girl is not living in his household but lives with her aunt, it is also not his concern to take her away and give her back to her husband against her will. A final solution should be sought in a divorce.

When the commission's investigation was already at its end, it learned of two cases in which married women had been removed from the camps and transferred to schools. The commission managed to fully ascertain the facts in one case: Yona Salem Sha'ar, thirteen years old, is now in a school in Nahalat Yehuda and is legally married. The social worker of Ein-Shemer Camp I, Penina Palmon, said that this was a similar case of an orphan whose "redeemer" did not want to let her go and would not agree to give her a divorce, because he had set his eye on property that his wife had inherited in Yemen. The husband is twice the age of the girl. She finds him repulsive, rebels against him, and goes into a state of hysterics every time she is about to meet him.

He lives in another camp, but occasionally visits the Ein-Shemer camp and wants to take his wife out in the evening in order to bring her back in the morning, as he was accustomed to do in Yemen. The Yemenite woman in whose custody the girl is living saw nothing irregular in this, so it was necessary to prevent it.

The social worker wanted to send the girl to Youth Aliya, as was done with other orphans, but Youth Aliya refused to accept married women who are not divorced. In order to hide the woman from her husband, she [the social worker] first transferred her to Alonim, a kibbutz of Hanoar Haoved, and thereafter to Ginnosar near Tiberias, a kibbutz of Hakibbutz Hameuhad, which received her temporarily as a private guest. When it turned out that the husband had tracked her down, she was again moved, this time to Kabara [Kibbutz Kabri] in Western Galilee; when the girl heard that the husband had arrived in Kabri, she became hysterical. Penina again raised the matter with Youth Aliya, which continued to refuse, and finally arranged a place for her in an agricultural school for girls in Nahalat Yehuda, but only as a guest until matters could be straightened out.

It is difficult to cast aspersions upon the social worker, whose constant concern was with the tranquility and physical and spiritual welfare of her charge.

But this is not the proper way. Should they succeed in hiding the girl from her husband, several years will pass and it will no longer be known that she is married, and this will in turn lead to a mishap.

When Penina was asked why she did not try at least to arrange a place for the girl in a religious kibbutz, she said that these were the only ones willing to accept her. She admitted that she did not approach a religious kibbutz.

The commission wishes to take this occasion to draw the attention of those in the government who are responsible for such matters to assure appropriate arrangements for such cases that will provide for both their humane-social aspects and legal-religious aspects.

CHAPTER 4

ACCUSATIONS IN THE PRESS

As the commission listened to witnesses, it did not ignore its second charge: to investigate the accusations made in the press and to examine the sources of the propaganda abroad. It posed questions concerning these issues to several witnesses, especially those "general background witnesses" whom one might assume were informed concerning this matter. The three cabinet ministers who testified before the commission, and Mr. Pinkas, a representative of the Religious Front in the Knesset, spoke extensively on this issue. Mr. Agron, director of the [State] Information Services, Mr. Arye Leib Gelman, chairman of the World Center of Hamizrachi, and Rabbi Z[e'ev] Gold, member of the presidium of the World Center of Hamizrachi, were specially subpoenaed to testify on this matter.

The [phrasing of the] second passage in the commission's writ of authority, charging it with "clarifying the accusations published in the press and those responsible for them," was not specific as to whether this referred to the Israeli press, the foreign press, or both; hence, one may assume that the intention was the general one. With regard to the foreign press, the commission was unable to examine everything that had been written there concerning this matter, apart from the well-known report in the *Jewish Chronicle* of 13 January 1950, which the director of the State Information Services described as "the only concrete item containing something like a very harsh accusation that he had seen with his own eyes," and the report in the *Times* (not that of New York, as erroneously stated by Minister Shapira, but that of London) from 23 November 1949, as well as items in the foreign press that were reported here and there in the local press. As for the Israeli press, almost daily over the past two months it was full of reports and articles, evaluations and criticism, concerning education in the camps, each paper in accordance with its own inclination and outlook and its particular party orientation and public tendency, while mutual accusations and attacks were not lacking, particularly in those papers that serve as the official organ of their parties.

As to the first question contained in this charge, whether the accusations leveled in the press were accurate, the answer may be found in the conclusions arrived at by the commission in regard to the major question of accusations concerning religious coercion in the camps. There thus remains only the second question, namely, who was responsible for the accusations made in the press?

We shall begin by discussing the foreign press. At the top of the front page of that issue of the [*Jewish*] *Chronicle* there appeared a telegram from the paper's correspondent in Jerusalem reporting the ultimatum submitted to the government by the Religious Front, threatening that sixteen Knesset members would leave [the coalition], and the resignation of three government ministers. This, as stated by Mr. Agron in his testimony, was known to every child, and was widely publicized in the Israeli press several days before the date of the above-mentioned publication. In that same issue space was also devoted to a report concerning the accusations of Hamizrachi, written by the journal's Hamizrachi correspondent, evidently the one in London, who of course articulated his party's viewpoint on the problem, describing it according to his own approach to and understanding of the issue. Responsibility for this report is the usual and accepted responsibility of papers and their correspondents for what they publish. The prominent and important place given to the telegram and the report by this paper are to be explained in terms of the great importance attached by public opinion abroad as well to a possible coalition crisis in the Israeli government against the backdrop of such a vital question pertaining to the spiritual integrity of the nation.

The article, "Immigration into Israel," published in the [London] *Times* of 23 November 1949, by the paper's correspondent in Tel Aviv, is to be seen in a different light. Referring to immigration of Jews from Oriental countries, the correspondent writes:

> With them they bring a multiplicity of problems, of which the obvious ones such as malaria, leprosy, and other tropical diseases probably give the least cause for anxiety. They have no comprehension of the modern materialistic life of Israel. Their language is Arabic, as are their customs and attitude to life. The Yemenites are intensely religious, but perhaps because in the Yemen religious observance is compulsory for Jew as well as Muslim, they often quickly revert to an amoral ungodliness when compulsion is lacking. One camp official estimates that 80 percent of the Yemenite immigrants forget the Messianic teaching and

break the Ten Commandments with a cynicism that appalls the sentimental materialist. Without religious support and understanding of
the duties required of a citizen in a modern State, they are an anchorless community.

It is well known that the religiosity of the Yemenite Jews has been deeply
rooted [in them] for many generations and is not the result of any external obligation imposed upon them that is liable to be easily undermined in the absence of
coercion. There is certainly not a grain of truth in the words of the correspondent
that 80 percent of them forget the doctrine of the Messiah and cynically break the
Ten Commandments (when they come to the camps). However, the significance
of the erroneous statement of this Gentile lies not in the mistaken view that he
presents, but in the fact that it is based upon information provided him by an official in one of the immigrant camps, and thus it reflects an opinion widely held
among the workers in the camps. And it is among such camp officials that the
source of the responsibility for spreading this type of groundless accusation is to
be sought.

As for the local press, the level of responsibility for what it publishes is on
quite a high level, and there is no need to lay the responsibility with others, except
insofar as a particular paper reflects the opinion of its party, in which case the
party also shares in the responsibility.

The commission wishes to note that it has not read everything that has been
published in the newspapers regarding these matters, apart from what was specifically brought to its attention by the witnesses, and apart from what was read by
each member in the course of his regular perusal of the newspapers that he reads
regularly. Nevertheless, on this occasion one article should be mentioned, not because of its contents but because of the irregularity of its very publication in opposition to generally accepted norms. The article in question is "For the Ears of
the Commission of Inquiry" (*Davar*, 6 February 1950), published over the signature of E. Lubrani, a regional supervisor of the Culture Department. Mr. Lubrani
asked to be called to testify before the Commission of Inquiry, yet nevertheless he
saw fit to publicize (before tens of thousands of outside readers) what he intended
to say to the commission.

Furthermore, in his testimony before the commission, he said that he had
asked the director, Mr. Nahum Levin, whether there was any objection to the publication of his article, and the director's answer was, according to Mr. Lubriani—
what is done is done. Mr. Levin confirmed that he had agreed to the publication
of the article.

From the extensive press clippings presented to the commission, one passage
from a professional journal and one passage from a paper that is not affiliated with
any particular party deserve citation.

In the journal of the Teacher's Union, *Hed Hahinukh*, of 29 Teveth [5710, 18 January 1950], there appears the following:

> Is it indeed impossible that the Ministry of Education and Culture should appoint and establish an authorized commission of inquiry on its behalf, before whom will be brought all the complaints, and that it be able to determine the absolute truth of the matter? Are there no longer honest and unprejudiced persons in the country, among its writers and teachers, who have an affinity for cultural values and know how to safeguard their purity? Such a commission might perhaps clarify and explain, to itself and to others, why and how matters of education in the camps were removed from the jurisdiction of the Education Division, a matter which is seemingly part and parcel of [the division]. Why did they see fit to place it specifically within the sphere of culture? It should, and could, get to the root of this seemingly strange arrangement, by which the education of children of Yemenite families, who are religious people and well versed in religion, was entrusted precisely to youngsters from "Hanoar Ha'oved," who are far removed from that world and from that way of life. As a result of its investigation, such a commission would also be able to close the breach and prevent such mishaps in the future. Moreover, Hebrew education, and especially education in our country, is first and foremost the creation of the Hebrew teacher. Every teacher teaches according to his pedagogic conscience in a place that suits his worldview. Moreover, the right to choose is given to the children's parents, so that both sides enjoy freedom of choice and the right to self-definition. What right and basis exists, therefore, for coercion and storming—by whatever side—of what is legally the right of others? True, that is the way "political" people behave, those for whom all means are legal! How good and appropriate it would be were our colleagues, the teachers of all streams, to bestir themselves, were it they who would set the limits and establish the framework. What is more precious than anything else—the education of the future generation—must not be left subject to passions.

The following is a passage from *Ha'aretz* of 22 February 1950:

> If education were really paramount (for both sides), it would be possible to come to an arrangement. But the truth of the matter is that the Workers Stream, which since the creation of the state is on the offensive, [together with] Mapai and Mapam have decided that since the present [wave of] immigration consists primarily of Oriental, religious Jews, according to the existing system of streams all this material [i.e., children] will go to the "religious streams" of Hamizrachi and Agudat Israel—in other words, it will be dominated politically by the Religious Front. For this reason, it has decided to expand the core of the religious

sub-stream of the Workers Stream. For it is clear even to the leaders of the Workers Stream that some day state education will be established in Israel; therefore, until then they must gain complete control of the educational sphere. Thus, they will have nothing to fear once education becomes state education.

As for the Religious Front, were it truly concerned only that children should receive a religious education, it would not need to be so apprehensive of the development of the religious school of the Workers Stream. On the contrary, it could consider this to be a great victory, that the Histadrut was also forced to establish a constantly expanding stream of religious education. But, in addition to their sincere suspicion that the religious school of the Workers Stream is no more than a tactic, and that its pupils will in the end be brought over to a non-religious framework, there exists within the Religious Front primarily the fear that this issue will undermine their organization and the prospects for their own development, for it will put an end to their monopolization of religious education in the state. [This is] a monopoly which, like the economic monopolization by Mapai, is the source of the Religious Front's political power in the state.

CHAPTER 5

SOURCES OF PROPAGANDA
ABROAD

Unlike accusations of religious coercion in the camps that were raised by religious circles both within and without the government, other government circles complained about the propaganda in other countries regarding these accusations, which they considered to be anti-Israeli activity.

The minister of education and culture referred primarily to the propaganda and publicity abroad, and his complaint was twofold: that the extensive publicity and protest rallies had been organized from here [Israel], and that even if the accusations of religious coercion were justified, a supposition with which he does not agree, these things should not have been made public to the world, not even among Diaspora Jewry, but a way should have been found to explain and influence from within.

In opposition to this, cabinet members and other personalities who came to the defense of the Religious Front argued that the propaganda had not been organized from here, and that the facts in themselves were sufficient to spark off emotions among ultra-Orthodox Jews, both in Israel and abroad. "A little bird told them" [as the saying goes]. Whatever is said and done here is immediately echoed abroad.

As proof that no propaganda was organized from here, Minister Shapira suggested that the commission get all of the telegrams that had been sent concerning this subject. Minister Levin supplied the commission with an exchange of telegrams between himself and New York, as did Mr. Pinkas, who gave [the commission] all of the material, apart from one telegram that he had sent and about which he told the commission, but of which he did not produce a copy.

Regarding Minister Shapira's suggestion to get hold of the telegrams that had been sent regarding this matter, the commission found that it was beyond its authority to summon witnesses of its own accord and instruct them to disclose information that had been submitted to the postal authorities for processing. However, from the testimony of Mr. Agron, it turned out that the minister of transport, as the person to whom the law had granted the authority which had previously been vested in the High Commissioner[1] under the Post Office Ordinance, was authorized by law to order the disclosure [of the content] of telegrams if the matter seemed justified to him under given circumstances. To enable the government to utilize this authority, the commission conveyed to the Government Secretary a preliminary decision that it had taken on this matter on 24 March 1950, stating that, according to Section 50 of the Post Office Ordinance, a court or a commission of inquiry cannot demand the disclosure of telegrams that had been sent. However, Section 49 of this same ordinance vests authority in the High Commissioner (or to whoever acts in his stead) in the event of a time of public emergency, or for public interest, to issue an order to disclose telegrams that had been sent by certain people or regarding certain matters to the High Commissioner or to whomever he should order. If such an instruction is issued, the person so designated by the government may appear before the commission and disclose [the content of] these specific telegrams.

Following the exchange of letters between the prime minister and the chairman of the commission concerning this matter, a directive was issued by the minister of transport to the effect that "any telegram that was sent abroad pertaining to the matter of education in the immigrant camps is to be disclosed to the chairman of the commission of inquiry."

This directive was based upon another one issued by the minister of transport, as follows:

> Post Office Ordinance (Paragraph 115), directive by the minister of transport, on the basis of Section 49: "By virtue of my authority under Section 49 (2) of the Post Office Ordinance (Paragraph 115), I, the minister of transport, hereby affirm that all acts performed under Section 49 (1) regarding any telegram sent abroad and pertaining to matters of education in the immigrant camps are for the public good."

On the basis of these directives, the director of the Postal Services disclosed to the chairman of the commission a number of telegrams that had been sent abroad from Israel during the months of December 1949 and January 1950 relating to education in the camps, from among which the chairman of the commission selected a number of telegrams having direct relevance to the matter, which the director of the Postal Services presented to the commission in his testimony.

The following is a summary of the material that was brought to the attention of the commission concerning propaganda abroad, from all the sources:

The first report about the dispute being publicized abroad reached the minister of education in a telegram dated 13 January [1950], concerning the widespread publicity given to the matter in the *Jewish Chronicle* of that date. The following is the text of the telegram, in its Hebrew translation,[2] as included in the material submitted to the commission by the minister of education:

> The lead article in today's *Jewish Chronicle* is a report filed by the Hamizrachi reporter, that the religious bloc is threatening to quit the government coalition because of the anti-religious policy of the Ministry of Education in the immigrant camps. The specific accusations are the following: the immigrants are denied the right to choose one of the four educational streams. Nahum Levin's Culture Department opened non-religious schools, despite the fact that the Ministry of Education denied (in a reply) to interlocutors on behalf of the religious [camp] that there is any intention of opening permanent schools in the transitory camps. Yeshiva students who attempted to open classes were expelled from the camp. The government (according to the *Chronicle*, the director of the camp) by means of threats extorted statements that the immigrants did not agree that the religious teacher should take 15 children from the camps near Haifa to a yeshiva in Jerusalem without the permission of the director of the camp, and accuse him of kidnapping the children. The storm that arose around this matter prompted the decision of the Ministry of Education to introduce the system of streams, which has not yet been implemented. Ninety percent of the 60,000 Oriental Jewish immigrants are religious. These accusations, on the eve of the United Jewish Appeal, are dangerous. Telegraph immediately your reasoned answer, which we will publish in our official journal, and perhaps we will publish [it as] a pamphlet. Bakshtanski.

Mr. Agron stated in his testimony that the article in the *Jewish Chronicle* was "the only concrete item containing something like a very harsh accusation that he had seen with his own eyes." It should be noted that it was published about two weeks after Mr. Pinkas' parliamentary query before the Knesset Committee on Education and Culture, and three days after the government session at which the problem was discussed in all its seriousness. But one cannot conclude from this chronological proximity alone that there was a direct appeal abroad by responsible persons or bodies in connection with the above-mentioned publication. Extensive publicity was given in the local press to the decision of the Religious Front threatening to quit the coalition (see *Davar*, 11 January, which relied upon *Haboker* of the previous day), presented to the government [at its] session of 10 January, nor does it make any difference if those close to the Religious Front also reported this to the foreign press, as one may assume that the *Jewish Chronicle* correspondent also relied upon what was published in the local press.

But news of the controversy was heard abroad even before the government session, as is made clear by a telegram from New York dated 5 January received by Minister Y. M. Levin, that reads as follows:

> The terrible news about the acts of forced abandonment of religion and the anti-religious inquisition in the camps of the Yemenite children and in other camps have greatly disturbed the rabbis and ultra-Orthodox Jewry in America. We need to know what means have been taken. The matter is extremely serious, and is likely to lead to destructive results, Heaven forbid. The Union of Orthodox Rabbis will not rest or be silent until the matter is completely taken care of.

This telegram arrived about one week after the parliamentary query of Mr. Pinkas in the Knesset Committee on Education and Culture (28 December 1949). In addition to the proximity in time, the use of the terms "forced abandonment of religion" and "anti-religious inquisition," used by Mr. Pinkas, also suggests a connection between the query and the telegram. How did the very fact of the query and its wording get abroad? Though the sessions of the Knesset committees are not public, it would appear that the discussions in the committees are also not kept secret. On the day of the parliamentary query the Tel Aviv evening paper, *Ma'ariv*, published an account of a stormy session of the Knesset Committee on Education in which "Mr. Pinkas said harsh things about the scandal of education in the camps, and spoke of the murder of Jewish religion and culture and the inquisition against religious education." Though the commission was not presented with any newspaper publications in New York between the date of the [parliamentary] query and the date of the telegram to Minister Levin, one may assume that the content of the query was conveyed to New York.

On 8 January Minister Levin responded to the above telegram:

> To the Union of Orthodox Rabbis, New York. Today I spoke regarding the contents of your telegram with the prime minister. We shall do our part, and inform you of the results in the next few days.

After the government meeting, Minister Levin again telegraphed as follows:

> 12 January 1950. To the Union of Orthodox Rabbis, New York. I raised the issue of education in the camps before the government, and if the matter is not dealt with, I proposed that we quit the government, and that [our] members in the Jewish Agency quit the Agency. I will inform you of further details.

A telegram with the same text was also sent to Rabbi Rosenheim in New York.

Four days later, on 16 January, uniformly worded telegrams were sent from the Religious Bloc in New York to the prime minister and to several ministers. The commission is in possession of the telegram received by Minister Shazar:

> To the honorable Minister of Education Zalman Shazar, Tel Aviv.
>
> The United Religious Bloc in America, including the following American movements—The Union of Orthodox Rabbis in America; the Union of Admorim [i.e., leaders of Hasidic communities]; the Rabbinical Council of America; the Rabbinical Alliance of America; Agudat Israel in America; Hapoel Hamizrachi in America; the Hamizrachi Federation in America; the Young Israel Council; Poalei Agudat Israel; the Union of Orthodox Congregations in America; Agudat Israel Youth—decided at a special assembly, unanimously and without reservation, to demand that the entire issue of absorption of the children be reexamined so as to prevent injustice to the children and their parents and to the foundations of religious Judaism, and in order to avoid a worldwide scandal with far-reaching and tragic consequences. Immediate action is essential. The United Religious Bloc in America.

The following is a telegram sent to the United Religious Front in Jerusalem:

> I telegraphed today the following people: Ben-Gurion, Sharett, Kol,[3] Shazar, Sprinzak[4] as follows: (Here follows the text of the telegram—see Shazar's copy of the telegram.) Ben-Gurion received the same wording, with the addition of an appeal to him as prime minister of Israel. Be strong on behalf of our God, our people, and our Holy Land. We await news from you. The United Religious Bloc.

The leaders of the Religious Front sent the following reply:

> Thank you for your efforts and your words of encouragement, for supporting us in our difficult struggle to save the souls of Jewish children. We are taking all possible steps to abolish the regime of coercion in the immigrant camps and in the new settlements. The issue is the subject of discussion by the government; the character of the young generation of the immigrants, nearly all of whom are religious, and particularly the immigrants from Yemen, all of whom observe the Torah and the Commandments, depends upon attainment of our just demands. We await positive results, with God's help. For the United Religious Front: David Zvi Pinkas, Elisha Tennenbaum.

The prime minister responded as follows:

> I received your telegram and conveyed its contents to the entire government. None of us denies the right of every Jew wherever he may be to voice an opinion and also to express criticism concerning matters in the State of Israel. However, it is rather surprising that you reached a decision on a serious issue with which you are not familiar, and that you passed judgment without hearing the accused, which is against the Torah of Israel. No one in the government knows the source of the information upon which you based yourselves.
>
> I am particularly astonished by the strange threat with which you address the government of Israel. The State of Israel is a democratic republic, based upon liberty, freedom of conscience, and freedom of religion, and all matters therein are determined by the decision of the majority of its citizens, according to their best judgment.
>
> You may rest assured that we shall do nothing under the pressure of threats, if the matter is not justified and necessary in its own right.
>
> If you wish to directly influence the direction which the State of Israel [is taking] and to strengthen a particular group among us, the most effective means of doing so is for you and those in whose name you speak to come to us and settle in the country. I promise you that every one of us will rejoice at your coming.
> Respectfully,
> D. Ben-Gurion.

The following are selections from several telegrams sent by the Chairman of the World Center of Hamizrachi, Mr. [Rabbi] Gelman:

In a telegram of the eighth of January to the Center of Hamizrachi in New York, it is stated among other things (based on the Hebrew translation):[5]

> I telegraphed the Union of [Orthodox] Rabbis requesting moral support for our struggle against discrimination in religious education in the camps. Please telegraph [to inform me] if the Jewish press has published reports pertaining to this tragic matter, which is an absolute repeat of the Teheran Affair.

The following is the telegram sent by Mr. Gelman sent on that same day to the Union of Orthodox Rabbis in the name of the World Center of Hamizrachi:

> For several weeks now the Hamizrachi movement, together with the chief rabbis, has been conducting a bitter battle against extreme discrimination regarding religious education in various camps that is a repetition of the tragic Teheran Affair.

The Hamizrachi delegation met with Ben-Gurion, demanding an immediate end to the discrimination and also a firm promise for full autonomy of religious education. He promised a thorough investigation. This struggle will be decisive for the very existence of religious freedom in Israel. We strongly request that you give us full moral backing, and if possible financial help.

And on 10 January Mr. Gelman telegraphed the Center of Hamizrachi in New York:

> After a stormy meeting of the World Center, together with representatives of the entire movement, it was decided unanimously that should the government refuse to change the system of discrimination and coercion against religious education in the camps and in other places in which there is similar discrimination, then its representatives must resign from the government and the Jewish Agency.
>
> Drastic action is necessary to finally resolve this tragic affair. Please pass on this information to the Union of Rabbis, to the Rabbinical Council, to Hapoel Hamizrachi, and to the press.

Following these things a protest rally, or as it was called there "a mass demonstration," was organized for the 23rd of January in Manhattan Center. The preceding day Mr. Pinkas was contacted by a telegram having the following text:

> To Pinkas, Tel Aviv,
>
> Tomorrow, Monday, there will be a public rally of Jewry in America to strengthen the ultra-Orthodox community and the Religious Front in your efforts on behalf of education of children in [the spirit of the] Torah and what is sacred to Israel. We ask [that you send] immediately telegrams of encouragement and support for the rally from the Front, the religious ministers, and the chief rabbis.
>
> Manhattan Center. The Religious Bloc in America.

In his testimony, Mr. Pinkas related that he was also contacted by telephone regarding the same matter, and that, in opposition to the view of Minister of Religious Affairs Rabbi Maimon, he expressed his opinion both over the telephone and by telegram that Hamizrachi should join in the demonstration. The following are the texts of the telegrams sent by Mr. Pinkas and by Minister Maimon just prior to the rally in Manhattan:

> If you do not participate in the rally of the Religious Bloc you are liable to undermine our efforts to achieve a satisfactory solution regarding re-

ligious education in the camps and the absorption of religious youth.
(Signed, Pinkas)

I advise Hamizrachi and all of Orthodox Jewry in America not to interfere in the internal affairs of the State of Israel. Your involvement
will only cause harm. We have here rabbis who are great scholars, God-
fearing, and having integrity, and they are capable by themselves of
battling on behalf of religious influence in the State of Israel, and you
should not become involved in this matter. (Signed, Rabbi Y. L. Maimon, Minister of Religious Affairs).

On 22 January Mr. Gelman sent a telegram to the Center of Hamizrachi in
New York that read in part:

We telegraphed today to the Religious Bloc, as follows:

The governmental commission of inquiry has begun its work. We
are awaiting a decision in a few days time. It is advisable not to take any
drastic action until the end of the inquiry. We are on our guard to safeguard the demands of religious Jewry. We will inform you of developments and advise regarding the necessary steps. It is advised that you
participate in the demonstration.

The commission was also presented with a similar telegram sent to the Religious Bloc and signed by Gold, Gelman, Shragai,[6] and Raphael.[7]

Telegrams of support were also sent by the Chief Rabbis, and there were also
telegraphic appeals from other rabbis, such as Rabbi Harlap and Rabbi Katz of
Petah Tikva.

On the day of the rally, huge ads appeared in the *Morgen Zhurnal*[8] calling
for "a mass demonstration of religious Jewry on behalf of Israel and our Holy
Torah." In the central ad, signed by the same organizations whose names appeared on the telegram to the ministers, with the exception of the Center of
Hamizrachi, the Religious Bloc called upon the Jews of New York to participate
en masse so as to express their support for the religious ministers and Knesset
members [in their struggle] on behalf of religious education in Israel. Among
other things, the ad declared:

American Jews will make heard today their strong voice against the unsolicited guardians who wish by force to impose a free-thinking and
alien education upon the children of religious immigrants in Israel.

Remember, the Chief Rabbis of the Holy Land, religious ministers and Knesset members, and the entire Religious Front in Israel appeal to us today to help them in their holy struggle for religious
education in Israel.

In addition to this general [joint] advertisement, separate ads appeared [signed by] several individual organizations which had signed the joint ad.

From all this, the commission concluded that what agitated ultra-Orthodox public opinion abroad was Mr. Pinkas' parliamentary query in the Knesset Committee [on Education and Culture], although it was not possible to clarify whether Mr. Pinkas or another of those responsible for conducting the affairs of the Religious Front here conveyed this directly to their colleagues in New York.

The commission sees nothing wrong per se in conveying information about the query to persons abroad, even if this was done by a member of the Religious Front, because it is only natural that they would want to inform their like-minded comrades of a situation which they believed to be most serious, and certainly one cannot ascribe to this any intention of undermining the foundations of the state. However, precisely because there was no intention on the part of Mr. Pinkas to conceal his query, and he could have surmised that the matter would elicit considerable publicity, he needed to be judicious in [the choice of] words and refrain from using such incendiary terms as "inquisition" with regard to people for whose actions the State of Israel bears responsibility. The man in the street who reads that word immediately conjures up images of torture, auto-da-fés, and the horrible atrocities of the Spanish period [in Jewish history]; whatever may be the government's degree of responsibility for the acts of coercion in the camps relating to religion, one cannot imagine [them to be] similar to an inquisition. The same holds true for such expressions as "cultural and religious murder."

It also became clear that religious circles in the state demanded help and encouragement from similar groups in the United States. This is particularly clearly stated in the telegrams of Mr. Gelman, who demanded full moral support. He also declared that it was necessary to take drastic action, and requested, among other things, that the press be informed of the situation.

The commission could have sufficed with a brief answer to the question it was asked—what was the source of the propaganda abroad—by saying that the signal was given by the parliamentary query in the Education Committee of the Knesset, which was widely publicized in Israel and abroad, and that aid was directly requested by responsible bodies here, such as the World Center of Hamizrachi, even to the extent of involving the press.

But the commission was also asked—albeit not in its writ of authority but by one of the cabinet members who appeared before it, Mr. Shazar—to express its opinion as to whether it was proper to call upon foreign elements for help, even if the accusations of coercion in the camps were true, and whether the external manifestations that resulted directly or indirectly from the calls for support issued here are to be considered acts against the State of Israel.

Two facts were brought before the commission regarding this point: the telegram to government ministers from the Religious Bloc in the United States, and the rally in Manhattan Center.

Regarding the telegram, two arguments were put forth:

(a) From the joint signatures of eleven religious groups, it was legitimate to think that this was [the outcome of] a one-time, united organizational effort, whose only purpose was to attack the State of Israel.

The commission does not believe this to be the case. Testimony was heard [to the effect] that upon the establishment of the Religious Front in Israel prior to the elections to the First Knesset, various religious groups in America also organized themselves into a religious bloc, and now they found an opportunity to express their joint will and a united approach.

(b) There were those who saw the wording of the telegram [of the Religious Bloc in the United States] as intervention in the affairs of the state, and as a threat. The commission finds no fault in the appeal on the part of the Religious Bloc in America to the government ministers as such. Even if there can be differences of opinion regarding the wording [of the telegram] and the accusations expressed therein, the [authority] to decide lies with the government of Israel, and the telegrams addressed to it cannot be considered [acts of] undermining [its standing]. Even the prime minister, in his reply to the telegram cited above, wrote: "None of us denies the right of every Jew wherever he may be to voice an opinion and also to express criticism concerning matters in the State of Israel."

Much bitterness has accumulated regarding the mass rally in Manhattan Center, which some members of the government saw as a severe action against the State of Israel. Minister of Education Mr. Shazar gave vent to these feelings by saying that the gathering was reminiscent of the meetings organized by New York Jews against Hitler, restrictions on *aliya*, and Bevin, and that the state could not tolerate such a thing.

Within religious circles too there were some who thought that the rally should not be held. Though the minister of religious affairs, in his telegram calling to refrain from involvement, does not relate explicitly to participation in the rally, it is a fact that his telegram was sent on the day of and in connection with the rally, in response to a request to send words of encouragement.

At first, the commission believed this also to be the view of the members of Hamizrachi and Hapoel Hamizrachi on the Jewish Agency Executive, who sent a telegram on the eve of the rally, together with the chairman of the World Center of Hamizrachi, calling upon [the American groups] to refrain from drastic measures until the commission of inquiry would conclude its work. Since the commission initially saw a certain contradiction between the joint request of the four signatories and the addendum of Mr. Gelman, after he quoted the wording of the joint telegram advising the Center of Hamizrachi in New York to participate in the gathering, it called upon Rabbi Gold and Mr. Gelman to provide it with an explanation of this matter.

Rabbi Gold's view was that the expression "drastic action" did not refer to the rally, which had already been organized and was impossible to call off, but to acts such as a boycott of the United Jewish Appeal, since reports had been received that there was a tendency to take such steps, as had been done at the time of the aliya of the Teheran Children. That is why they thought it to be precisely advisable to participate in the rally in order to calm things down, to announce that the government had taken measures [and] appointed a commission of inquiry, and that it was advisable to wait for the results.

A similar explanation was put forward by Mr. Gelman, who on the tenth of January had indeed demanded drastic action, but now that the government had entered into the thick of things, [believed that] this should be avoided. He did not consider the rally itself to be a drastic act, since the decisions adopted at that rally were very moderate; as evidence he presented the commission with the resolutions that had been adopted by the rally, as published in the *Morgen Zhurnal* of 26 January 1950.

One cannot deny those sectors of Diaspora Jewry who have been eternally connected to the Land of Israel and for generations have longed for the State of Israel the right to take an interest in what is happening in the state, particularly in matters spiritual, cultural, and religious. In particular, one cannot deny them this right at a time when their help and assistance is necessary for the establishment of the state, the absorption of immigrants, and the ingathering of exiles. If a large Diaspora community sees certain things that are not according to its inclinations, it has the right to comment upon them and attempt to influence affairs. But this right must be used judiciously, by voicing an opinion or even—in the words of the prime minister—by expressing criticism, but they must not intervene in affairs which in every democratic country are the sole responsibility of the authorities in the state, and they must also refrain from what might be perceived as such intervention. In particular, it should be taken into account that just as news of what is done in Israel is immediately heard in the Diaspora, so too the nations of the world closely observe how the Jewish world relates to the State of Israel.

The commission declares that as for the form [that the protest took], the organizers of the rally did not adopt the proper manner when they chose to express their opinion through a "great mass demonstration" in order to sound a "loud voice against the unsolicited guardians who wish by force to impose a free-thinking and alien education upon the children of religious immigrants to Israel."

On the other hand, the commission notes that the resolutions adopted at the rally in Manhattan Center were moderate in spirit and cannot be seen as pressure, or a threat, or intervention in the internal affairs of the state. On the contrary, the resolutions began with praise and thanksgiving for the creation of the state, noted the efforts being made by the government of Israel and its prime minister to improve the situation, and called for increased contributions to the United Jewish Appeal, while simultaneously demanding that the Jewish Agency build houses and structures for the religious children.

CHAPTER 6

CONCLUSIONS

1. COERCION IN THE CAMPS

> To investigate all accusations concerning religious coercion in the
> immigrant camps.
>> —Clause A of the writ of authority

The commission came to the following conclusions regarding religious coercion in the camps:

a. There was no intention on the part of the government of [imposing] religious coercion.

b. It was a fatal error to relegate the education of children in the camps in general, and of those from Oriental countries in particular, especially those from Yemen, Tripolitania,[1] and Morocco, to the "Department for Language Instruction and Cultural Absorption among the Immigrants," for the following reasons:

1. The composition of the personnel of that department, which from the outset was structured to care for adults, was not intended for the education of children. A number of the cultural coordinators, school principals, and teachers in the camps are lacking in pedagogic training or educational experience. The commission notes the strange fact that there was no contact between the Culture Department and the Education Division within the same ministry.

2. The composition of the personnel was not suited to the needs of a fundamentally religious element, for whom even a slight transgression of religious commandments would be likely to cause emotional shock and recalcitrance.[2] Regarding this, the commission notes the lack of contact between the Culture Department and the Torah Section of the Ministry of Education and Culture.

c. The same holds true for social mores which, while they do not involve any violation of religious precepts, nevertheless entail a severe danger that when such mores are suddenly imposed, they are likely to undermine general moral standards.

d. From this fact—i.e., the unsuitability of the personnel, both in relation to education and to the customs and way of life of the immigrants—followed superficial treatment of the religious problems of the immigrants and the children. The staff considered its prime objective to be the adjustment of the children to the Israeli milieu as it exists within [the staff's] own society and everyday life. The fundamental error was that it measured [the immigrants] using the same standards by which it measured itself or the standard by which it measured immigrants from European countries. It therefore chose a course that it believed to be easy and simple. Nevertheless, it should be noted that a heavy burden was placed upon the workers, under quite difficult conditions, and they acted with considerable dedication in their overall objective.

e. Regarding specific accusations, the commission asserts:

1. Cutting off of *payot*—this was done systemically and not by chance, and one must unfortunately note that the minister of education and culture was misled when told that there were only twelve such cases, and these because of ringworm.

2. Interference with religious studies was also systematic. The lack of religious teachers is not a sufficient argument, since in any event most of those engaged in teaching in the camps lacked pedagogic training.

3. They were not sufficiently assiduous about the observance of Sabbath and prayer, and there were also cases of interference with prayer.

f. All this was not the result of a deliberate campaign against religion, as a goal in itself, but as a means of hastening the desired process of adjustment. There was no justification for accusing government representatives in the camps of "inquisition" or "murdering national culture."

g. The struggle over education in the camps was not without partisan motivation. On the one hand there was a desire to prepare the immigrants and the youth for [membership in] the Histadrut, and not to strengthen the religious parties. On the other hand, though passions aroused in religious circles were indeed innocently sincere and only for the sake of Heaven, in order to strengthen religious sentiment among the immigrants, here too the wish to strengthen the religious parties and to weaken the influence of other parties on these immigrants was not lacking.

h. The commission has already asserted that the root of all evil, of the severe neglect of matters of religious education in the camps, lay in the fact that educational matters in the camps were relegated to the authority of the Culture Department. With whom does responsibility [for this situation] lie?

i. Responsibility does not lie with the director of the Education Divison, who demanded that education [in the camps] be transferred to his authority, and who, together with all his staff, was always willing to accept it.

One cannot explicitly blame Mr. Nahum Levin, who claims that he did not want to be responsible for education [in the camps], and proved that on several occasions he notified the minister of education that neither he nor his department were able to handle this task, demanding that education be transferred to the Education Division.

It is also difficult to place responsibility upon the administrative apparatus of the Ministry of Education and Culture, which was still in the process of being organized and structured, and lacked any [bureaucratic] tradition and experience.

This, therefore, leaves the minister of education and culture himself, who bears overall responsibility for everything in his ministry. However, responsibility cannot be placed upon Mr. Shazar, who for a considerable period of time during the development of these events was ill, and was therefore unable to give [the issue] his personal and fundamental attention. Hence, responsibility returns to its primary source—the government as a whole, that bears collective responsibility for all matters of the state, including education of the immigrants.

j. All this notwithstanding, direct responsibility for the severe harm to religious education in the camp lies with the director of the department, Mr. Nahum Levin, albeit the commission finds him innocent of such general and ungrounded accusations as "inquisitional acts" and "murdering national culture." Even if the commission does not hold him responsible for the very fact that educational matters in the camp were relegated to him and placed under his authority, nevertheless, so long as this state of affairs exists, he bears responsibility, towards both the government and the public, for his own acts and the acts of the extensive apparatus under his direction and supervision, since it was he who determined policy and appointed the personnel. The employees in the department and in the camps share in this responsibility, particularly insofar as they exaggerated even beyond the policy that was set for them, or were overly strict in its execution. The commission wishes to condemn particularly the leadership of the cultural coordinator in the Ein-Shemer camp, Mr. Aldema, and Ms. Zippora Zehavi, an instructor in the youth camp in Beit-Lid VII.

2. ACCUSATIONS IN THE PRESS

To clarify the accusations in the press and those responsible for them.
—Clause B of the writ of authority

k. The answer to the first part in the second clause, "if the accusations in the press are correct,"[3] is to be found above in the commission's conclusions regarding the basic question of the charges of religious coercion in the camps.

l. Responsibility for what was published in the local press lies, in the usual manner, with the newspapers and their correspondents and, insofar as the paper is the organ of a specific party, also upon that party.

3. SOURCES OF THE PROPAGANDA ABROAD

To examine the sources of the propaganda abroad concerning the accusations in question.
—Clause C of the writ of authority

m. The source of propaganda abroad concerning charges of religious coercion in the camps is to be sought in religious circles in the state and in the Israeli press. The signal was given by means of the parliamentary query in the Knesset Committee on Education [and Culture], and appeals for moral support were issued to rabbis and to the World Center of Hamizrachi. The latter sought to involve the press.

n. These requests are not to be seen as involving any intention to act against the State of Israel. Nor did the commission see any such intention in the organization of the Religious Bloc in New York, or in the telegram that it sent to the members of the government.

o. The public rally in Manhattan Center was not organized from here, although it may be ascribed, indirectly, to the information provided from here about the situation in the camps.

p. In its form the gathering was not proper, albeit one cannot find any fault with the content of its resolutions.

q. The commission believes that Diaspora Jewry has the right to take an interest in what is happening in the state, particularly in matters pertaining to the entire Jewish people, and insofar as this does not reach the point of intervention in the internal affairs of the state, it may address the Government of Israel with suitable proposals and demands.

Jerusalem, Tuesday, 22 Iyar 5710 (9 May 1950)
Chairman of the Commission: Gad Frumkin
Members of the Commission: Avraham Elmaleh
Izhak Ben-Zvi
Rabbi Kalman Kahana
Rabbi A. H. Shaag

ADDENDUM

List of Witnesses Who Testified
before the Commission

1.	Z. Shazar	Minister of Education and Culture
2.	M. Shapira	Minister of the Interior, Immigration and Health
3.	D. Z. Pinkas	Representative of the Religious Front
4.	Rabbi Hayyim David Kahana	Rabbi from Migdal Gad
5.	Yeshayahu Bernstein	Representative of [World] Center of Hamizrachi
6.	Rabbi Bezalel Cohen	Representative of [World] Center of Hamizrachi
7.	Rabbi B. Goldberg	Representative of Va'ad Hayeshivot
8.	M. D. Tennenbaum	Representative of Va'ad Hayeshivot
9.	Rabbi Y. M. Levin	Minister of Welfare
10.	Rabbi I. Y. Unterman	Chief Rabbi of Tel Aviv-Jaffa
11.	Mr. Wilner	Administrative Secretary, Absorption Department of the Jewish Agency
12.	Yehuda Rieder	Teacher at Ein-Shemer
13.	Moshe Segal	Teacher at Ein-Shemer
14.	Nahum Levin	Director, Department of Language Instruction and Cultural Absorption of Immigrants

15. Dr. B. Ben-Yehuda	Director of Education Division
16. Shlomo Kroll	Student at Poniewicz Yeshiva
17. Yehoshua Shklar	Student at Poniewicz Yeshiva
18. Avi [Zvi] Gartner	Director, Ein-Shemer II Camp
19. Ya'akov Trachtenberg	Director, Ein-Shemer I Camp
20. Rabbi Yitzhak Levi Yitzhak	Rabbi from Ein-Shemer
21. Rabbi David Yitzhak Jabara	Rabbi from Ein-Shemer
22. Rabbi Moshe Yitzhak Halevi (Levi)	Rabbi from Ein-Shemer
23. Rabbi Yihya Netanel Alchech	Rabbi from Ein-Shemer
24. Yihya Yehoshua Hassan (age 14)	Youth from Ein-Shemer
25. Y. A. Aldema	Cultural Coordinator at Ein-Shemer
26. Rabbi Y. Z. Diskin	Rabbi of Pardes Hanna
27. Yosef David Madmon	Immigrant at Ein-Shemer
28. Salem Yihya Naos	Immigrant at Ein-Shemer
29. Shalom Shalom Ya'akov Jarafi	Immigrant at Ein-Shemer
30. Shalom Shalom Boni	Immigrant at Ein-Shemer
31. Sa'adya Yarimi	Teacher at Ein-Shemer
32. Zippora Zehavi	Responsible for youth camp at Beit Lid VII
33. Yosef Govitz	Teacher at Beit Lid
34. Sa'adya Karwani	Responsible for school at Beit Lid VII
35. Hadassa Lipmanowitz	Director of Youth Bureau, Department for Language Instruction for Immigrants
36. Dr. E. Lubrani	Director of the Culture Department in the Samaria and Galilee District
37. Rabbi A. Y. Winkelstein	"Ahiezer," institute for establishing schools for Torah education
38. Simha Piltz	Teacher in Mahane Israel
39. Yitzhak Schneursohn	Teacher in Mahane Israel and Beit Lid VII
40. Dr. Yeshayahu Leibowitz	Ha'oved Hadati
41. Gitta Landau	Teacher in Beer Ya'akov
42. Lidia Nahias	Teacher in Beer Ya'akov
43. Menahem Adir	Cultural Coordinator in Beer Ya'akov
44. Simha Abir	Principal of Central School at Beer Ya'akov
45. Rabbi Farji Pitori	Immigrant at Beer Ya'akov
46. Rabbi Yair Hafita [Hafuta]	Immigrant at Beer Ya'akov
47. Gavriel Raccah	Immigrant at Beer Ya'akov

48. Shaul Baranitz	Teacher in the Hamizrachi school at the Agrobank immigrant camp (Hadera)
49. Yehuda Kasri [Kamri]	Immigrant at Beit Lid VII
50. Yehuda David Shar'abi	Immigrant at Beit Lid VII
51. Shalom Morhi	Immigrant at Beit Lid VII
52. Hayyim Haddad	Immigrant at Beit Lid VII
53. Shaul Yehuda Shar'abi	Immigrant at Beit Lid VII (a youth)
54. Sa'adya Yehuda Avraham	Immigrant at Beit Lid VII
55. H. Walbag [Ralbag]	Secretary, Samaria District of the Culture Department
56. Bezalel Gipstein	Cultural Coordinator and School Principal in Rosh Ha'ayin
57. Ophra Berland	Assistant to coordinator and teacher in Rosh Ha'ayin
58. Israel Fischler	Teacher at Rosh Ha'ayin
59. Zidkiyahu Haddi	Teacher at Rosh Ha'ayin
60. Yihya Salah Salem	Immigrant at Rosh Ha'ayin
61. Sa'adya Ovadya Ahraq	Immigrant at Rosh Ha'ayin
62. Israel Shim'on	Immigrant at Rosh Ha'ayin
63. Avraham Yehuda Shim'i	Immigrant at Rosh Ha'ayin
64. Hayyim ben Hayyim Kapah	Immigrant at Rosh Ha'ayin
65. Meshullam Arye	Immigrant at Rosh Ha'ayin
66. Shalom Zecharya Mani	Immigrant at Rosh Ha'ayin
67. Aharon ben Hayyim Dannin	Immigrant at Rosh Ha'ayin
68. Yosef Yihya Levi	Immigrant at Ein-Shemer
69. Yefet Hashai	Former Youth Leader at Beit Lid
70. Dr. Weinberg	Former Cultural Coordinator at BeerYa'akov
71. Dov Woltzer	Cares for immigrants at Rosh Ha'ayin
72. Dr. Deutsch	Supervisor in Ministry of Education
73. Ya'akov Halperin	Supervisor in Ministry of Education
74. Dr. Yahil	Absorption Department of Jewish Agency
75. Hayyim Zadok	Absorption Department of Jewish Agency
76. Michael Bergman	Cultural Coordinator and School Principal in Mahane Israel I and II
77. Rabbi Leib Dramer	Immigrant at Mahane Israel
78. Rabbi Fuchs	Immigrant at Mahane Israel
79. Yosef Bodniv	Director of Mahane Israel

80. Moshe Schwartzberg [Schwartzman]	Secretary, Hadera branch of Hapoel Hamizrachi
81. Shaul [Shmuel] Gilboa	Cultural Coordinator at Beit Lid camps
82. Ya'akov Katz	Poalei Agudat Israel Executive
83. Mordecai Breuer	Poalei Agudat Israel Executive
84. Moshe Glickman-Porush	Agudat Israel Directorate
85. Hayyim Balass	Teacher at Giv'at Shaul and Rosh Ha'ayin
86. Aharon Na'imi	Former teacher at Giv'at Shaul
87. Israel Grossman	Head of Karlin Yeshiva
88. Nahum Friedman	Rabbi of synagogue in Mahane Yehuda
89. Yitzhak Weingarten	Hayyei Olam Yeshiva
90. Docent [Hayyim] Lifschitz	Section for Torah Culture in the Ministry of Education
91. Ruth Heine	Former teacher at Ein-Shemer
92. Esther Shrager [Trager]	Former teacher at Ein-Shemer
93. Shoshana Lieberman	Former teacher at Ein-Shemer
94. Esther Perlman	Teacher at Rosh Ha'ayin
95. Rabbi Yitzhari	Emissary of Hapoel Hamizrahi among Yemenite immigrants
96. G. Agron	Director of [State] Information Services
97. Yona Salem [Sha'ar]	Young girl from Ein-Shemer
98. Penina Palmon	Social Worker in Ein-Shemer
99. Alfred Renen	Director of Postal and Telegraph Services
100. Rabbi Z. Gold	Member of Jewish Agency Executive
101. Mr. A. L. Gelman	World Center of Hamizrachi

NOTES

NOTES TO INTRODUCTION

1. *Reshumot*—the official gazette of Israel. A law or an ordinance goes into effect only after its publication in *Reshumot*.

2. The government compound in Tel Aviv.

3. Title used in Central Europe for an academic teacher or a lecturer of a lower academic rank than professor. Lifschitz, who was awarded this title in Poland, continued to use it in Israel.

4. *Hen tzedek*. Since Jewish law opposes the routine use of oaths, the "declaration of speaking the truth" serves the equivalent function in Israeli courts.

NOTES TO CHAPTER 1

1. See Glossary at the end of this book.

2. *Mori*—"teacher," a term used by Yemenite Jews to refer to their rabbis.

3. Bevin led the post–World War II British cabinet's anti-Zionist policy.

4. See Glossary at the end of this book.

5. Two socialist, secular youth movements.

6. A term literally meaning "going up" and indicating emigration to the Land of Israel.

7. See Glossary at the end of this book.

8. See Glossary at the end of this book.

9. A religious labor movement associated with Hamizrachi and Hapoel Hamizrachi and responsible for the Religious Workers Stream of education. See Chapter 7.

10. An Arab village in Galilee. The immigrant camp in its vicinity, first named Me'ona, developed into the town of Ma'alot.

11. An abandoned Arab village on the western outskirts of Jerusalem, now within the city limits.

12. Literally, "the mother of all sins."

13. See Glossary at the end of this book.

14. The afternoon prayers.

15. The authors of the report are undoubtedly referring to Chapter 3.

16. The "Displaced Persons" camps in Europe, in which Holocaust survivors were concentrated following World War II.

17. Youth movement affiliated with the *kibbutz* movement Ihud Hakevutzot Vehakibbutzim.

18. Youth movement of Hapoel Hamizrachi, founded in Jerusalem in 1929.

19. Youth movement originally founded in Germany, affiliated with ultra-Orthodox religious circles, particularly Poalei Agudat Israel.

20. *Haggada*, pl. *Haggadot*: a book containing the liturgy accompanying the family meal on the eve of Passover.

21. The Book of Esther, written on a parchment scroll, which is read in the synagogue on the festival of Purim.

22. A collection of then oral laws, based on the Bible, collected and redacted in the second century C.E.

23. The *Shulhan Arukh* is a compendium of Jewish religious law and customs compiled in the late fifteenth century. *Kitzur Shulhan Arukh* is a condensed version.

24. Literally, "The Life of a Man," a volume compiled by Rabbi Abraham Danzig (1748–1820) covering all laws of the *Shulhan Arukh* dealing with daily conduct.

25. Collection of prayers of repentance and pleas for God's forgiveness, recited in the period preceding the New Year and Yom Kippur.

26. Theodor Herzl, known as "the father of Political Zionism," passed away in 1904 and was buried in Vienna. His remains were re-interred on Mount Herzl in Jerusalem, Israel's national cemetery.

27. See Glossary at the end of this book.

28. No relation of Baruch Ben-Yehuda, Eliezer Ben-Yehuda is considered "the father of modern Hebrew." He labored for years to compile an etymological dictionary of the Hebrew language. Uncompleted at his death, it was continued by public efforts.

29. See Glossary at the end of this book.

30. The term "God-fearing" is evidently used here to refer to individuals who accept basic religious beliefs but are not necessarily observant.

Notes to Chapter 2

1. There is an inadvertent error in this column: all dates should read 1949.

2. This survey is not appended to the English version of the report, since it is long outdated.

Notes to Chapter 3

1. Teachers without pedagogical training who impart the rudiments of reading, the prayers, and the Bible to very young pupils.

2. The Fifteenth of Shevat, a festival known as "The New Year of the Trees."

3. *Mezuza*—a small case, containing specific biblical verses, which is nailed to doorposts in Jewish homes, signifying a Jewish house; *kashrut* certificate—a certificate affirming that the food being provided is kosher.

4. The person who performs the ritual circumcision.

5. During the Holocaust, many Jewish children had found refuge in Christian homes or institutions. After the war, some of the institutions were reluctant to return the children to be brought up as Jews.

6. On the Carmel Range, today part of the city of Haifa.

7. A neighborhood in the Zevulun Valley, north of Haifa.

8. In the Zevulun Valley, north of Haifa.

9. Israel Jacob De-Haan, a Dutch journalist who became an ultra-Orthodox Jew and an anti-Zionist activist, was assassinated in Jerusalem in 1924 by the Hagana, the labor movement's defense movement.

10. An ultra-Orthodox seminary for girls.

11. An abandoned Arab village, now within the Jerusalem city limits.

12. An abandoned village and neighborhood, respectively, now both part of Jerusalem.

13. Literally, a "House of Education," a term used for schools of the Workers Stream.

14. See Glossary at the end of this book.

15. A dance in which the dancers link their arms and dance in a circle. It became the symbol of the pioneers in the Land of Israel.

16. The first all-country organization of Jewish workers in the Land of Israel, Gedud Ha'avoda was founded in 1920. Its members worked as cooperatives in various occupations, such as laying roads and agricultural work. As a result of ideological differences of opinion—and a tendency on the part of some of the members toward Communism in the USSR—the organization was greatly weakened and finally came to an end in 1929. Its members founded the kibbutzim Ein-Harod and Tel-Yosef.

17. The distance prescribed in Jewish religious law, approximately 1 kilometer from the limits of the city or the settlement, beyond which it is forbidden to walk on the Sabbath.

18. A term used in several Oriental Jewish communities to denote a rabbi or a sage, learned in Jewish law.

19. See Glossary at the end of this book.

20. Literally, signs.

21. Penina Palmon, a social worker in the Ein-Shemer camp.

22. See Glossary at the end of this book.

23. In Orthodox circles, a married woman is forbidden to display her hair to anyone but her husband. One means of complying with the prohibition is by tying a scarf around her head.

24. Muslim religious leader, or the officiating priest of a mosque.

NOTES TO CHAPTER 5

1. During the British Mandate period, the highest authority in the Government of Palestine was the High Commissioner for Palestine.

2. The text provided here is an English translation of the Hebrew version in the commission's report, and not the original English, which we have been unable to locate.

3. Moshe Kol, a member of the Progressive Party.

4. Yosef Sprinzak, a veteran member of Mapai and the Speaker of the Knesset.

5. See n. 2, above.

6. Shlomo Zalman Shragai, a leader of Hapoel Hamizrachi, was at this time a member of the Jewish Agency Executive.

7. Yitzchak Raphael, who was to have a lengthy career as a minister in several Israeli governments, was at this time director of the Immigration Department of the Jewish Agency.

8. A New York Yiddish daily.

NOTES TO CHAPTER 6

1. Libya.

2. Literally, "throwing off the yoke."

3. This is not the phrasing of clause B of the writ of authority, though this is what is implied.

GLOSSARY OF HEBREW TERMS

Activist A person active in public affairs on behalf of a political party, a socioeconomic group, and so on is termed in Hebrew *askan*. For brevity, we have translated this term as "activist," albeit without the usual connotation in English of being a vigorous advocate of a political cause.

Agudat Israel When established, this was a purely Ashkenazic world Jewish movement and Israeli ultra-Orthodox political party seeking to preserve Judaism by adherence to *halakha* as the principle governing Jewish life and society.

Asefat Hanivharim The "Elected Assembly," the supreme organ of the Jewish community in the Land of Israel, 1920–1948. It elected the Va'ad Haleumi.

Bahad A contraction of Brit Halutzim Datiyim (League of Religious Pioneers), it was founded in Germany during the interwar years, later spreading to Great Britain and elsewhere, and affiliated with Hapoel Hamizrachi.

Bnai Akiva Youth movement of Hapoel Hamizrachi, founded in Jerusalem in 1929.

cantonists Young Jewish children in Russia who were forcibly conscripted to pre-military institutions with the intention that they would abandon Judaism. At age eighteen, they were drafted into regular army units.

chief rabbis Israel has two chief rabbis—one for the Sephardic community and the other for the Ashkenazic community.

coalition No party in Israel has ever had an absolute majority in the Knesset, necessitating negotiations and agreements to form coalition governments. These are often referred to simply as "the coalition."

First Aliya   The first wave of nationalist-oriented ("Zionist") immigration, (December 1881–December 1903). Some of the immigrants came from Yemen, and most from Eastern Europe.

Gadna   Abbreviation of Gedudei No'ar (Youth Battalions); deals with pre-military training of high school pupils within and outside of the schools, also involving its members in national projects of a constructive nature.

General Zionists   Zionist party whose roots go back to the early Zionist Congresses. Delegates who did not wish to be associated with Labor Zionism or Religious Zionism joined a loose affiliation of "General Zionists." Their organization in the Land of Israel began in 1922.

Gibeonites   See II Samuel 21:2: "Now the Gibeonites were not of the children of Israel."

Hakibbutz Ha'artzi Hashomer Hatzair   A union of kibbutzim founded in 1927 by the first settlements of Hashomer Hatzair; affiliated with Mapam.

Hakibbutz Hameuhad   A union of large collective settlements founded in 1927, primarily by pioneers of the Third Aliya; from 1948 affiliated with Mapam and from 1954 with Ahdut Ha'avoda.

halakha   The entire legal system of Judaism embracing all of the detailed laws and observances.

halitza   According to the *halakha*, when a man dies without offspring, his widow is obligated to marry her husband's brother in what is known as "levirate marriage." When this marriage does not take place, the woman is released from the levirate ties by the ceremony of *halitza* and is free to marry someone else.

halutziut   "Pioneering spirit," derived from *halutz* (pioneer). This involved a willingness to engage in any work that might be required at the time to build the new national society.

Hamizrachi   Religious Zionist movement founded in 1902 as a religious faction of the World Zionist Organization. Hamizrachi in the Land of Israel was founded in 1918 and from 1920 operated a network of schools providing religious education.

Hapoel Hamizrachi   Religious pioneering and labor movement founded in the Land of Israel in 1922, which became an independent political party that later united with Hamizrachi to form the National Religious Party.

haredi [pl. *haredim*]   Ultra-Orthodox Jews who at first did not recognize the Zionist movement or identify with its objective of establishing a Jewish state in the Land of Israel. After the establishment of Israel, some of them, particularly those associated with Agudat Israel, did join its first government coalitions (1948–52). Until the 1980s, the great majority of *haredim* in Israel were of Ashkenazic origin, a condition changed by the establishment of Shas. Since the mid-1980s, most of the political leadership of the *haredim* is comprised of Sephardim.

Hashomer Hatzair Socialist-Zionist pioneering youth movement founded in Eastern Europe prior to World War I with the objective of educating Jewish youth for life on the kibbutz in the Land of Israel.

Havatzelet Hebrew newspaper published intermittently in Jerusalem from 1863–64 until 1911 by Israel Dov Frumkin, father of Justice Gad Frumkin, who chaired the commission of inquiry.

heder [pl. *hadarim*] Religious classes for the youngest pupils, in which they are taught only the elements of Hebrew and prayer; generally private schools run by the tutor.

Histadrut Labor organization founded in 1920 that was much more than a trade union organization, handling all of the social, economic, and cultural affairs of the working class in the Land of Israel. Among its diversified projects were consumer and producer cooperatives, industries, housing developments, a publishing house, and the Workers Stream in education.

human dust A term used by David Ben-Gurion and many others in the 1920s and 1930s to denote Diaspora Jews, who had become dispersed throughout the world (in contrast to the authentic Jew, with strong connections to the land, in the Land of Israel). Ben-Gurion used this term much more extensively after the Holocaust—both in relation to Holocaust survivors and to Oriental Jewry—and was greatly criticized for it.

kashrut; kosher Used to denote food that is permitted to Jews by the *halakha*.

ma'abara [pl. *ma'abarot*] Literally, "transit" settlement, a temporary camp for new immigrants until they found or were supplied with permanent housing.

Mapam Left-wing political party; a contraction of Mifleget Hapo'alim Hameuhedet—the United Workers Party.

minyan A quorum of ten male adults, age thirteen and older, necessary for public prayer and certain other religious ceremonies.

moshav [pl. *moshavim*] Cooperative smallholders' agricultural villages combining some of the features of both cooperative and private farming, unlike the kibbutz, which was based entirely on collective principles.

Neturei Karta   Literally, "Guardians of the City" (in Aramaic); group of ultra-religious extremists that regards the establishment of a Jewish state not by God's hand to be a sin and a denial of God.

Pagi–Poalei Agudat Israel in Jerusalem   An extremist group in Agudat Israel that called upon that party to quit the government. It seceded from Agudat Israel and ran on a separate ticket in the elections to the Second Knesset (1951) but did not receive the minimum number of votes for representation in the Knesset.

payot   Sidelocks grown in accordance with the prohibition, "Ye shall not round the corners of your heads" (Leviticus 19:27). It is customary for Hasidic Jews and Yemenites to leave *payot*.

Poalei Agudat Israel   A religious party in Israel that called for the application of the Torah's social principles in daily life. It established several kibbutzim and *moshavim*.

redemption money   Money raised by Jewish communities to redeem Jews taken captive (generally by pirates or brigands) or imprisoned by the authorities.

Second Aliya   The second wave of Zionist-motivated immigration, 1904–1914.

Shulhan Arukh   *Halakhic* code for Jewish behavior in everyday life, compiled by Joseph Caro in the sixteenth century and widely accepted throughout Judaism.

state religious educational system   Established in 1953 to replace the religious educational network of *Hamizrachi*. See Chapter 12 of this book.

Talmud Torah [pl. *Talmudei Torah*]   Religious schools, generally maintained by the community (in contrast to the private *heder*), where children were taught the rudiments of Hebrew and prayer.

tefillin   Phylacteries—two black leather boxes containing the biblical injunction to put "these words" for "a sign upon thy hand and a frontlet between the eyes," worn by means of leather straps by adult males during the morning service (excluding the Sabbath and holidays) on the left hand opposite the heart, and on the head.

Tnu'at Hamoshavim   Literally, "Moshav Movement," an organizational framework for *moshavim*. During the early years of statehood, it was controlled by Mapai.

Va'ad Haleumi   "National Council"—the executive arm of the Jewish community in the Land of Israel during the British Mandate period.

women as witnesses   By Jewish religious law, Jewish women are not competent to testify in cases to be decided on the basis of *halakha*.

yeshiva [pl. *yeshivot*]   An institution for the pursuit of Talmudical studies and the ordination of rabbis.

Yevsektsiya   Jewish section of the Propaganda Department of the Communist Party of the Soviet Union from 1918 to 1930. It initiated and executed the liquidation of Jewish communal organizations, synagogues, *yeshivot*, and other schools, the closing of libraries, and the banning of certain books.

Yishuv   The term used to denote the Jewish community in the Land of Israel prior to 1948.

Youth Aliya   A branch of the Jewish Agency founded with the purpose of rescuing Jewish children and youngsters from hardship, persecution, or deprivation and giving them care and education in the Land of Israel. Though founded against the backdrop of the Nazi rise to power in Germany, Youth Aliya today cares for children from the Americas and Europe, Asia and North Africa, and children of families already in Israel.

SELECT BIOGRAPHIES

Gerson Agron (Agronsky) (1899–1959). Born in Minah, Chernigov District, Ukraine. In 1906, immigrated to the United States. In 1918, joined the "Jewish Battalions" (in the British Army) and after being demobilized settled in the Land of Israel. Among the founders and first editor of the *Palestine* [later: *Jerusalem*] *Post*. Director of the Israel Information Services. Mayor of Jerusalem (1955–1959), representing Mapai.

Rabbi Yihya Netanel Alchech (?–d. 1996). Born in San'a, Yemen. Served as a rabbi in Yemen, and after his immigration to Israel as the rabbi of the Ein Shemer II Camp. Later on the staff of the Ministry of Religious Affairs. Resided in Jerusalem.

Yehiel Aharon Aldema (1902–1955). Born in Russia; immigrated to Land of Israel, 1920. Member of Havurat Ha'emek in Haifa, before joining Kibbutz Ein Harod. Served as journalist for the paper *Doar Hayom*. Sent on missions by the Information Department of the Jewish Agency. In 1936, was appointed director of the Printers Union. In 1940, served as department director in the Office of Surveys. Called upon by Nahum Levin to help organize cultural activities in the immigrant camps. Served for one year at the camp in Ein-Shemer and was supervisor of cultural activities in all of the camps in Ein-Shemer. Following the report of the Frumkin Commission, he was removed from his position, but his friends in Mapai arranged his appointment as principal of a school in Migdal-Gad.

Zalman Aranne (Aharonowitz) (1899-1970). Born in Ukraine; immigrated to Land of Israel, 1926, serving inter alia as secretary of the Tel Aviv Workers Council, director of the Histadrut's Information Department, and member of the World Zionist Executive. Between 1948 and 1951, was the "strong man" in Mapai, serving as secretary general of the party. Member of the first six Knessets.

Minister without portfolio (1953–1955) and minister of education and culture (1955–60, 1963–1969).

Yeshayahu Avrekh (1912–1988). Born in Kiev, Ukraine; immigrated to the Land of Israel, 1935; engaged in writing and editing. Served in the Palestinian units of the British Army (1942–1945). Staff officer of the Hagana and its information officer in the Tel Aviv area. During the War of Independence he served as education officer of the Central Command. During the period of the Frumkin Commission he served as the first secretary general of the Ministry of Education and Culture and later as head of the Culture Department in this ministry. Active in Mapai. In 1986, awarded the Israel Prize for his literary and journalistic writing (including under the pseudonym "Yotam").

Rabbi Meir Bar-Ilan (Berlin) (1880–1949). Born in Volozhin, Russia; son of Rabbi Naphtali Zvi Yehuda Berlin; immigrated to Land of Israel, 1926. Among the leaders of Hamizrachi and its president from 1937 and among the founders of the Joint Jewish Distribution Committee, serving as vice president and head of its Culture Committee. From 1925 on, a member of the Jewish National Fund directorate. From 1944, member of Asefat Hanivharim and Va'ad Haleumi. Among the founders and organizers of the Religious Front. Editor of the newspaper *Hatzofeh* (1938–1949). Author of various books. Bar-Ilan University is named for him.

David Ben-Gurion (1886-1973). Born in Plonsk, Poland; immigrated to the Land of Israel, 1906. First prime minister and minister of defense of the State of Israel. Leader of Mapai and the Labor movement; secretary of Histadrut Labor Federation. Against his party's stance, Ben-Gurion opposed the system of educational streams and supported state education, just as he supported creating general frameworks and instilling a state ethos in other areas of society, education, and economy. Decided to appoint Frumkin Commission and chose its members. The Ben-Gurion University of the Negev and the Ben-Gurion Research Center in Sde Boker are named after him.

Dr. Baruch Ben-Yehuda (Leibowitz) (1894–1990). Born in Lithuania; immigrated to the Land of Israel, 1911. Teacher and educator at the Herzliya Gymnasium in Tel Aviv. Director of Education Division of the Ministry of Education and Culture, 1948–1951, and first director general of that ministry.

Izhak Ben-Zvi (Shimshelevitz) (1884–1963). Born in Poltava, Ukraine; immigrated to the Land of Israel, 1907. A leader of the Labor movement in Israel; a founder of the Poalei Zion Party, as well as of Hashomer (first self-defense organization); one of the initiators of volunteering for the Jewish Battalions during World War I. Participated in the establishment of the Ahdut Ha'avoda Party and the Histadrut. Chairman of Va'ad Haleumi from 1931 and its president from

1945. Engaged in research concerning far-flung Jewish communities and known for his positive attitude toward them. At end of 1947, established Ben-Zvi Institute for the Research of Oriental Jewry. Member of first two Knessets, representing Mapai. His personal and moral authority led to his membership in several investigating and inquiry commissions, including the Frumkin Commission. Served as second president of the State of Israel (1952–1963).

Yeshayahu Bernstein (1902–1988). Born in Ukraine; immigrated to the Land of Israel, 1922. A founder of Hapoel Hamizrachi, which he represented in the Va'ad Haleumi. Member of editorial board of *Hatzofe* and editor in chief until 1950. Member of World Center of Hamizrachi until 1968, serving as chairman of its Center for Religious Education. Considered one of the ideologists of Hapoel Hamizrachi, representing it at several Zionist congresses.

Dr. Mordecai Breuer (b. 1918). Born in Germany, son of Rabbi Dr. Yitzhak Breuer (president of Poalei Agudat Israel in the Land of Israel). Upon Israel's creation, was a member of the World Center of Poalei Agudat Israel and editor of its newspaper *She'arim*. In recent years, professor of Jewish history at Bar-Ilan University and chairman of the Israel Historical Society.

Dr. Joseph Burg (1910–1999). Born in Dresden, Germany; immigrated to the Land of Israel, 1939. Ordained as rabbi and doctor of philosophy. Elected to First Knesset as representative of Lamifne faction of Hapoel Hamizrachi, serving consecutively in eleven Knessets. Minister of health (1951–1952), minister of posts (1952–1958), minister of welfare (1959–1970), minister of interior (1970–1984, intermittently), minister of religious affairs (1984–1986).

Rabbi Bezalel Cohen (1902–1965). Born in Minsk, Bielorussia; immigrated to the Land of Israel, 1924. In 1931, emigrated to the United States, where he served as a rabbi in various congregations. In 1936, was honorary secretary of Hamizrachi in the United States and member of the Executive Committee of the Union of Orthodox Rabbis. After the establishment of Israel, immigrated for the second time. Headed the Education Department of the World Center of Hamizrachi and later directed the Center for Religious Education in Israel. Served as interim chairman of the World Center of Hamizrachi and Hapoel Hamizrachi.

Rachel Cohen (Kagan) (1888–1982). Born in Odessa, Ukraine; immigrated to the Land of Israel, 1919. Member of the Elected Assembly. A founder and leader of WIZO, chairman of the Israeli chapter, and world president of the organization. Member of the First Knesset, representing the Women's International Zionist Organization (WIZO) and a member of its Committee on Education and Culture. Member of the Fifth Knesset, representing the Liberal Party. Participated in many public committees devoted to diverse social issues. Opposed the system of educational streams and supported the introduction of a state educational system.

Arye Deri (b. 1959). Born in Meknes, Morocco; immigrated to Israel with family, 1968. After Shas' initial success in the 1984 elections, he became an advisor to the minister of the interior. In 1987, he was appointed director general of that ministry and in 1988 as minister of the interior, this before he had turned twenty-nine.

Dr. Avraham Deutsch (1889–1953). Born in Hungary. Served as teacher and supervisor in Jewish schools in Hungary. Chief supervisor of the Independent Educational System of Agudat Israel, and member of the Second Knesset representing that party.

Ben-Zion Dinur (Dinaburg) (1884-1973). Born in Horol, Poltava district, Ukraine; immigrated to the Land of Israel, 1921. Historian and educator, taught in teacher training institutes and at the Hebrew University. Knesset member from 1949. Minister of education and culture (1951–1955). During his term, the "State Education Law" was passed. Awarded Israel Prize for Jewish Studies (1958) and Education (1973).

Rabbi Yehoshua Zelig Diskin (1898–?). Born in Russia; immigrated to the Land of Israel, 1934. From 1948 to his death, served as rabbi of Pardes Hanna. Was a most trusted assistant of Rabbi Cahanmann in the Poniewiec Yeshiva in Bnai Brak.

Avraham Elmaleh (1885-1967). Born in Jerusalem; teacher and journalist. Founded and edited the newspaper *Herut*. Served in various positions, including member of the First and Second Elected Assembly (Asefat Hanivharim), member of the Va'ad Haleumi, president of the North African Immigrants Society, member of the Jerusalem City Council, and vice president of the World Sephardic Association. Spearheaded attempts to organize Sephardic Jewry within the framework of the World Zionist Organization. Member of the First Knesset, representing the Sephardic Party. Member of the Frumkin Commission.

Levi Eshkol (Shkolnik) (1895–1969). Born in Ukraine; immigrated to Land of Israel, 1914. A leader of the Labor movement in Israel and a founder of Deganya Bet, for many years a member of that kibbutz. From 1949, member of the Jewish Agency Directorate and head of its Settlement Department. Treasurer of the Jewish Agency (1949–1952). Member of Second through Sixth Knesset; minister of agriculture and development (1951–1952); minister of the treasury (1952–1963); prime minister (1963–1969); and, until May 1967, the eve of the Six Day War, also minister of defense.

Moshe Etz-Hayyim (Greenwald) (1917–1984). Born in Croatia; immigrated to the Land of Israel, 1936. A founder of Haoved Hadati, one of the heads of the

Religious Workers Stream of education and its chief supervisor. Directed it after the resignation of Dr. Y. Leibowitz in March 1950. From 1953, with the inception of the state religious educational system, was a supervisor of this system's primary schools.

Rafael Halevi Etzion (1885–1981). Born in Lithuania; immigrated to the Land of Israel, 1933. Educator, among the founders and shapers of national-religious education in Israel. Directed religious educational institutions in Lithuania; taught in Hamizrachi Teachers Seminary in Jerusalem. From 1943 until abolition of the educational streams in 1953, chief supervisor of the Hamizrachi Stream. Awarded Israel Prize for Education (1979).

Rabbi Yehuda Leib Fishman. See Rabbi Yehuda Leib Maimon (Fishman).

Gad Frumkin (1887–1960). Born in Jerusalem to a veteran family of the "Old Yishuv"; his father, Israel Dov Frumkin, had immigrated to Jerusalem in 1853. Studied law in Turkey and in 1918 was appointed justice of the peace by the British. From 1920 to 1948, served as the only Jewish justice on the Supreme Court under the British Mandate. Had extensive contact with the Arab community and was part of a group of five which, upon the outbreak of the Arab disturbances in 1936, tried unsuccessfully to bring about a peaceful agreement between the two sides to the national conflict. Upon the creation of Israel, Justice Minister Rosen opposed his appointment to the Supreme Court of the State of Israel. Headed the commission of inquiry that is the subject of this book.

Arye Gelblum (1921–1993). Born in Poland; immigrated to the Land of Israel, 1925. During Second World War, joined staff of *Ha'aretz* newspaper. His series of articles, "I Was a New Immigrant for One Month," published from April 1949 onward, aroused harsh controversy. The main criticism directed against him was due to his negative stereotypes of Oriental Jews, particularly North African immigrants.

Rabbi Arye Leib Gelman (1887–1973). Born in Wohlin, Ukraine; immigrated to Israel, 1949. Vice president of Hamizrachi in the United States (1930–1935) and president from 1935. Member of Jewish Agency Executive (1948–1953). In 1949, elected chairman of World Center of Hamizrachi and Hapoel Hamizrachi. Author of articles and books.

Moshe Glickman-Porush (1893–1983). Born in Jerusalem. One of the leading figures in Agudat Israel in Jerusalem and the Land of Israel. At the time of the Frumkin Commission, a member of the executive committee of the Center of Agudat Israel. Served on the supervisory board of the Agudat Israel Stream of education. Was for a time director of the Center of Agudat Israel and deputy mayor of Jerusalem.

Zecharia Gluska (1895–1960). Born in Yemen; immigrated to the Land of Israel, 1909. A founder of the Association of Yemenites and its chairman since 1925. Represented the Association of Yemenites in various Yishuv organs, at Zionist congresses, and in the First Knesset.

Rabbi Ze'ev Gold (1889–1956). Born in Poland; immigrated to the United States in 1906, where he served as rabbi in various communities; a leader of Hamizrachi in America; immigrated to the Land of Israel, 1924. In 1945, joined Jewish Agency Executive as representative of Hamizrachi. Member of Provisional State Council at the time of its creation. In 1951, served as head of the Jewish Agency's Department for Torah Culture and Education in the Diaspora. Also served as national president of Hamizrachi and member of its World Center.

Rabbi Baruch Pinhas Goldberg (1911–1984). Born in Jerusalem. Taught at Etz Hayyim Yeshiva and was supervisor on behalf of Va'ad Hayeshivot for religious educational institutions in the immigrant camps.

Israel Guri (Gurfinkel) (1892–1965). Born in Bessarabia; immigrated to the Land of Israel in 1919. Leading member of the Histadrut and Mapai and central figure in the Workers Stream of education. Member of the Tel Aviv Municipal Council. Member of Knesset, 1949–1965, serving for some time as chairman of its Finance Committee. Refused to be appointed minister or deputy minister of education and culture.

Rabbi Yair Hafuta (b. 1913). Born in Marrakech, Morocco; immigrated to Israel, 1949. Served as chief ritual slaughterer in Marrakech. Was in the Beer Ya'akov immigrant camp. Ordained a rabbi in Beer Ya'akov, served as a rabbi in that town.

Ya'akov Halperin (Niv) (1905–1976). Born in Poland; immigrated to the Land of Israel, 1921. Director of the Educational Center of the Histadrut (1941–1950); chief supervisor of the Workers Stream (1950–1953), later serving as director of the Tel Aviv Region of the Ministry of Education and Culture.

Rabbi Isaac Halevi Herzog (1888–1959). Born in Poland; received Torah and general education. Chief Rabbi of Ireland, active in Zionist movement, and among the founders of Hamizrachi there. Following Rabbi Avraham Isaac Kook's death, elected Chief Rabbi of Israel and immigrated to the Land of Israel in 1937. Served as president of the Chief Rabbinate and Rabbinic High Court; headed various religious organizations and Torah research institutes. Led the religious public in struggles on behalf of religious education, such as the episodes of the Teheran Children, the Yemenite children, and incidents involving children in the immigrant camps. Awarded Israel Prize (1958).

Ya'akov Herzog (1921-1972). Born in Dublin, Ireland; immigrated to the Land of Israel, 1937. Son of Chief Rabbi Isaac Halevi Herzog. Thinker and Israeli diplomat. Awarded rabbinic ordination and doctorate in international law. Active in intelligence services of the Hagana and in various diplomatic tasks. Served as Ben-Gurion's advisor and in his final years as director general of Prime Minister's Office.

Beba Idelson (Trachtenberg) (1895–1975). Born in Russia; immigrated to Land of Israel in 1926. A founder of "Women Workers Council" and its general secretary (1930–1974). Knesset member representing Mapai (1949–1968); Deputy Speaker of the Knesset (1955–1961).

Feige Ilanit (b. 1909). Born in Russia; immigrated to the Land of Israel, 1929. A leader of Mapam and active in social and educational issues. Member of the First Knesset, where she served on its Education Committee. Member of Kibbutz Gan Shmuel.

Dr. Giora Josephtal (1912–1962). Born in Germany; immigrated to the Land of Israel, 1938. Doctor of jurisprudence. Headed Hehalutz movement in Germany. Founding member of Kibbutz Gal'ed. Director of Absorption Department of Jewish Agency (1947–1952). Later served as Treasurer of Jewish Agency, Secretary of Mapai (1956–1959), and Knesset member (from 1959). In 1960, appointed minister of labor and in 1961 minister of housing and development.

Rabbi Dr. Kalman Kahana (1910–1991). Born in Galicia; immigrated to the Land of Israel, 1938. Graduate of Berlin Rabbinic Seminary; studied philosophy, Semitic languages, history, and pedagogy at universities of Berlin and Würzburg. Member of Kibbutz Hafetz Hayyim, serving as its rabbi. A leader of Poalei Agudat Israel and represented it on the Provisional State Council. Elected president of Poalei Agudat Israel. Member of First through Ninth Knesset. Wrote various books on religious topics, particularly concerning religious precepts that apply only in the Land of Israel. Editor of *She'arim*. Deputy minister of education and culture (1951–1952); member of Frumkin Commission.

Shlomo Kroll (b. 1928). Born in Russia; immigrated to the Land of Israel with his family, 1931. Lived in Kfar Hasidim. Studied at Poniewiec Yeshiva in Bnai Brak. Made a protest visit to the Ein-Shemer II Camp in February 1950 and was a witness to the altercation in which a resident of the camp was shot and killed. He was detained in the camp on the charge of incitement and illegal action. In later years, served as rabbi of Moshav Hemed and head of the *yeshiva* there.

Pinhas Lavon (Lubianiker) (1904–1976). Born in Galicia; immigrated to the Land of Israel, 1929. A leading member of the Labor movement, he led the Gordonia movement and was a member of Kvutzat Hulda. Secretary-general of the Histadrut (1949–1952), member of Knesset (1949–1961). Served as minister of agriculture (1950–1954) and minister of defense (1954–1955), a position from which he was forced to resign in wake of the failure of a plan to plant a bomb in Cairo, which for a period of time split Mapai into two opposing groups. Lavon was an ideological rival of Ben-Gurion, disagreeing with him over several issues, including the education of immigrant children.

Dr. Yeshayahu Leibowitz (1903–1994). Born in Riga, Latvia; fled with his family to Berlin at age sixteen; immigrated to the Land of Israel, 1935. Biochemist, physiologist, and highly controversial philosopher and thinker. Headed Ha'oved Hadati movement within the Histadrut during the 1940s. Fought for the right of religious Histadrut members to have kosher food in the workers' restaurants, no Sabbath desecration, and religious workers' education. His testimony before the Frumkin Commission, as representative of a group associated with Mapai, was of great importance. During the 1950s, he struggled, with others, against various forms of corruption. Professor at the Hebrew University of Jerusalem, editor of the *Encyclopaedia Hebraica*, author of numerous books and essays, and, in later years, outspoken critic of the ongoing occupation of the West Bank.

Rabbi Yitzhak Yitzhak Levi (b. 1903). Born in San'a, Yemen; immigrated to Israel, 1949. Served as rabbi in San'a; was in Camp Ein Shemer I. Described in the Frumkin Report as "an elderly and distinguished man." Served as head of religious court in the immigrant camp, was a ritual circumciser and slaughterer, and performed weddings.

Nahum Levin (1901–1959). Born in Bukhara, son of Shemaryahu Levin; immigrated to the Land of Israel, 1922. Studied at teachers seminary in Jerusalem and at University of Berlin, 1927–1933. Directed Culture Department of Association of Immigrants from Germany, and thereafter served as national supervisor in Culture Department of the Va'ad Haleumi. Staff officer of Jerusalem district of the Hagana, simultaneously serving as head of Information Bureau of the Hagana in Jerusalem. Chairman of Directorate for Education and Culture of Holocaust Survivors. From 1947 on, served as director of the Culture Department of the Va'ad Haleumi. After establishment of the Ministry of Education and Culture, served as interim director of its Department for Language Instruction and Cultural Absorption of Immigrants. Dismissed in the wake of the findings of the Frumkin Commission.

Rabbi Yitzhak Meir Levin (1894–1971). Born in Gur, near Warsaw, Poland; immigrated to the Land of Israel, 1940. A leader of the Gur Hasidic community, a founder of Agudat Israel in Poland, and one of the organizers of a network of Beit Ya'akov schools for religious girls there. Head of Agudat Israel in the Land of Israel and Executive Committee of the world organization. Knesset member from First Knesset until his death. At the time of the Frumkin Commission, he was minister of welfare.

Rabbi David Lifschitz (1907-1994). Born in Minsk, Belorussia. Studied at Grodno and Mir *yeshivot*; after the Nazi rise to power, immigrated to the United States. In 1943, was head of a *yeshiva* in Chicago, and from 1945 in Yeshiva University in New York. Very active in leadership of Orthodox Jewry in America. Member of the Union of Orthodox Rabbis and director of Ezrat Torah. Chairman of the Religious Bloc in America.

Hayyim Lifschitz (1898–1978). Born in Russia; immigrated to the Land of Israel, 1908. Studied in Herzliya Gymnasium, Tel Aviv, then returned to Russia (to complete his studies for a Ph.D.), where he remained as a "Prisoner of Zion" for ten years. Returned to the Land of Israel in 1936. Supervisor in the Department of Torah Education and Culture. Author of various books.

Hadassa Lipmanowitz (Ben-Ito) (b. 1926). Born in Poland; immigrated to the Land of Israel, 1935. Graduate of Beit Ya'akov and Ma'aleh High School in Jerusalem. Associated with Mapai. Appointed director of Youth Bureau in the Culture Department of the Ministry of Education and Culture by Yeshayahu Avrekh, from the summer of 1949 until the spring of 1950, when Ben-Gurion decided to abolish the special camps for Yemenite youth. Later served as district judge, retiring in 1991.

Dr Eliezer Lubrani (1898–1965). Born in Poland; immigrated to the Land of Israel, 1910. Member of *Davar* editorial board (1929–1936); first director of Hebrew programming at Jerusalem radio (1936–1944); director of Galilee and Samaria Branch of Culture Department (1949–1951); supervisor of special tasks in the Culture Department.

Rabbi Yehuda Leib Maimon (Fishman) (1875–1962). Born in Bessarabia; immigrated to the Land of Israel, 1913. One of the founders and leaders of Hamizrachi. A founder of the Hamizrachi educational system, he played an active role in the establishment of the Chief Rabbinate and founded the religious publishing house, Mossad Harav Kook. Elected in 1935 to the World Zionist Executive, where he worked closely with Ben-Gurion, the beginning of the long-standing cooperation ("historical alliance") between Hamizrachi and the Labor movement. Served in the provisional government as minister of religion and minister for the war casualties, and in the first elected government as minister of religious affairs; also a member of the Knesset. In 1951, he resigned over the issue of anti-religious coercion. The author of many books, he advocated the reestablishment of the Sanhedrin as an important step in the reconstitution of Jewish sovereignty.

Rabbi Yeshayahu Meshorer (1920–1998). Born in Yemen; immigrated to the Land of Israel, 1937. Headed the Department for Yemenite Jews of Hapoel

Hamizrachi. Rabbi of the Yemenite community in Petah Tikva and member of its rabbinical court. Member of the Rabbinical Court of Appeals in Jerusalem.

Dvora Netzer (Nossowitzky) (1897–1988). Born in Russia; immigrated to the Land of Israel, 1925. Active in the Zionist-Socialist and Hehalutz movements in Russia. Jailed in the USSR for her Zionist activities. Served some time as a teacher. Active member of Ahdut Ha'avoda and Mapai parties. Leading member of Organization of Working Mothers and the Women's Labor Movement. Member of the First to the Sixth Knesset, serving on its Committee on Education and Culture. Deputy Speaker of the Sixth Knesset. Wife of Shraga Netzer, who wielded much power within Mapai and greatly influenced appointments.

Rabbi Yitzhak Peretz (b. 1939). Born in Casablanca, Morocco; immigrated to Israel (via France), 1950. Appointed Sephardic Chief Rabbi of Ra'anana, 1963. Led Shas list to Knesset elections in 1984 and served as minister of interior in the government formed in their wake.

Shoshana Persitz (1893–1969). Born in Kiev, Ukraine; immigrated to the Land of Israel, 1925. Studied at universities of Moscow and Paris. Active in "Tarbut" Hebrew educational institutions in Russia. Member of Tel Aviv municipality and director of its Education Department (1926–1935). Simultaneously, member of the Education Committee of the Zionist Executive and of the Education Department of the Va'ad Haleumi. Represented General Zionists in First through Third Knesset. During First Knesset served as chairperson of its Committee on Education and Culture. One of the leaders of the campaign to abolish educational streams.

David Zvi Pinkas (1895–1952). Born in Hungary, immigrated to the Land of Israel, 1925. Educated in Vienna, where he served as one of the leaders of Young Hamizrachi. Following immigration, served in various public offices, including director of the Hamizrachi Bank, deputy mayor of Tel Aviv, head of the Tel Aviv Municipal Board of Education and the National Assembly of Hamizrachi. Represented Hamizrachi on the Provisional Assembly and headed its Defense Committee. One of the founders of the state religious educational system, he served two terms in the Knesset and was minister of transport from 1951 until his death.

Yitzchak Raphael (Werfel) (1914–1999). Born in Eastern Galicia; immigrated to the Land of Israel, 1935. A leader of Hapoel Hamizrachi and the Religious Front. Engaged in teaching. Member of the Va'ad Haleumi. Director of the Immigration Department of the Jewish Agency during the great wave of immigration in Israel's early years. Member of the Second to the Eighth Knesset. Deputy minister of health (1961–1965), minister of religious affairs (1974–1977). Wrote and edited extensively on Judaism and Zionism. His autobiography includes an important chapter on the great wave of immigration.

David Remez (Drabkin) (1886–1951). Born in Belorussia; immigrated to the Land of Israel, 1913. A leader of the Labor movement. Succeeded Ben-Gurion as secretary of the Histadrut (1935–1945). Chairman of the Va'ad Haleumi until the creation of Israel. Served in provisional government as minister of transport, but also was greatly involved in educational matters. Continued to serve as minister of transport in first elected government, but for many weeks filled in for Shazar (during the latter's illness and absence) as minister of education and culture. In October 1950, appointed second minister of education and culture of the State of Israel. Died half a year later, in May 1951.

Yehuda Rieder (b. 1928). Born in Germany; immigrated to the Land of Israel, 1937. Served in IDF and wounded at beginning of War of Independence. Recommended for work in camps by Young Agudat Israel. Began teaching at Ein-Shemer on 10 November 1949. Claimed that he was transferred to another position after publication of a protest letter to the editor of *Hatzofe*. Later a leader of Brit Hakanaim, an underground terrorist organization of extremist *haredi* youth, which from 1950 on engaged in various acts of violence, including torching some twenty cars whose owners drove on the Sabbath. They planned a terrorist attack on the Knesset during a debate in May 1951 on women's service in the army, which was nipped in the bud. He was arrested, along with forty other members of the group, and sentenced to the maximum sentence of one year of imprisonment. Lives today in Kiryat Arba.

Moshe Segal (b. 1929). Born in Poland; immigrated to the Land of Israel, 1935. *Yeshiva* student until 1949. Hired on 17 November 1949, to teach at Ein-Shemer by the Culture Department, upon the recommendation of Young Agudat Israel. Dismissed on 24 January 1950, according to his claim as the result of a letter protesting anti-religious coercion, published in *Hatzofe*.

Rabbi Avraham Hayyim Shaag (Zwebner) (1883–1958). Born in Jerusalem. A founder and leader of the Hamizrachi movement in the Land of Israel. From 1936 on, head of Religious Council in Jerusalem. Member of First Elected Assembly of directorate of the Va'ad Haleumi and the First Knesset. Member of the Frumkin Commission.

Moshe [Hayyim] Shapira (1902–1970). Born in Belorussia; immigrated to the Land of Israel, 1926. Leader of Hapoel Hamizrachi. Served as director of Immigration Department of the Jewish Agency (1935–1945) and from 1946 as member of the Zionist Executive and head of the Department of Immigration. Following the creation of Israel, was one of the leaders of the Religious Front in the First Knesset and served as minister of the interior, religion, and welfare. In 1956, was among the founders of the united National Religious Party, leading it and its Knesset delegation until his death.

Ya'akov Shimshon Shapira (1902–1993). Born in Russia; immigrated to the Land of Israel, 1924. Lawyer and political figure. First Attorney General of Israel (1948– 1949). Member of the First, Second, and Seventh Knesset. Minister of justice (1965–1974).

Zalman Shazar (Rubashov) (1889–1974). Born in Mir, Belorussia, into a family of Habad Hasidim; immigrated to the Land of Israel, 1924. Active in Poalei Zion movement from his youth. Received a broad Jewish and general education—studied at the Academy for Jewish Science in St. Petersburg and studied history and philosophy at universities in Switzerland and Germany. Member of the Executive of the Histadrut, edited its newspaper *Davar* (1944–1948), and a leader of Mapai and of the Labor movement in Israel. From March 1949 to October 1950, served as minister of education and culture; essentially, he ceased to function as minister as a result of the crisis surrounding the issue of education in the immigrant camps. Later served as chairman of the Jewish Agency Executive and as head of its Department of Education and Culture in the Diaspora. In 1963, elected third president of the State of Israel.

Bechor Shalom Shitrit (1895–1967). Born in Tiberias. Sephardic leader in the early years of Israel. Teacher in Tiberias, then filled several positions with the Police Force during the Mandate period, and from 1935 on, served as a civil court judge. Minister of police and minister for minorities in the Provisional Government. Later served as member of several Knessets, first representing the Sephardic Party and later Mapai.

Shlomo Zalman Shragai (1899–1995). Born in Poland; immigrated to the Land of Israel, 1924. One of the central leaders and ideologists of Hapoel Hamizrachi. Member of the Jewish Agency Executive (1946–1950), mayor of Jerusalem (1950–1952), and head of the Immigration Department of the Jewish Agency (1954–1968).

Yizhar Smilansky (b. 1916). Born in Rehovot. Author, public figure, and teacher. Mapai Knesset member from First to Fifth Knesset, representing Rafi in Sixth Knesset. Member of First Knesset's Committee on Education and Culture. Awarded Israel Prize for his literary work (1959). Wrote many important Hebrew novels, such as *Days of Ziklag*, under pen name S. Yizhar.

Avraham Tabib (1889–1950). Born in Yemen; immigrated to the Land of Israel, 1910. Leading member of the Yemenite community in the Land of Israel. Member of the First Knesset, representing Mapai. Died before completing full term in office. His brother, Mordechai Tabib, is recognized as being the first and leading author of Yemenite extraction in Hebrew literature.

Ya'akov Trachtenberg. Born in Ukraine; immigrated to the Land of Israel, 1921. Member of the Ze'irei Zion movement in Russia and of Gedud Ha'avoda in the Land of Israel. A member of Moshav Tel Adashim until 1923, when he moved to Tel Aviv. A member of the police force, later employed in the Ministry of Defense and finally in the Jewish Agency. On 15 August 1949, sent to establish the immigrant camps at Ein-Shemer and directed Camp Ein-Shemer I.

Moshe Unna (1902–1989). Born in Mannheim, Germany; immigrated to the Land of Israel, 1928. Member of Kibbutz Sde-Eliyahu and a leader of Hakibbutz Hadati, the religious kibbutz movement. Represented Hapoel Hamizrachi in First through Sixth Knesset (1949–1969). Deputy minister of education and culture (1956–1958) and chairperson of the Knesset's Committee on Law and Justice. Chairman of the council of the State Religious Educational System.

Rabbi Isser Yehuda Unterman (1886–1976). Born in Brisk, Grodno District of Lithuania; immigrated to the Land of Israel, 1947. Joined Hamizrachi in his youth. Served as rabbi in various communities of Lithuania, and in Liverpool, England. In 1946, elected Chief Ashkenazic Rabbi of the Tel Aviv-Jaffa District. Chief Ashkenazic Rabbi of the State of Israel (1964–1972).

Dr. Ephraim Elimelekh Urbach (1912–1991). Born in Poland; immigrated to the Land of Israel, 1938. Engaged in teaching and education. For a few months in 1950, was responsible for the education of children in immigrant camps, but resigned, claiming anti-religious coercion there. In 1953, was appointed lecturer in Talmud at the Hebrew University. Among the leading scholars in field of Talmud and Rabbinic Literature in Israel and in the world. President of the Israel Academy of Sciences and Humanities (1986–1988). Awarded Israel Prize.

Shmuel Ussishkin (1894-1978). Born in Dnieper-Petrovsk, Ukraine; immigrated to Land of Israel, 1923. Before immigration, had lived in Odessa from 1905 and studied law at Cambridge University. Practiced law in Tel Aviv and Jerusalem. His main work was as legal counsel to the Jewish National Fund (JNF). Member of the Directorate of the JNF, which was headed by his father, Menahem Ussishkin.

Dr. Zerah Warhaftig (b. 1906). Born in Belorussia; immigrated to the Land of Israel, 1947. Received religious education and studied law at a university, practicing since 1933. During World War II, fled to various countries, until reaching the United States, where he served from 1942 as vice president of American Hapoel Hamizrachi and member of the Steering Committee of the World Jewish Congress. In the Land of Israel, was member of the Va'ad Haleumi and the Provisional Assembly. Member of the first nine Knessets (1949–1981) and minister of religious affairs (1962–1974).

Yigael Yadin (Sukenik) (1917–1984). Born in Jerusalem. Second chief of the general staff of the Israel Defense Forces (1949–1952). After discharge, became archaeologist and professor of archaeology at the Hebrew University of Jerusalem. In 1977, was among the founders of the Dash Party, representing it in the Knesset and the government. Deputy prime minister, 1977–1981.

Hayyim Yahil (Hoffman) (1905–1974). Born in Moravia; immigrated to the Land of Israel, 1929. Active in matters of culture and trade union organization in the Workers Councils of Haifa and Tel Aviv, and member of the Executive Committee of the Histadrut. Member of Mapai. Headed Jewish Agency delegation to the World War II survivors in Germany (1945–1948). During the period of mass immigration, was assistant to Dr. Giora Josephtal, director of the Absorption Department of the Jewish Agency. Thereafter, held senior positions in the Foreign Ministry, including director general (1960–1964).

Sa'adya Yarimi (1918–1996). Born in Yemen; immigrated to the Land of Israel, 1939. Member of Mapai. In Aden, directed a youth camp on behalf of the World Zionist Organization; in the Land of Israel, was an instructor in a camp for immigrants from Yemen and Turkey, 1944–1945. Came to Ein-Shemer camp in November 1949 and was immediately appointed teacher and person responsible for the school.

Shmuel Yavnieli (Warshawsky) (1884–1961). Born in a village in the Kherson District, Ukraine; immigrated to the Land of Israel, 1905. In 1911, traveled to Yemen to bring Jews from there. Leading member of the Labor movement and of Mapai. Directed the Culture Department of the Histadrut and filled senior positions in the Culture Department of the Ministry of Education and Culture.

Israel Yeshayahu (1908–1979). Born in Yemen; immigrated to the Land of Israel, 1929. In 1935, founded the Yemenite Department of the Histadrut, and in 1948–1949, was among the main organizers of the mass immigration of Yemenites at that time, "Operation 'On Wings of Eagles.'" Chosen by Mapai as a member of the First Knesset in midterm, following the death of Avraham Tabib. Served as member of Knesset (1951–1977), minister of posts (1967–1972), secretary general of the Labor Party (1970–1972), and Speaker of the Knesset (from 1972). Was the secretary of the Frumkin Commission.

Rabbi Zadok Ben-Shalom Yitzhari (1901–1998). Born in Rad'a, Yemen; immigrated to Israel, 1949. Active in public affairs in Yemen. At age twenty, was appointed minister of supply for the Yemeni army (during the war against East Yemen). When the imam was killed and revolution broke out in Yemen, he was suspected of contact with the revolutionaries and managed to flee in chains to Aden, and from there came to Israel in 1949. From December 1949, responsible for organization of Yemenite immigrants in settlements, under auspices of Hapoel Hamizrachi. Left the party in 1950, claiming contemptuous attitude toward himself and other Yemenites. In 1955, established Bnai Teiman (Sons of Yemen) movement. Among the leading public figures in Rosh Ha'ayin, where there was a large concentration of Yemenite immigrants.

Rabbi Ovadia Yosef (b. 1920). Born in Baghdad; immigrated to the Land of Israel with his family, 1924. Ordained as a rabbi in 1940. Appointed to the Sephardic rabbinical court in Jerusalem, 1945. In 1947, elected to the office of Chief of the Rabbinical Court in Cairo and Chief Rabbi of the Jews of Egypt. Returned to Israel in 1950 and appointed member of the Rabbinical Court in Petah Tikva. In 1958, moved to Jerusalem to serve once again on its rabbinical court and simultaneously as one of the senior teachers of the Porat Yosef Yeshiva. In 1965, appointed to the Supreme Rabbinical Court of Appeals. Sephardic Chief Rabbi of Israel, 1968–1980. Upon completion of his term in office, became more active in political affairs, founding Shas (with the support of Rabbi Eliezer Menaham Schach) in anticipation of the elections to the Eleventh Knesset in 1984. Published many rabbinic works and was awarded the Israel Prize for Rabbinic Literature in 1970.

Zippora Zehavi. Third-generation Yemenite born in Israel. Member of Maccabee Youth movement and served in British Army during World War II. After demobilization, employed by Youth Aliya in Netanya and then asked to coordinate cultural activities in Beit Lid. Responsible for youth camp at Beit Lid VII camp. Frumkin Commission charged her with anti-religious coercion and caused her dismissal.

Aharon Zisling (1901–1964). Born in Russia; immigrated to the Land of Israel, 1904. A leader of Hakibbutz Hameuhad and Ahdut Ha'avoda, representing them in several Yishuv institutions such as Solel Boneh, Youth Aliya, and the Hagana. A signer of Israel's Declaration of Independence and minister of agriculture in the Provisional Government. Member of the First and Second Knesset, representing Mapam, and active on its behalf in educational matters. A leading supporter of the system of streams in education and a vociferous critic of the Frumkin Commission.

BIBLIOGRAPHY

Almog, Oz. *The "Tzabar" [Native-Born Israeli]: A Portrait* (Hebrew). Tel Aviv: Am Oved, 1997.

Arian, A., and M. Shamir, eds. *The Elections in Israel—1988*. Boulder, San Francisco, and Oxford: Westview Press, 1990.

———. *The Elections in Israel—1992*. Albany: State University of New York Press, 1995.

Arnon, Y. "The 'Hehalutz' Movement in Tripoli and Its Ties with the Religious Kibbutz, 1944–1948" (Hebrew). *Pe'amim* 44 (summer 1990): 132–57.

Barad, S. *History of the Zionist Movement in Tunisia* (Hebrew). Efal: Yad Tabenkin, 1980.

Barkai, H. *The Beginnings of the Israeli Economy* (Hebrew). Jerusalem: Mossad Bialik, 1990.

Bat-Yehuda, Geula. *The Life and Times of Rabbi Maimon* (Hebrew). Jerusalem: Mossad Harav Kook, 1979.

Ben-Gurion, D. *From Class to Nation* (Hebrew). Tel Aviv: Am Oved, 1974.

———. *The Restored State of Israel* (Hebrew), vol. I–II. Tel Aviv: Am Oved, 1969.

———. *Stars and Dust* (Hebrew). Ramat Gan: Masada, 1976.

———. "Uniqueness and Destiny: An Address on the Education of the Army before the Senior Command of the IDF, 6 April 1950" (Hebrew). Pp. 7–47, vol. II in *Vision and Path*. Tel Aviv: Mapai, 1951.

———. *Vision and Path* (Hebrew), vol. I–IV. Tel Aviv: Mapai, 1951.

Note: Titles of Hebrew books and articles are given in English translation and denoted by (Hebrew) after the title. Whenever the publisher of the volume or the journal has supplied an English title, we have used it, even if this has entailed some inconsistency in transliteration; in all other cases the translation is ours.

Ben-Zev, M. "The Political Level vs. Commissions of Inquiry: The Confrontation, the Tension, and the Fear." Pp. 234–44 in *Yitzhak Kahan Memorial Volume*, ed. M. Elon et al. Tel Aviv: Papyrus, 1989.

Bialer, U. "Jerusalem 1949: Transition to Capital City Status" (Hebrew). *Cathedra* 35 (April 1985): 163–91.

Carr, E. H. *What Is History?* Harmondsworth: Penguin, 1964.

Daniel, Sh., ed. *The Minister Haim Moshe Shapira: Portrait of a Religious Statesman* (Hebrew). Tel Aviv: Don Publishers, 1980.

Dayan, A. *The Story of Shas* (Hebrew). Jerusalem: Keter, 1999.

Dayan, D. *Yes, We Are Youth!: The Story of the Gadna* (Hebrew). Tel Aviv: Ministry of Defense Pub. House, 1977.

Don-Yehiya, E. "Cooperation and Conflict between Political Camps: The Religious Camp and the Labor Movement and the Education Crisis in Israel" (Hebrew). Ph.D. dissertation, Hebrew University of Jerusalem, 1977.

Doron, G., and R. Kook. "Religion and the Politics of Inclusion: The Success of the Ultra-Orthodox Parties." Pp. 67–83 in *The Elections in Israel, 1996*, ed. A. Arian and M. Shamir. Albany: State University of New York Press, 1999.

Douer, Y. "The Development of the Gordonia-Maccabi Hatzair Movement in Tunisia, July 1949–September 1950" (Hebrew). Pp. 47–92 in H. Avrahami and Y. Douer, *The Gordonia Movement in Tunisia*. Ramat Efal: Yad Tabenkin, 1990.

Duvdevani, B. "Chapters in the Aliya of Libyan Jewry" (Hebrew). Pp. 297–316 in *Libyan Jewry: Articles and Notes on the Life of the Jews in Libya*, ed. F. Zuarès a.o. Tel Aviv: Committee of Libyan Communities in Israel, 1960.

Eleven Years of Absorption: Facts, Problems, and Figures for the Period [of 15 May 1948 to 15 May 1959] (Hebrew). Tel Aviv: Division for Publications and Statistics of the Absorption Department of the Jewish Agency for Israel, 1959.

Elmaleh, A. "Yihya Tzaram, of Blessed Memory" (Hebrew). Pp. 243–51 in *Harel: In Memory of Rabbi Raphael Alshech of Blessed Memory*, ed. Y. Ratzabi and Y. Shavtiel. Tel Aviv: [no publisher], 1962.

Eram, Y. "The History of Education—Research Disciplines" (Hebrew). Pp. 105–20 in *Reshafim—Historical, Philosophical, and Sociological Aspects of Education: A Collection of Papers in Memory of Prof. Shimon Reshef*, ed. A. Kasher and R. Shapira. Tel Aviv: Tel Aviv University, 1991.

Eshkol, L. *In the Agonies of Settlement* (Hebrew). Tel Aviv: Am Oved, 1962.

Friedman, M. "The Chronicle of the Status-Quo: Religion and State in Israel" (Hebrew). Pp. 47–79 in *Transition from "Yishuv" to State 1947–1949: Continuity and Change*, ed. V. Pilowsky. Haifa: Haifa University, 1990.

———. *Haredi (Ultra-Orthodox) Society: Sources, Trends, and Processes* (Hebrew). Jerusalem: Jerusalem Institute for Israel Studies, 1991.

Friling, T. "David Ben-Gurion and the Catastrophe of European Jewry, 1939–1945" (Hebrew). Ph.D. dissertation, Hebrew University of Jerusalem, 1990.

Gelber, Y. *New Homeland: Immigration and Absorption of Central European Jews, 1933–1948* (Hebrew). Jerusalem: Yad Izhak Ben-Zvi, 1990.

Gorny, Y. "From Zionist Ideology to the Zionist Vision: On Ben-Gurion's Attitude to Zionism, 1906 to 1963" (Hebrew). Pp. 321–37 in *Transition and Change in Modern Jewish History: Essays Presented to Shmuel Ettinger*, ed. Sh. Almog et al. Jerusalem: Zalman Shazar Center, 1988.

———. "The Historical Roots of 'From Class to Nation' and Its Ideological Implications" (Hebrew). Pp. 73–90 in *David Ben-Gurion as a Labor Leader*, ed. Sh. Avineri. Tel Aviv: Am Oved, 1988.

———. "The Utopian Starting Point of Ben-Gurion's Social Thought" (Hebrew). *Mibifnim* 49 (1987–1988): 257–71.

Harel, I. *Security and Democracy* (Hebrew). Tel Aviv: Edanim, 1989.

Hayerushalmi, L. I. *The Domineering Yarmulke* (Hebrew). Tel Aviv: Hakibbutz Hamuehad, 1997.

Herzog, Hanna. *Political Ethnicity—Image and Reality: Socio-historical Analysis of the "Ethnic Lists" to the Delegates' Assembly and the Knesset, 1920–1984* (Hebrew). Efal: Yad Tabenkin, 1986.

Horowitz, N. "Shas and Zionism: A Historical Analysis" (Hebrew). *Kivunim Hadashim* 2 (April 2000): 30–60.

Israel Government Year Book, 1950 (Hebrew). Jerusalem: Government Printer, 1950.

Kafkafi, Eyal. *Truth or Faith: Yitzhak Tabenkin as Mentor of Hakibbutz Hameuhad* (Hebrew). Jerusalem: Yad Izhak Ben-Zvi, 1992.

Kanari, B. "The Kibbutz Movement in Transition from Yishuv to State." Pp. 187–97 in *Transition from "Yishuv" to State 1947–1949: Continuity and Change*, ed. V. Pilowsky. Haifa: Haifa University, 1990.

Keren, M. *Ben-Gurion and the Intellectuals: Power, Knowledge, and Charisma*. DeKalb, Ill.: Northwestern Illinois University Press, 1983.

Kimmerling, B. "Elections As a Battleground over Collective Identity." Pp. 27–44 in *The Elections in Israel, 1996*, ed. A. Arian and M. Shamir. Albany: State University of New York Press, 1999.

Klagsbald, A. "Tribunals of Inquiry in Israel (According to the Commission of Inquiry Law, 5729-1968)" (Hebrew). Ph.D. dissertation, Tel Aviv University, 1987.

Kolatt, I. "David Ben-Gurion and His Generation" (Hebrew). *Skirah Hodshit* 34:1 (March 1987): 16–39.

Lau, B. "The Struggle of Rabbi Ovadia Yosef to Revive Sephardic Halakha in Eretz Israel" (Hebrew). Pp. 214–27 in *The Challenge of Independence: Ideological and Cultural Aspects of Israel's First Decade*, ed. M. Bar-On. Jerusalem: Yad Izhak Ben-Zvi, 1999.

Levitan, D. "The Immigration of Yemenite Jews and Their Absorption during World War II: A Historical Precedent for Mass Immigration and Absorption" (Hebrew). *Afikim* 95-96 (September 1990): 39–48.

———. "The 'Magic Carpet' Aliyah As the Historical Continuation of the Aliyot from Yemen since 1882" (Hebrew). Master's thesis, Bar Ilan University, Ramat Gan, 1983.

Libai, Z. "Concerning Uniform State Schools" (Hebrew). *Beterem* 8 (20 July 1950): 20–23.

Lissak, M. "The Creation of Organizational Frameworks in Ben-Gurion's Thinking" (Hebrew). Pp. 108–17 in *David Ben-Gurion as a Labor Leader*, ed. Sh. Avineri. Tel Aviv: Am Oved, 1988.

———. "Some Historical Perspectives on Mass Immigration in the 1950." (Hebrew). *Hatzionut* 14 (1989): 203–17.

Lufban, H. *A Man Goes Out to His Brethren* (Hebrew). Tel Aviv: Am Oved, 1967.

Maimon, J. "Representatives of Tripolitanian Jewry at the 23rd Zionist Congress" (Hebrew). Pp. 165–66 in *Libyan Jewry: Articles and Notes on the Life of the Jews in Libya*, ed. F. Zuarès et al. Tel Aviv: Committee of Libyan Communities in Israel, 1960.

Medding, P. Y. "Ben-Gurion: Democratic Political Leadership and Statism" (Hebrew). *Yahadut Zemanenu* 5 (1989): 25–49.

———. *The Founding of Israeli Democracy, 1948-1967*. New York: Oxford University Press, 1990.

The Minister Rabbi David Zvi Pinkas of Blessed Memory: The Second Anniversary of His Death (Hebrew). Tel Aviv: The National Center of Hamizrachi, [1955].

Nardi, N. et al., eds. *The Education and Culture Annual 5711 [1950/51]* (Hebrew). Jerusalem: Ministry of Education and Culture, 1952.

Nir, Y. *Arye Deri: The Rise, the Crisis, the Pain* (Hebrew). Tel Aviv: Miskal, 1999.

Nishri, Y. "Plans for a State Youth Movement" (Hebrew). Pp. 205–10 in *The Youth Movements, 1920–1960* (Idan, 13), ed. Mordecai Naor. Jerusalem: Yad Izhak Ben-Zvi, 1989.

On the Talons of Eagles: All the Truth about Operation Magic Carpet (Hebrew). Bnai Brak: Torat Avot Organization, 1988.

Pappé, I. "The Lausanne Conference—An Early Indication of Different Approches in Israeli Policy towards the Arab-Israeli Conflict" (Hebrew). *Iyunim Bitkumat Israel* 1 (1991): 241–61.

Patai, R. "The Riots in Wadi Salib." *Midstream* (winter 1960): 5–14.

Press, Y. *Ethnic-Communal Relations in Israel* (Hebrew). Tel Aviv: Sifriat Po'alim, 1976.

Raccah, A., ed.. *From an Ancient Diaspora to Renascent Israel* (Hebrew). Tel Aviv: Association of Libyan Immigrants in Israel, 1983.

Rafael, Y. *Not Easily Came the Light* (Hebrew). Jerusalem: Edanim, 1981.

Rosenthal, Yemima, ed. *Documents on the Foreign Policy of Israel, May–December 1949* (Hebrew). Jerusalem: Israel State Archives, 1986.

Rubin, B. Z., ed.. *Echoes from the Diary* (Hebrew). Jerusalem: Association for the Heritage of Libyan Jewry, 1988.

Rubinstein, A. "The Secular Hourglass" (Hebrew). *Ha'aretz*, 8 May 1998.

Schein, Ada. "The Incident of the 'Teheran Children': The Yishuv in the Land of Israel in the Test of Absorbing the Children Rescued during the Holocaust Period" (Hebrew). Master's thesis, Hebrew University of Jerusalem, 1991.

Schmelz, U. O. "Mass Immigration from Asia and from North Africa: Demographic Aspects" (Hebrew). *Pe'amim* 39 (1989): 15–63.

Schoenfeld, M., ed. *The Teheran Children Accuse: Facts and Documents about the Snatching of Souls Perpetrated by the Jewish Agency in Eretz Israel with the Aid of Hamizrachi* (Hebrew). Jerusalem: Agudat Israel, 1943.

Segal, Z. "On Governmental Investigating Committees in Israel" (Hebrew). Pp. 177–91 in *People and State: Israeli Society*, ed. S. Stempler. Tel Aviv: Ministry of Defense Pub. House, 1989.

Sela, S. *Education among the Jewish Communities of Libya* (Hebrew). Nahalal: Yad Eliezer Yaffe, 1987.

Shaked, G. "'From the Sea?'—On the Image of the Hero in Hebrew Prose from the 1940s Onward" (Hebrew). *Mehkerei Yerushalayim be-Sifrut Ivrit* 9 (1986): 7–22.

Shapira, A. "Berl, Tabenkin and Ben-Gurion and Their Attitude to the October Revolution" (Hebrew). *Zemanim* 27–28 (spring 1988): 80–97.

———. "The Religious Motifs of the Eretz Israel Labor Movement" (Hebrew). Pp. 155–77 in *Reshafim—Historical, Philosophical, and Sociological Aspects of Education: A Collection of Papers in Memory of Prof. Shimon Reshef*, ed. A. Kasher and R. Shapira. Tel Aviv: Tel Aviv University,1991.

Shavit, Y. et al., eds. *Lexicon of Personalities of Eretz Israel, 1799-1948* (Hebrew). Tel Aviv: Am Oved, 1983.

Sheleg, Y. *The New Religious Jews: Recent Developments among Observant Jews in Israel* (Hebrew). Jerusalem: Keter, 2000.

Shetreet, Sh., ed. *Tearful Pioneers: Studies in North African Jewry* (Hebrew). Tel Aviv: Am Oved, 1991.

Shiran (Ben-Nathan), Vicki. "The Damning Label: The Oriental Communities in Israel Society" (Hebrew). Master's thesis, Tel Aviv University, 1978.

Sicron, M. *Immigration to Israel, 1948–1953* (Hebrew). Jerusalem: Falk Institute, 1957.

———. "Mass Immigration: Its Extent, Character, and Influence upon the Structure of Israel's Population" (Hebrew). Pp. 31–52 in *Immigrants and Transit Camps* (Idan, 8), ed. M. Naor. Jerusalem: Yad Izhak Ben-Zvi, 1986.

Spiegel, I. *On the Highway: Studies and Historical Episodes in the History of Agudat Israel* (Hebrew). Jerusalem: Mashabim, 1982.

Sprinzak, E. *Everyone Does as He Sees Fit* (Hebrew). Tel Aviv: Sifriat Po'alim, 1986.

————. *Political Violence in Israel* (Hebrew). Jerusalem: Jerusalem Institute for Israel Studies 1995.

Stern, M. "The Zealots and the Sycarii: Branches of a National Liberation Movement" (Hebrew). *Cathedra* 1 (September 1976): 52–55.

Surasky, A. *History of Religious Education in the Modern Period* (Hebrew). Bnai Brak: Or Hahayyim, 1967.

Survey of Immigration and Activities of the Jewish Agency. Jerusalem: Jewish Agency for Israel, 1950.

Tabib, A. *Explanations to the North Africans Concerning the Agreement Signed between the Center of the Yemenite Union in Eretz Israel and the Histadrut* (Hebrew). Tel Aviv: Center of the Association of Yemenites in the Land of Israel, 1944.

Tidhar, D. *Encyclopedia of the Pioneers and Builders of the Yishuv* (Hebrew), vol. I–XIX. Tel Aviv: D. Tidhar, 1947–1971.

Tomer, B. Z., ed. *Red and White with the Fragrance of Apples: The Teheran Children* (Hebrew). Jerusalem: Hasifriyya Hatzionit, 1972.

Tzur, Y. "The Ethnic-Communal Problem in the Second Decade" (Hebrew). Pp. 101–24 in *The Second Decade*, ed. Z. Zameret and H. Yablonka. Jerusalem: Yad Izhak Ben-Zvi, 2000.

Tzurieli, Y. *Education and Society in the Yemenite Community in Eretz Israel 1882–1948* (Hebrew). Jerusalem: Academon, 1990.

Unna, M. *By Separate Paths: The Religious Parties in Israel* (Hebrew). Alon Shvut: Yad Shapira, 1984.

Weintraub, D., M. Lissak and Y. Azmon. *Moshava, Kibbutz, and Moshav: Patterns of Jewish Rural Settlement and Development in Palestine.* Ithaca, N.Y. and London: Cornell University Press, 1969.

Weitz, Y. "The Attitude of Mapai towards the Destruction of European Jewry, 1939-1945" (Hebrew). Ph.D. dissertation, Hebrew University of Jerusalem, 1988.

Willis, A. P. "Shas—The Sephardic Torah Guardians: Religious 'Movement' and Political Power." Pp. 121–39 in *The Elections in Israel—1992*, ed. A. Arian and M. Shamir. Albany: State University of New York Press, 1995.

Yablonka, Hanna. "The Absorption of Holocaust Survivors in the Emerging State of Israel and Their Integration in Israeli Society" (Hebrew). Ph.D. dissertation, The Hebrew University of Jerusalem, 1990.

Yanai, N. "Ben-Gurion's Concept of *Mamlahtiut* and the Forming Reality of the State of Israel." *Jewish Political Studies Review* 1 (1989): 151–77.

————. *Political Crises in Israel: The Ben-Gurion Period* (Hebrew). Jerusalem: Keter, 1982.

Yeshayahu, Y. *Alone and Together: A Collection of Articles* (Hebrew), edited by. A. Wolfensohn. Tel Aviv: The Center for Culture and Education of the Histadrut, 1990.

Zadok, H. *Out of Distress—Epistles, Documents, and Letters: Eight Years of Yemenite Jewry's Extraction from its Imprisonment, 1943–1950* (Hebrew). Tel Aviv: [the author], 1989.

———. *The Yemenite Burden, 1946–1951* (Hebrew). Holon: [the author], 1985.

Zameret, Z. *Across a Narrow Bridge: Shaping the Education System during the Great Aliya* (Hebrew). Sde Boker: Ben-Gurion Research Center, 1997.

———. "Aranne and Educational Policy during the Second Decade" (Hebrew). Pp. 61–78 in *The Second Decade*, ed. Z. Zameret and H. Yablonka. Jerusalem: Yad Izhak Ben-Zvi, 2000.

———. "The Decision to Sanction the 'Fourth Stream': The Agudat Israel Educational Network." Pp. 121–43 in *Abiding Challenges: Research Perspectives on Jewish Education*, ed. Y. Rich and M. Rosenak. London and Tel Aviv: Freund Pub. House and Bar-Ilan University, 1999.

———. "Judaism in Israel: Ben-Gurion's Private Beliefs and Public Policy." *Israel Studies* 4: 2 (fall 1999): 64–89.

—"The Religious Workers Stream: An Unsuccessful Attempt to Bridge the Gap between Secular and Religious Jews" (Hebrew). Pp. 121–54 in *Reshafim—Historical, Philosophical, and Sociological Aspects of Education: A Collection of Papers in Memory of Prof. Shimon Reshef*, ed. A. Kasher and R. Shapira. Tel Aviv: Tel Aviv University, 1991.

Zamir, Yitzhak. "The Judicial Aspect of Commissions of Inquiry" (Hebrew). *Haperaklit* 35 (1983–1984): 323–27.

INDEX